Demystifying Game Studies

This book is an introduction to game studies, written in an approachable way that outlines useful perspectives that readers can use to interrogate games as a primary text. It provides the reader with a toolset that can "level up" their own critical perspectives.

This book is organized around several evaluative lenses, each supported with case studies. These lenses approach the analysis of games from different perspectives, outlining some of the important foundational work from game studies and other relevant disciplines, and then relating it widely across a corpus of modern titles. This book covers video games, role-playing games, and board games, along with digressions into other more obscure areas such as LARPs, Mega-Games, and Non-Games. Each of the main areas calls back to how each of the evaluative lenses of this book could be used to illuminate intersections of medium and theoretical perspectives. The provided case studies then offer deeper dives into titles of particular significance.

This book will be suitable for students in games-related courses at multiple levels of the curriculum, game critics, and those who simply want to develop more interesting and nuanced opinions on games.

Dr Michael Heron is Associate Professor in Games at the School of Computer Science and Engineering in Gothenburg, Sweden, and programme administrator for the Game Design and Technology programme. Michael is also the author of *Tabletop Game Accessibility: Meeple Centred Design* (CRC Press, 2024) and *A Case Study in Computer Ethics in Context: The Scandal in Academia* (CRC Press, 2024).

Demystifying Game Studies

Michael Heron

CRC Press
Taylor & Francis Group
Boca Raton London New York

CRC Press is an imprint of the
Taylor & Francis Group, an **informa** business

Designed cover image: Getty Images

First edition published 2026
by CRC Press
2385 NW Executive Center Drive, Suite 320, Boca Raton FL 33431

and by CRC Press
4 Park Square, Milton Park, Abingdon, Oxon, OX14 4RN

CRC Press is an imprint of Taylor & Francis Group, LLC

© 2026 Michael Heron

ISBN: 9781032869858 (hbk)
ISBN: 9781032868578 (pbk)
ISBN: 9781003530282 (ebk)

DOI: 10.1201/9781003530282

Typeset in Times
by codeMantra

Contents

Acknowledgements

This book is dedicated, as all my books are, to Pauline Belford. Nobody inspires me to do the things I do more than she does. There is a version of me in a parallel universe who never met her, and spent his life as a shiftless drifter running unsuccessful card-scams up and down the country. I'm glad I live in this universe where she never let that happen.

I offer my thanks to Staffan Björk, who was the examiner of Introduction to Game Research before I came along and who put in place many of the tracks my own iteration of the course would later follow. His thoughtful consideration of the topic was foundational.

I offer my usual thanks to Mafalda Samuelsson-Gamboa, who despite being no blood relation still occupies the position of "my brainy little sister" in my heart. Her passion and integrity is inspirational to me. Thanks too to Yin Liang, my equally brainy chosen daughter and my spiritual guide to Taylor Swift. It's often hard to judge what kind of an impact you have as a teacher – it's a melancholy profession where for every hello there's a matching goodbye that soon follows. Being adopted as a dad is about as meaningful a testimony I can imagine as to the kind of impact that *actually* matters. Friends are the family of the 21st century, and I draw strength and comfort from both of them.

Speaking of friends, I offer my thanks too to the many wonderful colleagues who have – directly or indirectly – smoothed the path to the production of this book. Cecilia Bjursell, our divisional genie, regularly works miracles that make my life measurably easier. Hanna Kvist, the study counsellor for our games programme, solves all those problems that would otherwise occupy literal hours of my time. I can sink myself into projects like this only because of the hard and often underappreciated work of others.

Family is also the family of the 21st century, and despite the fact I don't think my mother has read any of the books I've written it is immensely heartening to see how proud she is of their existence.

Thanks to Will Bateman, who has now twice been kind enough to roll the dice on a book proposal of mine. Working with him and the team at CRC Press is an experience I recommend to everyone.

Thanks to everyone who contributed work to this book – the guest chapters I found fascinating and each and every one of you is a star for giving your time, and insight, to make this book better than it otherwise would have been.

Finally, thanks to all of the students and teaching assistants I have worked with in Introduction to Game Research. Your collective enthusiasm for the course, the content, and the medium of games is the reason I had the confidence to write this book at all.

Michael Heron

Contributors

Nayat Astaiza-Soriano is a diligent scholar of English and Spanish Languages, Literature, and Linguistics, as well as Language Technology. She is currently working as a PhD student in Software Engineering at Chalmers University of Technology in Gothenburg, Sweden. She has been playing video games since 2002. She is trying to make interests converge by exploring topics such as the one contributed to this book.

Klara Aune attended the Introduction to Game Research initially as a standalone course in 2023. Having always been avid enjoyer of games but deeming it too fun to provide a real job, she had never engaged with the topic previously. The course, on which this book is based, opened her mind about many things, and some of the topics discussed in the paper are still what she actively engages with to this day. The course opened up a path to her current job as a part-time research assistant in the topic of *weird things* in relation to games. Indeed, she says she now has a job which is too fun to be real work.

Pauline Belford is a scholar of both Social Sciences and Software Engineering. She is a Lecturer in Game Development and Interaction Design at the University of Gothenburg, where she teaches courses on the Master's programme on Game Development and Technology. Pauline has been playing video games since the 1980s, and has been teaching game design and development for almost two decades. Her work focuses on critical analysis of games and professional ethics in computer science. In the latter capacity, she is the co-author of the book *A Case Study for Computer Ethics in Context: The Scandal in Academia* (CRC Press, 2024).

Anna Brannen has a multidisciplinary background, shifting between the Sciences, Humanities, and an MSc in Interaction Design. She is currently interested in exploring ludology, complemented by a passion for pen-and-paper tabletop. Her plight is penning perpetually purple prose.

Luise Donat is studying her Master's in Human-Computer Interaction at the Ludwig-Maximilians University of Munich, Germany, focusing on Mixed Reality and Game Development. You can find her at www.linkedin.com/in/luise-donat

Constantina-Edesa Filios is a power engineer passionate about the world, especially about people and what makes us do the things that we do. She is passionate about how the world works, what makes us choose one thing over the other, and what makes us act in a certain way. This interest led her to games, particularly in the social deduction genre, as a never-ending source of insight into human behaviour, decision-making, and the subtle dynamics of trust, persuasion, and deception.

Eleni Gianntizi's background is in Greek Literature with a specialization in linguistics from Democritus University. She completed her Master's in Language Technology at the University of Gothenburg, where she researched non-verbal communication with the Furhat robot, focusing on laughter and gaze, work that was published and presented at a few conferences, like the Laughter and Other Non-Verbal Vocalisations Workshop 2024, Belfast, UK and the upcoming HCI International in Gothenburg, Sweden. She is currently conducting her PhD research at KU Leuven in Belgium, focusing on avatars and virtual agents in Extended Realities.

Julius Simeon Lilie is a Master's Student of Computer Science at the Heinrich Heine University in Düsseldorf, Germany, with a focus on Machine Learning and Natural Language Processing. You can contact him at http://www.linkedin.com/in/julius-lilie.

Edvin Skog (or colloquially Ed) is a self-described expert at over-analysing. With a background in Tech and an MSc in Game Design, he hopes to contribute to what he believes is an iceberg of design problems. He hosts his games at his Itch page (https://edneedsbread.itch.io/), some things wacky and some things pretentious.

1

An Introduction to Game Studies

Michael Heron

Hello There

I don't know if you have noticed, but games these days are a big deal. The games industry dwarfs the combined annual turnover of the music industry and the film industry put together. In 2024, worldwide game industry revenue was estimated at 455 **billion** dollars and is projected to hit over 666 billion in 2029 (Clement 2024).[1] By comparison, the music industry in 2024 reported revenues of 28.6 billion (of which, we have to assume, around half was generated by Taylor Swift), and the film industry was worth almost 80 billion (we have to assume based on the sheer tonnage of them, 99% of that was due to Marvel movies). According to the Pew Research Centre (Gottfried and Sidoti 2024), in 2024, a total of 85% of teens said they played video games, with 40% identifying themselves as daily gamers. In 2023, there were a touch over 3 **billion** active video gamers worldwide. Games are a big business. They're wildly popular. And gamers are everywhere around us. Who knows, maybe you see one every time you look in a mirror.

Why then does it often feel like the world doesn't treat them seriously? Why does it feel like the games lack the credibility of albums, movies, the theatre, or literature? If you said to a culturally judgemental relative that you were reading Moby Dick, you'd likely get murmurs of approval and complimented for your willingness to take on challenging literature. If you said to the same relative that you'd just gotten a 100% completion on *Elden Ring* (FromSoftware 2022),[2] the response is likely to be quite different. Games may not have a popularity problem, but they certainly have a perception problem.

It hasn't always been so. Once upon a time, games had mystical – even religious – significance. Consider the trope of playing chess to cheat death, or how in the Mahabharata a prince gambled away his kingdom over the roll of some dice (Narayan 2016). Why are games, in their modern incarnation, comparatively low prestige? Why are they a target of jokes rather than accorded a measure of cultural reverence?

Perhaps it is because there hasn't really been time for an acceptance of games **for fun** to really seep into the cultural bones of civilization. When Elvis first gyrated his hips on the Milton Berle show in 1956, it was something of a scandal. Parents decried his erotically charged pelvis as something that shouldn't be shown on television.

DOI: 10.1201/9781003530282-1

Critics panned the appearance as vulgar, animalistic, and worse. It was, in other words, shocking – especially when paired to the almost Dionysian reaction of his, often young, often female, fans. In 2024, you might well chance upon the Cardi B/ Megan The Stallion collaboration *WAP*[3] simply by skipping through radio channels.

Novel incarnations of culture, in other words, lose their ability to shock as time goes by and they acquire credibility as a simple side-effect of familiarity. We become inured to its presence. Less likely to judge it for simply existing. The first home video game consoles began to appear in the early 1970s. And it's only really now that those of us who grew up with video games are becoming the societal elders who are supposed to mutter at the "kids today". In another 20 years' time, we'll likely all simply accept that video games are a thing people do. It'll be normalized past the point of opprobrium and well on its way to appreciation.

But why should we have to wait that long?

Part of the problem, I believe, is that much of the discourse around games lacks the kind of meaningful insight and "heft" that we'd see for other forms of entertainment. The analytical sophistication of everyday conversations around books and movies is considerably higher than for gaming. That's partly because there we have a pretty solid library of cultural touchpoints to rely on. The average cinema fan can expect that anyone they talk to will have seen, or at least heard of, a whole wide range of cinematic experiences. You can discuss The Irishman in relation to Goodfellas in relation to the Godfather and expect that everyone will at least follow what you're saying. They'll be aware, through osmosis, of significant themes, scenes and character moments. They'll have experienced second- and third-hand interpretations. A certain degree of cultural literacy comes simply through being a person who lives in a culture. If you're a fan of classical literature, you'll never have the experience of referencing Dickens and having someone say "Who is that?". Even the shallowest, surface-level familiarity is common ground that conversation can be built upon. If you want to have a conversation about Moby Dick, it helps if you don't need to explain that the book has a whale in it.

We don't really have that for gaming. We lack a shorthand, easily accessible cultural vocabulary. I believe it is rendering us incapable of expressing the richness, complexity and resonance of modern gaming experiences to those not already immersed in games as a hobby. When we talk about games, we lack a framework for how we can get across just how interesting games have become.

This problem gets even worse when you include experiences outside of the mainstream. Sure, your elderly relatives have maybe heard of *Grand Theft Auto 5* (Rockstar North 2013) (and have distorted perspectives as to what's involved), but how many of them have even heard of *Stardew Valley* (Barone 2016)? They might be aware of *Red Dead Redemption* (Rockstar North 2010), but likely they and nobody they know have ever heard the name *Sayonara Wild Hearts*[4] (Simogo 2019). Everyone has likely heard of Monopoly (Magie 1933) but who has heard of *Brass: Birmingham* (Brown, Tolman, and Wallace 2018)? That latter game is currently listed on popular enthusiast site BoardGameGeek as the #1 best board game of all time. Forget about it entirely if you want to talk about indie RPGs, or the growing popularity of Jubensha "parlour LARPs" or the fascinating phenomenon of Megagames.

You may think this is an overstatement of the situation, so let me belatedly introduce myself.

My name is Michael Heron (you may have seen that on the cover). I am a Scottish man, currently living in Gothenburg, Sweden. I am a Docent[5] at Chalmers University of Technology and the University of Gothenburg[6] and the administrator of our Game Design and Technology programme. One of the courses I teach is called Introduction to Game Research. Many of the students who take this course belong to my programme – it's their first mandatory course – but we accept students from across the university. We have language technologists, software engineers, interaction designers, and a lot of international students who attend through Europe's ERASMUS programme. They come from all kinds of cultural backgrounds. The only thing they all share in common is that they're all signed up to a course called Introduction to Game Research. It is the course that is the basis for this book.

I've been running this for several years, and every year I encounter the same problem – there is no subset of games I can reference that everyone knows about. Games I would think are prominent enough to receive universal recognitions are more obscure than I believe. I have had students who have only ever played The Sims (Maxis 2000). I have students who have invested hundreds of hours into every Soulslike on the market. I have students who have never heard of Assassins' Creed (Ubisoft 2007). And bear in mind, this is a group of people who have largely self-selected themselves onto a gaming course. For a large proportion of the wider population, as far as they're concerned, the only video game is FIFA (EA Sports 1993–2023).

Addressing this is part one of the job I'd like this book to do – to give us a kind of common ground that we can build future discussions on. There is no such thing as an agreed upon "canon" of significant games in the same way there is for art, for architecture, for film, or for literature. As part of our discussions in this book though, we'll start outlining the significant contributions of a number of games.

Once we get to that stage, we're at the point where we can begin to have some conversations that can build upon a shared understanding and familiarity. But then we get to the second problem that comes with the games discourse – how do we say something **interesting** about the games we love? Or even more challenging, how do we say something interesting about the games we **hate**?

That's the second job I would like this book to do. I want to provide a set of common lenses through which we can analyse games. I want us to be able to surface our personal insights in a way that lets us be **literate** about the game discussions we have. And as part of that, I want to give people the tools they need to say **original** things about games.

Don't get me wrong – there's a lot of genuinely insightful commentary out there around games. Video essays are often deeply thoughtful, but lack the robustness that academics like myself are accustomed to expecting from research literature. They are interesting, but often not **convincing**.

Academic literature, by comparison, is often convincing but not actually that **interesting.** Papers and books are often bound up in the context of rigorous formality, rendering them largely unreadable to an audience that isn't conversant with the forms and rituals of academic discussion.

Both extremes – enthusiast video essays and blog posts on one end, and academic output on the other – also suffer from Sturgeon's Law.[7] Engaging with the full range of discourse on gaming requires a lot of digging into literature, a lot of selective snipping, and often a requirement to translate from dense academic language into your first language of choice.

It doesn't have to be like that. That brings us to the third job of this book – to communicate the techniques by which you can have interesting and original opinions on games, but without the need to speak academese as your first language. This book is intended, in part, to be a Rosetta Stone to academic discussion around games. That's where the **demystifying** part of the book title comes in. Maybe at a later date, we'll do some **re**mystifying. For now, my goal is to help you develop meaningful, robust opinions through the process of performing research on games.

What Is Research? Why Is Research? How Is Research?

Many of you will have gone through an education process where, at some point, the word Research[8] has been brought up and left hanging. Depending on how far through the education system you've gone, you may have also heard other, associated terms. "Research question". "Literature review". "Hypothesis". In my experience, many of us in the education system sort of assume everyone is equally besotted with the vocabulary of our discipline and is equivalently familiar with what's being referenced.

Let's begin our demystification right here.

Research is, at its core, the process of gathering and analysing the evidence we need to understand the world a little better than we did before. That's it. The rest of what you have heard (or not heard) about research is all in service of that primary goal.

There is already a lot of insight to be found in gaming discourse. You don't need an academic framework to say something interesting about games. Your own opinions on the games you love, as a reader of this book, likely aren't shallow. However, my experience of teaching games for years is that where things often fall down is in the **robustness** of opinions – the extent to which they stand up to external critique and criticism. During the course of this book, I don't want to argue that you shouldn't have the opinions you have, or that you need better opinions. Rather, what I'd like to do is work with you (**with** you, mind) to help you shape your opinions so that they are bullet-proof. Shielded against reasonable critique. If in the process you find that your ideas don't survive the process – that the shielding doesn't hold up to criticism – then that's fine. That's normal. Sometimes things don't stand the tempering process we're going through. What I want to communicate throughout is that when our opinions don't stand up to critique, it's perfectly normal and natural to change them. I want to encourage you to develop an "evidence-based" philosophy for your opinions.

The key thing right now is that none of this is a mystical process. There are several stages through which we progress to take vague notions and turn them into hardened knowledge. Throughout this book, we'll be exploring each and every one of them. It's also important to stress here that while this book is going to do this within the frame of games, this is a general process that applies to all knowledge.

Research Scope

"Scope" is the term we use to describe the parameters of our inquiries. We say that a certain number of things are included, sometimes a combination of disparate disciplines or communities, and we essentially exclude everything else as irrelevant. The scope of our book is "gaming", which is a smaller subset of "fun", which is a tiny subset of "recreation", which is a tiny subset of "all human knowledge".

Note that our scope, in comparison to everything there is to know, is very small. We're not even going to concern ourselves with the "fun" topic as a whole, just the subset of fun that is covered by the concept of games. That's not to say we can't draw in concepts from elsewhere; it's just to say "this is the gravity well around which our thoughts will orbit".

Within this book, our scope is **games,** but you'll notice I don't say **video games**. We're also going to include board games, roleplaying games, and a bunch of other gaming forms of which you might not have even heard. Gaming isn't so much made up of different forms, but rather games exist in various intensities of hybridity. Pure board games, board games with digital components, digital games with physical components, and so on. As such, there are lessons to be learned for video game scholars by engaging with board games, and vice versa. We'll talk about all of these as we go on.

Specifically, within the frame of this book, this is our primary **knowledge domain**. It's not the only one we'll draw in, but it's the heart of our discussion.

Texts

As a budding games scholar, games are the primary texts of your discipline. It might feel odd to talk about a game as being a "text", but that's because modern usage has blurred the definition. In academic terms, a text is the original form of something that has been created – not the commentary about it, or the interpretation of it, but the primary form. Novels are one of the main texts of a literature scholar. Movies are the texts of a film critic. For us, the texts are games – and you should treat them with the respect other disciplines reserve for their core works. It's part of your job now to play games the same way a literature scholar would read books – thoughtfully, mindfully, critically, and regularly.

You cannot have a truly informed and interesting opinion on games unless you are aware of the context in which they are situated. You need to know the breadth of the discipline, but also the depth of it. To know if a game is doing something significant, or innovative, or novel – well, you need to have a sense for significance, for innovation, and for novelty. That only comes from subject matter expertise – from knowing the contours of your discipline. Nobody expects you to have played every game, or even have heard of every game. But you should have an understanding that allows you to make judgement calls on what are often very subjective criteria. Is the difficulty of the Dark Souls (FromSoftware 2011) series, or its various spiritual descendants, a novel feature? Or does it just **seem** novel because you didn't grow up with "Nintendo Hard" as a benchmark (Brandse 2017)? And if you feel it **is** novel, what is the **nature** of that novelty?

For context, the way in which Soulslike – the good ones at least – approach their philosophy of difficulty is likely genuinely novel. Articulating **why** requires you to be able to identify, integrate, and occasionally dismiss influences. Again, familiarity is the necessary pre-requisite for being able to do this.

You'll likely come to this book with whole families of games you have never played. As part of your construction of textual familiarity, you should play them. Games that are fun are not necessarily games that are interesting. You need to begin separating out that which is enjoyable from that which is meaningful. If you've never played a modern board game, go find a games night and join in. A few hours with Dominion (Vaccarino 2008) will teach you a lot about the roots and influences of Slay the Spire

(Mega Crit 2019), or Inscryption (Daniel Mullins Games 2021), or As We Descend (Box Dragon 2025). To begin with, nothing will connect up. After a while, everything will connect to everything else. The denser the knots of familiarity you have, the richer your scholarship will be. The more you can relate what you want to say to other examples, or counter-examples.

A lot of your mastery of the knowledge domain (or, your **domain knowledge**) is going to be based on your understanding of the primary texts of the discipline. However, you'll also need to dig into secondary and tertiary texts.

Secondary texts are those that offer commentary and analysis of primary texts. In our sphere, these might be academic critiques, or game reviews, or even social media commentary. We'll come back to that.

Tertiary texts are the ones that synthesize, aggregate, index, and process primary and secondary texts. These might include things like literature reviews (again, more on that later) or meta-analyses, systematic reviews, and so on. These are the texts that try to identify trends, or gaps, or unacknowledged assumptions.

In other words – how do you start to become an expert on games? You play games, you read about games, and you read what other people have written about what people have written about games. You'll probably never be willing to describe yourself as an expert – I certainly don't claim that title – but that's healthy. There's **always** something new to learn.

Directing Research

Where do we start then, when it comes to building this expertise? And what do we do with it when we've got it?

Remember our definition of research – it's about understanding the world better than we did before, and there are several ways in which that can be done.

First of all, you'll normally be working within a **problem domain**, which is an intersection of several **knowledge domains**. If you wanted to explore how simulation games represent the legal framework of aircraft traffic, you'd be combining several knowledge domains – games, simulations, the law, and air traffic control. In order to shift the needle on your understanding of your topic, you need to have a meaningful grasp of all of those domains. The more complex your problem domain, the more you need to know to understand **the context,** which is the set of interrelated elements within which a thing exists.

The level of mastery you might need in any single knowledge domain depends on the emphasis it's going to get in the work, but you basically need to know enough to be sure that what you're doing is building on state of the art (as in, working from the newest evidence we have) and is thus suitably informed to make new contributions to our understanding.

In this, there two main ways we do research.

Answering a Research Question

Let's say that you have identified a **knowledge need** as a result of your engagement with the texts of your discipline. By 'Exploring the wider context' you've found a topic on which we need knowledge that doesn't currently exist. You've dug into an ocean of commentary and literature and noted, "Okay, Sayonara Wild Hearts is clearly the best game ever... but nobody has really ever explained **why.** We've all just taken it as a self-evident truth, which we all agree with uncontroversially". What a knowledge need demands is a **research question** that outlines the scope and problem domain, and presents itself in a way that directs a scholar (that's you) to a meaningful answer.

So, "Why is Sayonara Wild Hearts the best game ever?"

That's a research question, and it's how a lot of research works. You either set yourself a question, or you answer a question someone else has identified.[9] Building good research questions is something of an art-form of its own, but there are some things we like to see in all of them. Specifically, good research questions promise:

1. **Novelty**. As a result of answering the question, you'll be saying something new and backing it up with evidence.
2. **Achievability**. The question should be sufficiently constrained in scope that you can make progress towards an answer.
3. **Interest**. When you advance the state of knowledge with your answer, someone out there should care.
4. **Answerability**. The question should be phrased in a way that you can fully answer it within a reasonable timeframe. It should be specific.
5. **Evaluative**. The answer implied by the question should require some analysis and consideration and often a filtering of the evidence.

So, "Why is Sayonara Wild Hearts the Best Game Ever" offers novelty, and it certainly offers interest.[10] However, it's likely not answerable in a satisfying way, and it certainly can't offer a full answer in a human lifetime. What do we mean by "best"? How do we provide a full answer to such a subjective question? Can we really say, amongst every game that has ever been made, that Sayonara Wild Hearts is the absolute uncontroversial best of them[11]? And since we don't say otherwise, we're going to have to compare it to board games, role-playing games, LARPs... and what does it even mean to say Sayonara Wild Hearts is better than Dungeons and Dragons? We're going to need to invent or discover a whole comparative methodology that works in that frame. And in that, what **is** a game? That's its own rabbit hole to fall down as we'll see a little later.

By the time you outline what's required to offer a full answer to this research question, we soon realize that it'll take a research team working around the clock for their full career to even explore a fraction of the problem domain. And by the time in late 2044 when you have that partial answer there's 20 years of new games to assess. The state of the art will have moved on.

So, we incrementally tweak the research question so it conforms more to the qualities we need.

- Why is Sayonara Wild Hearts the best **video game** ever?
  - More answerable, but still not answerable enough.
- **What are the qualities that make** Sayonara Wild Hearts the best video game ever?
  - The scope has been constrained, but it's still not answerable. "The best" still requires an exhaustive comparison. "What are **the** qualities" is

    implying a fully comprehensive list that starts up with things like narrative and aesthetics and ends with things like "the phase of the moon".

- What are the qualities that make Sayonara Wild Hearts **one of** the best video games ever?
  - Far more answerable – we don't need an exhaustive comparison, just a convincing one.
- What are **some of the qualities** that make Sayonara Wild Hearts one of the best video games ever?
  - Getting there, but we could end up focusing on the qualities that were easiest to identify rather than the ones that actually matter.
- What are some of the **most impactful** qualities that make Sayonara Wild Hearts one of the best video games ever?
  - Now we're pretty much where we need to be – we've implied an evaluative aspect that lets us constrict scope. More tweaking is always possible. Sometimes more tweaking is even necessary. But this is a solid research question that meets all of the five qualities we need.

Once you have a research question, you've essentially given yourself a nicely constrained project to explore the texts until this question can be given a satisfying answer. You need to spend a lot of time – ideally in conversation with someone who has gone through the process before – workshopping a research question. And there are other things to bear in mind too.

You're not required to know, or even suspect the shape of, the answer beforehand. If we knew what we were going to find, we wouldn't call it research. And while we aim for a question that is, at least in theory, fully answerable, it doesn't mean you **need** to fully answer it. All research is incremental.

Sometimes your research contribution is that you find out that – despite all your best intentions – the question cannot be answered from the state of the art as we know it. Sometimes your biggest accomplishment is clearing some of the "fog of war" from the topic. The next person who sets out to answer the question will be better prepared thanks to you having mapped out the difficult terrain for them. Sometimes our answer is just a better understanding of the questions we should have been asking. That's not only **okay**, it's absolutely critical to the whole endeavour.

Exploring a Research Direction

All of the research question stuff only matters though if you have a knowledge need to meet. What do you do if you're still looking for one?

That's when you pick up your go bag and strike out in search of one, which is done through **exploring a research direction.** This you do, usually, within a specific problem domain. You might want to explore politics in relation to Disco Elysium (ZA/UM 2019), but not have any real idea as to what we as a culture need to know about it. A research question is a ping on a map – you need to work out how to get there from where you are. A research direction is more like a psychogeographical Dérive (Gamboa, Heron, Sturdee, and Belford 2023), where you follow where the evidence leads you. You make notes of the landmarks, the gaps, and the unexamined assumptions. You immerse yourself in primary, secondary, and tertiary texts, and over time, you begin to see where there are opportunities for you to make your own mark. You might explore how politics are referenced in Disco Elysium. And then you might look at the real-world political contexts they draw from. You start digging into the messaging in the game, the ideological positions it supports and rejects. You find yourself immersed in Marx, Engels and the work of Thomas More and comparing Disco Elysium to how similar themes are expressed in other overtly political games such as Metaphor: ReFantazio (Studio Zero 2024). Over time, your aimless wanderings construct a map of your problem domain, and certain parts of that map will be less detailed than others. At a certain point, you switch over from undirected exploration to directed discovery – and at the end of that process lies a knowledge need (or likely, many knowledge needs) that you may well be the most qualified person in the world to meet. The knowledge need you find most interesting – the one that you're most excited about – is what you should craft a research question to answer.

I mentioned excitement there because I am firmly of the belief that the first person you should serve with a research question is **you.** You should fill a knowledge need that **you** want to see filled. After all, if you don't care about the answer, why should anyone else?

Days, weeks, or months into this exploration you emerge from the jungle of the academic and professional literature around your problem domain. Clutched in your hand is a research question. "Which of the major themes expressed in Disco Elysium are most relevant to the construction of meaning within an inherently political world".

And then, the work begins.

This might sound like it's the harder route to getting started, but the good news is that it isn't. Everyone needs to explore the literature in any case – the only thing that really changes is in what order, and to what end.

Doing Research

Now you have your question, or at least a strong idea of what it is. That either came about because you had a knowledge need ready to be filled, or you went out looking for one. The next thing is to build up the evidence base you need to actually answer the question. It's time for you **conduct a literature review.** The thing that characterizes academic scholarship from more general scholarship tends to be rigour and robustness. You've already seen why research questions tend to be so byzantine and woolly – they get workshopped so that they don't promise more than a researcher can deliver. The next part of the equation is why academic findings tend to have the same qualities – prevaricating, unwilling to commit, often in an argument with themselves. That's not by accident – it's the design of academia. And it's driven by two vital principles:

- All claims should be proportional to the evidence.
- Biases in thinking should be identified and addressed.

Academic literature is often unable to commit to claims that would pass without question (and often, with applause) in other settings. That's the robustness that we're looking to achieve in scholarship – that when we say something that is contentious, controversial, or dependent on further context, we provide it. We have the receipts, as I believe the kids say. Often evidence is only partial, or weak, or generally not strong enough to say the thing that we would – rhetorically – like to say. If we can't strengthen the evidence, we have to weaken the claim.

You've already seen an example of that when I said that Sayonara Wild Hearts is uncontroversially the best game ever. That's right, it was a trap all along.

I may believe it to be true (and indeed, it is my favourite game of all time) but in proper scholarship I can't make a claim like that and pass it off as a fact. There is no strength of evidence that can be proportional to a claim like that, for reasons we outlined when we talked about research questions. I can get away with it in a book like this, where I can employ rhetoric to make a larger point. It wouldn't even pass the laugh check in an academic peer review.

Formal research, in terms of what we look for in rigour, brings to mind the old joke:

> An economist, a mathematician and a statistician are driving down a Scottish country road. The economist looks out the window and sees a black sheep standing in the middle of the field. 'Look', the economist says, 'In Scotland, sheep are black!'.
>
> The statistician looks out the window and says, 'No, all we can say is that some Scottish sheep are black'.
>
> The mathematician thinks for a moment and says, 'All we can say is that in Scotland, there exists one field in which there is at least one sheep, of which at least one side of which is black'

This need for rigour is core to the heart of science – it's not that we don't know how to say interesting, exciting things. We're just bound by the evidence to not say more than we feel we can prove. "There exists at least one academic, who has expressed in writing, that Sayonara Wild Hearts is the best game ever". Not as catchy, not as provocative, but defensible. Rigorous.

The robustness that we seek comes from having a wide perspective on the problem domain that is capable of encompassing our work and all its contradictions. The research question is the ship, the literature review is the bottle... to misquote Garth Brooks for a moment. Robustness comes from having assessed a question from all its different possible perspectives. These perspectives include critical perspectives.

Think of how a lawyer prepares for a trial. They don't construct their case and leave it at that. They conduct opposition research. They know what their opposing counsel is likely to say, and they know what they're going to say in response, and what opposing counsel will likely say in response to that. Our work isn't weakened by taking into account conflicting perspectives – it is immensely strengthened because it shows that we have excised or addressed problematic biases and assumptions. That in turn brings to mind another old joke.

> A biologist, a mathematician, and a statistician are sitting outside a pub. Across the street they watch one person walk into a restaurant. A few moments later, two walk out.
>
> The biologist says, 'How interesting – they must have reproduced'
>
> The mathematician says, 'No – there must be some kind of flaw in our assumptions'
>
> The statistician says, 'You know, if one more person walks into that restaurant, it'll be empty'

We tend to see the world through lenses we don't even know we're using, and as part of robust research, we need to break out of those patterns of thinking to make sure that we're seeing things clearly. If an academic paper seems not to be saying much, and in an argument with itself about whether it is saying even that, it's this that you're seeing expressed. Academic papers rarely go viral. The average influencer probably has more impact on public discourse with a thoughtless tweet than an academic paper that may be the result of countless hours of expert attention. There is a reason though that we tend to consider academic literature in all its forms as the gold standard of knowledge.

Of course, the people making those rankings tend to be academics… and we all tend to see the world through the lenses that are comfortable to us.

So, from our research question, we continue on to the next stage – the literature review.

Conducting a Literature Review

A literature review, in its formal sense, is a written analysis that assesses, compares, and contrasts the texts (or literature) that are within the scope of a given academic exercise. In the terms we've discussed before, a literature review tends to take the form of a secondary or tertiary document, usually the latter in that they are built from investigating the secondary texts around one or more primary texts. They don't **have** to be written down, in the end, but it's good practice to do it – if you plan on doing anything academically with the work you do, a literature review (sometimes also called a **background**) will be expected.

The research that you do as part of a literature review is how you build your domain knowledge. Writing it down is how you communicate to people the fruits of your labour. In most academic works (dissertations and papers usually), this is a document with a job to do – it's to convince your reader that whatever follows is going to be built upon solid foundations. It should encompass the state of the art, familiarize your reader with everything they're going to need to know about your work, and it should **contextualize** your work. It should show people where your work contributes – as in, where it answers knowledge needs. It does this by identifying where those knowledge needs exist.

Part of what your literature review does is take into account the work of other people. You have a research question you're looking to answer, and the literature review sets the foundation of how others have attempted to answer the question, or questions like it. A literature review documents what's been left undiscovered in the research that others have done. As part of providing this understanding, you also create the intellectual foundation of your contribution. Let's go back to the workshopped research question we had earlier:

> What are some of the most impactful qualities that make Sayonara Wild Hearts one of the best video games ever?

Consider what we'd need to formalize to provide a satisfying answer to this question:

- What is a **quality** in this context?
  - We might answer this by looking at how other scholars have attempted to identify desirable qualities and traits in other forms of culture. Ideally, we'd want someone (or even more ideally, more than one someone) who has answered this in relation to games specifically. We can compare and contrast how quality is assessed in our knowledge domain and in

relevant other knowledge domains. Are the qualities that make for a good book the same as the ones that make for a good game? Why? Why not?

- What do we consider to be **impactful?**
  - And from what direction do we define impact? If we're considering what might be impactful on the production quality of the game, we might look at the effectiveness of tools and workflow. If we're interested in how people respond emotionally, perhaps we need to look at how players respond to aesthetic choices and musical selection. When we say "impact", what do we mean and how do we understand it?
- What is the frame of comparison for "one of the best video games ever"?
  - As we've discussed previously, there is no such thing as an accepted canon of great games. So, what games are you including as comparators (and why are you including them?), and what games are you excluding (and why are you excluding them)?

There are more things we'd need to do to situate our work in the wider literature. We'd need to identify what other people have said about Sayonara Wild Hearts, what studies have been conducted, and how they have informed our own. We'd need to look for similar questions being asked about other games and assess the ways in which **they** answered the question. And if we don't find anything that we can use to support our argument, we need to address that deficiency. Did we miss important texts, and if so, do we need to go back and change our process for finding literature? Or is this particular question, or this particular game, not actually very interesting to the field?

The literature review is then a discursive discussion of what you have found, including citations to all the papers that are relevant to your work. We won't concern ourselves particularly about all the different citation formats here – there are tools to simplify all of that. You'll see plenty of examples as we go through later chapters.

A question I'm often asked here is "how many texts do I need for a literature review", and the answer is an unhelpful "enough". There's no right or wrong answer, but generally for an academic paper, the key thing is that you should support all your contentious claims with evidence (and that evidence should be proportional to your claim), and you should cite other resources that are instrumental in setting your context. You want to demonstrate to your reader that you have sufficient mastery over each of the relevant knowledge domains. Your reader should be willing to accept your contributions on their own merits because you've built confidence in your scholarship. It's a credibility-building exercise in some ways.

However, alongside number of citations, a more significant element is **quality** of citations. When we say evidence should be proportional to claims, we mean in quantity (if you say something controversial, you'll need more citations to back it up than if you say something mundane) but also in quality. Fifty references to tabloid newspapers don't make for a robust argument. What we often hold to is a kind of hierarchy of evidence, where it is incumbent on you as a scholar to find the best quality evidence by converting low-quality citations into higher quality citations. Generally, this is how we rank it (from best to worst):

- Peer-Reviewed Academic Journals & Conferences
- Editorially reviewed academic journals and conference proceedings

- Academic books
- Academic workshops
- "Grey Literature" – pre-prints and whitepapers, although this can vary from field to field *.
- Other kinds of professional books
- Higher level periodicals (Wired/Edge/*New York Times*)
- Enthusiast Press (Polygon/IGN/Retro Gamer Magazine)
- Populist and General periodicals (New Scientist)
- Tabloids (Daily Mail/New York Post)
- Blog Posts/YouTube Videos *
- Social media Posts *
- Someone you met in the pub *

An asterisk means that it actually depends on the source rather than the format. If you meet Sid Meier in a pub, you can probably consider him a pretty good source of Sid Meier-related information. Cited in that case as "personal communication".

If you can't find higher quality evidence to support contentious claims, then it's time to soften those claims. "Everyone thinks Sayonara Wild Hearts is great" – contentious, heavy burden of evidence, even a single counter-example disproves it. "Most people think Sayonara Wild Hearts is great" – a testable claim that you can only satisfy with evidence that shows 50% +1 have expressed this view. "Many people think Sayonara Wild Hearts is great" – provide you are clear about what "many" means, you might be able to prove this with an academic survey, or with enough (lots and lots) tweets. "There are people who believe Sayonara Wild Hearts is great" – a handful of Reddit posts will be fine. In fact, at this point, you may not need citations at all, since it has become an arguably uncontroversial statement. And if you felt like being all belt-and-braces, a link to Steam's assessment of review sentiment would be absolutely fine.

How do you find all these texts though?

In the olden days, you'd find journals and conferences that work in the areas in which you are interested. You'd check journal editions and conference proceedings (the collection of all published papers). You might have to ask your local university library to order copies of what seem to be relevant papers. Nowadays, Google Scholar will hook you up to a world of literature, and I recommend this as your cheat-code to academia. Work out keywords and combinations of keywords, and then grab all the papers you can that seem relevant. You'll find many of them behind paywalls – if you have membership in a university library, you might be able to access their subscriptions through services such as OpenAthens or Shibboleth. If not – I recommend getting in touch with the authors directly. Most of us will be delighted at your interest. As to what games you should play – we'll talk about that as we go along. Intertextuality is going to be a major theme of this book.

You will find, for almost any search, that you end up with thousands of papers – and you don't have time to read thousands of papers. And even if you did, trust me – there are better uses of your time. Think of the list of all you find as your "candidate literature review", and you want to filter this down into a manageable number. Remember though that part of what a literature review is supposed to do is show your understanding of the state of the art, so there's a "soft" cut-off point in terms of dates. The general rule is "technology changes quickly, people change slowly". If you are researching cutting-edge graphical rendering techniques, a paper from 1992 may not be very relevant unless it is absolutely fundamental to understanding the present. And if it is, it'll show up repeatedly in your reading. If on the other hand you're researching how people respond to colour schemes, you might find a paper from the 1920s to still be relevant. It's always a judgement call, but I normally suggest as a rough rule of thumb:

- Cutting-edge technical techniques have an approximate half-life of about three years.
  - As in, after three years half of what's written in them will be obsolete.
- Papers discussing the culture of technology have an approximate half-life of about ten years.
  - Think back to what games were like in 2014 – the first Destiny (Bungie 2014) and Middle-Earth: Shadow of Mordor (Monolith Productions 2014) were dominating the charts. It's certainly feasible that papers from this era have something useful to say, but many of them will have faded into irrelevance.
- Papers discussing societal trends have an approximate half-life of 25 years.
  - In the year 2000, a cutting-edge handheld device was a Nokia 3310 – great if you want to explore the sociological context of Snake, but perhaps we've moved on a bit.
- Papers discussing low-level biological or psychological phenomena have a half-life of about 50 years.
  - Things like the Stroop effect (MacLeod 1991) or the Milgram Experiment (Miller, Collins, and Brief 1995) still have things to tell us about modern life. It's not that these findings are likely to be useless if they are from older papers, rather our understanding of the topic is likely to have become more sophisticated.

There is a particular way in which you should read an academic paper – you don't read them like an essay, but rather like a structured scientific document. Here's the order in which I recommend you read them:

- Start with the abstract. The abstract is a mini-version of the paper. If it doesn't seem like it is relevant, discard the paper. This underscores why writing a good abstract is so important, and we emphasize it so much in scientific writing.
- If the abstract seems interesting, read the conclusion. Most academic papers conform to the usual structure of "tell people what you're going to tell them; then tell them; then tell them what you told them". The conclusion should properly reference the key messages and themes and results that came from the work.
- If the conclusion suggests a link to what you're trying to answer, read the discussion. The discussion is where people self-critique the work they've done – talk about its limitations, its applicability, and what others can take away from it.
- If the discussion is relevant, read the whole paper and pay attention to its claims and the evidence that supports those claims.

When you find a paper that is useful to you, also read through its references. You'll find new papers to add to your candidate literature review.

Now let's say you've done the work. It's time to put it into an appropriate form, at which point you need to work out what **kind** of literature review you intend doing. There are some common forms:

- **The Argumentative Literature Review**, in which you say something provocative and then back it up with evidence. Usually applied to unseat deeply held entrenched viewpoints. Almost always structurally biased, but if you want to argue that – for example – the idea of a game's canon is inherently a colonialist viewpoint, this is the way you'd want to do it. Just... be sure of your evidence!
- **The Systematic Literature Review**, in which you adopt a rigorous, structural approach to a literature review with the intention of creating the context from which meta-analysis can be conducted. Which is to say – an analysis of statistically collected studies from which new knowledge can be derived, or verifiability of results can be assessed. You're almost certainly not going to be doing that.
- **The Scoping Literature Review,** in which you investigate how far the literature around a topic extends, and how dense it is. A good way of identifying knowledge gaps and thus knowledge needs.
- **The Integrative Literature Review,** in which your aim is to draw together diverse perspectives and results with the intention of generating new understanding, new theory, or new perspectives on that which is already there.
- **The Narrative Literature Review,** or the **traditional** literature review. This is a discursive critique and summary of texts connected to a particular problem domain, usually selectively chosen on the basis of their applicability to a research question. Here, you are looking to provide the intellectual and theoretical underpinning of everything that follows.

There are plenty of books and resources out there as to how you actually **write** a literature review, but the demystification of these steps leading up to it is essentially this:

- Research is the process of learning something new about the world and supporting your observations with evidence. Everything you do in service of this goal is research.
- Explore a research direction, and use that to identify a research question.
  - Or, identify a knowledge need and construct a research question that addresses it.
- Conduct a survey of the literature to find candidate texts.
  - If you've gone through the research direction route, you'll already have most of this to hand.
- Filter candidate papers down to a handful that are relevant to your understanding.
  - Read the abstract, then the conclusion, then the discussion.
    - Only if all of that is relevant, read the actual paper.

- Play games, become an expert in your discipline, and in the games that have something to say about the subject in which you're interested.
- Ensure that you take into account different perspectives, and that you are building your understanding on the best quality evidence available.

It should be stressed here that this isn't a "one and done" process. As you develop your ideas, you'll find you need to occasionally do a few directed "spot" literature reviews around particular topics. You may find as you go through the work that you end up thinking things and not having evidence to support those thoughts, at which point you go back into the literature and confirm or contradict your thinking. This is an ongoing part of research – you'll never escape the need to keep up to date. Sorry. It's estimated that the half-life of information generally is perhaps between seven and ten years (Stein 2014). Even if you grasp a topic completely, every ten years half of what you know will probably be obsolete or disproven. The state of the art is a moving target.

But all of this is about finding out what other people have said about a research question you want to answer. It's an important part of the process, but it's not really the fun part. That's what comes next – how do you actually say something new and interesting about games?

What Does an Answer Look Like?

Anyone who works in the educational system is almost certainly aware of Bloom's Taxonomy (Bloom 1956) – the assumptions of this are built into course syllabi, the length and breadth of the world. It's sometimes mistakenly discussed as a hierarchy, where simple forms of knowledge are built upon to arrive at higher forms. In its simplest, crudest application, it's sometimes used to make sure the form of a learning outcome is "at the right level" for the expected audience – a semi-mystical acceptance that certain nouns encode higher-level understanding than others. That it is more complex to "design" than it is to "select". And yet, real life provides us abundant evidence to the contrary – just ask someone choosing between equally credible courses of action in an emergency. Figure 1 shows it more correctly as a kind of wheel.

At the "lowest levels" of what's sometimes called the cognitive domain (Furst 1981; Huitt 2011), we see nouns such as "list", "define", and "describe".[12] At the highest levels, we see things like "judge", "evaluate", and "critique". The assumption is that – absent other considerations – that higher-level nouns are "more complex" than lower levels. Bloom's model isn't true – for every example of it being applicable, we can provide multiple counter-examples. However, the model is still **useful**. And it's especially useful when it comes to considering the level of intellectual "contribution" associated with an answer you provide to your research question (Figure 1.1).

I believe it's best not to think of this as a hierarchy, but rather a ladder. Higher forms of knowledge build upon lower-level forms, but no part is especially more important than any other. What **is** important though is the **proportion** of activity that you assign to each of these different cognitive domains. All of these levels come into play in critical thinking. In order to hypothesize, one must first define, interpret, organize, and analyse. That's what gives us the evidence upon which a response to a hypothesis is built.

When crafting an answer to a question, consider what you are actually saying with the answer. As an "original contribution to knowledge", most of what you do should

BLOOM'S TAXONOMY - LEARNING IN ACTION

recording speech photograph | implication conclusion model
drama diagram | from idea casual relations | outline analogy
cartoon | own statement | compare summary
story

text readings newspapers magazines | list drama sculpture jewelry
radio films television | painting poetry

match | explain
restate | defend
paraphrase | distinguish
rewrite | summarize
give examples | interrelate
express | interpret
illustrate | extend

videos plays filmstrips | illustration map solution project
events people recordings | question forecast diagram
follow an outline

select label
list identify
name locate | organize sketch
define recite | generalize apply
describe state | dramatize prepare
memorize recognize | produce solve
show draw paint choose

2 comprehension

1 knowledge **3** application

6 evaluation **4** analysis

5 synthesis

judge compare | compare differentiate
criticise critique | analyze subdivide
support recommend | classify infer
assess appraise | point out survey
evaluate compare | distinguish select categorize prioritize

self-evaluation conclusion recommendation | word defined statement
survey verdict court trial | argument identified conclusion
propaganda checked
questionnaire

standard compared standard established | discussion assessment

compose | construct
originate | produce
hypothesize | plan
develop | create
design | invent
combine | organize

survey syllogism breakdown
graph report

experiment play hypothesis | article invention
alternative action formulation book | set of standards game report
song set of rules machine

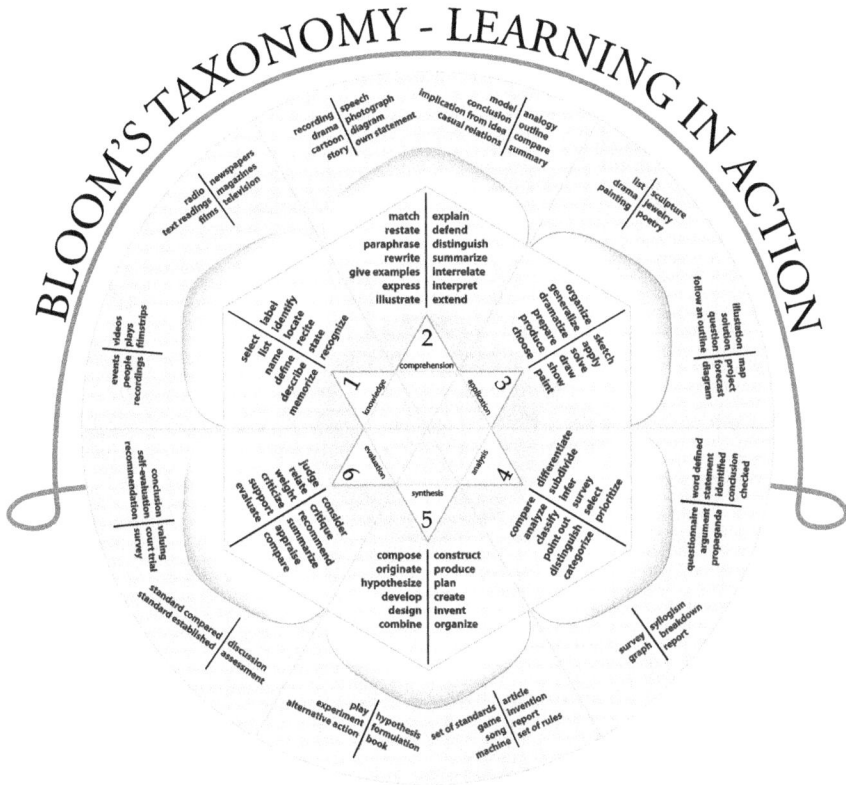

FIGURE 1.1 John Manuel Kennedy Traverso, CC BY-SA 3.0 <https://creativecommons.org/licenses/by-sa/3.0>, via Wikimedia Commons.

belong in the domains of analysis, synthesis and evaluation. If you spend most of your time describing and summarizing, your answer is probably too shallow to really advance the state of the art much. That's not always going to be true, of course – but as a general rule of thumb.

Each rung of this ladder then represents an intensification of the key deliverable of research – **insight.** Perhaps it's not even a ladder – perhaps it's best considered a kind of **refinery**. The more you refine, the more genuinely personal, reflective and critical your work will be. At the bottom, or start, of the process all you're really doing is shuffling words around – setting the scene, explaining important parts of how your subject matter works, familiarizing your audience with what they may need to know to understand what follows. You're not looking to baffle anyone with your brilliance here – just trying to make sure that when your brilliance manifests people recognize it. Almost everything that's expressed here is uncontroversial because it's statement of fact. That's an expression of **knowledge.**

We then move into **comprehension** in which we might summarize, restate or paraphrase the work of other people. Here we'll set the context of intertextual comparisons – "game A uses this system this way, game B uses it this other way". We then **apply** our knowledge, organizing it into a form for structured discussion and identify general trends. "From the way Game A, B and C do this we can see that system Y is used for this purpose".

All of this is about bringing in the work of other people and preparing it for when you crash the party like a record scratch.[13] You can happily write thousands of words in these parts of the cognitive domain without putting a single original thought into the mix. The top half is context. The bottom half – that's your time to shine. This is where research lives because it's where **you** come into it. You can't progress from the top half to the bottom unless you're willing to nail your colours to the mast.

Analysis, the next level, is when you build in your inferences, your comparisons, and your differentiations. "If Game A, B, and C use system Y to purpose Z, we can see that Game D is an outlier because it subverts this expectation", or "Authors Emily, Amy, and Lisa argue that System Y reflects assumptions of colonialism, but we can see that Bill, Bert and Amanda offer a contradictory opinion as a result of...'" You might infer. "Giving the following observations, we can infer a certain ideology that suggests...".

The form your scholarly output takes is largely irrelevant here – a blog post, a video essay, an academic paper, or a book. In all cases, if evidence must be proportional to claims, elements of the Bloom taxonomy should be proportional to the insight you hope to communicate. If the literature review makes your work robust, this is how you wield rhetoric to make it **convincing.**

Synthesis is when you start to formulate and test your hypothesis. Probe it for strengths and weaknesses. What does the choice of mechanisms, of narrative, of genre suggest in the scope of your research question? What claims are untested, and how does the subject of your work support or detract from the conclusions you have thus been drawing? What are the broader themes that you can originate on the basis of your experience?

And then, finally – an **evaluation** in which you consider all your evidence, judge it in context, weight its relative merits, and finally come to an answer to your research question.

Your work has a job to do. It should explain to people, clearly and with evidence, **why** we have arrived at a particular answer. An evaluation is important, but what is perhaps more important still is the reasoning. Many of us were constantly chided in school mathematics classes for simply writing down an answer without showing the working. Convincing rhetoric around research is all about showing your working.

What Even Are Games?

Knowing about research tells us a little bit about the **why** of what we're doing here. We do research – informally or otherwise – to understand a topic a little better than before. Sometimes this research is for our benefit– **we** are more informed as a result of our curiosity. Sometimes the research benefits society – the **world** is more informed as a result of our curiosity. The process is almost always the same regardless of what you're looking into – whether it's nuclear physics (what happens if I bang these two atoms together?), human psychology (what happens if we put someone in a room without a clock for a week?), or games (what is it about Sayonara Wild Hearts that makes Michael so giddy?). The skills we're developing here are skills that have general applicability.

This isn't a book on research methods though. It's a book about doing meaningful scholarship within the topic of games. It might then be a useful first step to actually define what it is we're talking about.

The scope of this book is broad – it includes video games; board games; role-playing games; mega games; LARPs; and even non-games (real-life systems we can understand as game-based systems). However, the word "game" is very well represented within our scope, and we haven't yet actually explained what a game **is**. How remiss of me!

Definitions are important in research, because they are inherently **scoping**. A child might say they want to grow up to be a doctor, but there's no such thing as a "doctor" other than as a broad descriptor of a socioeconomic category of activity. In reality, there are general practitioners, surgeons, gerontologists, psychiatrists, paediatricians and so on. If you want to cut people up with a scalpel, you need a different set of skills to what you need if you want to address mental health. By which I mean if you see your therapist pick up a brain saw, it's probably a sign to shift to a different provider.

A few years ago, I received an incredibly negative student evaluation for my Introduction to Game Research course. The syllabus is very clear what the course involves. It's an investigation into all kinds of video games, board games and role-playing games with the intention of furnishing a student with the necessary breadth of knowledge to say interesting things about the medium. This evaluation was "strongly disagree" for every single point. That's unusual – not to toot my own horn or anything but this course is traditionally very well reviewed. It was mystifying until I got to the open comments, which said "They should name this course something else because I joined it thinking it was about game theory and it's not".

We'll leave aside the fact that someone joining a course entirely on its title rather than its description suggests they need to develop research skills more broadly. The "feedback" though does highlight an important consideration – different disciplines use words differently. "Game" in mathematical theory is a very different thing from "game" as we discuss it. "Game theory" in economics relates to an assessment of human behaviour within which interdependent consideration give rise to complex outcomes. If you've picked up this book expecting us to break-down a Nash Equilibrium (Facchinei and Kanzow 2010) or delve into the structure of the Dictator Game (Engel 2011)... well, sorry but in future read the blurb on the back of a book before you buy it.

We're not going to be especially restrictive in how we talk about games here. I generally don't require students to adhere to a particular definition – for me, if someone can **convincingly argue** that something is a game, I'll happily accept their work. That in itself becomes kind of a mini-research project – to embed evidence and robust claims within well-crafted rhetoric that convinces the reader.

The problem with an all-encompassing definition is one common to all disciplines. It is **incredibly difficult** to define something in a way that excludes everything you want to exclude while including everything you want to include. Something always slips past the net. Stenros (2017) identified over 60 definitions of games from the 1930s onwards. Let's look at some common examples you may see in the literature.

Abt (1987):

> Reduced to its formal essence, a game is an *activity* among two or more independent *decision-makers* seeking to achieve their *objectives* in some *limiting context*.

So, that excludes Solitaire; solo board games; and Choose Your Own Adventure style gamebooks at a stroke. It also includes doing a buddy-read (an activity, between two or more people, to achieve the objective (reading a book) in some limiting context (a book that both have agreed upon). Kids playing dress-up, or musically inclined friends engaging in jam session, might qualify as games here.

Suits (1978) has a whole career worth of definitions and expansions upon definitions, but at one point tried to condense it down:

> Playing a game is the voluntary attempt to overcome unnecessary obstacles.

So, a kid leaping fences on her way back from school is "playing a game". Running
an obstacle course is playing a game. Throwing cards into a hat is a game. Running a
race **isn't** a game (no unnecessary obstacles), nor is it a session of "keep away" (invol-
untary). Putting together a jigsaw too becomes a game under this definition, as does
fortune-telling in many guises.

Some scholars make a distinction between play and gaming. Play is generally
unstructured and open-ended, reinterpreted and recontextualized on the fly. "I just
shot you with my laser!", "Nuh-uh, I have a laser deflecting shield!", and "My pet
shark eats your shield". Gaming, as a counterpoint, is usually structured and confined
within formal or semi-formal systems. Interpretation is usually limited to the construction of meaning where these formal systems are ambiguous.

There we introduce one of the common factors that unite most definitions – the
need for rules or limiting context. Crawford (1984) tried to frame games as having
four key factors they share – representation (a closed formal state that subjectively
represents a subset of reality), interaction between agents, conflict between agents,
and "safety", which is that the results of a game are always less harsh that the subset
of reality being represented. Again, the stress on interaction and conflict is problematic here – arguably excluding everything from Solitaire to co-op board games to The
Sims. However, the "closed formal state", or rules, again surfaces as a core element.

Huizinga (1971) spoke of games as free-standing activities quite consciously outside ordinary life. They were "not serious", connecting with no material interest (there
goes poker), and having no profit associated (there go many game-shows). He also
stresses though "it proceeds within its own proper boundaries of time and space,
according to fixed rules and in an orderly manner".

Jesper Juul (2003), in an influential keynote talk, talked about games as having six
key characteristics:

- Fixed rules, which is to say a formal set of mechanisms by which the state
  of a game can be modified.
- Variable outcome, which is to say that the outcome of a game is not deterministic or set in stone by starting conditions.
- Valorization of outcomes, which is to say that there are good outcomes and
  bad outcomes.
- Player effort, which is to say that the outcome should depend on the player's
  engagement.
- Player attachment to outcome, which is to say that players should care if they
  achieve good or bad outcomes.
- Negotiable consequences, which is to say that the play can **optionally** be
  assigned real-life consequences.

However, while Juul's definition suffers from the same issues as all definitions (it is
neither fully exclusive nor fully inclusive of outliers), he also offers a consideration of
games which fall outside of these factors. Specifically, he identifies borderline cases:

- Tabletop Roleplaying Games, where rules are often flexible and interpretations often at the whim and discretion of the referee. Whole subsystems of rules can be included or omitted largely at will.
- Open-ended simulations, where there is no particular valorization of outcomes.
- Games of pure chance, where player effort is completely decoupled from outcome.
- Chance and skill-based gambling, where the need for a financial stake and agreement on payouts enforce pre-negotiated consequences.

These exemptions also allow for compounds, such as "chance-based gambling", which doesn't offer negotiated consequences and **also** decouples player effort from outcome.

Juul also explicitly outlines several examples of things that are **not** games, including free-form play, warfare, storytelling, fire-watching, and many of the things classified as games in mathematics, such as the Game of Life (Conway 1970).

We could spend the rest of this chapter discussing these definitions and where they fall down. We could talk about the Crawford (2004) and Koster (2013) view that games are essentially learning tools where the provision of playful opportunities to make interesting decisions helps develop mastery. Or Esposito (2005) who argued that video-games in particular are games which we play thanks to an audiovisual apparatus and which can be based on a story. All definitions have their charms, their defenders, and their detractors. There is a definition that will encompass any "game" you want, and exclude any "game" you'd like. At this point, any new attempt to solve the problem will simply introduce more variability.[14]

For me, I tend to go back to one of my favourite philosophers, Wittgenstein. He argued for a principle called **family resemblance** (Wittgenstein 1958) in which we avoid strict definitions. We instead simply knuckle under to the fact that the universe is not required to be in alignment with our desire to order it. Often, things can't be connected by one or more **essential** common features and are instead connected by a subset of overlapping features. No one feature, Wittgenstein argues, is common to all things in a family. The more overlapping features, the more confident we can be that something belongs to a broader category. It's a kind of cluster analysis (Romesburg 2004), a technique now used to great effect in machine learning and data mining. We have a contextual checklist, and the more things on the list a thing checks the more likely it is that our categorization is correct. We'll come back to this idea later when we talk about the concept of genre and the importance of intertextuality.

For the purposes of this book, I'm happy to adopt the loose convenience of what the US Supreme Court said when facing a similar definition problem (Gewirtz 1995).

"We know it when we see it".

Not-Games

We might be on easier definition ground to look at a little outcropping of game studies – that of the **not-game**. These are formal systems that are explicitly **not** games (hence the name) but can still be understood in the context of a game. While we'll be devoting most of our time in this book to games as you will recognize them (you'll know them when you see them), a lot of the techniques and concepts we employ will also yield insights into a wide variety of other facets of life.

Consider for example the idea of how the education system works. Undergraduate studies, say. There's a win condition (emerge with a degree). It has a set of challenges (or obstacles) to overcome (assignments, cultural conventions). It has tactical and strategic elements (passing a course versus learning the material. What assignments get your A-Game and which get phoned in). It's replete in a meta-game context – what's often called the hidden curriculum (Bergenhenegouwen 1987; Giroux and Penna 1979; Gofton and Regehr 2006; Portelli 1993) in which all the unspoken rules are encoded. It has formal rules of engagement – plagiarism, deadlines, governance on the use of AI, and so on. In fact, consider how it fits into Juul's definitions:

- Fixed rules – codes of conduct, and attendance. Credits gained through participation in education. Credits awarded or rescinded according to set policies. Access to certain courses depends on previous engagement with other courses through pre-requisites.
- Variable outcome – everyone admitted starts, theoretically, at the same place. The actual outcome is independent of admission.
- Valorization of outcomes – passing versus failing, classification of degree, "with distinction", "summa cum laude". GPA, "top x% of the class".
- Player effort – the quality of the outcome is causally linked to the effort, talent and insight of the player.
- Player attachment to outcome – people take their results seriously.
- Negotiable consequences – well, perhaps not this one…

While it's not a complete fit for the definition of a game (and it would be kind of weird if it was), it overlaps very significantly. There is a clear family resemblance. And importantly, you can get **better** at academia, particularly as you master the principles of the hidden curriculum. Outcome is not just dependent on mastery of the topic, but also mastery of the system. I consider myself to be a "working class academic". I was never really expected to go to university, certainly not to gain a doctorate, and absolutely not to teach at one. I think a lot of people under-estimate the systemic advantage that comes from belonging to a family where academic achievement is part of the vocabulary of everyday life.

Not-games can be found everywhere. Software development is a not-game. Religious observance is a not-game. The stock market is a not-game. Dating is a not-game. And as such, we can apply research questions about these knowledge domains in a gaming frame.

- We could explore the game mechanics of academia.
- We could investigate the win condition of software development.
- We could analyse the experiential aspects of religious structures.
- We could assess the strategic or tactical implications of dating.[15]

As a priming exercise for the rest of the book to follow, consider how what we learn about games illuminates the world around you. Fun, after all, is a serious business.

A Final Note before We Begin for Real

As part of writing this book, I wanted to make sure you as the reader got a chance to see a range of different perspectives on how the various approaches might be applied. As a consequence, six of the chapters in the book are from guest contributors – all of whom who have a connection to the course from which this book was developed. These are primarily student contributions – largely, not entirely, revised versions of work that was submitted as the final assignment for the students in question. While I have done a little light editing here and there, the approaches, thoughts and gathered insights belong to the authors.

Chapter 4 is an experiential and critical reading of the board game Secret Hitler, contributed by Constantina-Edesa Filios (just Edesa to her friends). It's a great example of marrying intratextual and intertextual elements into a coherent hypothesis. Aya and Eleni's systemic exploration of categorization theory in Wilmot's Warehouse, drawing as it does from cognitive science, is a first-rate exercise in showing how theories from other disciplines may be brought in to illuminate our understanding of games. Klara's evocative meditation on melancholy in Hollow Knight – Chapter 8 – is a haunting look at experiential elements from a more philosophical perspective. Pauline's contribution on Animal Crossing, Chapter 10, is an autobiographical experiential application of psychogeography within the context of how place attachment can build emotional resonance into the virtual worlds we inhabit. Anna and Edvin look at the tabletop roleplaying game Blades in the Dark in Chapter 12 and build a systemic lens that can be used to explore and understand how its mechanisms contribute to developing and sustaining tension in play. Finally, Chapter 14 is a contribution from Luise and Julius looking at how Chants of Sennaar constructs its language to tell stories of cultural context and the power of translation – another systemic analysis with a critical bent.

I am beyond grateful to all of these contributors. Their work has broadened immensely the topics and games this book covers.

Notes

1 Let's start the demystifying process here. You'll find academic books littered with these little annotations. They're called **in-text citations** and they're essentially the audit-trail for ideas. Attached to every chapter in this book is a list of references, and this citation tells the reader which reference is the evidence for which claim. Here, you'd look for the 2024 entry for the name Clement. Work you do as a scholar should be built on a rigorous base of evidence, and this kind of thing is how you evidence that evidence.

2 Sometimes in-text citations refer to games, and in this case you look them up in the **ludography** rather than the references.

3 For those that don't know what this means, Google tells me that this is an acronym for Wireless Application Protocol and was a popular forerunner to the Internet on early mobile phones.

4 Which is, in my view, the best game ever made.

5 Yeesh, let's give this a go. For those reading in the UK and who are familiar with UK academic structures the closest thing is probably a Reader. For those in European universities, it's more like an Associate Professor. Associate Professor in Europe is

more like Full Professor in the US. Except in all the situations where none of this is true. In Portugal a Docent is just a word used for "teacher". Let's just sum it up as saying I'm a relatively mediocre academic with an obsession about games, and I have thus far managed to evade detection as the fraud I secretly believe myself to be.

6 I work in a blended department called Computer Science and Engineering, which is owned by two different universities with two different bureaucracies and two differ-ent sets of rules and procedures. If you think that sounds confusing and complicated, that's only because you don't have the five years of experience with the system I do. If you did, you'd know it's **much worse** than you'd imagine.

7 "Ninety percent of everything is crap".

8 The fact I instinctively capitalize it every time I type it is a sign of the Proper Noun status it has achieved in my mind.

9 A lot of published papers will explore a problem domain and conclude that "It sure would be nice if someone filled in the blanks of our knowledge as far as X, Y and Z goes!". That's **your** cue.

10 As you might pick up as we go through this book, I'm something of a fan of this game. At least one person in the world will care about your answer.

11 Yes.

12 We'll see in a little bit how complex something as supposedly simple as "define" can actually be.

13 Who's afraid of little ol' you?.

14 https://xkcd.com/927/.

15 Actually, that's exactly what pick-up artists do so maybe don't do this.

References

Abt, Clark C. 1987. *Serious Games*. Lanham, MA: University Press of America.

Bergenhenegouwen, Gerard. 1987. 'Hidden Curriculum in the University'. *Higher Education* 16(5):535–43. doi: 10.1007/BF00128420.

Bloom, Benjamin S. (Benjamin Samuel). 1956. *Taxonomy of Educational Objectives: The Classification of Educational Goals*. New York, Longmans, Green.

Brandse, Michael. 2017. 'The Shape of Challenge'. Pp. 362–76 in *Design, User Experience, and Usability: Designing Pleasurable Experiences*, edited by A. Marcus and W. Wang. Cham: Springer International Publishing.

Clement, Jessica. 2024. 'Video Game Market Revenue Worldwide from 2019 to 2029'.

Conway, John. 1970. 'Conway's Game of Life'. *Scientific American*.

Crawford, Chris. 2004. *Chris Crawford on Interactive Storytelling*. Pearson Education.

Crawford, Linda L., and Chris Crawford. 1984. *The Art of Computer Game Design: Reflections of a Master Game Designer*. Columbus, OH: McGraw-Hill Osborne.

Engel, Christoph. 2011. 'Dictator Games: A Meta Study'. *Experimental Economics* 14:583–610.

Esposito, Nicolas. 2005. 'A Short and Simple Definition of What a Videogame Is'. in *Proceedings of DiGRA 2005 Conference: Changing Views: Worlds in Play. DIGRA, Tampere Finland*.

Facchinei, Francisco, and Christian Kanzow. 2010. 'Generalized Nash Equilibrium Problems'. *Annals of Operations Research* 175(1):177–211. doi: 10.1007/s10479-009-0653-x.

Furst, Edward J. 1981. 'Bloom's Taxonomy of Educational Objectives for the Cognitive Domain: Philosophical and Educational Issues'. *Review of Educational Research* 51(4):441–53. doi: 10.3102/00346543051004441.

Gamboa, Mafalda, Michael James Heron, Miriam Sturdee, and Pauline Belford. 2023. 'Screenshots as Photography in Gamescapes: An Annotated Psychogeography of Imaginary Places'. Pp. 506–18 in *Proceedings of the 15th Conference on Creativity and Cognition, C&C '23*. New York: Association for Computing Machinery.

Gewirtz, Paul. 1995. 'On I Know It When I See It'. *Yale LJ* 105:1023.

Giroux, Henry A., and Anthony N. Penna. 1979. 'Social Education in the Classroom: The Dynamics of the Hidden Curriculum'. *Theory & Research in Social Education* 7(1):21–42. doi: 10.1080/00933104.1979.10506048.

Gofton, Wade, and Glenn Regehr. 2006. 'What We Don't Know We Are Teaching: Unveiling the Hidden Curriculum'. *Clinical Orthopaedics and Related Research®* 449:20–27.

Gottfried, Jeffrey, and Olivia Sidoti. 2024. 'Teens and Video Games Today'. https://www.pewresearch.org/wp-content/uploads/sites/20/2024/05/PI_2024.05.09_Video-Games_REPORT.pdf.

Huitt, William. 2011. 'Bloom et al.'s Taxonomy of the Cognitive Domain'. *Educational Psychology Interactive* 22:1–4.

Huizinga, Johan. 1971. *Homo Ludens: A Study of the Play-Element in Culture*. Boston: Beacon Press.

Juul, Jesper. 2003. 'The Game, the Player, the World: Looking for a Heart of Gameness'. in *Proceedings of DiGRA 2003 Conference: Level Up*. Tampere: DIGRA.

Koster, Raph. 2013. *Theory of Fun for Game Design*. Sebastapol, CA: O'Reilly Media, Inc.

MacLeod, Colin M. 1991. 'Half a Century of Research on the Stroop Effect: An Integrative Review'. *Psychological Bulletin* 109(2):163.

Miller, Arthur G., Barry E. Collins, and Diana E. Brief. 1995. 'Perspectives on Obedience to Authority: The Legacy of the Milgram Experiments'. *Journal of Social Issues* 51(3):1–19. doi: 10.1111/j.1540–4560.1995.tb01331.x.

Narayan, Rasipuram Krishnaswami. 2016. *The Mahabharata: A Shortened Modern Prose Version of the Indian Epic*. Chicago: University of Chicago Press.

Portelli, John P. 1993. 'Exposing the Hidden Curriculum'. *Journal of Curriculum Studies* 25(4):343–58. doi: 10.1080/0022027930250404.

Romesburg, Charles. 2004. *Cluster Analysis for Researchers*. Lulu. com. Morrisville, NC: Lulu Press.

Stein, Roger M. 2014. 'The Half-Life of Facts: Why Everything We Know Has an Expiration Date'. *Quantitative Finance* 14(10):1701–3. doi: 10.1080/14697688.2014.896123.

Stenros, Jaakko. 2017. 'The Game Definition Game: A Review'. *Games and Culture* 12(6):499–520. doi: 10.1177/1555412016655679.

Suits, Bernard Herbert. 1978. *The Grasshopper : Games, Life, and Utopia*. Toronto ; Buffalo : University of Toronto Press.

Wittgenstein, Ludwig. 1958. *Philosophical Investigations*. Cowley Road: Blackwell.

Ludography

It's not necessarily common practice to include a ludography (a bibliography, but for games) but I think it's a valuable way to allow people to see – at a glance – the intertexuality of your work. The convention here is that the authoring agent is listed as the author – the primary development house in the case of a company and the primary designers and developers in the case of small teams. Publisher is listed last.

Barone, Eric. 2016. Stardew Valley [video game] [Microsoft Windows]. Chucklefish.

Box Dragon. 2025. As We Descend [video game] [Microsoft Windows]. Coffee Stain Publishing.

Brown, Gavan, Matt Tolman, and Martin Wallace. 2018. Brass Birmingham [board game]. Roxley.

Bungie. 2014. Destiny [video game] [Microsoft Windows]. Activision.

Daniel Mullins Games. 2021. Inscryption [video game] [Microsoft Windows]. Devolver Digital.

EA Sports. 1993–2023. FIFA Series [Video games] [Multiple platforms]. EA Sports.

FromSoftware. 2011. Dark Souls [video game] [Microsoft Windows]. Bandai Namco Entertainment.

FromSoftware Inc. 2022. Elden Ring [video game] [Microsoft Windows]. Bandai Namco.

Magie, Elizabeth. Monopoly. 1933. [board game]. Self-published.

Maxis. 2000. The Sims [video game] [Microsoft Windows]. Electronic Arts.

Mega Crit. 2019. Slay the Spire [video game] [Microsoft Windows]. Humble Bundle.

Monolith Productions. 2014. Middle-Earth: Shadow of Mordor [video game] [Microsoft Windows]. Warner Bros Interactive.

Rockstar North. 2010. Red Dead Redemption [video game] [Microsoft Windows]. Rockstar Games

Rockstar North. 2013. Grand Theft Auto 5 [video game] [Microsoft Windows]. Rockstar Games.

Simogo. 2019. Sayonara Wild Hearts [video game] [Microsoft Windows]. Annapurna Interactive.

Studio Zero. 2024. Metaphor: Refantazio [video game] [Microsoft Windows]. Atlus.

Ubisoft. 2007. Assassin's Creed [Video game] [Microsoft Windows]. Ubisoft.

Vaccarino, Donald X. 2008. Dominion [board game]. Rio Grande Games.

ZA/UM. 2019. Disco Elysium [video game] [Microsoft Windows]. ZA/UM.

2

Critical Perspectives in Game Studies

Michael Heron

Critical Perspectives in Games

All of this talk of definitions, and "what do we mean when we say game?" and the idea of reading all formal systems as not-games falls under a broad umbrella of "critical evaluation". This is one of the lenses that we'll be using to focus in on ways in which we can be talking more deeply about games. This is a lens that looks to investigate **meaning**. A critical perspective is what we use to work out what a game is **saying** to us.

Games talk to us all the time, if only we know how to interpret the communication. Games communicate meaning to us through character design and through mechanical design. They communicate through story and dialogue, of course, but also through setting and thematic resonances. They talk to us in how they mediate the complexities of time and space. They talk to us in the way in which they give us control over the camera, and the ways in which they take that control away. They talk to us through visual effects. There is a language of gaming – a set of conventions, tropes and stylistic choices in which we eventually develop a kind of fluency. The term **game literacy** is often employed here (Buckingham and Burn 2007), and it's a fitting phrase.

Our job, when employing a critical lens, is to engage with what a game is saying – to participate in a conversation in which we interpret the vocabulary of game design and assign interpretation to its usage. In this, we employ the full toolkit of literacy and assess what we can say about a game based on how it upholds, subverts or inverts our expectations. Is a game saying something prosaic with how it works with and against our game literacy? Is it saying something provocative? And does it come out and say it, or does it imply it? In what way do you pick up on the messaging? Is that messaging intentional or accidental? Is it ideological or merely political?

Think of some of the conventions that you unconsciously ascribe to. Close your eyes and think of a game. A platforming game where you jump around and avoid goblins and trolls. It employs screen-based levels – when you get to the exit point of a screen, you warp to a new one. This isn't a real game, but... where does your character begin positioned on the first screen, and in what direction is the exit?

If you said "bottom left" and "to the right", you're visualizing a standard convention in gaming. We tend to interpret linear progress as going from left to right, and the first direction players will move – absent other cues – is usually rightwards. You're

DOI: 10.1201/9781003530282-2

probably not aware of that consciously, but it almost certainly feels true as an abstract case, right?

Now imagine the games where that convention is not enforced. Games where you begin at the right-hand side and move left. Or games where you exit one screen on the top right to find yourself starting at the top left. A game is saying something to you in these circumstances. It's saying something about how it models reality and the spatial arrangement of its geography. It is saying something about your expectations and how they can be manipulated. Our job, as scholars, is to drill into all the parts of a game to extract a meaning. Not **the** meaning – but **a** meaning.

One thing that is often said in gaming discourse is that "all games are political", which is instantly countered by something like, "No, that's nonsense. Where are the politics in Tetris?". As usual, the disagreement isn't actually in fact but in perspective. And it comes down to the question, "Well, what do you mean by politics?"

I sometimes say that all games are political but not all games are ideological. As soon as you get two people together in a room, you have politics. When multiple agents have contradictory opinions on how the world should be arranged, then politics is the system by which that gets mediated. Society is the minimum viable product which ensures we all agree not to kill each other. Within this kind of frame then even if two people agree entirely on every point, they've reached a political unity. If they disagree, you have political disunity. You can't escape politics, because you can't escape people. Trust me, I've tried.

Every game is the product of its politics as they are expressed in the beliefs and worldviews of the people who make them. Every player has an interpretation of the games they play. And games are made up of so many moving parts that they can't escape encoding political perspectives into them. They're to be found in the game and in the messaging around the game. They're in the code and they're in the aesthetics. They're in the mechanisms, and they're in the story. They're in where you buy the game and the rights you have over it. A PlayStation Exclusive game might be as apolitical as they come in terms of content, but the concept of platform exclusivity is inherently anchored in an economic model in which that exclusivity has value (Castro and Sant'Anna 2023; Mantena, Sankaranarayanan, and Viswanathan 2010). You maybe don't think of buying a PlayStation as a political act, but it is.

What it likely **isn't** is an **ideological** act. Politics is encoded automatically, but ideology has to be consciously engineered. Chess was once a battleground of East vs West – one of the many theatres of the Cold War in which a great ideological battle was being waged (Edmonds and Eidinow 2011). Tetris, emerging from Communist Russia, is mired in an economic system that distrusted outside commercialization and didn't valorize the individual accomplishment of its inventor (Ackerman 2016).

The win conditions in Civilization all centre around domination – beat your opponents to Mars; militarily dominate the planet; flood your competitors with your culture. Those are very political conceptions of victory (Krapp 2020). Where is the win condition that focuses on harmony? The one that focuses on happiness? Civilization, as a franchise, may not be pushing a specific agenda (it may not be ideological), but every game either upholds, subverts, or inverts its political context. No game can ignore it.

All of this is to say that even if a game doesn't seem to be intentionally saying anything – every game is saying **something, somewhere** in its design or its execution.

Interpretation

Essentially, what I'm getting at here is that games are ripe for **interpretation**. They are amenable to being put under an analytical lens and close-examined until they yield up their secrets. Interpretation, as a process, is one that is ideal for finding interesting things to say about the **meaning** of a game.

One of the scholars I find most insightful in this area is Terry Barrett, especially in connection to his excellent book *Criticizing Art: Understanding the Contemporary* (Barrett 2011). This is a book that is not written for games but offers a genuinely useful set of principles that strengthen a scholar's interpretation of all creative outputs. It's as relevant for movies as it is for paintings, as valuable for novels as it is for board games. It's going to do a lot of heavy lifting here.

Barrett outlined an approach that can help contextualize the role of interpretation and assist critics in making meaningful and insightful **critiques**. A critique is simply a detailed, thoughtful and evidenced analysis. We can critique practically anything – we might critique philosophies; models of thinking; and theories and frameworks. We can also apply it to the **outputs** of philosophies; models of thinking; and theories and frameworks. Anything that stands independently as a unit of creativity or knowledge is a valid target for critique.

Critique is something different from review or assessment. "Fortnite sucks" could charitably be considered a review. It's not really something we can consider to be a critique. It's not thoughtful, it's not detailed, and it's not evidenced. Reviews have a requirement to be evaluative (as per Bloom's taxonomy). Critiques **might** be evaluative, but their real value is that they are **contemplative**.

It's important here not to make the mistake many people make, which is to see the word **critic** and assume that a **critique** must be negative. A good critique will address the positive as well as the negative, but there's no requirement for it to emphasize one or the other. A critique is not something designed to tear down. It's something we use to **dig into** something. A way of surfacing subtle meanings, capturing and assessing nuance, and situating a piece of work or thought in a context.

Barrett's (Paraphrased) Principles of Interpretation

Barrett's approach encodes 18 key principles of interpretation that everyone should hold in mind as they attempt a critique. Here I have paraphrased them for games:

- **Games have an "aboutness", and that "aboutness" demands interpretation**. Aboutness is a concept in several fields (Hawke 2018; Hjørland 2001; Yablo 2014) – linguistics, information science, and the philosophy of mind. Here it means that games are *about*, *on* or *of* something. In philosophical logic, we might think of this as how a text relates to a topic.
- **Interpretations are built from persuasive arguments**. An interpretation is not factual. An interpretation is built up from many contributing parts, and it's the job of the critic to fuse them into convincing rhetoric. Barrett also has as one of his principles that **interpretations aren't right so much as they are reasonable, convincing or informative.**

- **Some interpretations are better than others**. The extent to which an interpretation is harmonious with its evidence, proportionate to its claims, and convincing in its rhetoric is what distinguishes good from bad. Barrett expands on this with another principle, which is **interpretations are judged by their coherence, how well they match the subject matter, and how complete they are.**

- **Good interpretations of games are more communicative about the game than they are the critic**. The New Games Journalism (Gamboa et al. 2023) was a brief movement in which the subjective perspective of the individual was centred and the game often shunted off to the sidelines. Barrett argues instead that when you talk about a game, you should decentre yourself.

- **Feelings are your guide to interpretation**. It's sometimes hard to work out where to start in a critique, so start with what affects you emotionally. If you feel happy, or sad, or disquieted, then that's your feelings telling you something interesting is happening.

- **There can be lots of interpretations about a game. It doesn't matter if they are contradictory.** You are not discussing **the** meaning, you're discussing **a** meaning. Barrett also states that **no single interpretation of a game is sufficient.** We all come from different backgrounds. We all have different perspectives. Many interpretations are needed to illuminate a text from all its angles.

- **Interpretations are often informed by a worldview, and often can't escape that context.** This is one of the reasons why it doesn't matter if interpretations are contradictory – we all view the world from a different perspective. It's possible for two things to be true **and** inherently contradictory.

- **A game is not necessarily about what the makers intended it to be.** Roland Barthes in his seminal work Death of the Author (Barthes 1967) dismisses the importance of biography or intention when it comes to interpreting a work. They are factors that can be taken into account, but they don't represent "ground truth". This inherently argues a stance that separates the art from the artist. One text, many meanings.

- **A critic is not a spokesperson or apologist for the artist.** In interpretation, it is the text that is the core of the work. The critic need not apologize for the artist, or the context of the times in which they work. They also need not incorporate artistic controversies unless they are integral to the interpretation. Or rather, as Barrett puts it, **the object of interpretation is the art, not the artist.**

- **Interpretation should focus on what's best, rather than what's weakest, about the work.** It's easy to pick holes, but if something is truly worthy of critique, it must have some qualities that make it so, and those are likely to be the most interesting elements.

- **All art is embedded in the world from which it emerged. All games have messaging embedded in them.** Every part of a game either upholds, inverts, or subverts expectations. No game is independent of its context.

- **All games are, in part, about other games.** This is an acknowledgement of a principle called **intertextuality** which we will get to in more depth in the next section. Similarly, **interpretation is, in the end, a collaborative process.** All critique is in ongoing dialogue with all other critique.

- **Good interpretations inspire us to our own interpretations.** We don't need to agree with the content of an interpretation, but a good interpretation will inspire us to a critique **of** the critique and encourage expansion, revision and refinement. Good critique starts a conversation; it doesn't end one.

These principles are almost universally applicable, but there are two features of games in particular that need special consideration within the framework. The first is that these principles were first outlined in relation to conventional artistic outputs – paintings, statues, photography and so on. In other words, they mostly assume a passivity on the part of the observer – that the conversation between the art and the artist transmits one way, even if it's received by different and unpredictable audiences. Games on the other hand have an almost **quantum** property (Heron 2017) in that they are interactive, and the form that a game experience takes will vary based on parameters that simply aren't relevant when talking about movies, theatre or music. A game comprises multitudes, and it is only through the act of play that those multitudes cohere into a single reading of the text. This is one of the things that makes games distinctive as a medium – their heavy focus on interactivity.

For games with a high social component, such as board games and role-playing games, there is a social aspect that also influences how people respond to play. I've often said that the dirty heart at the truth of board game design is that the game doesn't matter, it's the people who play it that generate the fun. That's why you can have a great time playing Monopoly (Magie 1933) – an objectively bad game[1] – with your friends, and yet a session of Brass: Birmingham (Brown, Tolman, and Wallace 2018)[2] with your parents might be so sapped of joy that it feels like you're attending a weirdly experimental yet intensely sombre funeral. In games, you can't ignore interactivity or social context in your interpretations. Indeed, to create genuinely distinctive interpretation, you should make every effort to **centre** those qualities in your discussion.

Intratextuality and Intertextuality

At the heart of critique is an understanding of **relationships** – as in, how elements within a work relate to each other. Interpretation isn't about description – or rather, it's only about description insofar as your reader has a sufficient frame of understanding to appreciate what it is you're saying. Description within critique is to set common ground between you and your audience. If you are spending half your intended word count recapping the plot of a game, you've strayed off of the true line of interpretation. It should be much more **why** and a lot less **what.**

The relationships – though – interrogating them is where you find most of the real meat in analysis. These relationships might be internal – something we can think of as **intratextuality**. That means that they are contained within a specific text. You might look at how certain game mechanisms work together to create an impression in play. You might look at how the design of the character helps tell the story. Or you might examine how well the story and the player agency mesh together into something coherent.

Let's say that a game gives you a certain amount of a resource every time you perform a certain action. And let's say that every turn, it taxes a certain amount of those gathered resources. Why does it do this rather than just giving you less of the resource when you perform the action? Why two separate mechanisms? Is it to encourage you to spend resources rather than hoard them? Is it to capture something thematic linked to its setting? Are there ways to circumvent taxation, making managing it something strategic? What, in other words, is the intention of the relationship between these parts of the game?

It's also important that interpretation is meaningfully **intertextual**, which is to say it's important to compare games against other games. And indeed, games against texts from other disciplines. Disco Elysium (ZA/UM 2019) almost demands an interpretation that draws in the work of social realist philosophers. Grand Theft Auto 5 (Rockstar North 2013) is illuminated by exploring its representation of organized crime against the genre of mafia movies it so gleefully channels. *Life Is Strange* (DONTNOD Entertainment 2015) is as much an emotionally charged Spotify playlist as it is an adventure game. Intertextuality means incorporating insights from relevant comparison texts, and not adhering too rigidly to the game that is right in front of you. As Barrett (paraphrased) says, all games are, in part, about other games. All **art** is, in part, about all other **art**. It is vital to explore intertextuality to construct convincing, meaningful interpretation.

Let's go back to the idea of intratextuality. One of the common ways in which we can talk about the relationship between parts within a game is in a common idea known as **ludonarrative dissonance** (Hocking 2009).

So...

Remember the title of our book? This is what I mean when I say my goal here is to demystify gaming discourse. Academia, often out of a kind of reflexive insecurity, has a tendency to inflate simple ideas and make them seem more complex, or important, through the use of obfuscating terminology (Kotwal et al. 2019; Markowitz and Hancock 2016). Here, we have **ludo**, from the Latin word Ludos, which means "relating to play". Then we have **narrative**, relating to story. Sort of. We'll come back to that. And then **dissonance** – which relates to a lack of harmony between two or more elements (Festinger 1962). So, ludonarrative dissonance or – sometimes the story and the mechanisms in a game don't seem to agree with each other.

You'll see this kind of unnecessary complexity a lot as you dig into the literature. "The subject, having underdeveloped motor and neurological sophistication found himself following an unanticipated trajectory upon an unexpected deviation in the mean height of the perambulating structure". Or, in human words, "the small child tripped and then fell down the stairs".

This is something I'd like to encourage you not to do – picking the right words is important, but clarity is always the goal of research. Obfuscation (the intentional process of making something overly complex or unintelligible) might fool some of the people some of the time, but all you do in the end is annoy people. As Nietzsche put it, you don't want to be someone who "disturbs their waters so that they may seem deep" (Nietzsche 1885, p151).

Anyway – this idea of ludonarrative dissonance comes into scope when the elements inside a game don't cohere properly, in this case, specifically the narrative and the gameplay elements. One of my favourite examples of this is from Shadow of the Tomb Raider (Eidos-Montreal 2018), in which Lara Croft is making her way through a camp of enemy soldiers. "They seem to be on edge", she muses to herself. "Something must be unsettling them". The story never really connects this to the fact that Lara is regularly emerging from the depths of muddy cliffs like a murderous Predator to slit the throat of unsuspecting enemies. "I wonder what they're so scared of?", she asks herself.

I don't know, Lara – **you**, maybe?

This is something that is particularly noticeable when it comes to tone and interpretation. The first Uncharted games (Naughty Dog 2007), starring Nathan Drake (the male Lara Croft, pretty much), were often taken to task for this. Drake is a charming rogue, a scoundrel, a wise-cracking guy who doesn't take anything all that seriously. The story reinforces this consistently. The tone is pure pulp – Indiana Jones and matinee television serials. The game however involves Drake and his companions mowing down dozens, if not hundreds, of enemies over the course of any one game. The intense gunplay is at odds with the narrative in a way that is often jarring. Or, in the terms of what we're talking about here – there is an intratextual relationship between story and gameplay that merits interpretation. The game **says** one thing but then encourages you to **do** something different. What does that say, then, about design intention?

One particularly egregious example of this (so bad it got patched out later) is in *Fallout 3* (Bethesda Game Studios 2008). The protagonist must enter a room flooded with lethal radiation in order to prevent a catastrophe. This is the final decision of the game – a moment of heroic glory in which you have the option give up your life for the greater good. And it's reasonably stirring unless you happen to be travelling with Fawkes as your companion. He's a friendly super-mutant, and super-mutants are completely immune to radiation. Mechanically, you should be able to say, "Hey buddy, do me a solid – go in there and pull that lever while I stand behind this lead sheet". The game though has narratively led you to this "moral choice" so if you ask Fawkes he says "No, this is your burden to bear". It's like having an asthma attack and asking your friend to pass your inhaler, only to be told "I'm sorry, I guess this is just how you die".

Elements within a game often don't cohere, and that's a good direction in which to aim your analysis. Or if they do cohere, that's also something worth analysing – we should talk about things when they are good as well as when they are bad. One of the coolest things that you can explore in game design is when mechanisms and narrative actually work so well together that they deliver a message that is more than the sum of their parts.

Celeste (Maddy Makes Games 2018), a rock-hard puzzle platformer, has a narrative focused on self-doubt, self-acceptance and imposter syndrome (Gadsby 2022). Every level of the game is difficult, and some of the additional challenges I am sure can only be completed with the intervention of literal witchcraft. Maddie, the main character, is beset with anxiety as she tries to climb to the top of the mountain. She keeps telling herself she can't do it, she's not good enough, it's too difficult. And you, as a player, are probably thinking "Yeah, this game is nails. I can't do it either".

Failure though in Celeste is designed to be a learning experience. The time gap between dying and restarting is tiny, allowing you to flow from failure into another attempt. The levels are structured in such a way as to permit muscle memory to develop in the pursuit of goals. And the exact sequence of movement required has peaks and troughs that allow you to psychologically compartmentalize your progress. You find yourself failing to jump on the first platform again and again. A few attempts later, you've absolutely mastered that part and have to focus instead on jumping up between two disappearing cliff edges. And by the time you're worrying about the last jump the challenges that were once insurmountable become trivial. The catharsis that comes at the end is not just visceral, it's philosophical. "Look at you", the game is saying, "You rose to this challenge". And having beaten one level, you know the next is beatable too. You climb your own mountain along with Maddie, and you learn exactly the same message, which is "You **can** do this".

Celeste is a phenomenal game, and sometimes the output of critique is to just stand back and applaud.

Another way to consider what we can say through focusing on intratextuality is examining how we come to know things about the game we're playing. For example, do we find things out through direct experience? Through exposition or audio diaries? Do we see cutscenes that aren't from our perspective?

One thing to be constantly aware of in interpreting a game is a principle known as the **unreliable narrator.** That is to say, the concept that the agent telling a story may not be accurately relaying all its elements. Perhaps they are intentionally, or accidentally, misleading the player. That's something very common in autobiographical and first-person narratives. But also, the agent telling the story (that agent might be **you**, based on how you direct the story and the camera) might simply not be in possession of all of the facts. This depends heavily on the perspective from which a story is told. You may have a reliable storyteller who presents an objectively true version of what happened, although even that doesn't mean that you are in possession of all the facts. Dialogue, for example, represents the internal understanding of a flawed observer. "They're keeping the nuclear bomb in the bunker". The dialogue doesn't define reality – at best, you might say that the speaker believes that's where it is. A disconnect between unreliable narration and what actually happens isn't dissonance – it's often a storytelling technique.

In Star Wars: A New Hope Han Solo is quoted as referring to the Millennium Falcon as "the ship that made the Kessel Run in less than twelve parsecs". Parsecs, in this sense, are almost certainly being incorrectly used as a unit of time as opposed to a unit of distance (Greenbaum 2008). That has been retroactively changed into consistency with scientific terminology (or it has been **retconned** in informal jargon) many times to define the Kessel Run as a measure of how close one gets to a network of black holes. We can also simply interpret it as Han Solo – a consummate con-man – attempting to bamboozle a couple of backwater rubes so they'll pay him for transit (Heron 2017). The dialogue doesn't create a meaning of the term, but it does mark Han Solo out as an unreliable narrator. A story might be made up of multiple unreliable narrators, within an otherwise reliable storytelling context. Nothing is ever as simple as saying "X means X".

The player themselves is an unreliable narrator – one of the things we naturally try to do when playing a game is to make sense of what is happening. In this, we rely on things such as the spatial relationship between the environment and the player, our control over the camera, cues given to us in the environment and our own sense of cause and effect. You might think of this as a game having a story, and a bunch of conflicting narratives about that story, which are unreliably interpreted by we the players to build a flawed model of what's happening.

When building an interpretation from intratextual elements, we need to be mindful of this. The source of information needs to be taken into account. Is it from a cut-scene? An audio-log? An in-game radio broadcast? How much can we trust the source, within the context of the game?

We can be aided here, most of the time, by considering whether the source of information is **diegetic** or **non-diegetic**. Diegetic means that it's something that is part of the world itself. If it's something your character would perceive in the game environment then it's a diegetic element. A song playing on a car radio – diegetic. That same song played as part of a cinematic soundtrack – non-diegetic. Dialogue is diegetic. User interfaces are (usually) non-diegetic. But these are in themselves loose yard-sticks. Consider how games and movies starring Deadpool explicitly break the fourth wall, such as in *Marvel vs Capcom 3* (Capcom 2011) where one of Deadpool's special moves is to grab his health bar and whack his opponent with it. Or how *The Stanley Parable* (Galactic Café 2013) is essentially a hilarious and passive-aggressive deconstruction of the very idea of a reliable narrator (Heron and Belford 2015).

One of my favourite examples of a game that plays with this is *Call of Juarez: Gunslinger* (Techland 2013). The framing is of an old grizzled cowboy telling a story in a bar. In the manner of pub raconteurs everywhere, many of the tales are wildly embellished. Each new story is a scenario you play through from his perspective. When he begins a story saying "And there I was, surrounded by fifty people on the cliffs above me", you find yourself in that situation and completely unable to do anything due to the instadeath that awaits you when you poke your head out of cover. Then one of the members of his audience scoffs, "You'd be dead if there were 50 of them. That's a lie", and the storyteller mumbles and says, "Could have been I miscounted. No fewer than ten though", and 40 of your enemies disappear. It's a wonderful system that makes for genuinely laugh-out-loud moments.

All of this is to say that we're always working from a partial conception of the world, the ordering of its elements, and its rules. We can't ignore that when it comes to interpretation.

When it comes to intertextuality, we have a wide range of things we might think about incorporating in a critique. Here are some productive questions to ask:

- What does examining similar games tell us about the game we're focusing our attention upon?
  - What can we say about Elden Ring (FromSoftware 2022) as a result of digging into Sekiro (FromSoftware 2019)? What do they do differently? What do they do the same? How does our view of the relationship change if we incorporate Bloodborne (FromSoftware 2015) or the mainline Dark Souls series (FromSoftware 2011)?
- What is the relationship between a game and a real-life (or fictional) political or philosophical context?
  - What is *Call of Duty* (Infinity War 2003) telling us about militaristic triumphalism? What are the historical themes that DEFCON (Introversion Software 2006) is playing on when it presents its view of nuclear annihilation? What does Papers, Please (Lucas Pope 2013) say about bureaucracy and immigration? What does Citizen Sleeper (Jump Over The Age 2022) have to say about what it means to be a person?
- How can games help us come to terms with difficult emotional content and trauma?
  - How does *That Dragon, Cancer* (Numinous Games 2016) tackle the death of a child? How does *A Night in the Woods* (Infinite Fall 2017) contextualize depression?
- How does a game engage with the historicity of its subject matter?

- Does *Black Myth: Wukong* (Game Science 2024) respect the cultural tropes of its source material – specifically the Journey to the West (Yu 2006)? How does Twilight Struggle (Gupta and Matthews 2005) encapsulate the nuclear brinksmanship of the Cold War? How does *Red Dead Redemption* (Rockstar North 2010) reflect our modern understanding of the passing of an age of freedom?
- How does the aesthetic design of a game trigger an external emotional response?
  - *Sayonara Wild Hearts* (Simogo 2019) makes me **feel things**, and it's been a long time since I felt anything. Why? Why does *Persona 5 Royal* (ATLUS 2022) make me feel so lonely? How do *Scanner Sombre* (Introversion Software 2017) and *Gone Home* (Fullbright 2013) make use of horror tropes to elicit a fearful response to fundamentally safe environments?

Intratextuality is entirely about how the elements of the text come together. Intertextuality is about how texts inform other texts. A good critique is made up of both of these elements. We will come back to this.

Time and Space and Presence

One valuable lens that you have available to say something of interest about a game is to assess how it represents important physical properties such as time and space. Also relevant is how your presence within time and space are represented. We've already talked about the idea of diegesis versus non-diegesis – the idea that sights and sounds are either part of our world (diegetic) or part of our interface (non-diegetic). Games often have to offload important elements from the world onto the interface, such as health, lives, score, ammunition, and so on. Occasionally, games try to blend non-diegetic data (health) into a diegetic interface (such as a HUD), but this is often an unconvincing approach unless handled very carefully (Marre, Caroux, and Sakdavong 2021).

Mimesis is another useful and related concept. Within game studies, we use this to capture the fundamental difficulty that comes with what a game must do – represent a complex world environment in a way that is comprehensible to us. Mimesis is an attempt to imitate that which exists in the abstract through a comprehensible set of metaphors. In this case, it relates to how a game mediates between elements such as local co-ordinates, world-co-ordinates, camera co-ordinates, data, behaviour, and physics to create something that feels harmonious.

Note here that within game studies, we use these terms differently from how they're used in other disciplines. In literature, for example, diegesis is mostly "telling" and mimesis is "showing". All disciplines borrow from each other in terms of concepts and terminology, but they are rarely differently translatable.

If you want a feel for how complex mimesis can be within a game, we can look at how Nitsche (2008) deconstructed it down into various analytical levels, all of which need to cohere to create a credible game experience.

- **Rules-based**, which is to say the rules that govern the underlying physics of the world. How fast we move, what we can see, where light comes from, etc.
- **Mediated**, where a complex world with objects made up of varied characteristics is rendered down into something that is perceivable by a player – such

as how a world of numbers ends up being projected as graphics onto a computer monitor.

- **Fictional**, where meaning is constructed and where the player imagines themselves as part of the game.
- **Play**, which is the environment we occupy while playing – maybe we're sprawled on a couch, or sitting in front of a TV, or upright at a desk.
- **Social**, which is the context of play when others are involved. This is where we draw in shared experiences, divergent perspectives on experience, and the perceptions of our companions.

Nitsche is essentially asking us to consider where a game exists. Is it what we see and control on the screen, or is it deeper in the rules? Is our immersion in a game (in the fictional layer) where real experience resides? One feature of remastered games I find most fascinating is in how I will be presented with screenshots and in-game footage and say "Well, it doesn't look like they've changed anything at all". Then I see screenshots and footage of the version I played back in the day, and it's striking how many differences there actually are. Much of the experience of play happens in our heads.

What about attitude and posture? Gaming is, at the end, a hobby that interfaces with our neurochemistry in many different ways (Kühn et al. 2011). Our neurochemistry is a physical property that is affected by our existence in a real world. The way in which we are immersed may have more to do with the angle of our chair than anything in the rules. Or they may have more to do with the social aspect. I vividly remember playing a particular wrestling game on the Commodore 64 with my uncle – not because of the game, but **because** it was with my uncle. Games exist in different places and some of them are in the spaces between us.

All of these layers are worth interrogating when it comes to working out what a game actually is, what it is saying, and how it is saying it. When I said earlier that the dirty secret of board games is that the game often doesn't matter… what I was saying on a more analytical level is that the rules are of lower priority than the social layer. For some people.

Consider too how a game presents itself to the player, and what that does to all the things we've already discussed. How does a video game handle its camera – does it give you full control, or does it direct your attention where it wants it to go? How does the removal of the physical constraints of a camera change the way that the game represents its world? How does a game move between different spaces, or levels? How does it translate or blend time and spatiality in those circumstances?

Cinema, as a medium, relies on the power of controlled camera angles and lenses. You go in for a close shot when you want the emotions to play out. You hold shots longer than we expect when you want to create discomfort. You project downwards to show vulnerability, and upwards to show dominance. There is a language of cinema that we often see at play in cutscenes in games, but that language is not available to a game designer when they turn over control to the player. Imagine Schindler's List if the audience member was represented in each scene and spent their time jumping randomly during long dialogue sequences.

What games give us, in most cases, is direct control and ownership over our attention. We look at what we want to look at, unless control is wrested from us. All of this combines together into the chokepoint of a mediated experience, in a rules-based system, where our perceived connection between ourselves and the action is one of the places in which the game can actually exist.

The flexibility that games give us to direct attention within our own environments gives developers a powerful tool for incorporating meaning, which is to say subtlety and implication. This is a function of time, space, **and** our presence in a game. Environmental storytelling, for example, can be something deep and comprehensive in a video game. Within cinema, we're constrained by the principle of Chekhov's Gun – a pistol on the mantle in the first act must go off by the third act.

We should also be mindful about what a game's relationship with time tells us about the way in which it helps us conceptualize a fictional reality. Games often make interesting use of time, bending and shaping it in service of narrative or mechanical goals. In Dungeons and Dragons (D&D, Crawford 2012), a journey of ten days might pass in a few minutes of vignette-based storytelling. On the other hand, a battle of ten ferocious rounds against implacable foes may only last a minute of game-time even if it takes an entire evening of play time. The convention in D&D is that each round of combat is six seconds long, and this is something used to help people conceptualize what they could feasibly do in the time they have available. People can imagine twisting open a potion and gulping it down in a round, but not constructing an elaborate trap.

The relationship between time and narrative is sometimes elastic and situational. If a cut-scene requires, for dramatic effect, a shadowy twilight, then that's when the event will occur. This is a utilitarian view of time that can sometimes be disorienting when we are used to a one-to-one relationship – that for every second of time that passes, a second of time passes.

We can even consider this in narrative frames – specifically, how **weird** the implications are. Consider the Civilization games, in which a single round of play may take 20 years of game-time in the earliest ages. That leads to an odd discontinuity where a unit of warriors may take several decades to get from one side of an island to another. In the days of the Romans, it would have been possible to walk from the north of Scotland to the south of England in around three months. In a game of Civilization, it could feasibly take a couple of centuries. And yet, as the game continues, the scale of time changes until full turns of play last mere months of game time. At this point, that same unit of warriors might find themselves breaking land-speed records as they traverse the better part of a continent at speeds reminiscent of the Flash. This gets even weirder when you think about who you are even playing in Civilization. Are you the ruler of a nation, somehow rendered immortal and anachronistically out of place? Or do you represent some kind of animus of a nation state? Who are you? Where are you? And what can we say about time and space in working out the answer to these questions?

Hauntology

Hauntology – a portmanteau of "Haunting" and "Ontology" – is a concept introduced by Jacques Derrida (Derrida 1993) to describe how certain obsolete ideas infect modern discourse long beyond the point they have relevance. It was originally used in relation to the spectre of Communism, a largely discredited economic model that is still the bugbear of Western political discourse. In recent years, the term has been appropriated by works such as the *Weird and the Eerie* (Fisher 2016) and *Retromania* (Reynolds 2011) to describe the characteristics of a society that has lost the ability to invent a future that is not some remix or reinterpretation of the past. We don't have room in this book to delve into this deeply, but I want to introduce it as a profitable frame of analysis.

There are several factors at play in hauntology:

- If you want to find inspiration, there's much more great stuff in the past – through sheer accumulation – than there is in the present.
- For most of human history, culture has been transient and as the years passed, it would fade away to make room for "modern" cultural innovations. In recent years, we have lost the very concept of loss.
- A growing reliance on algorithms for recommending cultural products has homogenized our tastes to the point that genuinely new things are vaguely alarming. Globalization too has resulted in cultural homogenization.

Derrida in his book *Archive Fever* (Derrida 1996) talked about the growing role of curators and collectors in relation to modern culture, and how in an attempt to reconcile Freud's idea of a "death drive" (Kernberg 2009), we have begun to fetishistically search the past as an escape from the future. Culturally, we seem to believe that by preserving knowledge we attain a form of cultural immortality even when there is too much knowledge for it to be routinely useful since the most valuable forms of it cannot be easily extracted.

In the short story *The Library of Babel* (Borges 2000), there exists an infinite library in which every book ever written exists. The problem is that every book that **can be written** exists there too. Given a fixed page count, word count, and character set – the vast majority of the books within the library are gibberish. Somewhere in the library is a book that tells you how to find all the real books – but how can you find it? The parallels with the release calendar of modern gaming are strong – there are too many games released annually for anyone to play even a meaningful subset. As such, we rely on others to identify the games worth playing. In the process, the games that don't get attention end up being lost in the stacks of the library regardless of their merits.

This storehouse of the past also creates a cultural gravity. Curation as an activity was once primarily about balancing the quality versus the quantity of emerging culture. Increasingly, it has become about unearthing treasures of the past (Borges 2000), and recycled cultural tropes have become the background of the world we all live within. Everything is a remix, a reinterpretation, or a homage. Mark Fisher talked about this as "the slow cancellation of the future" in which we see a situation where "new culture" is simply 20th-century culture on 21st-century screens.

For many of the products of popular culture, you could imagine a scenario where you sent it back 40 years in the past to the consternation and upset of an anachronistic generation. Rock and Roll scandalized a generation that associated music with Vera Lynn. Disco and Funk – a travesty for those who thought of the Ink Spots as being "somewhat controversial". Punk could be sent back pretty much any period of time to baffle everyone. It's hard to imagine that holding true with any movie, album, or novel from the 2000s onwards, right? For the first time in human history, we have a cultural era that is defined by the advancement of the medium as opposed to the message (Fisher 2016; Reynolds 2011).

Modern culture is haunted by the past. Try to imagine a version of the future that isn't a reinterpretation of how the future was imagined in previous decades. It's almost impossible. It's either Blade Runner; Alien; Star Wars; Dune; or one of any number of aesthetic derivatives.

Within games, there is a demonstrated half-life of relevance that comes from a lack of deep familiarity with intertextuality. Assessing games in hauntological terms – identifying their historical influences – is important if we are truly to be able to identify novelty and innovation. Games as a discipline did not spring into existence when we – as gamers – first sat down with a controller. There is a lineage and set of assumptions that we must recognize if we are to be able to break away from the ghosts of the past. We'll talk about some of this as we go through later chapters of the book, but it is worth in your critiques considering **why** conventions in games exist. There is a historicity to almost everything in games. Why do games have scores? Why is progress sometimes limited by a set number of lives? What is the emotional intent behind pixel art? Where did the concept of permadeath first originate in game design? What game had the first power-up? When did procedural generation become a common gameplay system? And importantly, how have all of these ideas evolved, or not, within the games you explore?

As part of critiquing games, it's worth considering the hauntological elements that have been adopted and examining the intentionality behind them. Sometimes games utilize well-understood systems to offer affordances in a design that are accepted largely without critique. If you want to include an assessment of innovation as part of your analysis, you first need to have a solid grasp on where an intellectual debt manifests and where a design or narrative deviates from well-worn paths. Engage with the hauntological – find the ghosts of the past, and identify evidence of where they have been intentionally exorcised.

Games as Art

We have so far been talking as if games are uncontroversially artistic outputs – we can see that as we apply Barrett's principles of interpretation to the reading of a game. However, that is not an uncontroversial assumption. Roger Ebert, a famous film critic, once declared that video games can never be art (Parker 2018). He had numerous reasons for making this statement, including:

- "No one in or out of the field has ever been able to cite a game worthy of comparison with the great poets, filmmakers, and novelists".
- You cannot win at art, you can only experience it. Games which have no win conditions cease to be games.
- The artistic merits of most games are closer to chicken scratches on a wall than they are what we traditionally consider to be art.

His argument was primarily in opposition to a particular TED talk which offered up games such as Braid (Number None 2009) and Flower (Thatgamecompany 2009) as compelling examples of games as art. However, in this he was taking a position that – certainly at the time – was as controversial as it was soporific.

My point here is primarily one of considering your audience when you talk about games – not everyone is going to be as charitable to your discipline as you'd like. Part of the core of a book like this is an entreaty – it's important that people take games seriously, and treat them as worthy of the same kind of respect that goes along with other artistic endeavours. In this though, we can't simply steamroller opposition and act as if games are art without engaging with the controversy.

It's not so useful for us to engage in disagreements about what is and is not art – one of the things that makes the debate largely fruitless is a lack of a shared common ground on how we can even define art. Where is the art in video games? Games contain artwork. They contain music. They contain writing. But games are more than the assemblage of their various constituent parts. They have qualities that aren't shared by other forms of art and to ignore those is to consider the primary texts of our discipline in the frame of inferior counterfeits. I would consider Portal (Valve 2007) to be a game worthy of the description of "art" because of the beauty of its core game mechanism.

If we subscribe to the perspective that games are art, we have to consider what we even mean by that. Is every game a work of art? If not, what are the qualities that differentiate games as art from games as… whatever else they are? Are parts of game art, or is the whole thing the art? Who is the artist? Does a game, given it is a (usually) commercial product developed (usually) by a team, contain enough "soul" to warrant the description? Are games art in the way paintings are art, or in the way architecture can be art? Is a cathedral art? Are video games comparable to cathedrals?

As with trying to formalize what we mean by "game", we can get lost in this definitional battleground.[3] It is worth considering though what you consider to be the artistic merit of a game you want to interpret. Because some games yield themselves more clearly to that descriptor than others. Choosing your battleground can be important when trying to convince people as to the merit of something as "serious" as a critique. Some hills aren't really worth dying on.

Social Commentary

One of the things that is sometimes used to identify art is the extent to which it engages in conversation with the societal context in which it is experienced. Social commentary is generally an expected part of modern art. You've probably heard the cliches – art is supposed to hold a mirror up to society[4]; art is supposed to challenge the status quo; art is intended to prompt introspection and make connections through juxtaposition. If we are to make a claim that games are worthy of the same kind of consideration as other media, then we do need to meet the discourse half way. One of the ways in which we can critique games is in terms of not just what they are saying – as in most of what we talk about in this chapter – but in terms of what they say about the world in which we live.

Lots of games are fun – a big challenge in our work is separating the games that are worthy from the games that are merely entertaining. Some games though aren't about fun in the sense that most people use the term. They're about arousal.[5] Fear is an arousal response. Anger is an arousal response. Sadness and despair – all arousal. That makes "fun" a difficult thing to pin down.

Is it "fun" to be scared? The many admirers of *Alien: Isolation* (Creative Assembly 2015) would undoubtedly say yes. Is it fun to be accelerated at high speeds towards a terrifying plunge into oblivion? Fans of rollercoasters sound off[6]! Is it fun to be frustrated to the point of a furious rage-quit? It can be!

On that latter point, a friend and I were once playing Blood Bowl (Hewitt, Hoare and Johnson 2016).[7] This is essentially Gridiron with Goblins. It's a turn-based board game of throwing and catching a ball with the intention of slamming it into the endzone, or banging your players into other players with the intention of slamming them into the hospital. It's a game with frustration built into the core, because every time you fail a skill check (and there are lots of them, often with poor odds), your turn is over and your opponent takes control of play. Essentially, when you fumble the dice, you are punished for it at the worst possible time.

We squared up to a game. I'd done some serious damage to his team in the past (we were playing in a league) so he started with many of his players off the field and on the bench. Or occasionally in the morgue. To balance this at the beginning of play, disadvantaged players are given a points budget to buy temporary replacements and freelancing star players, and that's what he'd done.

The first roll, of the first turn – I got lucky and straight up killed his most expensive star player. That's like losing your Queen in a game of chess – it's basically over at that point. In the second turn, I killed his other star player. Again, just luck – skill plays a part in *Blood Bowl* but it's more about managing risk than anything else. At that point, he quit the game and stormed off in a huff. And as I looked at the remains of the game all I could think was, "Yeah. That was actually the most rational response here".

Sorry John.

Later on in this book, we're going to talk about the idea of **frames** and **keyings**, which are ways of setting and understanding the context of social interactions. For now, let's just say that we'll take it as read that under the right circumstances, lots of things can be fun – provided the frame of our expectation is that our goal is the pleasurable arousal of strong feelings.

We don't need fun to be **fun**, in other words. That opens the door to games offering a lens on society through commentary upon that society. Some critics in the wider community find this idea borderline repellent – that mere frivolity like games can do justice to serious topics like death, grief, and politics. In fact, even the attempt is sometimes viewed as being irresponsible – that it is disrespectful at its very core.

We're going to ignore those people.

I'm not a fan of gatekeeping in the slightest, but sometimes you have to put some pre-requisites on who to take seriously. It's not okay to say to someone, "Oh, you like Dungeons and Dragons? Prove it – name every different kind of poisonous jelly". I think it's okay though to say, "Oh, you want to dismiss games as social commentary? Tell me five games that you think have tried to do it". If they can, then you've got common ground for a meaningful discussion. If they can't, well – they've got some research to do.

Game designers have long shown the potential of games – used correctly and with sensitivity – to deliver important messages about society, humanity, and the connections we make to each other. Sometimes these games have been provocative. Sometimes they have been intentionally ideological. Sometimes they have been autobiographical. We have no problems with books and movies tackling themes of mental health and societal isolation even if they are products of entertainment – commentary can rise above such concerns. The movie Joker – despite being ostensibly an origin story for a comic-book supervillain – is about as good a commentary as you could hope for with regards to society's disregard for mental health support.

So, let's talk about Train (Romero 2009), which was made by Brenda Romero as part of her *The Mechanic Is the Message* series of games (Ferrari 2011). These were designed to marry game mechanisms to social messages. The whole set is worth digging into if you want perfect examples of ideological and intentional intratextuality.

The game is very simple. Players are given typewritten instructions to load yellow pegs onto train carriages with the intention of routing them to different railway stations towards a goal. Trains are moved through dice rolls, and card play is used to change the momentum of play. That's the game – nothing remarkable at all. However at the end of the game, there is a reveal – the goal was a concentration camp in Nazi Germany, and the yellow pegs represented Jewish prisoners being transported. "The game is over when it ends", the game rules outline. The framing though is something that is only revealed once a player's train reaches the final destination.

The game was massively controversial at the time and received praise and opprobrium in roughly equal proportions. Given the nature of the game – more art installation than boxed product – few people have actually played it, and these days those likely to play it are already extremely likely to know the twist. Oh, sorry – spoilers for everything I just wrote.

However, those who played the game sometimes reported feeling shocked, upset, discomfited, or tricked. The revelation that they had "just been following orders" is intended to provoke players into considering their role in following procedures, about the importance of challenging assumptions, and perhaps even to reflect on the culpability of the everyman cogs in the Nazi's genocide machine. As with much social commentary, there is a slant in the game that directs the player down certain pathways of thought, but it otherwise leaves drawing conclusions to the player. The reveal at the end is not a "gotcha", but rather a provocation to reflect upon complicity.

Fun? Probably not.

We might also think here of games such as *This War of Mine* (11 Bit Studios 2014), in which the player controls a "safe" house within a warzone. Survivors occupy the house and must balance the needs to explore for supplies against the every-day forced banality of looking after their own physical or mental health. I first played the game properly during the early stages of Russia's invasion of Ukraine, and I confess half way through I just stopped playing and started crying. I had given the game a few tries in earlier years and never found myself moved. Sometimes the game happens in our heads (in the fictional layer) and is mediated by the empathy we have for others (in the social layer).

That Dragon, Cancer is the autobiographical story of a family coming to terms with the terminal illness of a child – it's a series of vignettes that explore significant moments during the period between the diagnosis and beyond. Again, the game was controversial in that plenty of people said it was in tremendously bad taste for the game to be made at all, even if its development was one of the forms that the grief of the parents took. The game was released after the death of Joel, the child in question, and final scenes in the game include real-life narration and voicemails (Coward-Gibbs 2020). Cards and letters from other grieving parents decorate scenes in the game. We have no problems with grief-memoirs such as *Crying in H-Mart* (Zauner 2021) or *I'm Glad My Mom Is Dead* (McCurdy 2022). Somehow though a game is considered to be a less meaningful vehicle to explore such themes, although I've yet to have someone convincingly explain to me why.

Holding On: The Troubled Life of Billy Kerr (Fox and O'Connor 2018) is a game in which a dying old man suffering from memory loss is taken into a hospital where the nurses must balance their own workloads, the need for his palliative care, and the desire to learn more about him as a person. I wrote an extended review of the game at the time it was released, and it's clear from that review how much it affected me (Heron 2024). Billy Kerr, when I played it, wasn't a fictional character in a board game. He was my father, in the earliest hours of my 21st birthday, as I watched him die from the brutally aggressive cancer that had robbed us of him. A month between diagnosis and death. Every time I saw the game on my shelves, it brought me back to those memories. At its heart, Holding On is a brutal satire of the care economy and an extended mediation on regret and empathy. But it has meaning beyond its own framing, and that's true of almost all art. We are not passive recipients of meaning – we are active in its construction.

Gone Home belongs to a family of games sometimes derisively called walking simulators. Personally, I prefer the term "empathic puzzler" (Heron et al. 2015), because these games are more about understanding a context than they are about simply exploring an area. The premise is that you are a young woman returning after an extended absence to find her family home empty. The house looks like it's in the process of being packed up. A note on the door from her sister begs Katie, our protagonist, not to investigate what has happened. Much as with having a loose tooth, you immediately begin probing the area to work out the damage. *Gone Home* leans heavily on aesthetics of horror – I spent my first hour with the game waiting for the devastating jump-scare I was sure was going to kill me.[8] The house is dark. Conspicuously empty. The weather is straight out of a Hammer horror movie. Thunder and ominous lightning. In the end, *Gone Home* turns out to be a story about belonging, familial tension and the intense passions of youth. It's about acceptance, rejection, and queer identity. There is value to be had in playing a game that gives you insights into the struggles and challenges of people not like you. Or like me, in this case. And in the end, it turned out *Gone Home* **was** a horror story – it's just one focused on the emotional consequence of someone's parents not willing to accept them for who they are.

These are games with intense social and cultural messaging embedded in them – down into the bones, in how they implement a setting, encode a theme, and incorporate a message that yields itself to interpretation. None of them are anvilicious about it, and they leave enough ambiguity that the player can contemplate their own relationship to the experiences they have had. Some games require you to dig deep to surface an interesting and nuanced interpretation. Some though have left helpful markers to show you where X marks the spot.

Dog Eat Dog

Let's finish up with a discussion of one of the most interesting indie *Tabletop RPGs* (TTRPGs) that have been released in the past decade or so – Dog Eat Dog (Burke and Press 2012). Unlike Dungeons and Dragons, this is a game that is about empathy rather than adventure. It's about emotional context and power differentials. It's about survival, and how power corrupts the powerless. And it's about as far from "fun" as I can imagine a game to be.

One player takes on the role of the occupier – a colonizing force that has come to an otherwise unspoiled nation. The game is canonically framed as being set in the Pacific Islands, but it doesn't necessarily follow that you're dealing with real natives or occupying forces. The key aspect here is that the occupier is dominant. Maybe it's because of their sheer numbers. Perhaps it's a technological advantage. Whatever the reason, the colonizer is in charge. The player who controls the occupier plays the part of **all** occupiers. They are a cohesive, unified, monolithic force.

Everyone else plays the natives, and each takes on the role of a character who must work for, or against, the occupying force. Each native gets a trait that they can use in the scenarios to follow.

Both sides get an allowance of tokens that represent abstract measures of an ineffable combination of willpower, autonomy, and agency. Occupiers get two tokens for each native plus one. Natives get three tokens each.

Going around the table, every player gives a descriptive trait to the natives – these represent easy stereotypes that will be used in later story elements. Perhaps the natives live in harmony with animals. Perhaps they solve all conflicts through negotiation. Perhaps they have no concept of cruelty. The traits don't need to be positive. Maybe the natives are vicious cannibals. Maybe they're lazy and feckless. Traits are also chosen for the colonizing forces in a similar way. "They are technologically superior". "They seek our natural resources". For reasons that will hopefully become clear later, a group may want to lean away from the encoding of "good" versus "evil" narratives.

The natives and the colonizers are then named. And then comes the first contentious rule in the game. The **richest player** takes control of the colonizers. That's an immediate point of discomfort for some people. Some are perfectly happy to talk about money, others were raised in cultures where money talk is taboo. And what is meant by **richest** is left open to interpretation. Is it net worth? Salary? Social connection? A conversation around this can be awkward, but the game is adamant that this is how it must be.

The **record** is then created, which is the collection of rules that will eventually form the core of interaction between the natives and the colonizers.

The game itself is played out in vignette form. Little self-contained scenes are narrated by players in turn. They begin based on the arrival of the colonizers, although as time goes by that will change. Natives can join any scene to which they are invited by the narrator, but the colonizers can join **any** scene without permission or an invitation. And in fact, they're incentivized to do just that – colonizers lose a token for every scene in which they don't participate.

When something in a scene happens that another player does not like, conflict arises. Conflict can be resolved through discussion, or if there's no agreement, it follows to a two-stage resolution process. First, there is negotiation, where everyone tries to find a compromise that is compatible with rules, traits, and personal goals. If that fails, then it comes down to chance – everyone involved gets a die, and an additional die for each trait (personal and collective) that is relevant to the conflict in question. Except… this is only true if a conflict involves only natives. If the colonizer is involved, then natives can't use personal traits. "To the occupation, Natives are all the same", as the rules put it.

The player with the highest total gets control and gets to decide what happens next. If anyone is dissatisfied by this result, the conflict escalates further to a decision by fiat. In this stage, the occupying force gets to decide what happens in any way they like. And this is true even if they were part of the conflict and even if **they** were the ones who were unhappy with the outcome in earlier stages.

When a scene ends, it proceeds to a phase called judgement. For each native that was in a scene, the occupier decides which adhered to the rules as outlined in the record. Disobeying natives (again, as judged by the colonizer) must give a token to the occupier for each broken rule. Natives who obeyed the rule get a token from the occupier. The occupier is also responsible for enforcing their own conduct – they abandon one of their tokens, permanently, for each rule they judge that they broke. Natives can certainly disagree with these judgements, but they can't challenge them.

Once this phase is over, the natives define a new rule based on the interaction between all the parties. As the rules put it, "If the game has a story, this is where you'd come up with the moral". Natives should consider how the occupiers responded to the situation, ruled upon it, and interpreted the record. A sentence describing this is added to the record and becomes binding for the future. Here, the occupier does not get to control anything.

There are some other rules, but this is the core of the experience. In the end, the game continues until either the natives or the occupiers run out of tokens, at which point you all resolve the story through a descriptive, narrative epilogue.

Encoded into the rules is an assumption – that the power belongs with the colonizers. It's more than that – it's a hard-coded rule that in all situations that natives are inferior to the occupiers. Every single scene progresses from that assumption. Scenes consist of natives attempting to placate their occupiers, who are incentivized to poke and provoke everyone else into snapping and breaking a rule. *Dog Eat Dog* is a system in which bullying has been gamified. Since all the power is in the hands of the occupier, the only way that natives can "win" in the end is through compliance. Natives get tokens from obeying rules. They lose tokens by disobeying rules. The win condition, such as it is, is that the natives get all the tokens the occupiers hold.

> The rule: 'We are required to pledge our allegiance to the occupier at the start of every day.'
>
> 'I am at home, and nobody can see me. I wake up, and begin my day with breakfast', says Michael, one of the natives. 'I invite my friend Pauline, who has had a bad time in the past few days and I want to comfort her because my trait is 'empathic''.
>
> Pauline joins the scene. They begin to talk about their budding resistance movement in tones that make it clear it'll never actually cohere.
>
> 'One of the nobles knocks on the door', says the Colonizer, inviting himself into the scene.
>
> 'We don't answer', says Michael.
>
> 'We duck down so we can't be seen through the window', says Pauline.
>
> 'I say, I know you're in there! Open the door, you little oik!', yells the noble. 'I look in the window, and I can see Pauline ducking down, and I shout at her to get up and let me in'
>
> The natives are always inferior, and so they can't refuse without risking the ire of judgement. Pauline opens the door, and the noble strides in. 'Have you pledged your allegiance today?'
>
> 'Yes', lies Michael. 'No', says Pauline whose trait is honesty.
>
> 'Well, pledge it right now. Both of you. Where I can see you do it'
>
> 'I mumble it resentfully', says Michael. The rule doesn't require enthusiasm.
>
> 'Not good enough', says the noble. 'Louder'.
>
> 'I mumble it louder'.
>
> 'No, do it properly. In fact, let's do it outside where everyone can see you. Set a good example to the people around you!'

It's the game equivalent of the bully pulling down your trousers so everyone gets to laugh at your underwear… except the bullies are the teachers, the board of governors, your parents, and the audience. All you as a native can do is seethe in your frustration and channel the spirit of malicious compliance in a situation where you don't get to decide on what level of compliance is acceptable. At the end of a game of *Dog Eat Dog*, everyone feels bad. Everyone feels complicit. And everyone understands something more about power differentials by being at the pointy end of them.

Sure, people may argue that games can't be art. That doesn't mean they're right. Sit them down for a session of *Dog Eat Dog* and see if they still believe games can't hold up a mirror to society.

Notes

1 Citation needed?.
2 At the time of writing, the highest rated game on BoardGameGeek.
3 Although Jack Donaghy of 30 Rock may have solved the problem for us when he says "We know what art is. It's pictures of horses".
4 Although in its original conception, this was Shakespeare (as usual) saying art holds a mirror up to nature. Again, we know what art is. It's pictures of horses.
5 Oh, get your mind out of the gutter. Arousal is the term we use to describe any emotion that is heightened to the point that we are consciously aware of it.
6 No, don't do that. It's a book, I can't hear you.
7 https://www.meeplelikeus.co.uk/blood-bowl-2016/.
8 In real life, I mean. I've sometimes said that if life gets too much for me I'm going to play Alien: Isolation on a VR headset because I don't think I'd survive the experience.

References

Ackerman, Dan. 2016. *The Tetris Effect: The Cold War Battle for the World's Most Addictive Game*. New York: Simon and Schuster.

Barrett, Terry. 2011. *Criticizing Art: Understanding the Contemporary*. 3rd edition. New York: McGraw Hill.

Barthes, Roland. 1967. 'The Death of the Author: Translated by Richard Howard'. *Literary Theory: An Anthology* 518–21.

Borges, Jorge Luis. 2000. The Library of Babel. David R. Godine.

Buckingham, David, and Andrew Burn. 2007. 'Game Literacy in Theory and Practice'. Journal of Educational Multimedia and Hypermedia 16(3):323–49.

Burke, Liam Liwanag, and Liwanag Press. 2012. *Dog Eat Dog*. Oakland, CA: Liwanag Press.

Castro, Henrique Ribeiro, and Dário ALM Sant'Anna. 2023. 'Playing against the Platform: A Research Note on the Impact of Exclusivity under Vertical Competition in Video Game Platforms'. Technological Forecasting and Social Change 191:122501.

Coward-Gibbs, Matt. 2020. 'Some Games You Just Can't Win: Crowdfunded Memorialisation, Grief and That Dragon, Cancer'. Pp. 173–88 in Death, Culture & Leisure: Playing Dead, Matt Coward-Cibb Leeds: Emerald Publishing Limited.

Derrida, Jacques. 1993. *Spectres De Marx*. Paris: GALILEE.

Derrida, Jacques. 1996. *Archive Fever: A Freudian Impression*. Chicago: University of Chicago Press.

Edmonds, David, and John Eidinow. 2011. *Bobby Fischer Goes to War: The Most Famous Chess Match of All Time*. London: Faber and Faber.

Ferrari, Simon. 2011. 'Train: From Black Box to White Cube'. Pp. 142–55 in *Tabletop: Analog Game Design*. Pittsburgh: ETC Press.

Festinger, Leon. 1962. 'Cognitive Dissonance'. Scientific American 207(4):93–106.

Fisher, Mark. 2016. *The Weird and the Eerie*. London: Duncan Baird Publishers.

Gadsby, Stephen. 2022. 'Imposter Syndrome and Self-Deception'. Australasian Journal of Philosophy 100(2):247–61. doi: 10.1080/00048402.2021.1874445.

Gamboa, Mafalda, Michael James Heron, Miriam Sturdee, and Pauline H. Belford. 2023. 'Screenshots as Photography in Gamescapes: An Annotated Psychogeography of Imaginary Places'. Pp. 506–18 in Creativity and Cognition. Virtual Event USA: ACM.

Greenbaum, Dov. 2008. 'Is It Really Possible to Do the Kessel Run in Less than Twelve Parsecs and Should It Matter-Science and Film and Its Policy Implications'. Vanderbilt Journal of Entertainment & Technology Law 11:249.

Hawke, Peter. 2018. 'Theories of Aboutness'. Australasian Journal of Philosophy 96(4):697–723. doi: 10.1080/00048402.2017.1388826.

Heron, Michael James. 2017. 'Pacman's Canon in C:A Quantum Interpretation of Video Game Canon'. The Computer Games Journal 6(3):135–51. doi: 10.1007/s40869-017-0036-5.

Heron, Michael James. 2024. *Tabletop Game Accessibility: Meeple Centred Design*. Florida: CRC Press.

Heron, Michael James, and Pauline Helen Belford. 2015. 'All of Your Co-Workers Are Gone: Story, Substance, and the Empathic Puzzler'. Journal of Games Criticism 2(1).

Hjørland, Birger. 2001. 'Towards a Theory of Aboutness, Subject, Topicality, Theme, Domain, Field, Content... and Relevance'. Journal of the American Society for Information Science and Technology 52(9):774–78. doi: 10.1002/asi.1131.

Hocking, Clint. 2009. 'Ludonarrative Dissonance in Bioshock: The Problem of What the Game Is About'. Well Played 1:255–60.

Kernberg, Otto. 2009. 'The Concept of the Death Drive: A Clinical Perspective'. The International Journal of Psychoanalysis 90(5):1009–23. doi: 10.1111/j.1745–8315. 2009.00187.x.

Kotwal, Sam, Edvin Pepeljak, Saumya Mathur, Angela Hug, and Fiona Rawle. 2019. 'Elucidate, Perfunctory, & Quagmire vs Fitness, Adaptation, & Selection: Overcoming the Jargon Barrier to Help Students Learn Scientific Terms'.

Krapp, Peter. 2020. '5. Sid Meier's Civilization: Realism'. Pp. 44–51 in How to Play Video Games, edited by M. T. Payne and N. B. Huntemann. New York: New York University Press.

Kühn, Simone, Alexander. Romanowski, C. Schilling, R. Lorenz, C. Mörsen, N. Seiferth, T. Banaschewski, A. Barbot, G. J. Barker, and C. Büchel. 2011. 'The Neural Basis of Video Gaming'. Translational Psychiatry 1(11):e53–e53.

Mantena, Ravindra, Ramesh Sankaranarayanan, and Siva Viswanathan. 2010. 'Platform-Based Information Goods: The Economics of Exclusivity'. Decision Support Systems 50(1):79–92.

Markowitz, David M., and Jeffrey T. Hancock. 2016. 'Linguistic Obfuscation in Fraudulent Science'. Journal of Language and Social Psychology 35(4):435–45. doi: 10.1177/0261927X15614605.

Marre, Quentin, Loïc Caroux, and Jean-Christophe Sakdavong. 2021. 'Video Game Interfaces and Diegesis: The Impact on Experts and Novices' Performance and Experience in Virtual Reality'. International Journal of Human–Computer Interaction 37(12):1089–1103. doi: 10.1080/10447318.2020.1870819.

McCurdy, Jennette. 2022. *I'm Glad My Mom Died*. New York: Simon and Schuster.

Nietzsche, Friedrich (1885). *Thus Spake Zarathustra*. Westminster: Penguin.

Nitsche, Michael. 2008. *Video Game Spaces: Image, Play, and Structure in 3D Worlds*. Cambridge: MIT Press.

Parker, Felan. 2018. 'Roger Ebert and the Games-as-Art Debate'. Cinema Journal 57(3):77–100.

Reynolds, Simon. 2011. *Retromania: Pop Culture's Addiction to Its Own Past*. New York: Farrar, Straus and Giroux.

Yablo, Stephen. 2014. *Aboutness*. Vol. 3. New Jersey: Princeton University Press.

Yu, Anthony C., tran. 2006. *The Monkey and the Monk: An Abridgment of The Journey to the West*. 1st edition. Chicago: University of Chicago Press.

Zauner, Michelle. 2021. *Crying in H Mart: A Memoir*. New York: Knopf Doubleday Publishing Group.

Ludography

11 Bit Studios. 2014. This War of Mine [video game] [Microsoft Windows]. 11 Bit Studios.

ATLUS. 2022. Persona 5 Royal [video game] [Microsoft Windows]. Sega.

Bethesda Game Studios. 2008. Fallout 3 [video game] [Microsoft Windows]. Bethesda Softworks.

Brown, Gavan, Matt Tolman, and Martin Wallace. 2018. Brass Birmingham [board game]. Roxley.

Capcom. 2011. Ultimate Marvel vs Capcom 3 [video game] [Sony Playstation]. Capcom.

Crawford, Jeremy. 2012. Dungeons and Dragons 5th edition. [roleplaying game]. Wizards of the Coast.

Creative Assembly. 2015. Alien: Isolation [video game] [Microsoft Windows]. SEGA.

DONTNOD Entertainment. 2015. Life is Strange [video game] [Microsoft Windows].Square Enix.

Eidos-Montreal, Crystal Dynamics. 2018. Shadow of the Tomb Raider [video game] [Microsoft Windows].Crystal Dynamics.

Firaxis Games. 2016. Civilization VI [video game] [Microsoft Windows]. 2K.

Fox, Michael, and Rory O'Connor. 2018. Holding On: The Troubled Life of Billy Kerr [boards game]. Hub Games.

FromSoftware Inc. 2022. Elden Ring [video game] [Microsoft Windows]. Bandai Namco.

FromSoftware. 2015. Bloodborne [video game] [Sony Playstation]. Sony Computer Entertainment.

FromSoftware. 2019. Sekiro: Shadows Die Twice [video game] [Microsoft Windows]. Activision.

FromSoftware. 2011. Dark Souls [video game] [Microsoft Windows]. Bandai Namco Entertainment.

Fullbright. 2013. Gone Home [video game] [Microsoft Windows]. Fullbright.

Galactic Café. 2013. Stanley Parable [video game] [Microsoft Windows]. Galactic Café.

Game Science. 2024. Black Myth: Wukong [video game] [Microsoft Windows]. Game Science.

Gupta, Ananda, Jason Matthews. 2005. Twilight Struggle [board game]. GMT Games.

Hewitt, James, Andy Hoare, Jervis Johnson. 2016. Blood Bowl [board game]. Games Workshop Ltd.

Infinite Fall. 2017. A Night in the Woods [video game] [Microsoft Windows]. Finji.

Infinity Ward. 2003. Call of Duty [video game] [Microsoft Windows]. Activision.

Introversion Software. 2006. DEFCON [video game] [Microsoft Windows]. Introversion Software.

Introversion Software. 2017. Scanner Sombre [video game] [Microsoft Windows]. Introversion Software.

Jump Over The Age. 2022. Citizen Sleeper [video game] [Microsoft Windows]. Fellow Traveller.

Lucas Pope. 2013. Papers, Please [video game] [Microsoft Windows]. Lucas Pope.

Maddy Makes Games. 2018. Celeste [video game] [Microsoft Windows]. Maddy Makes Games.

Magie, Elizabeth. Monopoly. 1933. [board game]. Self-published.

Naughty Dog. 2007. Uncharted: Drake's Fortune [video game] [Sony Playstation]. Sony Computer Entertainment.

Numinous Games. 2016. That Dragon Cancer [video game] [Microsoft Windows]. Numinous Games.

Rockstar North. 2010. Red Dead Redemption [video game] [Microsoft XBox]. Rockstar Games.

Rockstar North. 2013. Grand Theft Auto 5 [video game] [Microsoft Windows]. Rockstar Games.

Romero, Brenda. 2009. Train [board game]. Self-published.

Simogo. 2019. Sayonara Wild Hearts [video game] [Microsoft Windows]. Annapurna Interactive.

Techland. 2013. Call of Juarez: Gunslinger [video game] [Microsoft Windows]. Techland Publishing.

Thatgamecompany. 2019. Flower [video game] [Microsoft Windows]. Annapurna Interactive.

Thekla Inc. 2024. Braid [video game] [Microsoft Windows]. Thekla Inc.

Valve. 2007. Portal [video game] [Microsoft Windows]. Valve.

ZA/UM. 2019. Disco Elysium [video game] [Microsoft Windows]. ZA/UM.

3

Secret Hitler: Political Symbolism and Metagaming in Social Deduction

Constantina Edesa-Filios

Introduction

Since the beginning of time, people have developed an infinite number of ways, some more creative than others, to deceive the rest for their own personal benefit. They say that the first social deception game was introduced in Greek Mythology in the form of the Trojan horse in the 12th century BC.

It's probably fair to say that the people of Troy lost the first ever game of "Is this suspiciously hollow wooden horse full of soldiers or not?" so convincingly that it was never really played again. It was described as a massive wooden horse left as a "gift" by the former enemy – a ritual offering for a safe journey home and away from the field of battle. As we know now, Greek soldiers were hiding inside it. As a prize for years of war, the people of Troy dragged it into their city, only for it to spill those soldiers out onto the unprotected streets. The city fell almost immediately.

This was a brilliant and, let's be fair, deceitful, immoral and unethical way to conclude the ten years of bitter war with a happy ending for the Greeks. The story of this impressive event about the gullibility of the Trojans fuelled by their enthusiasm for success has been told for generations, ever since the days of the Odyssey and the Aeneid. You might be wondering how this event is related to our discussion topic, and the answer is: the Greeks tricked their enemies into lowering their defences by misleading them into thinking they were the winners of the war. The Trojan Horse is a compelling and universal symbol of how trust can be exploited even when nobody has reason to trust in the first place.

The Trojan Horse is only one example of this deceitful side of human nature. There are many more such examples. One incident in the late 19th to early 20th century concerns conman George C. Parker selling the Brooklyn Bridge multiple times to unsuspecting buyers, telling them they could set up toll booths and make a profit (Yadon and Smith 2011). Another example is Bernie Madoff's 65-billion-dollar Ponzi Scheme back in 2008 (Quisenberry 2017). This was the largest such scheme in history, defrauding thousands of investors – including individuals, charities, and institutions – as he promised consistent financial returns. In the end, he was simply

DOI: 10.1201/9781003530282-3

using new investors' money to pay off the existing ones. Deceit in war is common, in finance too. It's also a regular tool of political agents.

During Hitler's Reichstag Fire incident in 1933, the German parliament mysteriously caught on fire. The Nazis blamed the Communists. They used the fire to their advantage as an excuse to pass emergency laws that eliminated civil liberties (Tobias and Pomerans 1964). The Nazis used fear and deception to seize control and regularly employed crises so as to manipulate events and perception for political gain. Deception was a core property that allowed Hitler to rise to power, and an effective tool in the framework of propaganda that sustained his regime. It was used to gain acceptance from the public for some questionable policies and laws, which were in turn put into action through manipulation of the political mechanisms of that time – until those mechanisms could be changed to eliminate the need. Paranoia and fear were installed among the people – especially political opponents – through threats and the visible eliminations of those standing in the way of the Nazi regime.

The message was clear. The regime had eyes, ears, and fists everywhere, and no citizen knew who they could trust anymore. This resulted in a population of citizens that either fully supported the regime or were too scared and obedient to visibly oppose the regime – in some cases, it could be argued that these are functionally identical within a broken political system. We might argue that social proofing doesn't require authentic adherence to a cause.

Social Deduction Games

I brought this example to your attention because the main characters are a part of our topic, Secret Hitler, the social deduction board game.

The social deduction concept is rooted in human interactions, especially where people must figure out others' hidden intentions. Similarities are found within Nazi Germany's rule and politics, where it is nearly impossible to determine the true intentions of a person or group. When one cannot reliably infer intention, one must rely on fuzzier and less reliable social cues. When one cannot tell friend from foe and the trustworthy from the untrustworthy, it becomes necessary to deduce from softer evidence. Social signals, personal deductions and intuition are among the few tools one possesses in such circumstances, and they are often tools which can be manipulated.

We might think of social deduction games as "being good, or pretending to be good so you can do something bad". It focuses on the real social skills of the players around the table, who work to engineer the best possible outcome for themselves and perceived allies. They involve making convincing arguments within murky sets of data. They are games in which convincing rhetoric can be more compelling than the cold, unfeeling facts.

Social deduction games are often based on hidden roles as players are assigned secret allegiances and objectives through sealed envelopes or hidden role cards. The majority of those around the table will be assigned as part of the innocents' group – the good guys – while the remaining ones form the traitors, or the baddies. There is a specific intentional asymmetry in social deduction games, which is for the numbers of players in each group: the innocents are always more common than the impostors, but this is balanced through the fact that those imposters get to know who is on their team right from the beginning of the game. For the good group, this information will not be available until the end of the game. A second characteristic is the elimination of players often through voting mechanics. As the name "social deduction" implies, the genre is mostly based on social interactions and negotiation, alliances, deduction, deception, logical reasoning, misdirection, and manipulation. All these attributes play a role in deciding who to vote out of the game. The accumulation of data points based on how others vote, abstain, or engage in objectives helps narrow the window of uncertainty regarding loyalty – except everyone knows that the traitors know that too and will be leveraging this to present themselves as loyalists. Players are eliminated based on suspicions and only a vague idea of what the real state of play is. Traitors are incentivized to make loyalists look untrustworthy. A reputation for being a "strong" manipulator can win or lose the game for your team. The best pattern recognition or behavioural analysis skills can help with deductions, but they're always drawing from unreliable data. The last characteristic of social deduction games is keeping the victory conditions simple. Within Secret Hitler, they are (Temkin et al. 2016):

The Players on the Liberal team win if either:

- Five Liberal Policies are enacted.

OR

- Hitler is assassinated.

Players on the fascist team win if either:

- Six fascist Policies are enacted.

OR

- Hitler is elected Chancellor any time after the third fascist Policy has been enacted.

There exist many games belonging to this genre. Mafia is, arguably, the first such game that can be unambiguously identified, as well as the most influential. The game was designed by Dimitry Davidoff, a psychology student from Moscow State University in 1986. In a later version called Werewolf, the game was given a new theme but remained mechanically very similar.

While Mafia is often regarded as the first social deduction game, the foundations for the genre had already been laid by the time of its release. The genre is really a merger between two other genres: social games and deduction games. As discussed elsewhere in this book, genres are emergent, and it's true here too.

Social games, where the main premise is social interaction, had been in existence for a long time. Examples are *Dungeons and Dragons* (1974), and the broader genre of LARPing, circa 1977. One might also identify earlier prototype social games such as *Charades*, *Bridge*, and the whole wider genre of parlour games. Deduction games, where players use deductive reasoning to draw conclusions, also existed before Mafia. An example of this is Cluedo (1949), but one might also point to classics such as 20 questions, and parlour-based murder mysteries.

While neither the first social game nor the first deductive game, Mafia appears to be the first game known to bridge the gap between the genres: information is mainly gained through social interaction to make more informed deductions. Mafia became an international success and set the framework for how many social deduction games would appear: asymmetrical teams, with a minority fighting a majority; the main source of information is gained through social interactions; the minority party operates in secrecy; and player elimination through public voting.

Mafia's concept is simple: players are assigned secret roles as either mafia or villagers, some with special abilities. These abilities may include healing or revealing privileged information. Allegiance is kept secret through the "night" phase, where everyone closes their eyes until instructed otherwise. Mafia requires one of the players to act as the storyteller – a referee of sorts – keeping their eyes open and giving the rest instructions such as "now the healer opens their eyes and heals someone"

The goal of the game is to eliminate the opposition through deception. During the "night" phase, the players will exert their powers, if any, while during the "day" phase, the players will debate and vote on who they believe the mafia members are. All this time, the mafia members will try to deceive the rest of the players into believing they are innocent. This game was so popular that a digital version was created, Town of Salem (BlankMediaGames 2014), where players can receive more unique roles, such as Arsonist, Jailer, and Sheriff. It would take Among Us (InnerSloth 2018) though before social deduction games really took off among the general public at large. This is a game that has been on the lips of many people since its explosion of popularity during COVID. The Resistance (Eskridge 2009) is also a team-based social deduction game. It is set within an explicitly ludic framework where the loyalists must successfully build teams that complete missions before they can be sabotaged by the traitors.

It could be argued, and convincingly so, that all these are basically the same game, but with the emphasis on different aspects of the social deduction formula. The Resistance shifts away from role abilities and puts emphasis on pure trust and deduction. The mission structure adds stakes to the game, and success and failure in missions provide concrete data points for players to interpret. No players "die" during the game either, unlike Mafia, allowing deception and manipulation to develop and grow across rounds. However, teams may be voted for or against before they set out on missions.

The Structure of Secret Hitler

Secret Hitler (Temkin et al. 2016) is a social deduction game. The designers said, in response to criticism of the theme: "this is a time when art needs to be fearless about remembering and teaching history". From the first look, the title hints towards a social deduction game through the word "secret", while "Hitler" gives a chilling reminder of the brutal events of the history.

The story of the game takes place in Germany in 1932, several years before the start of the Second World War. During the set-up stage, a role is secretly allocated to each of the five to ten players. A randomly selected brown coloured envelope is distributed to each player, containing a party card (liberal or fascist) and a role card. These roles can be Liberal, fascist, and Hitler. There is only one "Hitler" and the rest of the roles are given in a distribution depending on the total number of players. The number of liberal envelopes varies from three to six, while the fascist envelopes vary from one to three in addition to the Hitler envelope. As soon as every player checks their role inside the given envelope, the game can start.

As is common in games like this, the fascist players get to know who their fellow fascists are, while liberals get no knowledge on player allegiance. This is the perfect recipe to create paranoia among the liberals, as they cannot ever know who to trust. The fascists by contrast can cooperate in secrecy. This mechanic, as most mechanics in the game, is a strong representation of the political context and parallelism this game operates within. This mechanic refers back to Nazi Germany, where the Nazi party often operated in small secretive groups against a larger divided opposition, keeping their intentions and plans hidden. The fascist party is aware of who Hitler is, but at a larger player count Hitler is not aware of who his supporters are until the end of the game – again, creating a sharp parallel where the leader cannot truly know the hearts of his allies.

Each round follows three phases. The first is an election phase when the President of the round nominates a Chancellor and the rest gets to discuss and vote on the government. A legislative phase follows when the elected government works towards enacting a new policy by selecting from one of three policies drawn at random from a deck. Players must expect liberals to choose liberal policies where they can, although it is entirely possible none will be available. In the event a chancellor acts against their claimed role, the partial information of the mechanics provides plausible deniability. Players must rely on the word of the chosen government, which is free to lie.

Finally, there is the executive action phase when, depending on the number of players, certain enacted policies grant executive powers, such as investigating roles or "executing" players. This is one way in which the game can end with a win for the Liberal team, in the case an executed player was Hitler. Hitler, in other words, must remain secret if he is to survive.

Political Symbolism

Past Versus Present

Secret Hitler is replete with political symbolism. It deftly uses its mechanics and narrative to represent the rise of authoritarian regimes. The game parallels the historical events in the late 1920s and early 1930s Germany, where political instability paved the way for fascism. The central premise of preventing or enabling Hitler's ascent to power is an abstraction of those historical events. The fascist faction works covertly to undermine democratic processes, whereas the liberals strive to maintain public stability.

The game's overall mechanics reflect the gradual degradation of democratic norms. The passing of fascist policies, even when forced or when there is no choice to be made, mirrors the real-world steps through which authoritarian regimes gain power. This underscores how seemingly small concessions can cause large political shifts. We can see that in Germany through the Reichstag Fire Decree – the passing of legislation that nullified many citizens' liberties in hope of heading off a communist uprising. However, this decree was used as the legal basis to imprison all opposition to the Nazi party. To the public, this decree likely seemed the best option to maintain public safety.

The hidden roles of the fascists and Hitler as utilized by the game highlight the dangers of covert operations and propaganda as seen in the real world. The fascist faction must use deception and manipulation of others to achieve their goals of political domination. One such strategy is where a fascist party chancellor might be given the choice between a fascist and a liberal policy to enact. The fascist member has the option to play the fascist policy and call out the president for giving no other choice. The reasoning behind this is to get a fascist policy on the board and simultaneously attempt to frame the president as untrustworthy.

Trust and distrust are a central dynamic in the game. Liberal players must rely on deduction, strategy, and communication to identify members of the fascist faction and complete their goal. However, the inherent uncertainty of the hidden roles creates opportunities for miscommunications, lies, betrayal and conflict. This dynamic is core to democratic fragility as seen throughout history. An example of this is the "Night of the Long Knives" in 1934. This was a purge at Hitler's orders of the SA (Sturmabteilung), the original paramilitary arm of the Nazis. Hitler deemed them as a threat to the success of the party. He accused the SA of planning a rebellion and coup, justifying the purge and execution of most of the SA leadership. The accusations created distrust among the population, resulting in many Germans approving of the purge in the name of stability. The scourge of McCarthyism is another compelling example.

The inability to establish trust among key actors and politicians, and people placing too much trust on untrustworthy actors, can lead to an institutional breakdown. This is reinforced in the game through the use of the president and chancellor roles. These roles require collaboration between the two players, as well as voting approval from the rest of the table. This not only leaves a barrier of trust and distrust between the government and the rest of the players but also a trust barrier between the president and chancellor. The possibility of one of the political party members betraying the other by deliberately attempting to pass fascist policies always looms. For instance, the president has the power to discard one of the policies without any witnesses. A fascist president can use this in their favour to force the choice of fascist policy by discarding a liberal policy followed by a sigh and a claim they had no other choice. No one can know whether they are lying or telling the truth. The same concept applies the other way around. The chancellor can play a fascist policy even if they had a choice and attempt to frame the president as having given them no choice.

Choosing the chancellor requires a lot of trust, as a wrong decision can cause the liberals to lose the game. This balance of trust and distrust between and among political parties can be observed in history. For instance, Hitler as chancellor managed to persuade the president Von Hindenburg into passing multiple policies that set in motion the rise of Fascism and Hitler's dictatorship.

The veto mechanic, which is introduced later in the game, represents a last effort to prevent a rise of authoritarianism. This highlights the importance of political safeguards in the maintaining of democracy but also showcases the danger if used with malicious intent. This highlights the crucial step of gaining the right to pass policies without influence from the parliament that caused fascism to rise to power in Germany.

In political democratic scenarios and elections, the choice is only rarely between "good" and "bad" anymore. More often, it is between "bad" and "worse", with the difference being a very fine line. The same is seen in Secret Hitler. Political necessity for choosing between "bad" and "worse" has long been used to justify the passing of horrible policies and laws, undermining democracy and the general public.

Secret Hitler shines light on these conditions and contradictions and encourages players to consider and reflect, through its abundance of symbolism, on the factors that contribute to democratic decline and the rise of authoritarian leaders. Not just in the pages of history, but also in the present day. The game's depiction of propaganda, mistrust, and misinformation as the primary strategy of the fascist faction shines a clear light on the role of polarization of the masses through media and technology. This is a topic that is worthy of consideration in today's technological era.

Symbolism in Design

The game puts a large emphasis on symbolism within the design and style of the game. sThe most straightforward use of this, which is immediately also the most provocative, is the title and the box. The title is paired with the design of the bright orange box depicting a pistol, dagger and a snake crawling around a skull. For a lot of people, the title and presentation are where they stop paying attention to anything else. For instance, in Australia, a Jewish Anti-Defamation Commission condemned retail stores for selling the game. Some quotes from the group's chairman Dvir Abramovich include[1]:

- "This is beyond normal. What's next, a board game set in the gas chambers and ovens of Auschwitz?"
- "There is nothing funny, entertaining, laughable or enjoyable about Hitler".
- "Just ask those who lost children, parents and relatives to his cruel and demonic regime"

However, the symbolism is in more than just the mechanics and name. According to colour psychology, the bright orange colour of the box is associated with positivity, optimism and confidence as well as arrogance and superficiality. This shows the good and bad duality and encourages social communication.[2]

Beyond this box is a gorgeous and delicately crafted game with premium components. The colours associated with the liberal side, such as the board and policies, are depicted as a bright blue colour. This colour is perceived with a feeling of protection, security and confidence.[3] The colour used for components of the fascist side is bright red. This colour is perceived with a feeling of strength, danger, caution, sorrow, aggression, and defeat.[4] In addition, the tropes of game literacy, especially within video games, would suggest that blue and red are commonly used to depict teams. Blue is commonly associated with the good team or allies, whereas red is commonly associated as the bad team or enemies. Reasoning for this ranges from the aforementioned psychological associations of the colours to historical evidence such as blue and red being used to represent friend and foe in traditional wargaming such as the Prussian Kriegsspiel. This usage of the colour spectrum gives insight on who is perceived as good and bad and can evoke emotional responses in players while reinforcing the seriousness of the theme of the game (Filios and Schroeter 2023).

The art style of the game is visually pleasing. The liberal board is decorated with ancient pillars, olive leaves, and a dove. The symbolism here draws from ancient Greece and Roman culture. The pillars refer to the majesty of Greek and Roman architecture, conveying a feeling of democracy, intellect, and power. The olive leaves represent peace and victory in both ancient cultures. The dove is associated with peace and love. The board is littered with positive symbolism conveying peace, order, and democracy.

FIGURE 3.1 The role cards in Secret Hitler.

On the other hand, the fascist board is decorated with chains, swords, skulls, and snakes. The symbolism here is broader. The chains can be associated with oppression and captivity. The swords convey aggression, military power, and authoritarianism. The skulls can be connected to death, fear and destruction. The snake is associated with deceit and betrayal. Overall, the fascist board is covered with negative symbolism, conveying oppression, betrayal, and authoritarianism.

These polar opposites in messaging and symbolism put strong emphasis on which party should be perceived as "the good", and which should be perceived as "the bad". With regards to the role cards, the liberal roles depict era-accurate cartoony illustrations of citizens. The roles of the fascists are depicted as reptilian. This adds another layer of symbolism. In various cultural contexts, reptiles and serpents are associated with cunning, trickery and deceit as well as the cold-blooded and emotionless. In addition to this, the usage of reptiles plays into the famous "Lizard people" conspiracy (Lewis and Kahn 2005). This conspiracy states that the world is secretly controlled by alien lizard overlords unconcerned with the norms of human morality (Figure 3.1).

Secret Hitler uses this to play into the theme of hidden power structures. The addition of this satirical and humorous exaggeration, paired with explicitly refraining from using human characters for the fascist roles, helps distance the roles of fascists from the people playing them. The game avoids directly depicting historical events and characters, besides using the name Hitler, and tries to remove the "human" from "fascist". This softens the game's heavy theme, reassuring the player that it is "just a game", not a historical reenactment nor a reflection of present-day reality. The game attempts to offer some refuge within the magic circle (Duggan 2017; Montola 2005).

Controversies and Critiques

Part of why this game is so well known is through how it is intentionally provocative at first sight. Indeed, the largest criticism lies in the theme and the title of the game. Although there is never any explicit reference to the horrible events associated with the

Second World War besides the usage of the name "Hitler", it can still be experienced as offensive by those who are emotionally struck by the events of that time period. For instance, a daughter of a Holocaust survivor, part of the same Jewish Defamation group as aforementioned, was shaken when she first saw the game and stated[5]:

> I started shaking, I literally saw the Holocaust flash in front of me. I felt as if there were Nazis about to storm into the store. I could barely look at the shopkeeper.

It can be argued that the game glorifies fascism and Hitler through its overall theme. On the other hand, as covered earlier, there is a significant amount of political commentary encoded in the game that suggests vilification of fascism instead. Another point of critique on the game is on the other end of the spectrum, suggesting that the game is not historically accurate enough to the actual events of the rise of fascism in Germany. It lacks references to the key events that brought about the rise of fascism. Furthermore, certain aspects of the game lack political realism. For instance, a win condition for ending fascism is to kill Hitler, which not only seems like a very unlikely scenario to be carried out by a liberal party, but these actions will also not end an entire political shift, and would likely only add fuel to the fire by creating a martyr – a symbol around which a movement could cohere.

As argued by reporter Kemp on Podculture at the Daily Northwestern[6]:

> I wasn't sure if the game trivialized the Holocaust or not, and I was wondering why the creators decided to make this game about Hitler, because nothing about the game is very specific to fascism. The policy cards don't include any real historical info. They're just labelled 'fascist' or 'liberal.' In fact, Secret Hitler is so unspecific to fascism that there are spin offs of the game that situate it in different contexts.

Secret Palpatine and Secret Voldemort are popular reskins of the game, although one might argue that they lack the situated context for the political commentary to really take hold.

Metagaming in Secret Hitler

Defining Metagaming

Elias, Garfield, and Gutschera (2012:203) define the metagame as "the game outside the game". Metagaming represents bringing external knowledge that a character or player would not normally have access into the gameplay (Carter, Gibbs, and Harrop 2012). "It is how the game interfaces with life" (Garfield 2000).

Let's look at an example: *Dungeons & Dragons* is probably the most played and loved tabletop role-playing game out there. The in-game characters are defined by abilities and skills represented on a character sheet. While in a battle with a monster the players – as opposed to their characters – may have access to information about the monster's weakness. This is encoded in various instructional books that define game rules. This is information the characters would have no way to know otherwise. Using player information to strengthen a character is a metagaming activity. Another example from the same game is how players sometimes make decisions based on the dungeon master's reactions, rather than what is currently happening in-game. A player about to open a door only to be asked "Okay, in what order are people going through the door?", may change their decisions in response to the obviously sinister implication.

Hemmingsen (2024) defines metagames, "at the most general level, [...] activities that are separate from a game, but are about or tied to that game in some way" and continues by identifying four such kinds of metagames:

- **Social metagames** – "What players bring to a game, what players take away from a game, what happens between games, and what happens during a game" (Donaldson 2016).
- **Strategic metagames** – Popular strategies or overarching ways of play that appears optimized for an individual player or team based on both their perceived strengths and weaknesses as well as those of their respective opponents, using information contained both in and outside the game and its surrounding environment (Kokkinakis et al. 2021).
- **Intertextual metagames** – "Games that are themselves about games, that make reference to or comment on other games".
- **Ludic metagames** – "Games that are played on top of games".

As each person is different, the same game played by different people at different times will also vary, even though the rules do not change. We could even say that the people create the game given a set of rules. We could also say, and we would not be wrong, that there is no game without a metagame because each player, on top of everything else, is a blend of experiences and feelings.

When it comes to social deduction games, metagaming becomes crucial, as the need of the "game beyond the game" is vital. In Mafia or Among Us, the metagaming usually increases once a player recognizes other players' real-life behavioural patterns and when others start using them to their advantage. Of course, already knowing the other players is a major help in being able to identify one's emotions, as most humans lack skills when it comes to detecting deception. "Deception detection accuracy tends to hover around 54%, with truths being evaluated more accurately than lies because people are truth-biased" (Levine, Park, and McCornack 1999; Markowitz 2024)

Strategies of Metagaming in Secret Hitler

In Secret Hitler, players use various metagaming strategies, such as social trust and alliances, and behavioural analysis coupled with playstyle recognition and pattern recognition.

Social trust is defined as our faith that other people will follow established norms. Boslego (2005) writes that "social trust can entail perceived honesty, objectivity, consistency, competence and fairness". This trust is a vital, but fragile component in Secret Hitler. Players are in need of putting their trust on other players and creating alliances to proceed with pursuing their goals. However, liberal players will never know for sure that the members of their alliance are pursuing the same goal and are not actually part of the other faction. Betrayal is inevitable and likely originates from your most trusted allies – after all, it is difficult to be betrayed by someone in whom we have placed no trust. We see the same concept reappear when it comes to actual politics. The general public puts their trust in politicians by casting their vote and expect the politicians to follow their norms and stick to the promises that they make. We are often disappointed.

Behavioural analysis focuses on observing and understanding how people behave in different situations. Recognizing the types of behaviour helps the observer or the interlocutors to figure out intention. Players may analyse tone, body language, and playstyle to determine which faction to which another may belong. This becomes especially clear when the game is played repeatedly with the same selection of people, where minor changes such as a player's presence or even a slight change in the way they talk are noticeable and may give away their intentions. Poker is in many ways built on the identification and manipulation of these subconscious "tells".

Pattern recognition represents a data analysis technique that uses observation and recognition of patterns to predict the next steps of a player. For instance, a player who has been involved with fascist policies being played is likely to lose the trust of their fellow players as it's starting to show a fascist pattern. Furthermore, patterns in chancellor selection and voting can give large insights into the trustability of a player.

As the metagaming means bringing the real-life knowledge into the game, behavioural analysis, pattern recognition, and historical playstyle recognition play a major role in altering the gameplay environment. The observer can gain valuable information that can help improve the game or shape it towards the desired outcome.

The Double-Edged Sword of Metagaming

Metagaming is what makes the game an actual experience, but it also comes together with a dark side. We can explain this using the example of the halo effect (Nisbett and Wilson 1977), which represents the tendency for positive impressions of a person to positively influence one's opinions or feelings. For example, a wide smile and similar expressions of joy or contentment will never scream out loud fascist. The opposite of the halo effect is the horn effect (Noor et al. 2023), and it is associated with negative attributes. Facial expressions like frowning and grimacing will make the interlocutor unconsciously associate them with a negative role, such as the fascist. A player's reputation from previous games can also unfairly influence their standing in the current round.

I think we are at a story time point. A couple of years ago, I started a Masters course on games. This is the course that actually opened my eyes towards a new unexplored world for me. This book is based on that course. The course involved a lot of research, which meant a lot of reading but also playing games during organized games nights and workshops. During the first two such events, I had found a group of people excited to play Secret Hitler after all the discussions we had during the lectures. The beginning was interesting, we were all curious to find out what all the fuss was about, but we were also ready to hate it and demolish the already controversial game concept. As soon as the role envelopes were dealt, I impatiently opened the one right in front of me to find out I was playing a fascist. I will not lie, it felt unsettling to be assigned this role, even if it was just a game. Just the thought of playing this role gave me goosebumps. It was neither my background, my beliefs or my expectations of the game. Funny how only one word, fascist, can have such a big impact on someone, I thought.

As it was the first time interacting with the game for most of us, it ended soon, with a win for the Liberal Party and without much debate.

We decided to play another round and, again opening the envelope impatiently, I was surprised to find the fascist card inside. It felt like this role stuck to me, and it also started to grow on me (as alarming as this might sound to you, I would kindly ask you to never forget the power of habit goes beyond what is considered good or bad). After the previous loss, it was time for us to put more effort into creating alliances while betraying the competitor team. This time, there was a lot more communication, debate, and manipulation which brought us the win. As it was a 1-1 tie between liberals and fascists, we decided to play another round. I was a fascist, for the third time. Everyone's gameplay was improving; we were all testing different strategies and alliances. I enjoyed playing this role as it provides the privilege of knowing my allies from the very first moment. It gives "knowledge is power" vibes. It also plays well to my love for spoilers and hate for surprises. I was curious though about the other side of the game, as it involves less knowledge and different strategies.

Some of the other players observed the intriguing situation: me being assigned the fascist role during all three games and while we were preparing to begin a new round (another one, yes), the jokes started: "Are you a fascist again?", "She is a fascist, let's eliminate her", together with people voting against elections where I was President or nominated as the Chancellor. For me it was hilarious as this time I was a part of the "good" team and did not give too much attention to the jokes or exclusion I was subjected to. The vilification of the fascist role and fascism in general, through symbolism and design, made me seem untrustworthy though to the new friends I was playing with. I did not know back then that the idea of me being a fascist in Secret Hitler would become a permanent association. It ruined my experience with the game when at least one of those new friends was playing – they represented a store of community knowledge that passed on the implication even when playing with new people. As much as I thought this was going to be a magic circle, the game extended to our real lives where the jokes continued: "Don't trust her, she will betray and backstab you".

Similarities are found in the real world, where someone's political view or opinion can nullify all their actions and opinions. This was the sad moment I felt the other edge of metagaming, and I understood that it can create social exclusion, and it will – if the players are unable to understand the difference between the game environment and reality. Luckily, this was not the case for me in the end, and until this day, we still joke about it. As new or less experienced players struggle against established group dynamics, leading to an uneven playing field, balancing metagaming remains a key challenge in social deduction games. And in real terms – we all carry with us a history decided for us by those around us.

Conclusion

Secret Hitler is a provoking experience that can change your perception of games. It functions as both an entertainment medium and a platform for political and psychological exploration. It encourages us to reflect on historical and contemporary governance issues. It provides an immersive and learning experience, where we can explore the role of deception in politics; and group psychology; and decision-making. It is important to remember to avoid harmful stereotyping and encourage critical reflection and, most importantly, to have fun!

Notes

1 https://www.dailymail.co.uk/news/article-6579671Jewish-Anti-Defamation-Commission-demands-Australian-retailers-stop-selling-Secret-Hitler-board-game.html
2 https://www.color-meanings.com/orange-color-meaning-the-color-orange/
3 https://www.color-meanings.com/blue-color-meaning-the-color-blue/
4 https://www.verywellmind.com/the-color-psychology-of-red-2795821
5 https://www.sbs.com.au/news/article/australian-holocaust-survivors-shaken-by-secret-hitler-board-game/51nfva1vv
6 https://dailynorthwestern.com/2021/04/14/audio/podculture-secret-hitler-monopoly-and-the-historical-board-game/

References

Boslego, Jordan. 2005. 'Engineering Social Trust'. *Harvard International Review* 27(1):28.

Carter, Marcus, Martin Gibbs, and Mitchell Harrop. 2012. 'Metagames, Paragames and Orthogames: A New Vocabulary'. Pp. 11–17 in *Proceedings of the International Conference on the Foundations of Digital Games*. Raleigh North Carolina: ACM.

Donaldson, Scott. 2016. 'Towards a Typology of Metagames'. Pp. 1–4 in *Proceedings of the Australasian Computer Science Week Multiconference*. Canberra Australia: ACM.

Duggan, Eddie. 2017. 'Squaring the (Magic) Circle: A Brief Definition and History of Pervasive Games'. Pp. 111–35 in *Playable Cities, Gaming Media and Social Effects*, edited by A. Nijholt. Singapore: Springer Singapore.

Elias, George Skaff, Richard Garfield, and K. Robert Gutschera. 2012. *Characteristics of Games*. Cambridge: MIT Press.

Filios, Constantina-Edesa, and Pia Schroeter. 2023. 'Ways in Which Sensitive Themes Can Be Effectively Handled Within Games: A Study on Secret Hitler, the Board Game, and Other Similar Games'.

Garfield, Richard. 2000. 'Metagames'. *Horsemen of the Apocalypse: Essays on Roleplaying*, pp.14–21. Sigel: Jolly Roger Games.

Hemmingsen, Michael. 2024. 'What Is a Metagame?' *Sport, Ethics and Philosophy* 18(5):452–67. doi: 10.1080/17511321.2023.2250922.

Kokkinakis, Athanasios, Peter York, Moni Sagarika Patra, Justus Robertson, Ben Kirman, Alistair Coates, Alan Pedrassoli Pedrassoli Chitayat, Simon Demediuk, Anders Drachen, and Jonathan Hook. 2021. 'Metagaming and Metagames in Esports'. *International Journal of Esports* 1(1).

Levine, Timothy R., Hee Sun Park, and Steven A. McCornack. 1999. 'Accuracy in Detecting Truths and Lies: Documenting the "Veracity Effect"'. *Communication Monographs* 66(2):125–44. doi: 10.1080/03637759909376468.

Lewis, Tyson, and Richard Kahn. 2005. 'The Reptoid Hypothesis: Utopian and Dystopian Representational Motifs in David Icke's Alien Conspiracy Theory'. *Utopian Studies* 16(1):45–74.

Markowitz, David M. 2024. 'Self and Other-Perceived Deception Detection Abilities Are Highly Correlated but Unassociated with Objective Detection Ability: Examining the Detection Consensus Effect'. *Scientific Reports* 14(1):17529.

Montola, Markus. 2005. 'Exploring the Edge of the Magic Circle: Defining Pervasive Games'. P. 103 in *Proceedings of DAC*. DAC 2005 conference, Vol. 1966. Copenhagen: IT University of Copenhagen, Citeseer.

Nisbett, Richard E., and Timothy D. Wilson. 1977. 'The Halo Effect: Evidence for Unconscious Alteration of Judgments'. *Journal of Personality and Social Psychology* 35(4):250.

Noor, Norzalina, Sukor Beram, Fanny Khoo Chee Yuet, Kumaran Gengatharan, and Mohamad
    Syafiq Mohamad Rasidi. 2023. 'Bias, Halo Effect and Horn Effect: A Systematic
    Literature'. *International Journal of Academic Research in Business & Social Sciences*
    13(3):1116–40.
Quisenberry, William L. 2017. 'Ponzi of All Ponzis: Critical Analysis of the Bernie
    Madoff Scheme'. *International Journal of Econometrics and Financial Management*
    5(1):1–6.
Tobias, Fritz, and Arnold Pomerans. 1964. *The Reichstag Fire*. New York: Putnam.
Yadon, Laurence J., and Robert Barr Smith. 2011. *Old West Swindlers*. Charleston: Arcadia
    Publishing.

Ludography

BlankMediaGames. 2014. Town of Salem [Video game] [Microsoft Windows]. BlankMedia
    Games.
Davidoff, Dimitry. 1986. Mafia [Board Game]. Unpublished.
Eskridge, Don. 2009. *The Resistance* [Board game]. Indie Boards & Cards.
Hasbro. 1949. Cluedo [Board game]. Waddingtons.
Innersloth. 2018. Among Us [Video game] [Microsoft Windows]. Innersloth.
Temkin, Max, Mike Boxleiter, Tommy Maranges, and Mac Schubert. 2016. Secret Hitler
    [Board game]. Goat, Wolf, & Cabbage.

4

Systemic Perspectives in Game Studies

Michael Heron

Systemic Perspectives in Games

If the critical perspective makes us consider what a game is saying, and the experiential perspective makes us consider what a game makes us feel, then the systemic perspective is about how a game actually **works**. Here, we're not going to talk about how to **design** games – that's a whole other book that should be written by a whole other person. What we're looking to do here is consider some ways in which we might **deconstruct** the various moving parts of a game to get a handle on how they function as systems. Systems, in this frame, being collections of interdependent mechanisms (hence the term, **game mechanism**) that work together towards a harmonious (or semi-harmonious) goal. What is the machinery, in other words, that performs the alchemical magic of transmuting your time into fun?

We can think of games in the abstract as being comprised of **state** and the **mechanisms** that act upon that state in order to produce **gameplay**.

Ah, "gameplay". That hoary old chestnut. A term used almost reflexively in gaming discourse, and yet so ill-defined that it might as well be replaced by the grunting of monkeys. "The gameplay is good!", says a review. What does that mean? What do you **mean?**

As with the definition of game itself, I don't think it's especially useful to get into the minutiae of attempts made to define this. Let's go with something loose and useful rather than something tight and confusing. For our purposes, we'll talk about gameplay as what emerges as the cogs of the mechanisms grind away – essentially, the **game** is the interaction of those cogs, and they crush player time and player choice together into **gameplay**. The interaction between mechanisms and state in other words.

Note that this definition doesn't require a human player. We see gameplay whenever we watch bots battle it out, or when we see automata (simulated players) interact with a board game rule-set. Gameplay is independent of fun – fun isn't a natural, reliable, guaranteed output. Good gameplay should **generate** fun, but it's not mandatory. I'm sure we've all played games that take our time and convert it not into fun but into tedium and frustration.

A lens that we have on games then is to assess them in terms of their gameplay, which requires deconstructing that gameplay into its constituent parts. We identify

DOI: 10.1201/9781003530282-4

state – that is, the data being stored about all the elements in a game. We identify the mechanisms that act upon that state. And then by analysing how these constituent parts interact, we can say something about **why** particular games evoke particular outcomes. We're looking here to determine whether things align as expected – the intended effect of a mechanism may be different from the **actual** effect. Barthes (1967) is as relevant here as he was in our chapter on critical perspectives. Intent is not the primary determinator of outcome. Few people set out to design an irritating game.

Mechanisms

Let's begin our discussion by talking about what we mean by a **mechanism**[1]. As with anything when you get into the weeds of scholarly discourse, there's plenty of disagreement on what the term means. We'll be drawing from Miguel Sicart's definition (Sicart 2008), which he defined as "methods invoked by agents for interacting with the game world". Mechanisms shouldn't be thought of as rules, because those are often made up of compound mechanisms. "On your turn, take a coin from the supply and buy a card from the marketplace" is a rule, but it's made up of at least two mechanisms (taking a coin, and buying a card).

Other definitions include:

- Fullerton, Swain, and Hoffman (2004) who described mechanisms as rule-bound actions or methods of play, which create interactions and guide player behaviour. I don't really like this definition because I don't agree that mechanisms create interactions, and also that they guide player behaviour.
- Cook[2] who talked about mechanisms as rule-based systems or simulations that facilitate and encourage a user to explore and learn the possibility space through the use of feedback mechanisms. I avoid this definition because I've usually forgotten how it started by the time I've gotten to the end.
- Jarvinen (2008) talks about how game mechanics take a primary role in shaping the user experience, acting as limiters on the possibility space with the intention of eliciting particular behaviours. Again, I take issue with the idea that mechanics guide behaviour since that implies an intentionality that is often absent.
- Gee (2003) talks about game mechanisms as being based on loops, where particular behaviours are rehearsed through increasingly challenging scenarios. This is a bit too "game designy" for me, and not useful for doing constructive deconstruction.

There are other definitions, because that's academia for you. One in particular we'll explore in more depth later on. For the moment Sicart is the definition we'll stick to and it's the one that will inform our discussions.

Critical points here – mechanism isn't **state**. The amount of health you have isn't a mechanism. The amount of money your character possesses isn't a mechanism. The set of items your character carries (their inventory) isn't a mechanism. Those are state values – variables encoded into the game somewhere. State is **information** – which is to say data existing alongside an explanatory context (Heron and Belford 2024).

It sits there, inert, until acted upon by a mechanism. Being hit by an enemy, which causes you to lose health – that's a mechanism that alters state. Selling an item to increase money, two mechanisms (one to remove the item from your inventory, the other to increment your money). Mechanisms are often packaged up into sets which are intended to act in a holistic way, at which point they become **systems,** which are then labelled with some descriptor of intent.

Consider for example a simple "inventory system", which is made up of multiple mechanisms:

- Add an item to the inventory, removing it in the process from the world.
- Removing an item from the inventory, adding it in the process to the world.
- Moving an item from one inventory (say, a pocket) into another inventory (say, a backpack).

However, there are broader mechanisms at play too. Does the game pause, for example, when a player accesses their inventory? That creates a different texture to the game experience in contrast to a game that keeps running while someone is struggling to find a health potion in the middle of a tense fight. That's why an understanding of mechanisms is so important – the experience of play is fundamentally constructed from tiny design choices made with regards to independent but interlocking mechanisms.

Other definitions of mechanisms focus on the idea of a possibility space, which is to say all the different configurations in which state can exist within a particular game. Mechanisms define the **decision space** – the subset of the possibility space to which a player can intentionally and legally navigate. The places a pawn can move in a game of chess are limited – it can only move forwards and attack diagonally. As such, parts of the possibility space that require a pawn to move two spaces to the side are not within the legal **decision space** even if we could easily represent it within the **possibility space**.

Rules, in this conception, refer to the legal architecture of movement within a possibility space. The mechanism may be that a chess piece can move to another place on the board, but each piece has its own rules which constrict that mechanism.

Mechanisms tend to belong to one of a few different common types:

- **Spatial**. Spatial mechanisms are those which alter the position or size of elements of a game. Movement can change the position and rotation. Elements might get bigger or smaller as they are scaled. Collisions will often trigger "collision responses" which result in momentum being imparted or halted. However, some spatial mechanisms also prevent movement – being afflicted by a hold spell, or being grappled by an enemy.
- **Temporal**. Temporal mechanisms handle time, specifically the ordering and duration of elements. When the flow of a board game is managed into rounds, and each round is broken up into turns, and each turn into actions – that's a temporal mechanism. Races, and the clocks that govern them, are temporal mechanisms. Effects that manipulate time (bullet time, for example) also fall into this category.
- **Change**. These are the mechanisms which primarily act upon state. Taking damage, spending money, and gaining factional reputation – all of these are change mechanisms.

- **Rule-Altering**. Some mechanisms act to change or qualify other mechanisms. A mechanism that changes an attack from one type to another or
  protects a character from a change mechanism (a protection from fire spell,
  that kind of thing). Sometimes games are built entirely on the idea of mechanisms that change other mechanisms. Fluxx (Looney and Looney 1997) or
  Nomic (Suber 1982) being especially interesting examples.

You can spend your entire life subdividing mechanisms into categories, but that's not
what we're about here. It's not that it's a useless exercise to fret about the categorization of mechanics in a game – it's actually a good way to get a sense, at a glance, where
systems might be under- or over-developed. It's just best used as a rule of thumb rather
than something we think of as a definitive taxonomy.

There's an additional part of the Sicart definition we haven't yet unpacked. What do
we mean by an **agent**?

Agents, for our purposes, are sources of instruction with regards the machinery of
the game. They are what trigger mechanisms within a rule-based framework. Players,
AI bots, automata – these are all agents. Agents represent intentional engagement with
how often, and in what order, mechanisms are triggered. In this, agents undertake
three key activities.

- They **observe** the game environment. They take in game state, contextual-
  izing its meaning appropriately.
- They **contemplate** their response to the game environment, deciding upon
  competing courses of action.
- They **act** upon that contemplation, choosing the desired course of action
  amongst all the competing possibilities.

Different agents do all of this in their own unique ways. A chess grand-master doesn't
brute-force their understanding of a game in progress. Instead, they draw in conclusions and create hypotheses on the basis of their superior understanding of the relationship between elements on the board (Chase and Simon 1973). A chess AI will use
depth and breadth-first search with mini-max pruning and a heuristic for assessing
board strength to build a model of the value of the current state and possible future
states (Rivest 1987).

Not all phases need to be equally emphasized. You can have a chess agent that
makes random moves. You can have people who simply skip over the contemplate
part of the process and move straight to action. My father was, at one point in his life,
a professional gambler and was adept at the psychological aspect of rattling his opponents. When playing poker, he'd sometimes take a replacement card and not look at it
(he'd refuse to observe the game environment) because it often discomfited people to
the point they'd play more erratically in future rounds.

Game Loops

Mechanisms are almost always embedded within what is known as a **game loop**. This
isn't the same loop that is at the core of a game engine, which takes the form of a regulated timing system that ensures everything happens when it's supposed to happen.

Game loops exist as ways to define the core experience of play. More correctly, we should think of mechanisms as being embedded in loops within loops.

Early games at Nintendo were often designed, to begin with, as little more than coloured geometric shapes on the screen – a gameplay-first prototyping process that is championed by Shigeru Miyamoto. Core game mechanisms would be put in place. Running. Jumping. Leaping atop enemies. All of this before a single character model was developed. The reasoning was that if a game felt fun when you were just moving shapes around a screen, it'd only become more fun as it got refined and polished. If it wasn't fun with the shapes, no amount of polish was going to save it. This is, at the heart, what we mean by a **core gameplay loop** – the moment-to-moment experience of playing a game.

Some genres of games – and we'll get to the idea of genre later in the book – have core gameplay loops that are a few seconds long. Run, jump, fire a gun. It's important that those few seconds are enjoyable and satisfying. It should feel **good** to shoot an enemy. It should feel **good** to jump over an obstacle. Polishing those few seconds means that the game – a strung-out chain of a few seconds of gameplay repeated again and again – is fun. Other games have longer, more sedate loops. The core gameplay loop in Doom (Id Software 2016) is "identify enemy", "choose weapon", "fire until dead". I've sometimes described Doom as a puzzle game, where the solution is always some variation of "use gun on demon".

Other genres of games are glacial in their pace. In *Baldur's Gate 3* (Larian Studios 2023), the core loop is "explore, face encounters, level up". Sure, it has its combats and its dialogues and its puzzles. Those have loops of their own. *Baldur's Gate 3* though is a game that is best understood when the adventure itself is the loop upon which we focus.

Consider the core gameplay loop in *Stardew Valley* (Barone 2016) as a comparison.

- You wake up in the morning.
- You check your plants to see if any can be harvested.
  - If they can, you harvest them. Doing so is accompanied by an extremely satisfying **pop** sound. Remember, every part of the loop should be satisfying.
- You plant new crops to replace the ones just harvested.
- You water and fertilize the unharvested plants.
- You sell the produce you harvested.
- You use the money from the sale to buy new seeds to replace the ones you planted, or new equipment to optimize the process.
- You go to bed.

Whole weeks can go by in game without you substantively deviating from this core loop. Sure, you'll do other things as you follow its grooves. When you go to buy new seeds, maybe you stop and talk to a villager. Maybe before you plant new seeds, you clear away some rocks and debris to make room. The loop will change and refine itself. Steps will be added and removed. And if you want, you can even completely ignore the loop. Do you want to play a terrible action-RPG in the *Stardew Valley* engine? You can go down the mines and battle samey monsters over a bunch of samey levels!

The thing that defines *Stardew Valley* as a game though is the loop above. It wouldn't be *Stardew Valley* if this wasn't the core – if all the systems didn't eventually feed into this general machinery.

However, in this each loop is itself made up of a number of sub-loops. There are crafting systems, upgrade systems, and relationship systems, and they can all be decomposed into mechanisms of their own. Seeing a game as loops within loops can help clarify what the game is actually supposed to be, and whether its systems are harmonious with its own framing.

Identifying game loops is important for a number of reasons:

- Understanding the mechanical structure of a game is a matter of identifying its loops and how they interact with its systems.
- The core loop of a game is immensely communicative of the genre of a game, which in turn is a way of understanding cultural expectations and assumptions about systems.
- Core gameplay loops define core gameplay experience, and if they don't, then there's profitable analysis to be done in working out why. Remember, everything either upholds, subverts or rejects its context. Sometimes the fun isn't where designers expect it to be[3].

The secondary loops in a game tend to be primarily categorized by how they change the experience of the core gameplay loop. Upgrade loops, advancement loops, narrative loops – all of these create a texture to the core gameplay loop that ensures players never become tired by doing the same thing over and over again without variation. Game loops must evolve in line with the growing familiarity of their players if they are to remain satisfying.

Verisimilitude

Imagine a game in which you take your standard Xbox controller, and in time with prompts on screen, you press buttons to simulate your ability to play a guitar. It flashes up X, and Y, and B, and RT, and RB, and you execute the instructions – the closer you are to the beat, the better you score. These sorts of games have fallen out of fashion of late, but there are plenty of them out there. Imagine a similar game where you do the same thing, but to simulate dancing instead of playing guitar. Or to sing Karaoke, rather than dance. It's often fun – everything from *Yakuza 3* (Ryu Ga Gotuko Studio 2021) to *Persona 4: Dancing All Night* (P-Studio 2015) have made use of this to great effect. However, it feels disconnected – the mapping between the concept of the interaction and the physicality of the mechanism isn't very tight. You're always aware that you're engaging with an abstraction – that you're explicitly doing a gamey thing to achieve what is purportedly a non-gamey outcome. None of us know what it feels like to summon a fireball into existence through the channelling of our magical abilities[4], but we **do** know what it feels like to play an instrument, sing a song, or dance along to the beat. The distance between our experience and the way we interact with the mechanisms stands between us and the ability to truly inhabit what's happening on the screen.

As a counterpoint, think of *Guitar Hero* (Harmonix 2005) – a game where your controller is a plastic guitar. Or *Just Dance* (Ubisoft Paris 2009) where it is your body that provides the input. Or *Rock Band* (Harmonix 2007) in which an algorithm attempts to match the pitch of your voice to the pitch of the vocal track via a microphone. In these games, it **feels** like you as a player are engaging with the game through an abstraction that is much less **abstract** than the alternatives we have discussed. I don't feel like a guitar god when I have a controller in my hand. Give me a plastic guitar and a decent song, and there's not a power in the "verse that would convince me I'm not secretly Jimi Hendrix".[5]

What we're talking about here is a quality known as **verisimilitude,** which is the property that we give to something that appears to be real, or true, or authentic. It's the extent to which the abstraction of a mechanism is distant from the interaction we perform.

If you have a key to a door, many games will simply let you pass through that door with a button press, and sometimes not even that. *Indiana Jones and the Great Circle* (Machine Games 2024) handles it by requiring you to equip the key, insert it into the lock, rotate it with thumb-sticks before pushing through to the other side. Does this improve the experience? That's up to each player to decide for themselves.[6] It is though more "authentic".

There's a famous cliché that gets used when we talk about representations of reality, and it goes "all models are wrong, but some models are useful" (Box 1979). Every time we simulate the real world, we need to choose an appropriate level of abstraction that captures what we need while omitting things that are extraneous. Consider what is needed to pick a lock in real life – physical dexterity, special tools, hours, and hours of dedicated practice. There's nothing stopping you making Lockpicking Simulator 2025 and immaculately modelling the physics right down to the quantum level. It's just not going to be a lot of fun for most players. Imagine playing an open-world RPG and every time you came to a locked door, you needed to spend ten minutes wrestling with it through the limiting factor of your own clumsy fingers. You don't want people focusing on this mechanism to the expense of others, so you abstract it. In *Skyrim* (Bethesda Game Studios 2016) and *Fallout 3* (Bethesda game Studios 2008), lockpicking is done through twiddling a rake and pick at angles represented by the thumb-sticks of your controller. In *The Outer Worlds* (Obsidian Entertainment 2020), it's done by pressing a button and passing a skill-check. Games must abstract reality in order to gain an appropriate balance between realism and playability. Essentially, the degree of verisimilitude depends on the importance of a mechanism to play.

Attaining meaningful verisimilitude is one of the unique challenges in game design. Nobody really cares if you press a button to print a document, versus select an option from a menu. Nobody cares if it's a key combination. What people care about is that the document gets printed. However, the reality of game development is that the way in which you map a mechanism to its execution has significant gameplay impact. It's worth considering – as part of your investigation of a game – what the mapping of input to interaction says about the priorities of the game developer.

Chance

The way in which mechanisms deal with probability is also an important element of system deconstruction. Chance is a major component of many games, and managing it correctly has a great impact on the experience of play. Consider *XCOM: Enemy Unknown* (Firaxis Games 2012), in which every attack is given a percentage chance of being successful – that chance depends on a range of factors including relative elevation, skill, distance, angle of attack, enemy cover, and so on. Making the odds manipulable changes the whole tenor of play, which we'll talk about in more detail when we discuss the Mechanics-Dynamics-Aesthetics (MDA) model later in the chapter. *Warhammer 40,000: Chaos Gate – Daemonhunters*[7] (Complex Games 2022), a very similar game, uses a mechanism where if an attack is legal, it always lands even if it might be resisted or dodged. The same basic mechanism (does damage at range), but interpreted differently according to game design priority.

It is sometimes said that "Luck is probability taken personally" (Kucharski 2016) and nowhere is that more true than in gaming. Sid Meier, one of the true legends of the field, has said that players expect two-to-one odds to play out in their favour around 90% of the time. He is channelling here Terry Pratchett's narrativium maxim that "million to one chances happen nine times out of ten" (Pratchett 1990). Genuine probability often feels arbitrary. Understanding the ways in which games present chance, and how they actually **honour it**, is an important consideration when it comes to understanding how mechanics work in practice.

Sometimes games are lying to us. As an example, the last sliver of health in a player's health bar is often represented more generously in the mechanisms than it is in the interface. Showing 5% health for what is actually a 15% health pool gives players an artificial buzz – the exhilaration of feeling they only just scraped through a difficult encounter by the skin of their teeth. Similarly, just because a game shows you 2:1 odds, it doesn't mean that's how the dice will roll because reality won't **feel** real.

Part of this comes from the fact that people are terrible at estimating probabilities. As a matter of course, only six-sided dice (d6) are regularly tested for fairness when they are mass manufactured. The average person throws enough d6s in their life that they have a reasonably intuitive sense of when they're balanced. The average person hardly ever throws a d4, or a d20. If you feel, as a player of D&D, that you have a die that is cursed… well, you might well be right.

Probabilities offer us a lens into the complexity of the states a mechanism might create. Mechanisms can be made up of elements that are:

- **Deterministic**, which is to say from a given starting state, they will always produce the same results.
- **Stochastic**, where from a given starting state, the outcome will incorporate uncertainty or randomness.

Randomness sometimes gets a bad rap in game design, but one of the key benefits it gives is that it creates interesting game states that may not otherwise come about through tactical or strategic play. These interesting game states require players to adapt strategies, or reconsider their options, or perhaps even re-evaluate their likely success or failure. Randomness comes in a range of flavours, and each has a role to play in creating mechanistic outcomes.

Two primary categories of randomness exist, as outlined by Geoff Englestein[8]. The first is **inbound randomness**, which relates to a randomness of context. A game in which the map is randomized every time you start a campaign is exhibiting inbound randomness, as is a game in which abilities of your character are chosen from a random sub-set of all possibilities. Games which place enemies in random areas, or randomly spawn encounters, all represent forms of inbound randomness. The outcome of this form of randomness is that the state of the game places constraints on what a player should do, but doesn't necessarily alter the likely results of what they **do** do.[9] A hand of cards in poker is another example of inbound randomness. Your hand doesn't change your options, but it does change your strategy.

Outbound randomness comes into play when the outcome of an action is uncertain. "Roll a d20, add your modifiers, and beat a difficulty check of 15". Monopoly's (Magie 1933) "roll to move" mechanism is an example of outbound randomness.

Within these categories, there are also flavours of how that randomness might be applied.

- **White** randomness is pure, unweighted, and gives an even chance of any result within a minimum and maximum. A die roll is a perfect example of white randomness, if we assume the die is properly balanced and doesn't favour any particular face. If we want to enforce a certain probability, we do it through – for example – rolling multiple dice together.
- **Brown** randomness is what we see when we take a starting value and adjust it within certain ranges. If we start with the value five and change it by +1, 0, or –1 every round, for example. You won't see a five becoming a one in a single turn, but you might find it becoming so after several rounds. *Thousand-Year-Old Vampire* (Hutchings 2020) is a game that uses brown randomness as a way to move through narrative sections in the book – you roll a d10, subtract the value of a d6, and read that text passage. As such, the number tends to grow, but sometimes it shrinks. It does this though within particular boundaries.
- **Pink** randomness is something we observe when we have small changes of state that can jump up or down in larger increments. For example, you see this in the concept of "exploding dice", when rolling the maximum number might result in rolling additional dice as a reward or punishment.

These are combinatorial, so you might have white inbound randomness or pink outbound randomness. Each has a role to play, and sometimes the role of a player isn't to "roll better" but to plan better around the randomness that they are presented. *Blood Bowl* (Hewitt, Hoare, and Johnson 2016) is a game in which any failed roll leads to the end of your turn, so it's a game of triaging your actions to minimize the risk of catastrophe. *Yahtzee* (Lowe 1956) and other dice rolling games sometimes offer a poll of rerolls and the ability to bank good rolls for the future. *Dungeons and Dragons* (Crawford 2012) offers skill modifiers, and *Blades in the Dark* (Harper 2017) offers negotiation over optimal skill application.

A systemic lens you have available as a games scholar is assessing how randomness is used in a game, and how it underpins or undercuts game mechanisms. Monopoly – white, outbound randomness – offers few opportunities for demonstrating genuine skill. As a result, the skill ceiling is low and easily met. Settlers of Catan (Teuber 1995) uses a combination of inbound and outbound randomness. Relies more on probability than chance. Mechanisms are provided for (somewhat) mitigating luck. The ways in which chance is wielded give us opportunities to say much about the systemic properties of a game.

Games as Systems

If collections of mechanisms working to a common purpose are a system, then we can think of games are being made up of discrete but interconnected systems. A game might have a combat system, or a crafting system, or a magic system. Or it might have all of them. The clarity of our conception of a mechanism is valuable – it considers each part of a game as being independent, and the interaction of discrete mechanisms is a consequence of manipulating shared state. The heal mechanism takes mana and turns it into health. The damage mechanism takes a sword blow and converts it into negative health. Neither the heal mechanism nor the damage mechanism needs to know about each other. It is only through their shared interest in a particular piece of state that they are linked.

That's not true when we start thinking of things on a system level – at this point, we need to think of higher-order interactions. A crafting system produces a weapon, for example. That's a formal link between all the mechanisms involved in crafting, and all the mechanisms used in combat. In this, we don't need to think of all the micro-interactions at play but should instead think of systems as largely independent units that produce outputs and take inputs. The crafting system outputs a weapon, which is an input to the combat system. The gathering system may output raw components (metals), which are the input to the crafting system. Thus, the gathering system links to the crafting system which links to the combat system.

Systems may require inputs from multiple related systems. Perhaps you need raw components (gathering) and a powerful spell (magic) to craft higher level swords. Perhaps the output of gathering produces components that can be used for crafting, but also chewed directly for a combat bonus. Identifying the interrelationship between systems is an important part of understanding the characteristics of a game.

It's here we can introduce two distinct but often confused outcomes of the relationships between systemic elements – **complexity** and **complication.**

A complicated game has lots of interrelationships between mechanisms (through shared state), as well as lots of interrelationships between their larger systems. The impact of each of these interrelationships can vary in intensity, as can the applicability of interactions. One of the hall-marks of complication is a small set of qualifying words when used to describe how they work: *if*; *or*; *except*; *unless*; *however.* Assessing the consequence of an action will require taking into account a lot of factors of varying levels of importance.

A complex game tends to have a smaller number of interrelationships, both between mechanisms and systems, but those interrelationships tend to be more impactful and their effect more subtle. The possibility space also tends to be greater as a result, and the decision space is more difficult to navigate competently. A complex game is not necessarily complicated, and vice versa.

Take for example, the game *Go* (Unknown, -2200). This has a handful of rules, but the possibility space is so vast that it takes a lifetime to master the intricacies of play. It's no surprise that artificial intelligences capable of playing *Go* at the highest level took much longer to develop than their Chess equivalents (Burmeister and Wiles 1995) – 1997 for chess and 2016 for *Go*. The cliché of "simple to learn, but a lifetime to master" succinctly captures the quality of complex games.

Consider Figure 4.1. Here we see the index of the rule-book for *Twilight Struggle* (Gupta and Matthews 2005), along with a rules extract and some of the cards you'll be

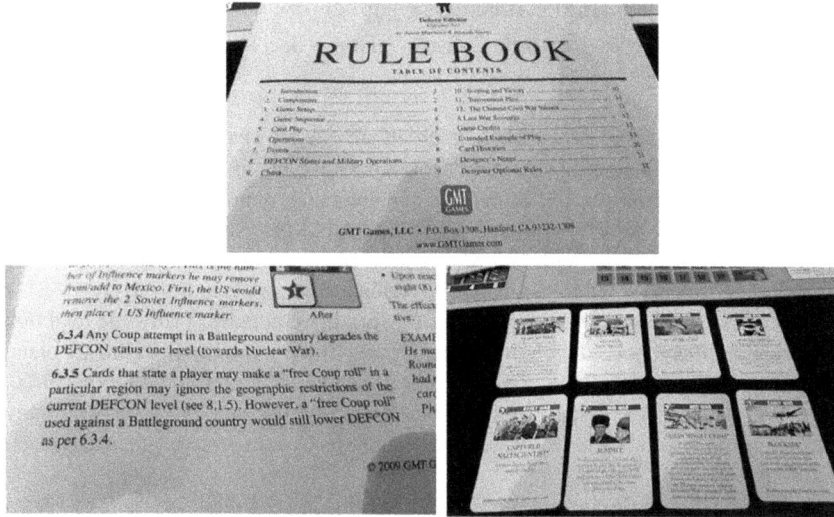

FIGURE 4.1   The rulebook, and some cards, from *Twilight Struggle* (Photographs by the author).

playing with. Any manual that has sub-subsections is one you know is going to epitomize complexity. The rules are dense. Consider rule 6.3.5 from the figure – executing upon this requires the interaction of cards that have a particular description, an assessment of DEFCON levels, an analysis of geographical placement, and an assessment as to whether a country is a Battleground country and reference to a second rule (6.3.4) with its own subtleties. I'm not picking on *Twilight Struggle* as an example of why complicated is bad – *Twilight Struggle* is actually a genuinely excellent game. It's just a really good example of what complexity looks like in play.

Emergence

One of the features we occasionally see when interdependent systems are allowed to interact is a property known as **emergence,** which is higher-level behaviour that comes about through often unexpected subtleties in how mechanisms relate to each other. Any time systems come together and you're surprised by the result because it wasn't actually embedded in the design – that's a sign that emergence is in play.

One of the most striking examples of the property of emergence is to be found in the Game of Life (Conway 1970). Remember how in the first chapter we spoke about how games, as discussed by mathematicians, are a different thing to games as **we** talk about them? This is an example of that – the Game of Life isn't a game so much as it is a system of rules with striking effect – a form of grid-based simulation known as a **cellular automaton** (Codd 2014)**.** Consider an infinite two-dimensional grid made up of individual cells. Each cell can be alive or dead – or it can be either one or zero. The "game" runs in generations, and each generation is essentially a round of calculation performed where the next generation's state is defined by that of the current generation. The Game of Life has only four rules:

1. Any live cell with fewer than two live neighbours will die through loneliness.
2. Any live cell with two or three neighbours will survive into the next generation.

3. Any live cell with more than three live neighbours dies through overpopulation.

4. Any dead cell with exactly three live neighbours becomes a live cell through reproduction.

These four rules, and how they interact, create a system of baffling complexity. You can build a fully functioning computer using the Game of Life. As a result, it's actually Turing Complete (Rendell 2016). You can create configurations of cells that create what are called "gliders", which are self-replicating patterns that move across the grid. You can create AND, OR, and XOR gates – when gliders come in to these, they output other gliders on the basis of a logical comparison.

Four rules, from which you can build a functioning computer. That's the textbook definition of emergence. You can see this property at work too in Minecraft (Mojang Studios 2011), or in *Legend of Zelda: Tears of the Kingdom* (Nintendo EDP 2023). Whenever a game gives you room to be creative and doesn't try to put too many restrictions on it, you'll find players using the systems to unexpected, and often hilarious, ends.

We can see this at play in games as diverse as Sim City (Wright 1989) and The Sims (Maxis 2000); Dwarf Fortress (Bay 12 Games 2002); Skyrim (Bethesda Game Studios 2016); and XCOM: Enemy Within (Firaxis games 2012). Emergence is the property that creates mechanical complications that a design cannot predict, or even potentially control for. When a dragon lands in Riverwood in Skyrim and kills Faendal, the archery teacher… well, that's just had a permanent impact on how easily certain players with certain skill builds will be able to progress through the game. There was no narrative reason Faendal had to die; it was just a consequence of everyone in the village coming to fight the dragon and the dragon not pulling its punches to honour the idea of plot armour[10].

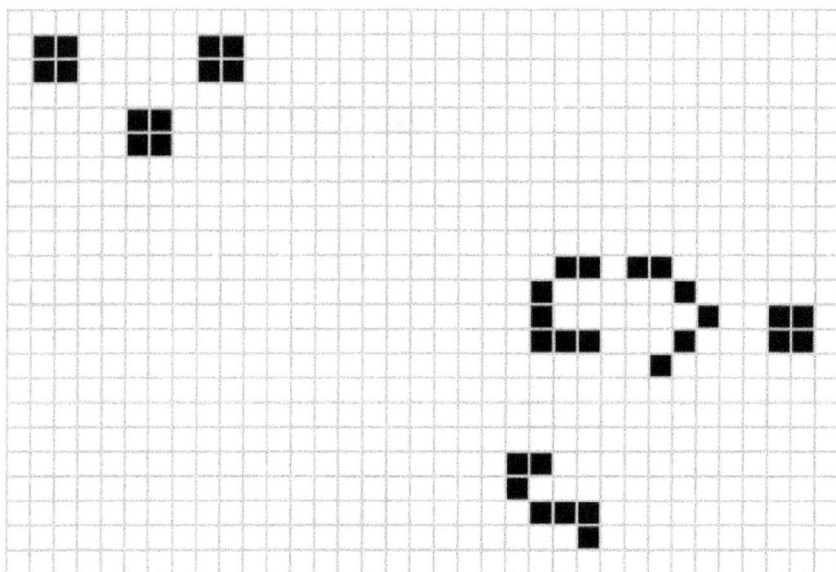

FIGURE 4.2   The *Game of Life*. Public domain image.

In Sim City, most of the environmental effects are emergent. You build a factory next to a residential district, which makes the latter less attractive so only poorer people live there. If the quality of a commercial district depends on the economic power of the nearest residents, you'll find higher quality shops replaced by lower quality shops, which might make those living in neighbouring residential districts move where there are better amenities. The effect isn't coded as a chain of "if this, then this" but rather a series of smaller, interconnected consequences. Before too long, the factory you just placed has to close because none of the people who would work at it live close enough to bear the commute. Much like Conway's Game of Life, this is often done through a primarily independent analysis of cell-neighbourhoods that ends up having complex effects (Johnson 2002).

When your sniper is at risk of being brutally bludgeoned by a Berserker in XCOM as it climbs up the roof to reach him, a stray grenade thrown by an enemy might evaporate the roof it's standing on, sending it plummeting to the ground to land in a pool of plasma. Simple rules – "you fall when there's no ground below you" and "grenades can destroy terrain" can create these kinds of spookily compelling narrative outcomes.

Focus of Attention

There are numerous other considerations that a game scholar can use to get a grip on the mechanisms of a game experience, particularly when it comes to how agents interact with these systems.

Consider for example the principle of the **focus of attention**. Or, "the place where players spend most of their time looking". You can argue – convincingly, in my view – that life is the sum of the things to which we choose to pay attention. If that's true, then we can also reason that a game is the sum of the things to which we gave our focus. In this, we can consider where a player is looking and where the core gameplay mechanisms exist. If the two are aligned, that's great. However, often they aren't.

The best games are effective marriages of user interface and gameplay expectation. We look for games where we essentially melt into the play. Games though are also engines for enforcing **context** or **task switches**, which is the term we give when our attention moves from one task to another, or one understanding to a different one (Egner 2023; Monsell 2003). We are walking through a forest. It's beautiful – God rays filter through the leaves and mingle with the golden haze of the day. We see a tree. It's a nice tree. Underneath the tree is a dog. It's a nice dog[11], so you go a little closer. Wait, that's not a dog. That's a wolf! The adrenaline kicks in, and you move into a combat state, becoming flustered and inefficient as you shift from one task to another. Enjoyable, satisfying context switches are what keep our attention focused on what's happening.

The issue is that context switches are cognitively expensive to process – they involve mentally ramping up to deal with the new context and then mentally ramping down once we switch back to our original (Mark, Gudith, and Klocke 2008). Psychology experiments have shown alarming impact when considering productive activities – switches in the form of interruptions increase error rates; increase the time cost to get back into a productive mode; and negatively impact the overall time to complete tasks. Games aren't spreadsheets[12], and productivity is not an ideal measure of satisfaction. Our measurements are far more subjective, our goals more ephemeral. But the cost of redirecting attention away from where we are currently focusing can be impactful in terms of enjoyment.

FIGURE 4.3   The map, and moment to moment gameplay of *Legend of Zelda: Breath of the Wild* (Screenshots by the author).

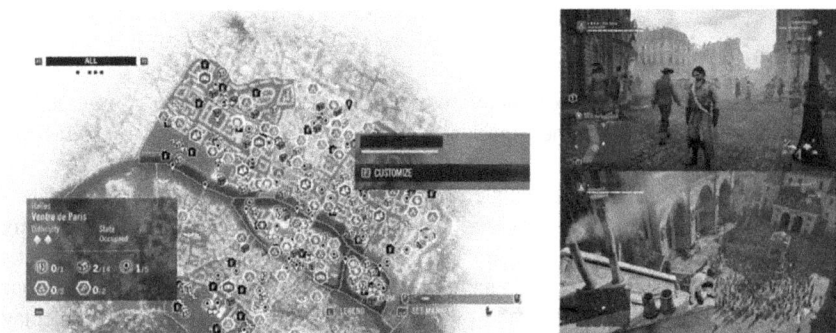

FIGURE 4.4   The map, and moment to moment gameplay of *Assassin's Creed: Unity* (Screenshots by the author).

Consider two examples here – *Legend of Zelda: Breath of the Wild* (Figure 4.3) and *Assassin's Creed: Unity* (Figure 4.4). In *Breath of the Wild*, markers of interest are sparse. The map is primarily a **map** – it doesn't direct the player to many places of interest. Play, as a result, tends to focus on the game itself – you're focused on what the game camera is showing you, and as a result, you tend to be present in the moment. It takes an organic approach to exploring and trusts the player to find their way without abundant non-diegetic interface cues.

Assassin's Creed, on the other hand, fills its map with markers – quests, shops, collectibles, and mission waypoints. It's less a map and more a checklist. As such, when you play, the temptation is to focus on the mini-map in the bottom right to see what's in the immediate vicinity. Focus on the beautiful architecture and atmospheric sights of Paris is harder to maintain because each of those markers is attention grabbing. In *Breath of the Wild*, you're already focused on the main view of the world. In *Assassin's Creed*, you're constantly shifting the focus of your attention.

I'm not saying here one is necessarily better than the other – that's a subjective judgement, and not one about which I'd like to nail my colours to the mast. They are though I think uncontroversially different in their philosophy of how they represent a game to a player.

Flow

If games are at least partly engines for generating interesting context switches, they're also engines for generating the experience of flow. We might think of this as an experiential topic, but flow is also systemic in that it comes about through the careful engineering of systems. If a task is too easy, we become bored. If a task is too difficult, we become frustrated. When there is a good match between our skills and our challenges, we may achieve what's often considered the golden goal of game design – we may experience a state of **flow.**

Flow is a mental state in which our activity is so immersive, so inherently absorbing, that it takes no mental effort to keep us engaged (Csikszentmihalyi, Abuhamdeh, and Nakamura 2014). We are effort averse as a species (Kahneman 2011), and our minds are usually looking for ways to avoid spending energy (Le Bouc et al. 2023). The little voice in your head that says "You know, you'd be so much more productive if you stopped doing this difficult thing and tidied the room" is essentially cost-aversion given psychological weight. Our brains want us doing the easy thing rather than the hard thing. Those same brains will also try to convince us to do nothing rather than the easy thing if we let them. When we enter a state of flow, that little voice quietens, and you can simply inhabit the moment.

We experience flow when we get lost in the pages of a good book or find ourselves in harmony with a musical instrument. And, of course, when we sink ourselves into an especially enjoyable game. That "just one more turn" effect so often associated with Civilization (Firaxis Games 2016) is one that comes wrapped up in a package of flow. If we let ourselves fall prey to the siren call, we may find we skip from 10 pm to 4 am without having a lot of conscious memory of the period in-between. Flow is the state of effortless engagement with a task that enables that to happen.

We can't design for a flow state – if we knew how to do that reliably we'd never have to play a mediocre game again. The best we can do is know when we're actively designing **against** it. We know the factors that **prevent** the emergence of flow. Figure 4.5 shows the likely emotional outcome that comes from combinations of challenge and skill.

Flow as it is outlined here bears a close similarity to the pedagogical concept known as the **zone of proximal development,** or ZPD, which is the window within which learning is most effective. I, being an exceptionally poor chess player, am unlikely to learn much from what Garry Kasparov may have to teach me. I am not such a bad chess player however that I will learn much in the circumstances of playing against a complete beginner. I am most likely to learn and get better by playing someone of approximately the same skill level. That's the core idea of the zone of proximal development – that we want to face challenges that are at the periphery of our current skill level. We aim for a target slightly beyond our ability, because that way our ability will grow to meet the new challenge. Figure 4.6 shows the band within which this happens, which you can overlay neatly onto the model of flow in Figure 4.5.

Koster and others (Crawford 2004; Koster 2013) talk about games in an almost pedagogical framing – that they exist as opportunities to present players with interesting decisions so as to encourage learning. "The young of all species play" notes Koster, pointing out that this is how big cats learn to hunt, and how dogs learn to socialize. Those of us in educational fields like to believe education is an inherently enjoyable activity, forgetting perhaps Churchill's grumbling that he "always enjoys learning, but

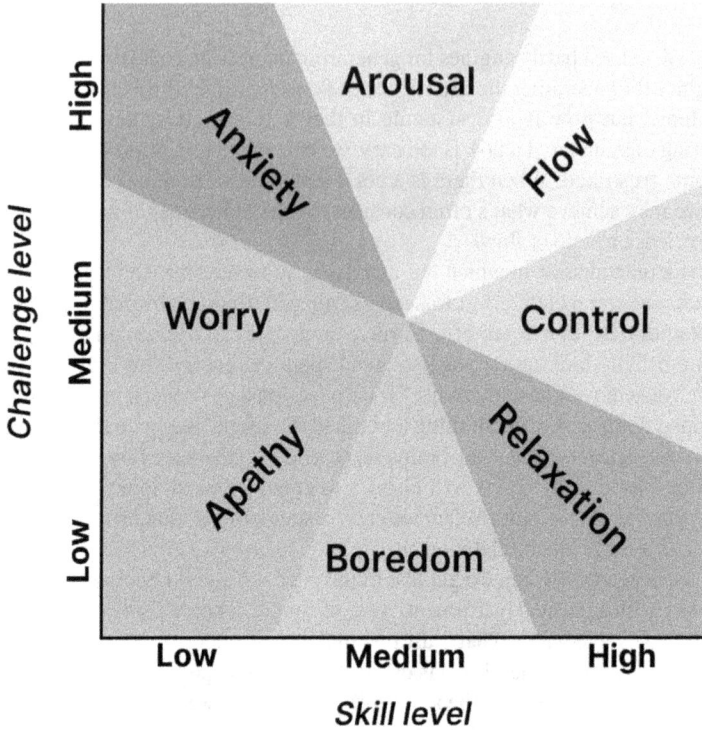

FIGURE 4.5   Flow.   Public domain image. https://commons.wikimedia.org/wiki/File:Challenge_
vs_skill.svg.

doesn't enjoy being taught". Many of the most genuinely satisfying games though take
their role as instruments of instruction seriously. Consider *Dark Souls* (FromSoftware
2011) through to *Elden Ring* (FromSoftware 2022) and encompassing alleyways such
as *Jedi Knight: Survivor* (Respawn Entertainment 2023) and *Black Myth: Wukong*
(Game Science 2024). While they have well-deserved reputations for being difficult,
they also have equally well-deserved reputations for being **fair**. Mastering difficult
encounters is well within the zone of proximal development that the games work
within, and any time that you find that isn't the case it's an excellent sign that you
maybe need to backtrack and explore until you find an area where it is. We can see
this translate into flow states in boss battles especially, where the ZPD works to build
in us a vocabulary as to how attacks are telegraphed and executed, which brings us
elegantly from a state of anxiety, into a state of arousal, into a state of flow. The **experience** is what matters to the player, but the way in which the game is mechanically
designed is a systemic frame through which we can **deliver** that experience.

Resource Management

One particularly useful way for understanding what's happening within a game is
through the lens of resource management. We can think of games as collections of
systems, made up of mechanisms. We can also think of them as economies, made

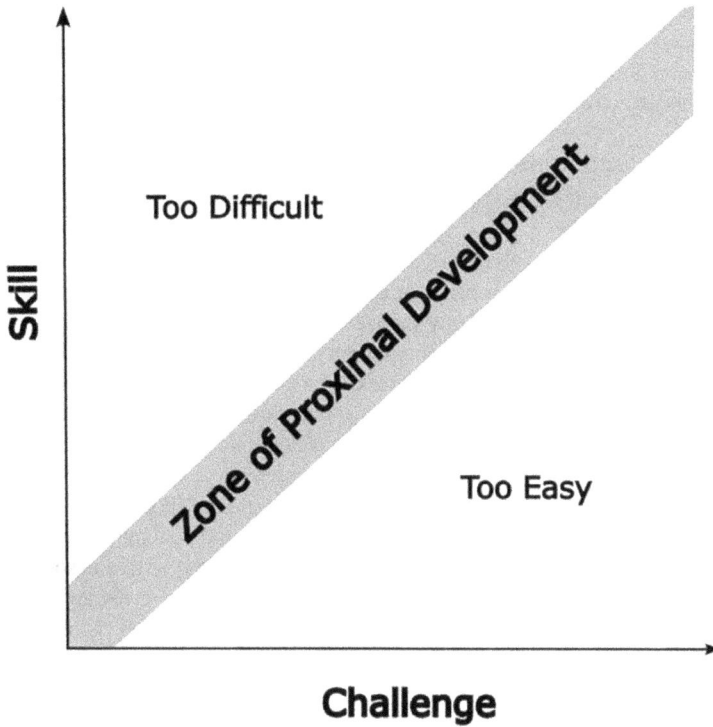

FIGURE 4.6 The zone of proximal development. Author's image.

up of resources that flow as they are spent and accumulated. It's sometimes said that the single most important tool for game development is Excel, and that's because few tools are quite so good at allowing you to explore subtle interactions between resources in a system.

Consider everything within a game as representing a currency to be gained and/or spent. And in this, I mean **everything.**

- Time
- Energy
- Actual in-game money
- Speed of advancement
- Progress through areas
- Enthusiasm

By modelling all of these in a spreadsheet, you get to understand a game on a broader scale. That in turn lets you identify issues such as balance and over (and under) supply. Judgement is still needed when it comes to assessing intention – as in, what was a designer aiming for – but as a game design and analysis tool this has significant utility. If you want to work out a levelling curve in an action RPG, you can calculate the availability of enemies, how much experience they are worth on average, and how many experience points are needed to level up. Work out how much time a player needs to spend per experience point, and that tells you both how long it'll take a player to progress and also how many enemies you need to seed in an area.

To do this effectively, you need to assess a game in terms of two key components.

- **Sinks**, which are mechanisms that take a resource out of a system.
- **Sources**, which are the mechanisms that add resources into a system.

A spawn point generates enemies (a source), which are killed (a sink) through time-consuming combat (a sink), to generate experience points (a source), which are spent on skills (a sink). Hitting an enemy damages equipment, which must be repaired (a sink) with money gained by completing quests (a source). Balancing the flow between sinks and sources is one of the primary tasks of a game designer. Think of these as an overlay on top of the systems that underpin a game – resources often cut across systemic boundaries to offer a larger view of the macro-economics of play. One might model a boss fight for example in terms of how many attempts it should take a competent player to win (a target flow rate), how long the average attempt should take (a time sink), how frustrating it's expected to be (an enthusiasm sink), and how much elation is to be expected at the end (an enthusiasm source). You can break these sinks and sources down into whatever level of detail you need – perhaps modelling things as damage per second versus likely damage mitigation (as in, "how long the average attempt should take" may be a resource calculation of its own). Valve, the company that owns Steam and used to make games, tends to treat every playtest like an experiment with its own hypothesis (Drachen, Mirza-Babaei, and Nacke 2018). In order for a hypothesis to be testable, it needs to be declarative. Sinks and sources give a way to predict outcomes in testable ways. "This boss will be defeated after an average of five attempts, and each attempt will last an average of three minutes".

All games have sinks and sources, and this explains why you often encounter odd irritants in gameplay experiences. Why does Legend of Zelda: Breath of the Wild have weapon degradation? It's a sink (of weapons) to compensate for the number of weapons you find in the game (a source). Identifying sinks and sources doesn't say anything about their **desirability**, but that's for you as a game scholar to assess.

One other thing to bear in mind is that sinks and sources also provide excellent ways to texture game loops, as we discussed earlier. Perhaps in an open world RPG, players have several key resources they need to gain – experience, money, equipment, and reputation. Areas and enemies that are particularly "flavoured" for each of these can be distributed around a map, incentivizing players to seek out variation rather than simply land upon the optimal return of investment. A bunch of easy enemies that occasionally drop a rare item will have a different game feel to a single difficult enemy with a high experience yield.

Remember what we've already talked about in terms of the interconnectedness of systems. Exploring the flow of resources emphasizes this through situating sinks and sources within their surrounding context. Sources should be mapped to sinks – even if it's only that enemies produce useless items that count purely for "vendor trash". Sinks **perhaps** should be mapped to sources, although it depends on the overall goal. If you want an infinite number of experience points, then add a source for spawning enemies. If you want a fixed pool of experience and money available, then maybe you don't add a source. In other words, consider whether you are dealing with closed systems (sources are designed in such a way that they don't add anything to the "economy", perhaps as a "once and done" process at the start of the game) or open systems (where sources are constantly adding new resources to sink). And in this, you might want to consider how to turn off the "tap" of a source, or plug a sink. You might have infinitely spawning enemies but reduce how much experience and money they drop over time. As a scholar, the presence of these taps and plugs is also something that tells you much about the design intent in the game.

Feedback Loops

If we consider mechanisms to be methods of influencing states, and systems to be collections of interrelating mechanisms, then we also need to consider **directionality.** In what direction does that influence apply? Sometimes we change state in a way that makes certain other changes more likely in the future, and sometimes we do the opposite.

Some systems, due to the way in which their mechanisms interface, tend towards a state of **homeostasis**. They become self-regulating, with their internal state changing but not deviating from a certain range of configurations. In happier times, we might have talked about the climate as an example of that. Other systems can become chaotic if left to their own devices. Some systems reinforce and intensify their internal states, and some trend towards placidity. We often talk about these in the framing of "feedback loops".

We see positive feedback in a system where one of its mechanisms increases the reactivity of that system. Let's say we have a target number that players must roll over on a d20 in order to succeed at a task. Every time they fail, the target number increases. To begin with, they need to roll higher than a one. Then they need to roll higher than a two, then a three. To begin with, there's a 5% chance of failure. Then 10%, then 15%. Every failure makes another failure more likely. This is positive feedback. It's also an example of brown randomness, for what it's worth.

Negative feedback reduces the reactivity of a system. In our example above, let's imagine every success halves the target number. After a failure, success becomes more likely until a state of relative homeostasis is maintained – failure will hover around the 30–70% mark over the long term.

Whether feedback is positive or negative becomes incredibly important when systems are reinforced by themselves or by other systems, because then they can become out of control (see Figure 4.7).

A positive feedback loop is what happens when outcomes get reinforced. You took a piece in chess, and because you took that piece, you are in a stronger position than your opponent, and as a result, you're more likely to take other pieces in the future, which will put you in an even stronger position. Despite the phrasing, **positive feedback** doesn't mean it's a loop with an outcome we **want**.

A negative feedback loop tends to suppress extreme states. You are in last place in a racing game, and because you're the current loser, you get a special speed boost to bring you back into alignment with the pack, at which point the speed boost is no longer required. Again, despite the word "negative", we're not talking about outcomes we wouldn't like.

Understanding the nature of feedback loops in a game gives us perspective on how gameplay and balance manifests. They are, like most things in game design, not inherently desirable or undesirable. They are tools with a role to play. That role though should be consciously chosen.

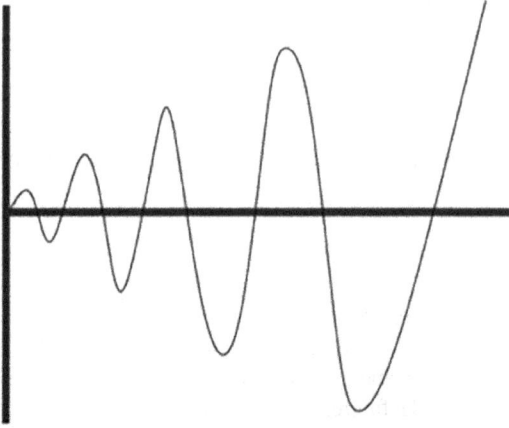

Positive feedback loop – state gets more extreme over time

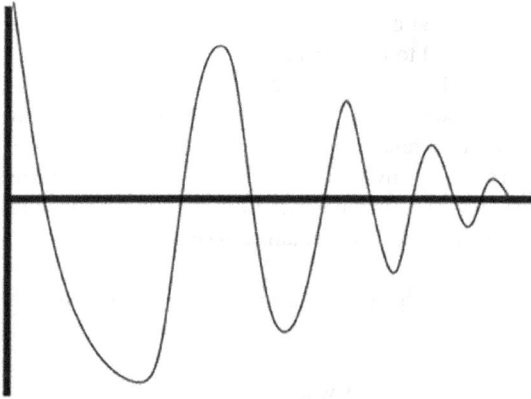

Negative feedback loop – state regresses to the mean over time

FIGURE 4.7 This shows how systems either stabilise or become ever more energetic depending on the type of feedback system employed.

Some examples of feedback loops that you might have encountered:

- Games where the winner of a round gets a special bonus in the next round (positive feedback), which creates a scenario often referred to as the runaway leader. The Matthew Effect, as outlined in the bible, is an example of this. Or, more colloquially – the rich get richer (Rigney 2010). Highly upvoted posts on Reddit attract more attention than other posts, which draws in a greater number of upvotes, which increases the amount of attention they get.

- When on a killstreak in certain online arena shooters, the "hot" player might receive bonuses that increase speed and damage, allowing that killstreak to continue and trigger new bonuses (again, positive feedback).
- When you're the seemingly obvious leader in games of diplomacy and trading, other players are discouraged from trading with you and you tend to find yourself the target of aggression and penalties (negative feedback).

Positive feedback loops – the better you are doing, the better you'll do in the future. The worse you are doing, the worse you'll do in the future. Negative feedback loops – the farther you are away from the average, the more the game (or other players) will act to "rubber band" you back into a pre-defined idea of normal.

Identify, analyse, and evaluate feedback loops to understand the nature of the systems you are working with, and you'll reveal some important dynamics of the mechanisms that drive them.

Tools for Systemic Analysis

Finally in this chapter, we're going to talk about a couple of scholarly concepts that have been shown to be generally useful for those looking to structure systemic analyses in a kind of academically appropriate form. These are:

- **The MDA Framework** (Hunicke, LeBlanc, and Zubek 2004), which acts as a top-down, or bottom-up, lens through which we can explore games in terms of the relationships between their mechanisms, dynamics, and aesthetics.
- **Game Design Patterns** (Björk and Holopainen 2005), which systemize examining games as interlocking systems, each of which has a particular role to perform in creating specific experiences.

Earlier on in this book, we spoke about "talking academese as a first language". If you want to be able to participate in scholarly discourse at the level of contributing to academic literature, one of the basic expectations is that you can talk the talk. You might think of what we've been doing so far as a kind of lesson in what you should say, but academic frameworks represent the expected grammar at the level of units of publication. They're **how** you should say things.

The MDA Framework

The MDA Framework is one of the more dominant ways in which academic debate about games tends to be structured. It's a multi-directional framework. It can be used top-to-bottom as an analytical tool. It can also be used bottom-to-top as a design tool. Within the MDA Framework, we break the moving parts of a game down into three key components – **mechanics, dynamics,** and **aesthetics.** Dynamics emerge as a consequence of mechanics acting upon the input of an agent – they are higher-order behaviours not encoded in mechanisms but emergent from their interactions. Aesthetics are the emotional responses that are triggered by dynamics.

Mechanics in this model are a little different from how Sicart defines them. Not so different that they are incompatible, but that we need to be a little careful about how we think about them. Within the MDA, mechanics are usually considered at a higher level of abstraction and are definitionally conflated with rules. The original paper gives some examples:

- The mechanics of card games include shuffling, trick-taking and betting;
- The mechanics of shooters include weapons, ammunition and spawn points;
- The mechanics of golf include balls, clubs, sand traps and water hazards.

Our discussion so far would have something like "trick-taking" as a system of interacting mechanisms, rather than a mechanism itself. The MDA formalizes its language thusly:

Mechanics are the various actions, behaviours and control mechanisms afforded to the player within a game context. Together with the game's content (levels, assets and so on), the mechanics support overall gameplay dynamics.

If you're struggling to get started in identifying the mechanics within a game, I recommend a simple act of natural language analysis. Write out a description of a system. Any verbs in that description are likely to imply mechanisms. Any adjectives imply state. Nouns probably represent objects, and proper nouns imply agents. This won't get you 100% of where you want to go, but it will give you a starting point and from there, the rest is inevitable.

As with many definitions – as we have discussed – this conception of mechanic is not wholly satisfying on a philosophical basis. The key element is that mechanics here are not just interrogable in isolation, but rather they need to be considered with regards to the role they perform in offering structural elements for the analysis of **dynamics.** And it's here that things get more interesting.

Dynamics, within the MDA, are the higher-order interactions that are implied by the existence of certain mechanics. The paper again talks about how spawn points can lead to emergent behaviour such as spawn-camping or sniping. There's nothing in the mechanical design that requires, or even encourages, such behaviour. It just happens because players are (usually) people. The existence of a hidden-hand of cards in poker can lead to dynamics such as bluffing or betting with real money. The game of poker requires neither, in terms of its mechanics. However, both are so intrinsically linked with our conception of Poker that it is a deviation to think of the game without them.

"Playing for toothpicks", as an example, is perfectly valid. However, it's often viewed as a diminishment, or neutering of the game itself. You play with toothpicks when someone has shown they can't be trusted to play with money. Or when nobody involved wants the interpersonal conflict that comes from introducing genuine stakes. This shows the power of dynamics in game systems – while they aren't necessarily encoded into the mechanics, they are essentially a way of understanding the **soul** of a game. From a top-down approach, we can examine a particular behaviour of people playing a game, and extract from it the mechanics underpinning that behaviour. As a design exercise, we could take a set of planned mechanics and "theorycraft" the expected dynamics.

I say theorycraft because I am a strong believer that you don't design games on paper, or even in a game engine. You design games in playtesting, because that's the only time you actually test the assumptions you make. However, some designs are more likely to survive their "first contact with the enemy" than others, and thoughtful consideration of the relationship between intended mechanics and expected dynamics can strengthen that survivability.

Game design is sometimes called a **second-order design problem.** We don't design a thing, and people have fun with it. What we do instead is design the mechanisms (first order), which then create the dynamics (second order). It is the dynamics, more than the mechanics, where the systems of a game find room to really shift into gear. If a game mechanic is a cog, then the system is the wheel, and the dynamic is the smoothness of the journey.

Next up comes the **aesthetics** layer. Here, in a typical reversion to the mean of academic readability, the term isn't used like normal people would use it – as a way of talking about the beauty of its subject. No, here it's used to reference the different ways that "fun" might manifest. From the top-down perspective, we can capture particular aesthetic responses to a game and unpick the contributing dynamics before deconstructing those dynamics into their constituent mechanics. From the bottom-up, we can look at how dynamics emerge from mechanics, and how those dynamics come together to create aesthetics.

The original paper outlines eight example areas of aesthetic categorization. These were never intended to be exhaustive, but are often treated as if they are. For the sake of completeness, they are:

- **Sensation (games as sense pleasure).** The extent to which a game is inherently satisfying to play. Games that look attractive, or have wonderful music, or have enticing tactility. Or emit a wonderful pop when you harvest their virtual vegetables.
- **Fantasy (games as make-believe).** This is when games give us opportunities to explore imaginary worlds and engage with imaginary people.
- **Narrative (games as drama).** Here, a game's fun comes from the story it tells and the progress it permits us to make towards a thematically satisfying conclusion.
- **Challenge (games as obstacle courses).** Here the focus is on overcoming difficulties and developing mastery of a game's systems.
- **Fellowship (games as social framework).** This relates to games where being part of an active community – in or out of the game – is one of the primary motivators for engaging with it.
- **Discovery (games as uncharted territory).** The game world presents itself as a playground of mysteries for an explorer to uncover.
- **Expression (games as self-discovery).** The extent to which a game allows us to present ourselves authentically, or allows us to explore different conceptions of ourselves.
- **Submission (games as pastime).** Here, the holistic appreciation of the game is to be found in the extent to which we can immerse ourselves within it.

Games will have multiple aesthetics, stressed differently. We might think of Elden Ring in terms of its challenge and its discovery – a game full of subtle secrets and difficult boss fights. However, that's not to say it lacks sense-pleasure – beautiful environments and haunting vistas certainly count in this category. We might think of Sayonara Wild Hearts (Simogo 2019) as a game focused primarily on sensation (the art, the visual effects, the stunning soundcraft) as well as a game of narrative (in that the story is satisfying and delivered in a compelling way). Challenge is also there, but delivered differently to *Elden Ring* as a consequence of its dynamics. The *Outer Wilds* (Mobius Digital 2019) – a heavy focus on discovery. *The Sims*, a big focus on fellowship (through its many vibrant fan communities) and expression.

A lot of this is woolly and ill-defined – in its original form the MDA is more of a notion than it is a formal framework. The good news is we're not talking about a tool that needs to have mathematical rigour and comprehensive classification. It doesn't matter that much of the way in which it defines mechanisms is inconsistent and lacks a consistent level of abstraction. The MDA is flexible enough that such concerns need not overly worry us – an approximate analysis will give us what we need to understand how a game works, and that should be the goal that we're trying to reach.

Game Design Patterns

If this bottom-up approach of designing sounds difficult, you're not wrong. Even professional game designers find it hard to reliably identify second-order effects, and it's almost impossible to generate fun from a cold start (Schreier 2017). Game design, in my view, only truly happens in evaluation. It's almost impossible to succeed with theory alone. Judgement and experience help to reduce the error-bars that go along with theory-crafting a game design, but they are still subjective, erratic, and unreliable tools.

If you know what **kind** of experiences you want someone to have in a game, you might consider "packages" of mechanisms that have been generally shown to work well together. In many design fields, "design patterns" represent battle-tested solutions to commonly recurring problems. Design patterns in architecture exist to provide good, if not optimal, configurations of architectural elements to achieve a goal (Alencar, Cowan, and Lucena 1996). Design patterns in software do the same thing (Gamma et al. 1994) – provide developers with a library of reliable approaches to satisfy otherwise difficult recurring requirements. Game design has its own pattern library. In fact, it has several pattern libraries (Björk et al. 2005; Engelstein and Shalev 2022). So, if you know what you want your game to do – why not make use of a pattern that documents a reliable way to achieve that goal[13]?

While you as an individual can take a game design and deconstruct it with the MDA, the idea of a game design pattern library implies some research work on your part. If you've ever tried to find a particular narrative cliché on TV Tropes (Martin 2013), you'll have encountered the problem – the taxonomy of patterns is often not particularly comprehensible to someone who doesn't live and breathe the collection. You may know what you want, but lack the vocabulary to know how to search for it. That's an unfortunately intractable problem in this kind of work, but you can close the gap by dipping into a pattern collection and allowing yourself to pick up navigational clues through osmosis. Björk's pattern library, based on his published work, is an excellent place to get started. Each pattern documented in this library comes with a comprehensive analysis. We've spoken about spawn points earlier, and these are one of the patterns available to consider[14]. Outlined in the pattern language are likely dynamic consequences (can instantiate camping, challenging gameplay, flanking routes, illusion of open space, etc.) as well as the modulating effects the use of the pattern has on a game. The pattern talks about diegetic considerations (they can compromise thematic consistency). In other words, the pattern shows you a solution to a problem and provides you with a way of systemically analysing what will happen if you use this particular solution.

You might find yourself confused here though by what is again a definitional inconsistency – there is an overlap between mechanic as outlined in the MDA, and how mechanisms are defined by Sicart, and also in how patterns are explained and used. Our field, alas, does not have a reliable universal dictionary. Björk defines the difference thusly:

- Patterns encode relations more deeply than how Sicart talks about mechanisms.
- Patterns can also include higher-order behaviours – not only the verbs of mechanisms but also observable features.

Patterns, in other words, are kind of a mid-level between mechanisms and systems, and between mechanics and dynamics. They don't necessarily result in dynamic behaviour, but the likely consequence of it can be inferred through how the pattern has manifested in games that use it. They are a way of capturing the "lived experience" of game designers. A good game design pattern is valuable not just because it solves your current problem, but because it has been built upon the hard-earned experience of those who have come before.

That's the value of game design patterns as a design tool, but they also offer a formal short-hand for analysis. Often when communicating the results of analysis, we have to balance readability, comprehensibility, and brevity. Being able to point to a pattern that covers what you want to talk about is a way to communicate complex ideas without having to reinvent the wheel every time. If the MDA offers a form of grammar through which we can talk about systemic elements of game design, it can be argued that game design patterns are where we should look to develop the vocabulary.

Notes

1 Some people use the term "mechanic" here. There is a lot of passionate debate on whether that is grammatically correct. This tells you a lot about the kind of people who talk about games on the Internet. Use whatever you like, it's fine.
2 https://lostgarden.com/2006/10/24/what-are-game-mechanics/comment-page-1/.
3 Sim City (Wright 1989) was originally the level editor for a game called Raid on Bungeling Bay (Wright 1984). Will Wright found out that developing the editor was more fun than the game it was for, and that enhancing the sophistication of the infrastructure that the player would bomb was a more satisfying task than actually bombing it. He delved into the texts of urban planning to develop a model for the evolution of these virtual cities. The game became so influential that universities would use it to demonstrate important principles to people studying urban planning degrees (Gaber 2007).
4 Right? If that's not true for you, drop me an email. I have some incriminating evidence I wouldn't mind incinerating in style.
5 Ask your parents. Bear in mind they might have to ask their parents in turn.
6 But no. It doesn't.
7 A game with a title so convoluted you need to take a breath in the middle of saying it.

8 As per his GDC talk – White, Brown and Pink: The Flavours of Tabletop Game Randomness.
9 Haha. Dodo.
10 A trope that comes into play when heroes and other important figures are protected from death because they are important to the plot.
11 Which logically follows from the indisputable fact that all dogs are, in fact, the best dog.
12 Although I did have some students a few years ago – Johnny Hamnesjö and Arturs Umbrasko – who put forward a compelling argument that all games are basically either Excel or Mafia. Later, after much discussion, they refined this into the Greater Game Categorisation theory, which states that all games are either Excel, or Mafia. Or Jenga.
13 My colleague Staffan Björk has his own wiki of patterns he and others have developed. You can find it here: http://virt10.itu.chalmers.se/index.php/Main_Page.
14 http://virt10.itu.chalmers.se/index.php/Spawn_Points.

References

Alencar, Paulo S. C., Donald D. Cowan, and Carlos J. P. Lucena. 1996. 'A Formal Approach to Architectural Design Patterns'. Pp. 576–94 in *FME'96: Industrial Benefit and Advances in Formal Methods*. Vol. 1051, *Lecture Notes in Computer Science*, edited by M.- C. Gaudel and J. Woodcock. Berlin, Heidelberg: Springer Berlin Heidelberg.

Barthes, Roland. 1967. 'The Death of the Author: Translated by Richard Howard'. *Literary Theory: An Anthology* 518–21.

Björk, Staffan, and Jussi Holopainen. 2005. 'Games and Design Patterns'. *The Game Design Reader: A Rules of Play Anthology* 410–37.

Box, George Edward Box. 1979. 'All Models Are Wrong, but Some Are Useful'. Robustness in Statistics 202(1979):549.

Burmeister, Jay, and Janet Wiles. 1995. 'The Challenge of Go as a Domain for AI Research: A Comparison between Go and Chess'. Pp. 181–86 in *Proceedings of Third Australian and New Zealand Conference on Intelligent Information Systems. ANZIIS-95*. New York: IEEE.

Chase, William G., and Herbert A. Simon. 1973. 'Perception in Chess'. *Cognitive Psychology* 4(1):55–81.

Codd, Edgar F. 2014. *Cellular Automata*. Cambridge: Academic press.

Conway, John. 1970. 'Conway's Game of Life'. *Scientific American*. 223:120–123.

Crawford, Chris. 2004. *Chris Crawford on Interactive Storytelling*. New Jersey: Pearson Education.

Csikszentmihalyi, Mihaly, Sami Abuhamdeh, and Jeanne Nakamura. 2014. 'Flow'. Pp. 227–38 in *Flow and the Foundations of Positive Psychology*. Dordrecht: Springer Netherlands.

Drachen, Anders, Pejman Mirza-Babaei, and Lennart E. Nacke. 2018. *Games User Research*. Oxford: Oxford University Press.

Egner, Tobias. 2023. 'Principles of Cognitive Control over Task Focus and Task Switching'. *Nature Reviews Psychology* 2(11):702–14.

Engelstein, Geoffrey, and Isaac Shalev. 2022. *Building Blocks of Tabletop Game Design: An Encyclopedia of Mechanisms*. Florida: CRC Press.

Fullerton, Tracy, Chris Swain, and Steven Hoffman. 2004. *Game Design Workshop: Designing, Prototyping, & Playtesting Games*. Florida: CRC Press.

Gaber, John. 2007. 'Simulating Planning: SimCity as a Pedagogical Tool'. *Journal of Planning Education and Research* 27(2):113–21. doi: 10.1177/0739456X07305791.

Gamma, Erich, Richard Helm, Ralph Johnson, and John Vlissides. 1994. *Design Patterns: Elements of Reusable Object-Oriented Software*. London: Pearson Education.

Gee, James Paul. 2003. 'What Video Games Have to Teach Us about Learning and Literacy'. *Computers in Entertainment* 1(1):20–20. doi: 10.1145/950566.950595.

Heron, Michael James, and Pauline Helen Belford. 2024. *A Case Study for Computer Ethics in Context: The Scandal in Academia*. Florida: CRC Press.

Hunicke, Robin, Marc LeBlanc, and Robert Zubek. 2004. 'MDA: A Formal Approach to Game Design and Game Research'. P. 1722 in *Proceedings of the AAAI Workshop on Challenges in Game AI*. Vol. 4. San Jose, CA: Association for the Advancement of Artificial Intelligence.

Järvinen, Aki. 2008. *Games without Frontiers: Theories and Methods for Game Studies and Design*. Tampere: Tampere University Press.

Johnson, Steven. 2002. *Emergence: The Connected Lives of Ants, Brains, Cities, and Software*. New York: Simon and Schuster.

Kahneman, Daniel. 2011. 'Thinking, Fast and Slow'. New York: Farrar, Straus and Giroux.

Koster, Raph. 2013. *Theory of Fun for Game Design*. California: O'Reilly Media, Inc.

Kucharski, Adam. 2016. *The Perfect Bet: How Science and Maths Are Taking the Luck out of Gambling*. London: Profile Books.

Le Bouc, Raphaël, Nicolas Borderies, Guilhem Carle, Chloé Robriquet, Fabien Vinckier, Jean Daunizeau, Carole Azuar, Richard Levy, and Mathias Pessiglione. 2023. 'Effort Avoidance as a Core Mechanism of Apathy in Frontotemporal Dementia'. *Brain* 146(2): 712–26.

Mark, Gloria, Daniela Gudith, and Ulrich Klocke. 2008. 'The Cost of Interrupted Work: More Speed and Stress'. Pp. 107–10 in *Proceedings of the SIGCHI Conference on Human Factors in Computing Systems*. Florence Italy: ACM.

Martin, Jennifer. 2013. 'Crowd-Based Information Organization: A Case Study of the Folk Ontologies in Wikipedia and TV Tropes'.

Monsell, Stephen. 2003. 'Task Switching'. *Trends in Cognitive Sciences* 7(3):134–40.

Pratchett, Terry. 1990. *Guards! Guards!*. London: Corgi Books.

Rendell, Paul. 2016. *Turing Machine Universality of the Game of Life*. Vol. 18. Cham: Springer International Publishing.

Rigney, Daniel. 2010. *The Matthew Effect: How Advantage Begets Further Advantage*. Columbia: Columbia University Press.

Rivest, Ronald L. 1987. 'Game Tree Searching by Min/Max Approximation'. *Artificial Intelligence* 34(1):77–96.

Schreier, Jason. 2017. *Blood, Sweat, and Pixels: The Triumphant, Turbulent Stories behind How Video Games Are Made*. Harper New York.

Sicart, M. 2008. 'Defining Game Mechanics'. *Game Stud*.

Ludography

Barone, Eric. 2016. Stardew Valley [video game] [Microsoft Windows]. ConcernedApe.

Bay 12 Games. 2002. Dwarf Fortress [video game] [Microsoft Windows]. Bay 12 Games.

Bethesda Game Studios. 2008. Fallout 3 [video game] [Microsoft Windows]. Bethesda Softworks.

Bethesda Game Studios. 2016. The Elder Scrolls V: Skyrim Special Edition [video game] [Microsoft Windows]. Bethesda Softworks.

Complex Games. 2022. Warhammer 40,000: Chaos Gate – Daemonhunters [video game] [Microsoft Windows]. Frontier Foundaries.

Crawford, Jeremy. 2012. Dungeons and Dragons 5th edition [roleplaying game]. Wizards of the Coast.

Firaxis Games. 2016. Civilization VI [video game] [Microsoft Windows]. 2K.

Firaxis Ganes. 2012. XCOM: Enemy Unknown [video game] [Microsoft Windows]. 2K.

FromSoftware Inc. 2022. Elden Ring [video game] [Microsoft Windows]. Bandai Namco.

FromSoftware. 2011. Dark Souls [video game] [Microsoft Windows]. Bandai Namco Entertainment.

Game Science. 2024. Black Myth: Wukong [video game] [Microsoft Windows]. Game Science.

Gupta, Ananda, and Jason Matthews. 2005. Twilight Struggle [board game]. GMT Games.

Harmonix. 2005. Guitar Hero [video game] [Microsoft Xbox]. RedOctane.

Harmonix. 2007. Rock Band [video game] [Microsoft Xbox]. MTV Games.

Harper, John. 2017. Blades in the Dark [roleplaying game]. Evil Hat productions.

Hewitt, James, Andy Hoare, and Jervis Johnson. 2016. Blood Bowl [board game]. Games Workshop Ltd.

Hutchings, Tim. 2020. Thousand Year Old Vampire [roleplaying game]. Tim Hutchings Makes Games.

Id Software. 2016. Doom [video game] [Microsoft Windows]. Bethesda Softwarks.

Larian Studios. 2023. Baldur's Gate 3 [video game] [Microsoft Windows]. Larian studios.

Looney, Andrew, and Kristin Looney. 1997. Fluxx [board game]. Looney Labs.

Lowe, Edwin. 1956. Yahtzee [board game]. Public Domain.

Machine Games. 2024. Indiana Jones and the Great Circle [video game] [Microsoft Windows]. Bethesda Softworks.

Magie, Elizabeth. Monopoly. 1933 [board game]. Self-published.

Maxis. 2000. The Sims [video game] [Microsoft Windows]. Electronic Arts.

Mobius Digital. 2019. The Outer Wilds [video game] [Microsoft Windows]. Annapurna Interactive.

Mojang Studios. 2011. Minecraft [video game] [Microsoft Windows]. Mojang Studios.

Nintendo EDP. 2017. Breath of the Wild [video game] [Nintendo Switch]. Nintendo.

Nintendo EDP. 2023. Tears of the Kingdom [video game] [Nintendo Switch]. Nintendo.

Obsidian Entertainment. 2020. The Outer Worlds [video game] [Microsoft Windows]. Private Division.

P- Studio. 2015. Persona 4: Dancing All Night [video game] [Playstation Vita]. Sega.

Respawn Entertainment. 2023. Star Wars Jedi: Survivor [video game] [Microsoft Windows]. Electronic Arts.

Ryu Ga Gotuko Studio. 2021. Yakuza 3 Remastered [video game] [Microsoft Windows]. SEGA.

Simogo. 2019. Sayonara Wild Hearts [video game] [Microsoft Windows]. Annapurna Interactive

Suber, Peter. 1982. Nomic [board game]. Self-Published.

Teuber, Klaus. 1995. Settlers of Catan [board game]. KOSMOS.

Ubisoft Montreal. 2014. Assassin's Creed Unity [video game] [Microsoft Windows]. Ubisoft.

Ubisoft Paris. 2009. Just Dance [video game] [Nintendo Wii]. Ubisoft.

Unknown. Go. -2200 [board game]. Public Domain.

Wright, Will. 1984. Raid on Bungeling Bay [video game] [Commodore 64]. Broderbund.

Wright, Will. 1989. Sim City [video game] [Commodore Amiga]. Maxis.

5

Box Classification and Puzzle Logic in the Video Game Wilmot's Warehouse: Its Relation to Language and Semantics Categorization and Language in Wilmot's Warehouse Gameplay

Nayat Astaiza-Soriano and Eleni Gianntizi

Introduction

Wilmot's Warehouse (Hollow Ponds 2019) is a puzzle game that requires the player to sort different box items in a large space representing a warehouse and then deliver them in a timely fashion to customers who request those boxes. The game encourages the player to resort to what is considered an innate human capacity (Goldstone and Kersten 2003; Rosch 1978): the extraction of features, the formation of concepts, and the process of categorization. In this research, we focus on the dissection of the categorization process players engage in during gameplay and the connection between this process and language.

This contributed chapter offers a small sample of literature on the topic of puzzle solving. We present our proposal on the game's connection with the semantic process of categorization, along with an example of what we believe of the gameplay as experienced from the player's perspective. We highlight a few other processes that intervene in gameplay. We do this in relation to data gathered from other players working in single-player and co-op modes.

Background

There is little research one can find directly related to Wilmot's Warehouse in the academic record, and as such, our literature primarily concerns the areas of cognitive science. For example, Megalakaki et al. (2012) present an overall review with regards to a player's processes while solving puzzle games – a genre to which Wilmot's Warehouse belongs. The puzzle-solving process, they argue, is the following: we first determine

DOI: 10.1201/9781003530282-5

the goal, we then look at the shortest path in a series of states, starting from the initial state, and then finally execute an action that will move us towards the goal state. However, some puzzles, like the somewhat problematically titled Missionaries and Cannibals (Berlekamp and Rodgers 1999) (categorized generally as a river-crossing puzzle) or the Chinese Ring Puzzle (Kotovsky and Simon 1990) – a disentanglement puzzle – demand the disruption of this behaviour: they want us not to think about the shortest path, but rather consider the whole puzzle first. Doing the former will not give us the answer, but instead will stick us within an insolvable loop.

As an a priori comment, we could say that something similar occurs in Wilmot's Warehouse, where the first and fastest classification style one may think of involves colour or basic shapes (Goldstone and Kersten 2003). However, the player soon realizes that with a greater number of boxes to classify, these become an inefficient way of sorting them. Megalakaki et al. argue the importance of understanding the specific rules of a puzzle in order to solve it. To develop a set of steps to solve the puzzle – i.e., a series of intermediate states that would lead to the goal state – the characteristics of the objects it consists of and the actions one can perform must be clearly understood. In other words, we must understand how the possibility state can be manipulated through puzzle mechanisms. Wilmot's Warehouse does not have a standard path of action to successfully classify and deliver the boxes, which may be a factor contributing to the game's difficulty. We argue that the game's structure progressively demands the use of memory and turns it, in essence, from a puzzle game into a memory game.

The game designer, Richard Hogg, makes an explicit comparison to Tetris (Pajitnov 1984) to address the specific issue of puzzle solving in the game[1]:

> … [Wilmot's Warehouse] incorporates what I call emergent puzzles. […] What I mean by it is that the puzzles in the game are a function of the player's behaviour. Rather than solving puzzles that have been 'authored' by a game designer, you are solving puzzles that are a byproduct of how you solved the last puzzle.

Tetris and Wilmot's Warehouse behave similarly in this respect. The difference lies in that Wilmot's Warehouse does not have any other constraints: in Tetris, the pieces need to fit precisely; in Wilmot's Warehouse, they go wherever there is a space for them to go.

Semantics and Language

We believe these factors require the consideration of the cognitive process of categorization to fully understand the way the game presents its puzzle to the player. This constitutes the main strategy to efficiently complete tasks presented in the gameplay loop. In this section, we will see how categorizing assists the process; how this process is carried out (together with some examples of players' decisions in categorization); a comparison of this process to the gameplay loop of other games; and the contribution of language to such a process.

Categories and Memory

Starting a new game in Wilmot's Warehouse guides the player through a tutorial. The tutorial explains basic controls and, while doing so, makes the player transport boxes of icons to a space delimited by dash-dotted lines. There we find the only moment

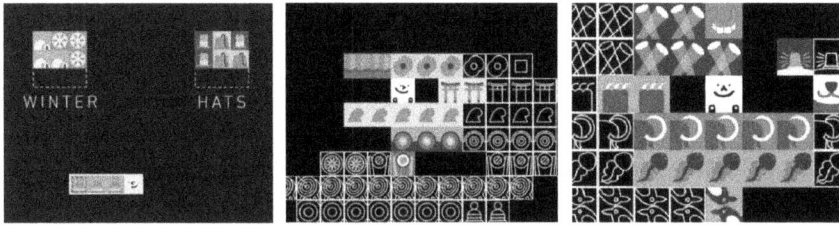

FIGURE 5.1 Left – word categorization of icons. Centre – the possibility space of categorization. Right – colour-based classification.

when we see any sort of linguistic label in the game: the space is captioned by the name of the item represented in the boxes (e.g. BANANA, HORSESHOES). After a couple of training screens, the tutorial presents the player with an option. There are two categories of items, labelled as WINTER and HATS. After the player takes the boxes representing an igloo, a snowflake, a fez, and a fedora to their respective category spaces (see Figure 5.1, left), they are presented with knitted hats in the next tutorial screen. We will see the importance of this labelling later.

The tutorial not only provides an introduction to the mechanics but also presents a strategy to deal with the main loop of the game: organizing items in space according to a pattern. What it doesn't stress at this point is **why** this organization is relevant.

As the name of the game reveals, the player controls Wilmot, who works in a warehouse. The warehouse is the only location where the gameplay unfolds: a wide, rectangular room where Wilmot is expected to arrange all the incoming boxes. The main loop consists of a couple of successive rounds where the player receives boxes with new items at the start of every session – this is the DELIVERY PHASE. Wilmot is then asked, after a too brief unloading process, by four coworkers in the service hatch to deliver a concrete quantity of specific boxes – this is the SERVICE PHASE. The player has two minutes and one minute, respectively, to operate during these phases.

Sorting diverse boxes in an organized way is relevant because the amount of time given in the service phase is too restrictive for slapdash curation of the warehouse. Since new and different boxes arrive every round, it becomes increasingly difficult to keep track of the different illustrations, shapes or icons in the boxes. As rounds keep passing, the space available for managing the inventory becomes smaller as the room has been taken up by previous delivery phases. It is relevant to mention here that when the player completes 100% of the game, they would have seen a total of 200 items, but these are drawn from a set of 500 different potential items. Due to this, categorization schemas must be invented for each playthrough of the game. Wilmot's Warehouse is essentially a memory challenge: a variant of a find-the-pair game, where the boxes shown in the service hatch need to be matched with other boxes somewhere in the warehouse. Insofar as it is a puzzle game in the purest sense, it is made so only because of the incompatibilities between the spatiality of the warehouse and the player's own organizational scheme.

Categorization, Concepts, and Memory

Both categorization and memory are relevant concepts in Wilmot's Warehouse. In order to attempt an explanation of how the player's cognitive process works during the game, we refer to foundational work on concepts and categorization (Goldstone and Kersten 2003). This work provides a thorough summary of relevant models and theories.

We adopt their definition of category: "a set of entities that are grouped together". This definition is contrasted with that of concept: "a mentally possessed idea or notion" (Goldstone and Kersten 2003:608). The tutorial of the game introduces those notions in a practical way by explicitly giving labels to the categories WINTER and HATS. This produces a sort of cognitive clash when the "knitted hat" box is introduced. The concept of winter and the concept of hats both contain features that match with the features of "knitted hat" (e.g. "used when it's cold" and "goes on the top of your head"). This contextual and time-limited comparison of features is constant during gameplay.

Different proposals on how concepts are mentally represented include the following models: the **rule-based model**, the **prototype model** and the **exemplar model**. The rule-based model posits that a single rule determines the classification of an entity in a specific category. In the prototype model, category membership is determined after the account of the "most common attribute values" of an entity. The exemplar model proposes that categorization occurs after the consideration of all entities and their features in a category is done (see pp. 612–616 for more on these). After a few hours of executing multiple categorization tasks in the game, it is difficult to opt for one or another model, but what becomes clear is that categories that include consistent traits will be challenged. Because of this, it could be said that a single rule being the sole marker of category membership may be unlikely. The player either creates a prototype with the best predictor feature or compares the new entity (box) to the entities in the target category.

Regardless of how the system for category membership detection works, the disparity in features related to boxes in the game allows for different types of categories/concepts. Goldstone and Kersten propose that the different types of categories "can be arranged roughly in order of their grounding by similarity: natural kinds[…], man-made artefacts […], ad hoc categories[…], and abstract schemas or metaphors […]" (2003).

The closer a category gets to the abstract, the fewer requisites there are for entities to enter that category. At the same time, such categories do not allow for "inductive inferences" as they would if they were, say, a natural kind, which contains categories with multiple features in common.

Categories such as animals (natural kind) and everyday objects (artificial kind) may be created easily during Wilmot's Warehouse. However, and this is where the mechanics of the game truly excel, the game will challenge the player into creating ad hoc categories: *things seen during camping*; *food*; *stuff related to food with red and purple backgrounds*; *cultures of the world*; and *concentric circles*. These categories are situational, emerging from the specific subset of icons made available in any one playthrough. The job of the player becomes to fit unexpected items into imperfect categories, and occasionally this task is so conceptually cluttered that it requires a complete re-architecting of the categories that were previously identified. There is a spatial component to this too – reordering the warehouse requires physical space in which to do it, and that space is often littered with the evidence of discarded conceptualization.

This re-architecting is due to a number of different constraints: these include time, warehouse space, and the number of the same type of boxes received during the delivery phase. If it is not always possible to preserve even ad hoc categories intact, that is precisely what is outstanding about the categorization process as it manifests within Wilmot's Warehouse: categorization helps us understand new entities, but new entities help update concepts (Rips, Smith, and Medin 2012). In the case of the game at hand, we would rather say that new entities force us to update concepts and categories. Concepts that are formed as a product of our interaction with the world benefit from such a feedback loop, but that is exactly what is being challenged during gameplay.

Rips et al suggest that ad hoc concepts and categories are used to instantiate goals such as "what to bring on a night finishing trip". This capacity makes Wilmot's Warehouse's gameplay make sense, but at the same time, such capacity is challenged by concept feedback as new entities enter continuously in the game. The game thus takes full advantage of these abilities and finds the right amount of difficulty to make it both plausible and entertaining.

The process of categorization as a cognitive tool for learning about the world is inseparable from memory. The very existence of categories eases the cognitive load when multiple entities are introduced. By the consideration of specific features of a set of entities and their categorization and labelling, it is possible to consider larger amounts of entity data. As Rips and colleagues summarize for their proposal: "A key part of our story is what we call 'the semantic memory marriage,' the idea that memory organisation corresponds to meaningful relations between concepts" (p. 39).

Boxes and Instances of the Categorization Process

Concepts are equivalence classes (Goldstone and Kersten 2003): once a concept is formed, the different perceived features are ignored, and the entity is classified as belonging to that set. But what are the features that get perceived in Wilmot's Warehouse's boxes?

A constant across final warehouses is the tendency to classify boxes by background colour, followed by the combination of shape resemblance and colour. This is consistent with the fact that colour is a salient feature in the context of the game: the colour palette of the boxes is contrasting – blue and red are common background colours, and so are purple and yellow. Another tendency, unsurprisingly, is to classify according to natural kinds and artificial kinds. The reason for this last aspect ought to be related to the concentration of features: when background colour stops being useful for discerning between boxes, new features need to be taken into account and old ones discarded or incorporated and summed (see Figure 5.1, centre).

The game could be observed in terms of semiotics, the process of interpretation of symbols or signs. On different occasions, the boxes are not totally discernible but rather represent ambiguous shapes. This process of interpretation, we believe, is derived from feature observation and overlaps partially with categorization. However, we believe that this process does not affect the game loop in the way categorization does, since there are many items which do represent clear objects or shapes. That is why we decided not to look at this aspect in this chapter, even though such a process is interesting and relevant because it is linked to subjectivity and interpretation aspects. One interesting way to study semiotics in the game would be to interview players on their entity (not category) classification for ambiguous boxes.

Another aspect that we suspect interferes with the classification process is priming (Goldstone and Kersten 2003:614) in the form of box adjacency when items are delivered to the warehouse and requested through the service hatch. The request of a box representing "plate of soup and spoon" and "cupcake" together may condition the player to create a "food" category faster. The arrival of the "soap dispenser" box (oriented to the right) next to the "pipe" (oriented to the right) may condition the player to create a category based on the orientation of the shape. The observation of previously arranged boxes in specific categories may also contribute to priming: the arrival of the "vampire fangs" box may end up near the food category and form the base for mouth-related objects just because food was close to the delivery space. The box for "dentures", on the other hand, may go together with the category of objects that we use in everyday life because objects in that category have the same background colour and do not enter the previous ad hoc category.

Process

Given the observations accounted for here, we could establish a typical categorization process as follows, with concrete examples (see Figure 5.1, centre). This stems from the basic, overarching understanding that the categorization task is beneficial for smoother gameplay:

1. The player identifies boxes with similar colours (either background or shape colour) and groups them together.
   a) For example, the box representing a "poppy" (*red*) gets placed near the box representing a "medieval castle" or "medieval banner" (*red*) since they share similar colours. To the red category, the "tori gate" may get added, but another feature becomes salient: it represents a cultural or historical object (*cultural*).
2. Colour grouping becomes inefficient as more complex and distinct shapes appear and new categories are formed.
   a) For example, the box "taiko drum and sticks" (*purple*) gets added to the *red* & *cultural* categories, expanding it and ignoring irrelevant features (*purple*) and preserving relevant ones (*cultural*).
3. The previous ad hoc category gets renewed, as a new entity presents similar features to specific entities in such a category, thus expanding and reforming it.
   a) For example, the box "target and arrows" gets placed in the previous category (*cultural*) because of its round shape (*round*) and similarity to the "taiko drum and sticks" box. As we can see, more and more features get activated for the category.
4. Finally, items that had nothing to do with the original category may get included even when they could represent categories on their own.
   a) For example, our original *red* & *cultural* category ends up including many boxes that contain simple shapes of concentric circles (*circle*), since both "taiko drum and sticks" and "target and arrows" present the *circle* feature.

In this example process, we can see the constant update categories undergo during gameplay, favouring the creation of ad hoc categories rather than the creation of separate new categories. We could argue that this is done for memory optimization, but further research should aim to confirm such a claim. The process described above we do not argue as a rule, but rather as a cognitive route some players may follow. In other words, it is illustrative rather than definitive.

Another example process (see Figure 5.1 – right) illustrates the expansion of a category:

1. The boxes with "mammoth" and "bear paw" form the category: *extinct or wild animals*, both because of their *animal* feature and because of their colours (*blue*, *purple*).
2. To this category, the box "penguin" gets added for the same reasons: the *animal* feature and the blue colour scheme (*blue*, *dark blue*) (ignoring *purple*).
3. The colour scheme of the previous box makes it easier for the box "searchlights" to fit into that category (*blue*, *dark blue*) and by the addition of this entity, the category gets updated: *extinct or wild animals* becomes the ad hoc category *zoo objects or extinct or wild animals*.

Other Processes and Interferences

It is not only feature observation that plays a role in category classification. Sometimes a box can be categorized in a faster manner by checking shape resemblance to other boxes, at the cost of the box's most immediate interpretation. For example, the interpretation of "short blonde hair cut" or "short blonde wig" (see Figure 5.2) is related to the box representing a "tent", because of its visual similarity (wedge-shaped opening at the right side of the shape). This might be done, again, for economic reasons, since the search for more abstract features and relations to other boxes and categories might be more cognitively costly. As a result, the box might become part of the "camping" category. The entity may then be relabelled as an "aerodynamic tent". We believe, nonetheless, this process is closer to the domain of semiotics than to the domain of semantics.

The process may be interrupted by constraints in time and space. Such constraints may lead you to force-memorize the position of items. For example, because space gets too narrow in a specific category, attaching an item to an adjacent category space forces you to remember that position. This could happen especially towards the end of the game, when there are too many objects in the warehouse. In an opposite manner and as a way to economize cognitive resources, some items simply may be left in the first place they were seen.

Here, a distinct process may play the part: association of images that we have previously seen may help cement a memory related to that particular box. For example, a box that can be interpreted as both a "wizard hat" or a "Christmas tree" might be interpreted as the former because of its proximity to "dinosaur". Why would this make sense? If one has recently seen the image of a dinosaur wearing a wizard hat (or other whimsical images via, say, the internet), association may be the fastest way to form a concept and a category.

How Language Assists Categorization in Gameplay

Finally, to determine the connection between language and gameplay in Wilmot's Warehouse, we look back to where we started – to the tutorial: the only instance of

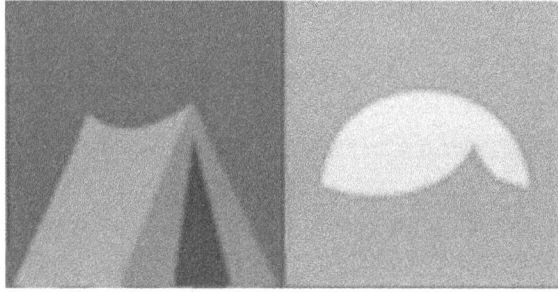

FIGURE 5.2   A tent and a short blonde wig, perhaps categorized by the shape of the opening.

linguistic labelling of categories in the game. We could argue that, with such labelling, the tutorial is priming players to label their categories or choose specific concepts. At the same time, this could condition the player to think about entities (boxes in the game) in linguistic terms.

Following Goldstone and colleagues, when learning unlabelled categories (i.e. categories without a name attached to them), one may resort to finding the most relevant features that make up an element of that category (p. 623), making it easier to scan for similarities when a new member is considered for inclusion. According to our observations, labelling may be beneficial when there are several categories to be considered and when basic salient features such as colour or shape do not come easily to mind. In our previous example for the category "red and cultural stuff", the presence of such a label makes it easier to include entities such as "taiko drum with sticks", since the label quickly identifies a feature that can be connected to the entity ("cultural") in opposition to a category labelled "everyday objects".

We have also observed how language may interfere with feature focus and memory in a specific instance of the game. If instead of keeping in mind the visual features of a requested box, the player instead resorts to memorizing an associated word – especially if that word is ambiguous or easily confused with another – problems may arise. In our specific observation that we will discuss in the next section, an order requiring a box representing a "microscope" was erroneously labelled as a box of "binoculars". The player did not memorize visual information, favouring a linguistic representation over a visual representation. They then doubted their linguistic labelling and brought the wrong box to the counter. This specific instance is consistent with the literature on findings on labels in categorization tasks (Cohen and Lefebvre 2005; Rosch 1978; Sloutsky 2003).

As a final comment for this section, we would like to mention how the knowledge of a second or a third language can affect the semantic categorization process. Specifically (Zareva 2007):

> First, L2 learners may rely on different categorisation strategies compared to native speakers of the language. This can be due to differences in linguistic and cultural backgrounds, as well as the influence of their native language. For example, L2 learners may categorise words based on their L1 knowledge or use translation equivalents as a category cue.

However, the author clarifies that L2 speakers show different levels of accuracy and flexibility while categorizing, due to their language fluency:

> [...] lower proficiency learners may rely on more basic or surface-level categorisation strategies. [...]. L2 learners may experience difficulties in categorising words that have ambiguous or multiple meanings.

This may result in major difficulty or even inability in categorizing words without "direct equivalents in their native language". The implications for cross-linguistic categorization within Wilmot's Warehouse are significant but unfortunately outside the scope of this chapter.

Observations

To develop a more solid evidence base and to provide a qualitative sample of the process outside our own, short interviews were conducted with one player who had finalized the game and with a team of two players who had completed more than 40% of the game. We looked at how they made use of the *Timelapse* or *Map* feature to explain their sorting, and whether they developed specific labels for the categories they made. Irrespective of their participation in a team or as an individual, each player walked through the game without prior knowledge of our research topic or inquiries, to avoid unintended influence.

Results

The players were advised to end their gameplay either when approaching the game's completion –marked by the availability of the Timelapse feature in their inventory – or when passing the midpoint of the game (60%) – this is marked by the availability of the Map feature in their inventory. Subsequently, we recorded their final outcomes and proceeded to explore our research topics. The categorization results and their labels are depicted in Table 5.1.

Result Analysis

In the single-player walkthrough, more items were delivered in each session as the game progressed, altering the categories formed initially. However, the multiplayer gameplay, despite involving fewer items, featured a greater number of categories.

When asked about their sorting choices, the single player emphasized that "as more and more items start coming, it is hard to keep your sorting as you expected", an observation that matches remarks made earlier in this chapter. This becomes increasingly evident as a player advances within the game. In the single-player experience, the cognitive process and adaptive thinking seem to govern the gameplay, requiring the continuous reassessment and reorganization of the warehouse to meet the game's demands.

Conversely, the multiplayer walkthrough unveiled an interplay of internal categorization and conceptualization achieved through cooperation. The successful categorization of items mirrors the success of a conversation requiring shared common knowledge, background, and context. It is noteworthy that, most of the time, both

TABLE 5.1

Item Categorization and Labelling in a Single-Player and Multiplayer Mode

Single Player: Item categorization	Single Player: Labels per Category	Multiplayer: Item Categorization	Multiplayer: Labels per Category
	Objects and signs		Flowers
	Fauna and feed		Volcano like things
	All that is related to the sea		Fruits
	Blue background and uncategorized objects		Shapes
	Similar colours		Trees
	Similar colours (same as above)		Camels
	Blue background colour		Colours and food
	Intense colour backgrounds		Sun and sunset-like things
	Hearts and purple colours		Beach and ocean things
	Abstracts with shapes		Bathroom and colour blue

(Continued)

TABLE 5.1

(Continued)

Single Player: Item categorization	Single Player: Labels per Category	Multiplayer: Item Categorization	Multiplayer: Labels per Category
	Blue background		Stationary and colour blue
	Nature, Hearts and others		Yellow patterns
	Intense colour backgrounds		Rope, candles
	-		Random

players arrived at similar concepts for categorization. However, as in any conversation, differences and disagreements occasionally arose, such as an exchange regarding whether an item most resembled "lungs" or "camel footprints". Compromise is occasionally required, with a subsequent increase in cognitive load to navigate shared agreements.

When asked about their choice of sorting, the players highlighted the ease of categorization and recollection when items were grouped according to the spaces they are found in. For example:

> We put the toilet paper with the hairdryer, because you have them together in a bathroom. It's easier to remember and you know where to look.

And

> P2: The fire match with the fire and the bomb and that thing that looks like a mushroom, because when you camp on a forest […]. P1: Really? I thought these are lamps! That's why we were placing it there!

Equally notable is that the emergence of mental notions happened while playing. A clearer review of the "final" warehouse after playing gave the players a different insight:

> P1: We put the bird here, but now that I think about it, we could add it with the camel. P2: Yeah, both animals! But I think we put it there because it is blue. P1: Yeah, because it's blue.

We see a shift from colour-based sorting to conceptual categorization, highlighting an active engagement of semantic processes in gameplay. Shared common knowledge and background are crucial in the multiplayer mode, resembling conversation dynamics. The player's preference for item sorting based on "natural kind" or "man-made artefacts" driven categories further highlights the importance of semantics in facilitating categorization and memory recall. However, we consider this but a sample of what further research could expand on in terms of contrastive singleplayer and multiplayer gameplay.

Differences between Wilmot's Warehouse and Puzzle-Linguistic Games

Whereas games like Tetris, often compared to Wilmot's Warehouse, present clear constraints, they differ greatly in the processes players utilize for completion. Tetris does not appeal to the use of concepts; it requires only spatial processing. Even though the latter is a component of Wilmot's Warehouse, we could still say that the games are fundamentally different because of the nature of the mechanisms, the dynamics, and the expected aesthetics (Hunicke, LeBlanc, and Zubek 2004).

If language and concepts are at hand, then games like *Baba Is You* (Hempuli 2019) could make for a relative comparison. In this game, players can re-order linguistic elements to create new rules that can be manipulated to solve logic puzzles. The statement "Baba Is You" determines who you control when you move. Creating instead a rule that "Wall Is You" means that when you move, every wall in the level will move instead. However, even though one could argue that language is an important part of both games, it is so in different ways. For Baba is You, the simplest form of syntax (predication) and meta-language are the main mechanisms that propel gameplay. Those are in a different domain that does not overlap with categorization. Despite being games ostensibly about language, one is about simple rules, and the other is about concepts and categorization.

A board game that does incorporate concepts meaningfully is Wavelength (Warsch, Hague, and Vickers 2019), but it does so differently to Wilmot's Warehouse. In this, teams of players work together to decide where on a specified spectrum a certain clue belongs. The spectrum may be "hot" to "cold", and the clue-giver may need to give a clue that is closer to hot than it is to cold (see Heron 2024 for an outline of the complexity associated with this task). Wavelength is inseparable from the social component: success in the game depends on how closely concepts are understood and shared by the players – in short, we all need to have a shared conception of what "hot" and "cold" mean. We need to get the players of our team to see categories in the way we do. Categories may be more subjective or objective (soft/hard, underrated game/overrated game), but to get players to guess our rating, one must come up with a specific prototype of a category, with the right amount of features that would place our clue at the right spot in the category spectrum. An interesting comparison could be made by comparing Wilmot's Warehouse co-op gameplay to a Wavelength session.

Be that as it may, the mechanisms of all three games (*Tetris, Baba Is You, Wavelength*) require very specific actions to be performed flawlessly. Unlike them, Wilmot's Warehouse's only requirement is not as strict: as long as the delivery of items is performed, the player has complete room for creativity in warehouse organization.

These intertextual comparisons are not given in an exhaustive manner, but rather represent a small sample of the potential of contrasting the game with superficially similar puzzles. Further research would benefit greatly from a more thorough comparison of Wilmot's Warehouse with these games, as well as comparisons with other relevant board games and video games.

Conclusion

The exploration of this topic has led us to conclude that the relation between Wilmot's Warehouse and semantics is clear: the categorization process is at the core of gameplay. Even though it is not a restrictive process, it is, arguably, the most effective mechanism for a successful completion. Categorization may be used as a system for saving memory resources, as the game requires the player to recall items in space. At the same time, because of time and space constraints, the game fosters creativity in the categorization process: quickly categorizing and coming up with newer and more intricate categories benefits gameplay overall.

We do not dive deep into the theories that interlink language and categorization; further research should focus on this aspect. Nonetheless, we believe that language is an important part of the categorization process when categories are labelled. It can be argued that this labelling also enhances memory. It can be detrimental, as we have seen, when labels are not established from the beginning of the memorization process. Not only this, but the player's native language may also influence the process of both understanding features and classification, as lexicalization predetermines categories and may intervene in perception. We acknowledge, though, that this is a highly controversial assumption.

All in all, we consider Wilmot's Warehouse a playground for observations on categorization, category perception, and feature detection. Semantics, semiotics, perception, psychology, and language all play a part in gameplay. Further research should expand on the topics dealt with in this paper, and we advise those interested in applied cognitive science to contemplate the game's utility as a low-cost and fun laboratory for exploration.

Note

1 https://www.gamedeveloper.com/design/game-design-deep-dive-the-creative-camaraderie-behind-i-wilmot-s-warehouse-i-.

References

Berlekamp, Elwyn R., and Tom Rodgers. 1999. *The Mathemagician and Pied Puzzler: A Collection in Tribute to Martin Gardner.* Florida: CRC Press.

Cohen, Henri, and Claire Lefebvre. 2005. *Handbook of Categorization in Cognitive Science.* Amsterdam: Elsevier.

Goldstone, Robert L., and Alan Kersten. 2003. 'Concepts and Categorization'. Pp. 597–621 in *Handbook of Psychology.* New Jersey: John Wiley and Sons, Ltd.

Heron, Michael James. 2024. *Tabletop Game Accessibility: Meeple Centred Design.* Florida: CRC Press.

Hunicke, Robin, Marc LeBlanc, and Robert Zubek. 2004. 'MDA: A Formal Approach to Game Design and Game Research'. P. 1722 in *Proceedings of the AAAI Workshop on Challenges in Game AI*. Vol. 4. San Jose, CA: Association for the Advancement of Artificial Intelligence.

Kotovsky, K., and H. A. Simon. 1990. 'What Makes Some Problems Really Hard: Explorations in the Problem Space of Difficulty'. *Cognitive Psychology* 22:143–83.

Megalakaki, Olga, Charles Tijus, Romain Baiche, and Sébastien Poitrenaud. 2012. 'The Effect of Semantics on Problem Solving Is to Reduce Relational Complexity'. *Thinking & Reasoning* 18(2):159–82. doi: 10.1080/13546783.2012.663101.

Rips, Lance J., Edward E. Smith, and Douglas L. Medin. 2012. 'Concepts and Categories: Memory, Meaning, and Metaphysics'. P. 0 in *The Oxford Handbook of Thinking and Reasoning*, edited by K. J. Holyoak and R. G. Morrison. Oxford: Oxford University Press.

Rosch, Eleanor. 1978. 'Principles of Categorization'. in *Cognition and Categorization*. Abingdon: Routledge.

Sloutsky, Vladimir M. 2003. 'The Role of Similarity in the Development of Categorization'. *Trends in Cognitive Sciences* 7(6):246–51. doi: 10.1016/s1364–6613(03)00109-8.

Zareva, Alla. 2007. 'Structure of the Second Language Mental Lexicon: How Does It Compare to Native Speakers'. *Lexical Organization?' Second Language Research* 23(2):123–53.

Ludography

Pajitnov, Alexy. 1984. Tetris [Video game] [Electronika 60]. Academy of Sciences of the USSR.

Hempuli. 2019. Baba Is You [Video game] [Microsoft Windows]. Hempuli.

Hollow Ponds. 2019. Wilmot's Warehouse [Video game] [Microsoft Windows]. Finji.

Warsch, Wolfgang, Alex Hague, and Justin Vickers. 2019. Wavelength [Board game] [Tabletop]. Palm Court.

6

Experiential Perspectives in Game Studies

Michael Heron

Experiential Perspectives in Games

Let's begin this chapter with a question for you to answer. Can a game make you **cry**?

As we touched upon in our discussion of games as art, our field has for a long time had a perception problem when it comes to convincing people that it matters. Old attitudes are hard to shift. Ossified perspectives are mostly swept away by time rather than actually changed – or as the quote perhaps mistakenly attributed to Max Planck goes – science advances one funeral at a time (Azoulay, Fons-Rosen, and Graff Zivin 2019). There exist disagreements on the extent to which the games industry has the largest portion of its soul in art, versus craft, versus business.

The real truth is that its soul is everything, everywhere all at once because there is no such thing as the "games industry" and we're doing ourselves a disservice when we pretend otherwise (Keogh 2023). It's instead a complex ecosystem of smaller industries, with their own set of requirements, incentives, and roles to play. When someone points at manipulative microtransactions and asks "How can this possibly be art?", they're choosing to assess the industry within starkly economical frames. The people adding loot-boxes to pause screens generally aren't the same people working late into the night to find the exact right inflection of a word for a piece of throwaway dialogue.

Many early critics set eliciting ocular waterworks as a threshold for the point at which we take games seriously, setting up a kind of ludic *Turing Test*. If games **can't** make you cry, then it surely follows that they can't tell meaningful stories? Sure, they might make you excited, or angry, or frustrated – but if they can't access our tear-ducts, then there are higher-level emotions that are just inaccessible. We accept that games are **affective** – they affect their players. Convincing the unconvinced about the depth and sophistication of that affective property is more challenging.

Ironically, it was *Electronic Arts* – in the modern era not exactly looked upon as a progressive force engaged with philosophical purity – who tackled this topic most directly. The company took out full-spread ads in popular periodicals during the early 1980s, directly positing the question. The approach was provocative, self-consciously "artsy", and perhaps even a touch defensive in how aggressively these adverts confronted the reader. It's also a clear challenge to the perceptions that EA itself would undermine decades later.

DOI: 10.1201/9781003530282-6

At the time, you'd find few people who would go to the mat for an affirmative answer. Nowadays, with the benefit of 40 years of talented people working within a massive ecosystem of interlocking industries, the answer for me at least is an unambiguous yes. Not even just a manly tear as my on-screen character is forced to kill his own buddy in order to save a building full of nuns and children. I mean **ugly crying.** Head down, weeping – tears and snot everywhere. It's not even as if this happens only in a tiny, rare subset of the games I have played. Here though are some especially memorable examples.

- The final episode of the first season of *The Walking Dead* (Telltale Games 2012). I won't spoil it, but there is a single narrative choice in the last few minutes of the game that makes me well up whenever I think of it. Which I just did. And then did.
- In *Life Is Strange: Before the Storm* (Deck Nine 2017), there is a sequence where Chloe, the main character, is in a junkyard with a baseball bat, reflecting on her life and her loneliness. Narrative choices in this game normally permit you to choose between a range of actions to let you shape the story as you like. In this moment of heightened sadness and despair, all you are ever allowed to do is "smash".
- *Sayonara Wild Hearts* (Simogo 2019). Anyone who can play through this to the final level, reach the point where the narrative plays out in reverse, and not burst into tears has something wrong with them (Heron 2026. This book). If it doesn't make your heart fill to overflowing from the inside out, maybe it's time to do some digging to make sure your soul is still where you expect it to be.
- To *The Moon* (Freebird Games 2011), and to a lesser extent its sequel, which is a largely narrative exploration of the wish for someone to die with a satisfying memory rather than an authentic reflection on a life lived imperfectly.
- Assassin's Creed: Black Flag (Ubisoft Montreal 2013). This is on the surface a relatively straightforward action game of assassins and pirates (which is to say, it has perhaps the single most perfect framing in all of games), but the time in which the story is set is really the sunset of an age of legends. The final scene, reflecting upon all the friends you lost along the way, is effective. Sarah Greene, who plays *Anne Bonny* in the game, pairs this with a haunting rendition of a traditional Scottish song, that is mostly often sung when a gathering of friends parts. The song is called The Parting Glass, and thanks Sarah – I enjoyed the cutscene just as much when I wasn't able to see it for the tears.

Honestly, I could fill this chapter with examples. Just like with movies and music and books. One might argue at this point that the common factor is me and perhaps what I think is affective storytelling is actually just deep-seated depression. To those people I say – please don't say that again, it's much harder to live in denial if people confront me about it. I am reasonably sure the games are the proximal cause of the tears.

This isn't about me though – I posed the question to you. If you answered yes, then you are expressing an inescapable experiential truth – games can make you **feel**, and they can make you feel emotions that cynics may not believe are accessible to the medium.

As hinted at above, this isn't a quality that is at all constrained to video games. I'm not arguing here that games are **better** in this respect than other media, although they certainly can be in individual cases. I'm arguing that games are **just as good** at providing meaningful experiences, but in a different way.

The primary differentiating factor is interactivity. As players, we each have a role in shaping a game experience. These might be in trivial ways, such as how we progress through a linear level. Maybe everyone goes exactly the same way and does the same things, but you can control at the very least the pacing, or the camera, or whatever else the game puts in your sphere of influence. If you don't control anything, then you're actually watching a movie or perhaps reading a book.

We often have more significant control over more substantive things. We can choose between branching narratives or employ tools and tactics to our own goals. We pick dialogue options, select companions, and decide to save or sacrifice antagonists – that kind of thing. Games have long been an experimental medium for playing with conceptions of **agency** – or the extent to which we are instrumental with regards to the means and mode of our actions. Are we the surgeon, or are we the scalpel? Who, in other words, is wielding our character – the player, or the game?

This then brings in an uncomfortable aspect to how we engage with games – to what extent do we acquire **culpability** for what happens in a game in which we exert that agency?

On one hand, this is a ridiculous question – it's a game, who cares? But on the other hand, we've already spoken about how one of the places a game lives is in our own head. It's never an entirely clean separation. Games fulfil a lot of roles in our lives, and some of those roles are psychological (Granic, Lobel, and Engels 2014). While you are almost always free of real-life consequences for what you do in a game (we'll get to that **almost**), we still have psychological relationship to our actions. If I kill an innocent civilian in a video game, can I genuinely declaim all consequences? Real consequence, sure – but as Buddha once said, "With our thoughts we make the world". It's not so easy to discount that our actions in a game may reflect upon us, and be reflected back by us in return. If I weep uncontrollably at the thought of my darling Clementine, in *The Walking Dead*, being sent out into a hostile world to fend for herself… and if the thought of that brings back tears every time I contemplate it… well, doesn't that say that there has been a permanent real-life consequence of the choice I made?

I think it does. Feeling is an experience, and we are shaped by our experiences. Some have argued that our lives are "the sum of the things to which we choose to pay attention" (Wu 2016). Whether you subscribe to the view that games genuinely matter, I don't think we can authentically wriggle out of deconstructing how our choices in games reflect upon us as people.

Are you, as the player, responsible in part when your character in a game performs an atrocity? Are you a bad person if you play games in which you do bad things? Should **you** feel bad if your **character** is bad?

The Magic Circle

One of the ways in which scholars have attempted to come to terms with this idea is through what is sometimes known as the **magic circle** (Consalvo 2009; Heron and Belford 2014, 2015; Stenros 2014) – a morally discontinuous space in which the usual rules of society do not apply for a period of time, or under certain circumstances. A magic circle isn't necessarily a physical space. It's not necessarily a period of time. It's whatever it needs to be, in the circumstances to which it applies.

One of the canonical examples is a boxing match. In real life, if you see two people attempting to punch each other into unconsciousness, you'd expect intervention. You'd expect people to pull them apart, to hold them distant until the red mist clears and they can engage once again as rational people. You might even intervene yourself, putting your body between the combatants in the hope of enforcing a moment of clarity in which their reluctance to hit a third party cools the situation. And intervention, in this case, would be considered a social good. Proof to everyone involved that people were working the way people are supposed to work.

Imagine though if you intervened in the course of a boxing match. Two fighters, squared up, and you stand up from the crowd and yell "Stop! If this goes on much longer someone is going to get hurt!". You then burst through the crowd, under the ropes, to intervene. In this scenario, this **isn't** people working the way people are supposed to work. The boxing ring is a magic circle – we have collectively agreed that within the constraints of a boxing match that it's okay for two people to hit each other for the purposes of our entertainment. The match comes with its own rules, conventions, and expectations – not a lessening of societal obligation but a reshaping of it. Collectively, we have largely agreed that what happens within this magic circle does not connect in the usual ways – philosophically, emotionally, morally, and sometimes legally – with what happens outside of it.[1] The magic circle of a boxing match has a transmutational property – it turns a brawl into "good, clean sport".

In many situations, we assume a complete moral separation. Games represent a magic circle, and it is this protective pentagram that inoculates us – substantively – from the moral consequence of our choices. Leaving aside that nobody is actually hurt from your murder rampage in *Grand Theft Auto 5* (Rockstar North 2013), the instantiation of a game as a magic circle is a philosophically convenient way to abnegate any lingering awkward feelings.

Except as always it's not actually that simple. Particularly when we consider actions that may cross over boundaries that we might hope are inviolable. The magic circle is, unfortunately, porous. We often bring bits of ourselves into the circle, and we are often changed as we exit its environs.

Before we get too deeply into that though, let's talk about good and bad.

Morality Systems in Games

Many games make use of a **morality system** where the game changes based on what you do within the narrative. This might reflect in environmental changes; attitude changes in NPCs; conclusions and epilogues; and occasionally even whole mechanical systems. I'm not going to touch on any deep philosophy of ethics in this book – it's out of scope, and I couldn't hope to offer a better introduction to the topic than *The Good Place* (Benko and Pavelich 2019) did. I am though someone with a long-term interest in ethics in professional environments (Heron and Belford 2024), and it's not surprising I would be compelled by this topic within a game framing. But more than my own personal interest, morality systems represent an interesting quirk of many game designs in that they are explicitly engaging with the idea that choice reflects upon us, at least within the magic circle of play.

We do need to perform some scene setting though before we dig in, because the nature of games as formal systems bound by rules (as useful a definition as any, for our purposes here) has consequences for how sophisticated moral models can be. Real life has a fidelity of one-to-one with reality, but games need to start from zero and add everything needed in from an empty base. You want a physics system, then you need to add a physics system. Games can be thought of as a form of abstraction, or perhaps even simulation. If you design an apartment complex, you don't need to model noise leakage through walls – the universe provides that for you. You're welcome. If you build a **simulation** of that same apartment complex, you need a model of noise leakage if you want it to be part of the system. As such, games are only ever partial models of the game world. Nitsche's conception of the rules-based layer of games (Nitsche 2008) comes into relevance here again. The rules governing the underlying physics and interrelationships of objects are in some ways a reflection of the priorities of the developer.

However, the fact that everything must be built into a game means that there are functional limitations to what a game can model. Modelling has to be rules-based, it has to be represented by state, and it has to be manipulable by mechanisms. As such, games have no access to the internal states of a player. Much moral philosophy is about introspection. It's about self-reflection, and the tension between intentions and outcomes. They're often about situational awareness, such as the concept of **moral particularism** (Dancy 2017). This argues that the right thing to do is not based on unyielding rules or principles but rather a nuanced deconstruction of the implications and relevant considerations unique to a particular scenario. I'm not saying it's impossible for games to capture at least some of this complexity. Just that unless that game is made by a moral philosophy professor[2], it's probably not going to be something that's a high priority in a medium where you also need to worry about how physical collisions and momentum are working.

As a result, most games have a focus on **consequentialism**, which is to say that they assess "goodness" and "badness" on the basis of an evaluation of outcome (Driver 2011). That stands in contrast to **virtue ethics**, in which we assess things on the basis of the characteristics of the agent. There are games that do a good job in exploring virtue ethics, even moral particularism, but they tend to be games where character exploration is the core of the game. I'd argue for example that *Disco Elysium* (ZA/UM 2019) is a game that engages deeply with the protagonist through a lens of non-judgemental virtue ethics.

Games are often **utilitarian** in this framing, arguing the "rightness" should be assessed on the basis of how an action maximizes benefit and minimizes harm (FOOT 1985). You killed a bandit; therefore, you have performed a good action. It doesn't matter **why** you did it (maybe you just like killing), but within the moral judgement of the game universe you made the world a better place. Have ten "being a good person" points.

Other games enforce a **deontological** perspective, which is to say that they encode inviolable moral principles, and "rightness" is a function of evaluation against those principles (Alexander and Moore 2007). We might say, "killing is always wrong", or "killing a civilian is always wrong, killing an aggressor is fine", or "you can kill everyone except children". Deontological principles are also sometimes enforced from "on high" as a consequence of decisions made by developers. For example, it is possible to kill children in earlier versions of the Fallout franchise, but not from *Fallout 3* (Bethesda Game Studios 2008) onwards.[3] Each game's encoding enforces an Overton

Window (Russell 2006) that represents an almost literal "word of God". Absent mods, glitches and bugs, you cannot thwart the will of the developers in exactly the same way you can't escape the pull of gravity.

For a long period of time, games would often come with what is somewhat derisively known as a **karma meter** – a value in your save file that indicates how much of a good person your character is. Nowadays, games may still use them but as a hidden value that is used to assess the path a story takes. You may have seen karma meters in *Fallout 3* (Bethesda Game Studios 2008) and *Fallout: New Vegas* (Obsidian Entertainment 2010) where it was literally called a Karma meter. *Star Wars* games that permit you to choose your character path encode this as a choice between Light Side and Dark Side. *Star Wars: Knights of the Old Republic* (Bioware 2003) and games in the Jedi Knight series such as *Jedi Knight: Dark Forces II* (Lucasarts 1997) allowed players to make "evil" choices to unlock dialogue options and dark-side powers. The Mass Effect series (Bioware 2008, 2010, 2012) framed it as Renegade versus Paragon, or informally "Kirk versus Picard". Bioshock (2K Boson and 2K Australia 2007) had the option to harvest or rescue little sisters – to save them or exploit them. Undertale (tobyfox 2015) encoded a Pacifist versus Genocide morality but in typical Undertale fashion, with a twist.

There are many reasons developers might want to include a morality system in a game. They encourage replayability – story beats, equipment and powers can be doled out depending on whether or not someone plays a "good" or "bad" character. They create the impression of actions having weight to go with them. They let players immerse themselves by feeling like they have a greater degree of agency. Few of the reasons though are to teach the player something about themselves. So why do we see these systems so often, why are they so often framed as being explicitly about morality, and under what circumstances do they breach the magic circle? At what point does a moral system inspire genuine reflection?

Essentially, there are two big sins that are committed by this kind of "push me pull me" style of system, where choices move players along a line that represents goodness and badness.

- These systems tend to be **reductive**, as in they reduce a complex issue to a simplified form. Choices are rarely meaningful in any deep sense. They rarely require you to reflect upon the implications of your decisions. And, since morality systems are often primarily about encouraging replayability and enabling choice, they need to be "balanced" from a game design perspective. Whether you go Light Side or Dark Side, most games will be designed in such a way as you end up in roughly the same place by the end.

- The choices tend to be **cartoonish**. In *Fallout 3*, one of the early moral dilemmas that you are confronted with arrives when you enter the post-apocalyptic city of Megaton, a stable settlement built around an unexploded atom bomb. In the city, you meet an agent of a rich man who would like the bomb to be triggered so he could enjoy an uninterrupted view of the surrounding wasteland. Your choice is "explode a bomb, wiping a settlement and all its inhabitants from the map", or... don't. This is a far cry from the Trolley problem (FOOT 1985).

There is no reason with these morality systems to believe there is meaning beyond the magic circle. They are all **system** and no **morality.**

Ultima IV

One of the first video games to take a serious magnifying glass to how they encoded ethics and virtue was Ultima IV (Origin Systems 1985). Richard Garriott, the master-mind behind the series, had been growing increasingly concerned about the way in which parents wrote to him about his games (Contato 2019). With reflection, he wanted to build a game where players had to **think** about what it means to be a champion. In service of this aim, he built a relatively complex religious system focused on medita-tion upon virtues, and on manifesting these virtues in the game (Figure 6.1). A hero couldn't run from combat and still consider themselves courageous. Likewise, abstain-ing from charity was not something one might expect of a compassionate soul. The job of the player was to become the Avatar, a perfection of all of the game's core virtues.

Mechanically, in the end all boiled down to a series of intersecting morality meters. Embodying virtues was profoundly deontological. If you gave money to a beggar, it nudged your "compassion" meter upwards. It didn't matter how much, or how often, or

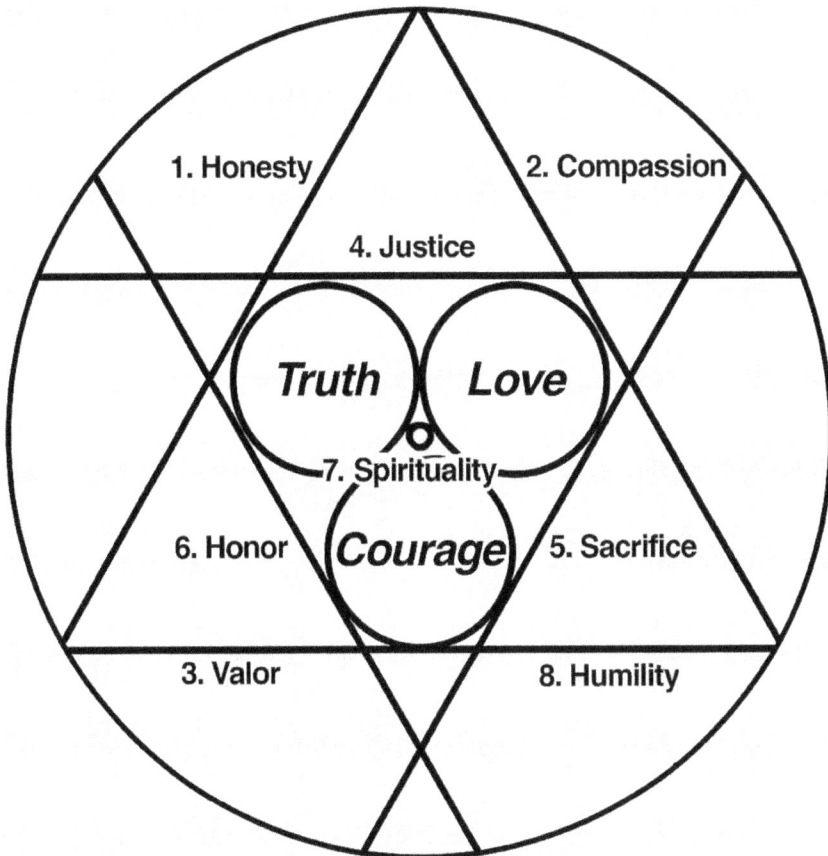

FIGURE 6.1 Ultima 4's model of virtue, available under a CC-SA Licence at https://commons. wikimedia.org/wiki/File:Ultima_codex_symbol.svg.

to whom you gave support. You could thus "game" these meters by doling out money in minute quantities but doing it often. There was no requirement to consider need or larger societal impact. Give money == good. But still, the game through its framing explicitly surfaced an obligation to think about – in an era before easily available walkthroughs – how one might actually exemplify the theoretical virtues of the world.

Ultima IV was also interesting in its approach to character creation. Many Tabletop Roleplaying Games (TTRPGs) would have extensive character creation systems and this was a common design choice in early video game design too. The standard *Dungeons and Dragons* (D&D) model was to roll three six-sided dice (3d6) for each of your six main attributes in turn (strength, intelligence, wisdom, dexterity, charisma and constitution). What you rolled determined your best choice in terms of character class (fighter, magic user, and so on). Later versions of D&D would offer more sophisticated choices of class and race (dwarf, elf, halflings) as well as more subtle choices for attribute distribution (roll 3d6, assign results as desired; roll 4d6, drop lowest number, assign in order; distribute a fixed number of points amongst attributes as desired). Ultima IV eschewed all of this in favour of a series of moral vignettes. For example:

> Thou art sworn to uphold a Lord who participates in the forbidden torture of prisoners. Each night their cries of pain reach thee. Dost though A) show Compassion by reporting the deeds, or B) Honor they oath and ignore the deeds?

Answering these questions would situate your character within the game's mesh of virtues, and where you landed determined which of the eight different character archetypes you began as – a pool varied enough to include honourable knights and humble shepherds. While there may be raw, simple mechanisms at the back-end, the game tries to inculcate in its players a more nuanced perception of how their choices in play reflect on them as players.

What's perhaps most notable about this system is how ahead-of-the-curve it was at the time, and how spectacularly it failed to inspire contemporary game designers to engage more deeply with moral themes. The virtue system of Ultima IV became absolutely critical to the architecture of all subsequent Ultima games. Ultima V (Origin Systems 1988) dealt with the obvious criticism of the system – the extent to which virtues could be corrupted through fanatical and literalist interpretations of the principles. Ultima VI (Origin Systems 1990) deals with a flavour of moral relativism (Harman 1978) and how differing but equally convincing readings of scripture can create disagreement and tension. We know that – we've already had our introduction to Barrett's Principles of Interpretation (Barrett 2011).

Ultima IV remains a fascinating example of what early games could do with regards to breaching the confines of the magic circle. There are abundant personal testimonies that tell of people who were compelled to model the virtues of the avatar in their real life. Even if the heart of the system remains mechanistically trivial and is a victim of the fact you need to **encode** morality into a game… it just goes to show that a thoughtful exploration in a game can yield dividends far in excess of the sum of its parts.

Dungeons and Dragons

TTRPGs offer an interesting counterpoint to the idea of moral systems, because they have a powerful game component not available in video games – human judgement.

Since its early days, *Dungeons and Dragons* has had a conception of morality that it encoded into its **alignment** system. Technically, this is much like a simplified version of the Ultima IV virtues. It represents a character's placement on two intersecting axes – specifically between **good** and **evil** and between **law** and **chaos.** While some campaign settings and rulesets track individual movements within these axes, for the most part, players simply choose one end of the scale or the other, with the midpoint being a third possible choice. The end result is one of nine categories that define the character's philosophy of how the world should work:

- **Chaotic good**, which captures the kind of person who believes that systems are inherently broken and working within them towards good ends is limiting.
- **Neutral good**, which represents the view that the end justifies the means in service of making the world a better place. Rules are made to be broken, unless you can accomplish more within a system.
- **Lawful good**, which represents the view that it is important to work within a system to bring about consistent good outcomes. If injustice is found, lawful good characters will work to change the system.
- **Chaotic neutral**, which represents the mindset of your typical anarchist, acting primarily in service of their own self-interest.
- **True neutral**, which represents a balanced attitude where good and evil, law and order are merely intellectual constructs. Those who seek balance, or coherence with universal forces, might be considered in this frame.
- **Lawful neutral**, in which the moral outcome of an action is independent of the need to follow the rules and strictures of a system. Stability and consistency are more important than specific moral outcomes.
- **Chaotic evil**, in which characters are driven by the impulse to satisfy their own desires at the expense of others, especially if it results in a slide towards societal anarchy. These are the "some people" that want to watch the world burn.
- **Neutral evil**, where characters act in their own self-interest independently of the societal context in which they function.
- **Lawful evil**, where the strict rigidity of systems is used as a tool for gaining personal advantage over the weak.

These interpretations of alignment aren't likely to find universal agreement. That is one of the things that has plagued the idea over the years – that it's not rigidly defined enough to serve its original purpose as a game mechanism. In early conceptions of D&D, alignment was tightly coupled to gameplay effects – spells that would target only good creatures, or identify chaos, and so on. The accessibility of various supernatural powers was limited to working within certain moral limitations – good gods likely would not answer the prayers of evil people. Players were rewarded by the Dungeon Master (DM) for behaving in a way compatible with their alignment and punished for deviating from their moral code. Some character classes (the Paladin, for example, a kind of holy warrior) were only available to those of particular alignments. Given the ambiguity in both the rules and their interpretation, this often led to disagreements and arguments. Increasingly, the idea of alignment has been de-emphasized as a mechanic and left almost entirely as a role-playing aid. You only need to turn to an internet forum to see how diverse the viewpoints regarding alignment are. Ask "What alignment was Emperor Palpatine?", or "what alignment was the Joker?"[4] and you'll find a wealth of opinions and justifications. What about Malcolm Reynolds from Firefly[5]? Captain Picard[6]?

When it had prominence as a mechanical system, however, what the social context of *Dungeons and Dragons* gave is an opportunity for people to justify, explain, and interrogate their decisions within a moral framework. When a Paladin commits an act outside of their enforced lawful good alignment, they can lose access to their class powers until they atone. The game can pause while the DM and the player discuss the mindset behind the character's actions.

> 'Yes, I agree it was unlawful of me to free the prisoner from the jail-cell, but I felt a system that would imprison and execute a child for stealing food is inherently unjust. In this particular case, I didn't feel it was possible to conform to both aspects of my alignment, and that to behave ethically would be to behave immorally. I think given my God's principles, in situations where I can't satisfy both I am obligated to satisfy the desire for goodness'.

Video games can't (or rather, they **don't**) interrogate motivations and reasoning. Within the frame of a social game, this might actually become a character-defining moment, or establish a precedent for future themes a campaign might explore. More than this, the relative freedom of play in *Dungeons and Dragons* and other such games doesn't confine players to a limited set of coded choices. A player who engages deeply with the morality of their character is free to propose courses of action that nobody anticipated in advance.

In a video game, the choice would likely be "Free the child", "refuse to free the child", or "talk to the authorities on behalf of the child". In a *TTRPG* maybe you find this scenario playing out as an elaborate jail-break farce. Or perhaps the paladin steps in as legal counsel and defends the child in court.

The availability of reflection as a process for the DM, and for the player making moral choices, offers deeper opportunities for contemplation. The personal relationship between a player and their character (more on that later) offers a lens onto the internal life of fictional constructs that video games generally can't offer. It's still difficult to truly assess alignment in anything other than consequential terms since we still get what is essentially a rationalization of behaviour rather than access to the moral machinery in a character's mind. And those assessments are still in the frame of a system in which the definitions are woolly and unreliable.

Alignments in D&D represent not so much sophisticated moral positions as they do vaguely over-lapping archetypes. The reason why people disagree so much on the alignment of well-loved fictional characters is that no believable personality resides fully within one of these nine philosophical positions. As Walt Whitman wrote in the poem Song of Myself: "Do I contradict myself? Very well then, I contradict myself. I am large. I contain multitudes".

Why Are Moral Systems so Hard to Do Right?

Essentially here, in our quest to see if the magic circle is permeable, we are confronted with the fact that sometimes experiences are difficult to systemize.

In real life, **morality is hard.** There's a reason we have literally centuries of deeply thoughtful work on the topic. Moral quandaries are often small, complex, and form a kind of "wicked problem" (Rittel and Webber 1973). A wicked problem, if you haven't encountered the term, is an issue that is difficult, if not impossible, to solve because of one or more characteristics:

- Information about the context of the problem may be incomplete or contradictory.
- The characteristics of a good solution may not be fully understood or may be evolving as the problem domain is clarified.
- The solution can only ever be partial, and we may not ever be able to truly assess the effectiveness of that solution over time.
- There is no obvious point at which the solution may manifest itself, and no obvious point at which you should stop thinking about it.
- The problems are unique and not amenable to trial-and-error when formulating and executing upon a solution.

If we knew how to behave morally, or ethically, in all situations, then none of us would have any excuse for behaving otherwise. It is precisely because of the wicked (complicated, rather than evil) nature of reality that we are often doing the best we can rather than the best that can be done. However, none of this necessarily makes for good game design – typically in games, we are choosing between what end up being roughly equivalent paths through a game because players want choice, but they are less keen on real consequences. They don't want a murder-spree to end up with literal years of in-game imprisonment. *Grand Theft Auto* would be a very different experience if it ended in a lethal injection for your character.

There are also no rewards in real life for doing the right thing over the wrong thing. In fact, it is often the unethical path that yields the best results for the individual. At best, doing the right thing saves us from the consequences of doing the wrong thing. Or perhaps more cynically, from the consequences of being **caught** doing the wrong thing.

The experience of playing the game *Alter Ego* (Favaro 1986) is one that has stayed with me for pretty much my entire life. I played it as an eight-year-old, loading it from a floppy disk into a Commodore 64. I probably didn't fully understand it at the time, dealing as it often did with adult themes. However, I vividly remember one part of it cementing in me an appreciation of the fundamental unfairness of the universe.

The game played out in a series of narrative vignettes. It was a text-based game in which you'd select a card that represented a life experience during a particular phase of life, from being a baby all the way through to dying of old age. You'd have the scenario explained, such as "You're in a mall with your mom. You lose sight of her for a moment, and when you look back, you can't see her. There are people everywhere".

Then you get to choose a response, such as "look for her", or "start crying", or "ask an adult for help". You'd also get to choose an emotional state, such as "calm", or "anxious", or "frightened". Incompatible responses were prohibited – you couldn't calmly burst into tears for example. This was in the days before TikTok of course when performative grief couldn't be monetized. Your character had various personality traits that developed over time, and the game would also stop you from doing things that were contrary to the personality you'd built up through previous decisions.

If you'd been an anxious child, you might not be able to be "calm". It was a seriously innovative game for its time and allowed you to live a semi-convincing life, albeit one framed in the context of its own time and place.

My main point here though is that there was one particular vignette that I still hold as being genuinely formative for me. You are hungry, and there are some snacks in the fridge. They're not for you though – they're for the family. You can eat them, satiating your current hunger. Or you can leave them, because they don't belong to you. If you leave them, the game asks you how you feel about the fact nobody will ever say thank you for your self-denial. You can say essentially, "Goodness is its own reward", or "Wow, that sucks now you point it out".

It does suck, but that's how real life works. You don't get rewarded for doing the minimum work needed to get along in society. It's just expected of you. Games though work differently – we expect to be, and generally are, rewarded when we do good things.

Even within *Alter Ego* though, we still encounter situations where the choices – nuanced by emotional state – remain limited. In real life, morality is granular. We're not usually choosing between good or bad, or light-side and dark-side. We're choosing between two different kinds of bad, or two different kinds of good. Or more accurately, we're choosing between 50 options, none of which are clearly good or clearly bad, and there are also secret choices you never encounter. Or more accurately still, we're working with an infinite number of things that are morally incomparable. In fact, the board game *Trial by Trolley* (Houser 2020) is essentially one big long exploration of this theme.

Finally, the big problem – agreement on what **good** and **bad** even are is almost impossible to achieve. You just need to look at modern political discourse to see how we all draw our moral lines in different places, and how polarizing discussions about right and wrong have become.

Morality is a wicked problem, as we've discussed, and wicked problems are perhaps impossible to systemize.

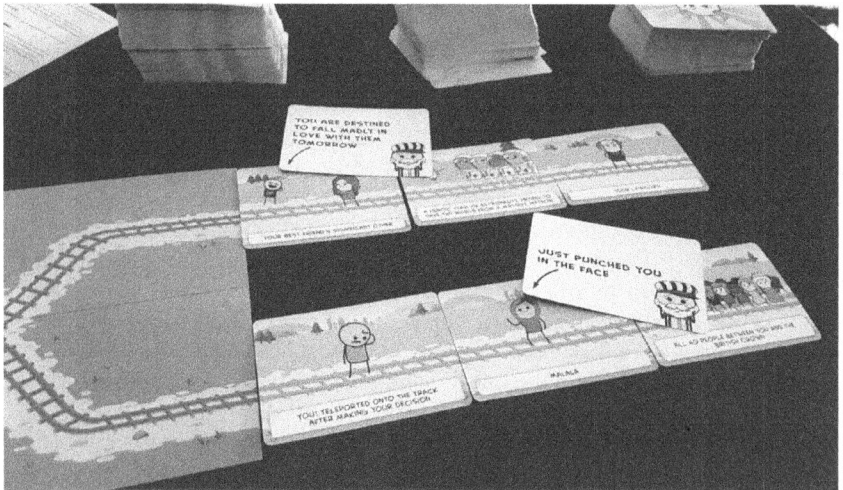

FIGURE 6.2 The Trolley Problem as expressed through the game *Trial by Trolley*. To which line are you directing the oncoming train? (Photograph by author).

Breaching the Magic Circle

If systemized moral decisions fail to really breach the magic circle, are there games that actually **can** encourage the player to contemplate the decisions they make?

I'd say yes, but I must caution here that this is very much a "your mileage may vary" situation. Everyone will have their own opinions but in this section, I present a few examples of games that have certainly made me reflect on my decisions, on my moral compass, and sometimes even on my own complicity in virtual atrocities.

The idea of simple morality meters has fallen a little bit out of favour in recent years. The comically cartoonish decisions and the predictability of "the good ending" and "the bad ending" knocked much of the shine off the idea. They're still used, but primarily in the background. The better class of modern games tend to adopt more narrative explorations of morality and consequence. *Red Dead Redemption 2* (Rockstar Games 2019) doesn't have much of a morality system (although it does have something of a wanted system), but the whole game is an extended morality tale in the literary tradition. Undertale (tobyfox 2015) is one big long extended commentary on the nature of binary morality systems among other things. Undertale is really an extremely clever satire on many tropes of role-playing games, choice being among them. *Baldur's Gate 3* (Larian Studios 2023), despite drawing from D&D and thus having that alignment system within its mechanical orbit, assesses moral action through storytelling consequence. But a few games do things differently still.

Telltale Games: *The Walking Dead*

I've already hinted in this chapter that I found *The Walking Dead* (Telltale Games 2012) – henceforth TWD – to be tremendously affective. That final conversation, in the final chapter, broke me. That wasn't because it, by itself, was particularly clever or moving or resonant – but rather, the game was designed along a trajectory. Every single thing you did aligned to make you **care** about that final decision. And it did this through a tremendously simple system.

TWD places you in the shoes of Lee, a man being carried off to prison for killing his wife. The police car in which he's travelling crashes down the verge as the officer swerves to avoid a figure on the road. I don't think it's possible to spoil a game called *The Walking Dead* with this next revelation – the figure was a zombie! The cop is now a zombie. It's zombies all the way down.

As Lee escapes his situation, he finds himself in a garden where a young girl in a tree house is looking down at him. Her parents are missing, and she is alone. At this point, the cynical part of you thinks, "Oh great, an annoying escort mission". And you're partially right. Clementine, the young girl, becomes your charge and yes – you are escorting her through the rest of the game. But rather than getting stuck on scenery, leaping out of stealth directly into the path of an approaching guard, or running into the arms of hostile enemies, your relationship with Clementine is narrative. You are her saviour, her protector, and a reluctant moral guide to her future. You become her surrogate father figure, and she looks up to you as you engage with the realities of a newly hostile world.

Here's where that "tremendously simple system" comes in – every time you do something and Clementine witnesses it, the game will flash up a little piece of text that says

Clementine will remember that. The game never places **any** moral judgement on what it means. Mechanically, this statement indicates a branch in the narrative – a point of consequence that **might** have future knock-on effects. Sometimes these consequences are minor – a changed line of dialogue, for example. Sometimes they are literal life or death, and you don't necessarily know in advance what kind of consequence you're dealing with. A wicked problem, in other words. Your advice for Clementine to cut her hair short **might** be the thing that saves her life a few hours down the line.

This simple notification though – for me – breached the magic circle as if it were drawn in dust on a windy day. I care what Clementine remembers, and the small changes in timing and intonation of that notification add a subtlety that stops it ever becoming rote. "Clementine witnessed what you did". "Clementine will remember".

You are teaching Clementine by example, setting up the way she understands the world. What is it you're putting in her head, and is it what you want to be there? **What**, in other words, does Clementine remember and are you happy that she does?

There were more than a few times that notification made me pause, consider my actions, and then reload from an earlier save file. There **are** mechanical consequences for some of these decisions, but I cared less about them than I did about what my fictional adopted daughter thought of me. I didn't want her numbed by a hard world, but I wanted her hardened enough that she could survive it. I wanted to give her as many opportunities as I could to retain her childish innocence but not at the expense of making her naïve and credulous. TWD employs this device like a dagger to the heart. The most effective psychological horror is built on implying a threat and letting your mind fill in the blanks (White 1971) – nobody knows how to scare you better than you. An actor in a rubber mask is less frightening than the suggestion of movement in the corner of your eye. Here, Telltale Games employs the same approach. They encourage a response – don't systemize, empathize.

A similar system later got explored in more depth in *Life Is Strange 2* (DONTNOD Entertainment 2018), in which you take the role of a big brother modelling moral behaviour for his younger brother. They are fleeing a supernatural incident that

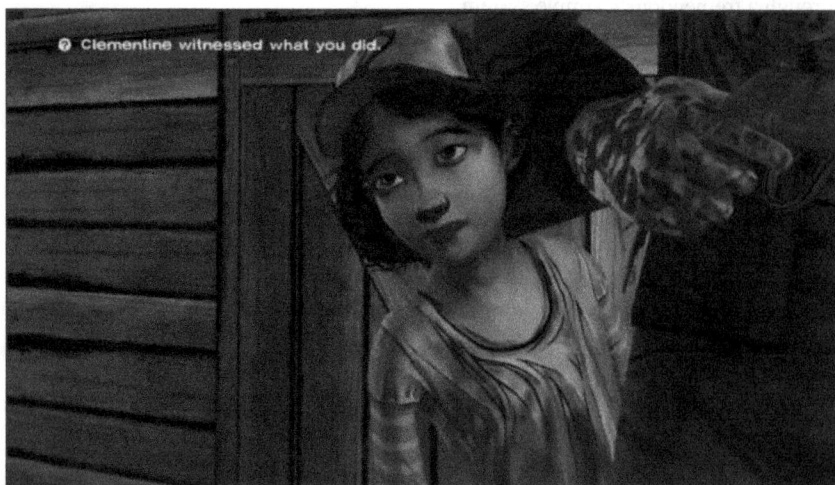

FIGURE 6.3   Time to reload a save file (Screenshot by the author).

exploded after a police over-reaction resulted in the killing of their father. In this, not only does the game incorporate the values you have inculcated in your sibling, but it also makes the accumulation of these lessons a feature of the interactions you have with him. *Life Is Strange 2* is, surprisingly, perhaps weaker in this respect because by externalizing the consequence they are basically showing the rubber mask. I still worry about my darling Clementine. She has been the recipient of all the affection and care I would have pointlessly squandered on children of my own. I hope she also remembers **that**.

Papers, Please

TWD gives us a game that encourages contemplation as to what messages we impart upon those we care about. It's explicitly narrative in its framing – even the consequences are narrative. The kind of introspection it inspires is essentially about meaning in relationships. Papers, Please (Pope 2013) on the other hand encourages us to reflect on how we, as hopefully compassionate people, encode small cruelties in how we engage with bureaucratic systems. Again, this is not a game that judges you for your choices. Instead, it encourages you to judge yourself. All the game does is give you a puzzle.

You are an immigration officer, standing at the border to a fictional soviet-style country called Arstotzka. Your job is to allow legal immigration while denying entry to those that that 'the powers that be' have deemed unwelcome. Your job is to decide whether to approve passage, or not. And deciding on this is handled by a set of rules – largely, simple rules – that determine what legal entry looks like. For every person, you correctly let into the country, you're paid a small amount of money.

And then the game gives you two additional considerations. The first is a time limit per day. The second is that narratively your wages must go to support your extended family. You need to feed them, shelter them, and keep them healthy and doing so for everyone is financially punitive. Inevitably, you'll need to make some decisions about who gets to eat and who gets the heat.

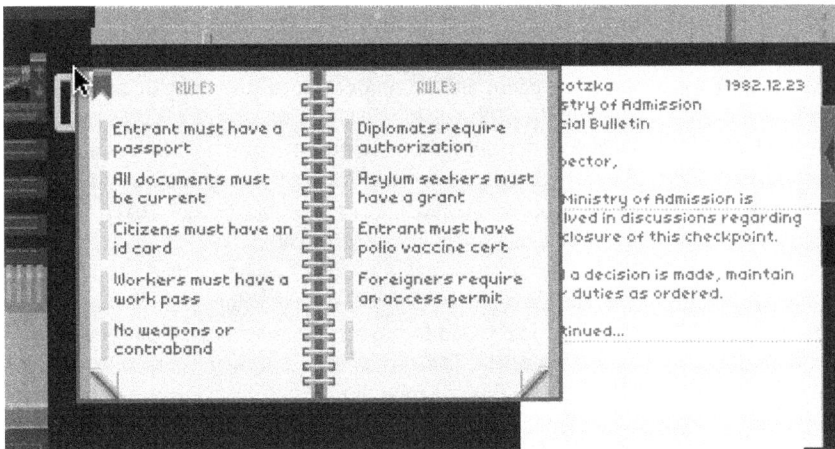

FIGURE 6.4   The rules of entry for later in the game (Screenshot by the author).

To begin with, your job is very easy. The rules for day one are simply that everyone needs a passport, and only Arstotzkan citizens are permitted entry. People walk up to your booth, show a passport, you check their citizenship and then stamp yay or nay appropriately. You're able to process quickly and correctly, and you'll probably be able to put aside a healthy surplus of your wages against future calamities. The problem is that this is a country full of political turmoil and the target of international pressure – the rules change daily. And they get more and more complex, incorporating larger amounts of cross-checking of separate documentation. See Figure 6.4 for an example of how byzantine it can get.

Each rule adds a cognitive cost (Sweller 2011) to your decision-making. Each new document introduces a lag in your processing. Every single document might be invalid – out of date, or a forgery. Every single person might be trying to get by using someone else's documentation, so you need to check passport photos against the person in front of you, cross-referencing photos, weight, and height. Sometimes documents are only valid if issued with a legal stamp from another country, and so you need to check official seals against the seals Arstotzka recognizes. You will go from processing, say, twenty people a day to processing five, or six. And every so often, the game will offer you an opportunity, or present you with a plea.

- "Please don't let this person in, they are a sex trafficker".
- "If you detain people rather than send them away, I'll give you a portion of my salary for each".
- "Let me into the country, I will pay you extra".

There are no morality meters here, just a creeping sense of fatigue. You have so much processing to do, and you have so little time to do it. You'll begin to introduce efficiencies. If someone comes in with complicated paperwork, perhaps you deny them entry rather than accurately process them. You don't need a reason to deny someone, until a few weeks into play – at that point, you need to fill out a denial slip. If you deny someone with proper paperwork, it'll lead to a citation in the same way as letting someone illegally into the country. Two citations per day are warnings, simply denying you the money for correctly processing an entrant. Further citations result in fines. The game is over if those fines can't be covered.

So, perhaps you play the system and deny a couple of the complicated requests knowing that you'll make up the difference in faster processing of easier cases. A foreign diplomat needs an access permit, polio vaccine certificate and diplomatic authorization, the latter of which needs cross-referenced against recognized nations. So perhaps you say "no", take the citation, and hope the next person is a citizen who only requires a passport, an ID card, and the vaccine certificate.

Or...

What will almost certainly happen is that you'll stop being quite so merciful in the edge cases. Sometimes people forget to provide documentation, and you need to ask them for the missing documents. Sometimes they'll argue or debate, sometimes they'll just provide it. It is not a violation though to reject someone on the basis that they didn't present you a passport, even if they had one they'd show you on request. Negotiating for the documentation people should have had upfront is a time delay you can't necessarily afford. For the crime of leaving their passport in their pocket, away they go. Stamped rejected.

It's certainly easy to play Papers, Please as a simple *immigration 'em up*. It's fun enough in that frame. If you let your mind focus inwards though, you may find yourself disquieted by how easily you fell into the role of the merciless bureaucrat. Systems, when rigidly enforced, are dehumanizing. Here, you are the dehumanizer, acting as the dehumanizing agent of a dehumanizing regime.

One of my favourite quotes from the Expanse series of books is in Tiamat's Wrath (Corey 2019):

> 'Easy to make systems with a perfect logic and rigor. All you need to do is leave out the mercy, yeah?'

Papers, Please is an extended lesson in what happens when we remove the mercy from systems, and when we remove the compassion from ourselves. As an educator, my philosophy is to **try** to talk to all of my students as if they were having their worst week of their lives, and I might be the only positive interaction they get to have. You never know what's going on in someone else's life, and only occasionally do people risk the vulnerability that goes with revealing themselves. Papers, Please shows me that given the right circumstances and right system, perhaps I too would find kindness an impossible standard to which I could hold myself.

Spec Ops: The Line

The Walking Dead implicitly asks us to reflect on how we might be viewed by others. Papers, Please makes us think about how systems can grind away the better parts of our nature. In both cases, this is an **interpretation** of the experiences that the games provide. *Spec Ops: The Line* (YAGER 2012) is different in that it has an explicit message it wants you to consider, and it keeps on asking you to think about what you're doing and how it makes you feel. This was something of a surprise to everyone who played it, because on the surface this was the latest in a line of non-remarkable military shooters, and nobody expected the makers to do anything remarkable.

You play *Captain Martin Walker*, leader of an elite Delta Team sent into a post-catastrophe version of Dubai on a recon mission. Your brief is to find out what happened to the previous recon team. You find out they're still there, and in trouble. Walker makes the decision to turn the recon mission into a rescue mission. However, you find that the previous squad have gone rogue and renounced their allegiance to the United States. Your brothers-in-arms are now your enemy. Lock and load, boys, we're going in.

The whole game is a Trojan horse. It's not the game it pretends to be. It's actually a complex, nuanced deconstruction of player complicity in glorifying violent narratives in media. And in this, it is uncompromising in the focus of the deconstruction. This is not a story about Walker, in the end. This is a story about **you**. It explicitly makes your choice to play the game a moral decision. It casts your diegetic engagement with the game scenario as a non-diegetic choice you made. It begins doing this subtly, but with increasing insistence as the game goes forward.

At first, you're killing terrorists – largely stereotypical "others" (Brons 2015). It's okay to kill them, says the language of game design, because they don't look like us. Right away you might recoil from that characterization until you think a bit about how consistent the vocabulary of entertainment is on that score.

After a while, you're killing American soldiers. But you know, the bad ones. The traitors. Them, not Us. And then you're killing civilians. And after a while you're just... killing. Everything. And everyone. The escalation is justified narratively, creating a kind of seamless transition from Heroic American Exceptionalism to indiscriminate war-crimes. It happens so incrementally you might not even notice it's happening. After all, every game adds enemy variety to the experience. The language of game design is being employed as expected.

Spec Ops: The Line has no branching narratives. It is linear in almost every respect. You never make a story decision in the game. You're riding on Walker's shoulders, and the only choice you have is to play or not (Heron et al. 2014). For a lot of people, that's enough for them to absolve themselves over any responsibility for the atrocities they are conducting. It's not like anyone asked them if they were okay with it, right?

But Spec Ops: The Line isn't willing to accept this as an answer. Increasingly stridently, through its loading screens and other elements, it begins to ask you a simple question. "Why don't you just stop playing?". After all, if you stop playing, then the atrocities will end.

What happens if you stop playing?

Nothing. No recognition. No achievements. No fanfare. All you have is the knowledge that you made a moral choice to stop playing the game. You'll never experience the ending except, perhaps, through YouTube videos but that's not the same thing. That's you voyeuristically observing an ending that someone else earned. It's stolen valour. In other words, this is a true moral choice – nobody applauds you for doing the right thing. And you may find it difficult to convince anyone you even did anything of note. It's only a game, right?

The game becomes increasingly strident, and explicit, in its framing as it goes on. It never lets you ignore your complicity in what is happening. Some of the loading screen "tips" it gives you as the game goes on:

- "The US military does not condone the killing of unarmed combatants. But this isn't real, so why should you care?"
- "To kill for yourself is murder. To kill for your government is heroic. To kill for entertainment is harmless".
- "If you were a better person, you wouldn't be here".
- "Can you even remember why you came here?"

As the game cajoles you, it changes. Walker becomes increasingly unpleasant to play as he loses track of himself and his mission. He essentially turns feral. In the earliest hours of the game, he is a consummate professional. Kills are surgical, precise, and always necessary. He takes no pleasure in an unpleasant job done well. Gradually, he begins to ease into the violence. He no longer employs minimal necessary force – instead of knocking an enemy unconscious with his rifle, he breaks their legs. He quips, like he's in a Marvel movie. He makes jokes. He banters with his team. Takedowns become increasingly brutal and violent, uncomfortable to watch. Walker begins to take joy in the visceral catharsis of killing – he starts screaming insults and challenges, revelling in the slaughter.

"Cognitive dissonance is an uncomfortable feeling caused by holding two conflicting ideas simultaneously", the game reminds us.

His comrades, Lugos and Adams, are increasingly alarmed by this and they make their views known. They try to talk him down. They try to remind him of the actual mission. They can't get through to him, because he's having a blast. Because you, as the player, are having a blast. At least to begin with. Over time, Walker goes from a character you control to a wild, violent beast that you're only "sort of" steering. The only thing you can do to stop him, and the celebration of violence you are enabling, is to stop playing.

Do you, though?

You wanted to feel a certain way. You wanted to blow off some steam. You wanted to put yourself in the shoes of a hero. The game was supposed to give you the opportunity to do that. But... is it? Can you, in fact, even remember why you came here? Why don't you stop it all? All you have to do is **stop playing.**

Do you feel like a hero yet?

It's a brave game that keeps insisting that you stop playing it. *Spec Ops: The Line* forces you to reflect on what role violent media may have in the coarsening of our attitudes towards atrocity. Nobody expected *Spec Ops: The Line*. That's what made it so effective in delivering the message encoded within.

The Psychogeography of Imaginary Places

Psychogeography is a largely ill-defined reflective practice that exists within the uneasy liminal space between psychology and geography. Giving it a full treatment is well outside the scope of this book, but it can be an invaluable tool for those seeking to illuminate experiential perspectives within games. Hon Je Bek is quoted as defining psychogeography thusly (O'Rourke 2021):

> Psychogeography is the fact that you have an opinion about a space the moment you step into it.

The discipline finds academic safe harbour within a variety of fields. It's sometimes considered an outcropping of urban design (Ellard 2015); of literature (Holloway 2022); and of political activism (Bridger 2013; Holloway 2022; March-Russell 2013). In connection with what we are discussing in this chapter, psychogeography is a kind of "emotional dowsing" – a way to let the worlds in which we wander inhabit and enrich us on a personal level.

In cinema and theatre, there is a concept known as *mise-en-scene* (Lathrop and Sutton 2014) – the assembling of props, set-dressing, lighting, and so on to create a particular impression in the minds of the audience. Authors like Baudelaire, Ballard, and Poe created almost psychological profiles of urban environments to underscore the themes in their writing. Guy Debord and the Situationist International movement stressed undirected exploration of physical environments as a way to engage with the neurosis of a place (Smith 2010). Modern psychogeographers like Will Self (Self 2007) and Iain Sinclair (Richardson 2015) often talk about psychogeography as a form of communion with the landscape, and a way to connect more resonantly with the factors that shaped it.

In this frame, we might think of the experience of playing a game as a form of practical psychogeography because what is a game environment other than a representation of a place that ensures we have opinions the moment we enter it?

The New Games Journalism comes into play again here. Perhaps with psychogeography, we are not so much travel journalists but rather travel therapists, seeking to connect our experiences to our own intuition as to their meaning and then exploring the relationships that emerge. Many players talk of the world of Dark Souls (FromSoftware 2011) as being melancholy, and they're right – but what are the factors that make it so? Miyazaki once chided one of his artists who, upon attempting to design an undead dragon, focused too much on making it unpleasant to look at. He instead counselled (Software 2014):

> Can't you instead try to convey the deep sorrow of a magnificent beast doomed to a slow and possibly endless descent into ruin?

This ethos is expressed everywhere in the environmental design of Dark Souls. Magnificent structures worn away by time; sweeping landscapes that invade the bones of lost civilizations; the bosses – all of it comes together to create this sensation of "deep sorrow" and a "slow, possibly endless descent into ruin". The graphical design, audio design, narrative design – it all serves the purpose of reinforcing an almost singular vision. And we, as players, can meditate upon how that vision is communicated to us and how it makes us feel.

Video games offer a lens on telling stories of which more traditional, passive media can't take advantage. We control, in most circumstances, the locus of our own attention. We look where we want to look. We linger where we want to linger. In a movie, the director has control of what we see and when. In a book, we can only experience that which we have been told. In a video game, if I want to stand by a lake and simply observe the play of colours on the surface, I can do so – provided of course the game gives me a lake and time to reflect upon it.

If the magic circle insulates us from the consequences of what happens in a game, we can think of psychogeography as an explicit rejection of the convenience of emotional distance. Psychogeography is an interrogation of what the game makes us feel – angry, sad, melancholy, confused – the whole gamut of the human experience. It's about extracting **meaning** about how we, as players, exist within and without the imaginary environments in which we find ourselves.

Consider Iain Sinclair and his book *London Orbital* (Sinclair 2003) in which he engages in a psychogeographical exploration of the M25 ring road that surrounds London. He talks of the different way acoustics work depending on the combination of concrete and verge. He talks of the waterways that the roadways supplanted, and how ancient geology dictates modern infrastructure. He inhabits the moment, engaging all of his senses, to be **present.** We can do the same thing in the context of play.

Here's a simple exercise. Pick an open-world game. Open its map. Take a screenshot. Now, draw a circle around an area of the map. Follow that circle without deviation. It doesn't matter whether this is *Skyrim* (Bethesda Game Studios 2016) or *GTA 5* (Rockstar North). Your job is to follow that circle and simply engage mindfully with the journey. Make a note of what you see – it doesn't matter how mundane. Make a note of what you hear, no matter how prosaic. Imagine how the game would smell. Those notes can be textual, or visual (Gamboa et al. 2023). Imagine how the ground underneath would feel. Consider your character's inventory, if it has one, and how its weight would press against you in the journey. Is it smooth going, or hard? Flat, endless desert or vertical, stabbing mountains? Take time to inhabit each moment in the journey. Do you feel a sense of wonder, or a sense of boredom? If the core game loop is defined by second-to-second gameplay, the game's emotional resonance can be defined by second-to-second experience.

This is a flavour of the directionless wandering Debord and his collective wanted to make core to the experience of practical psychogeography – a concept known as the dérive. It conjures up the sauntering of a Baudelaire-style flaneur (Mazlish 2014) simply soaking in the atmosphere with no particular place to be, no particular time to arrive. From games such as *Shadow of the Colossus* (Team Ico 2005) to *Legend of Zelda: Breath of the Wild* (Nintendo EDR 2017), we see landscapes that encourage losing oneself in an agenda-free drifting through the world.

Before you move on from a place in the traversal of your drawn circle, ask yourself – **how does this moment make you feel**? And what does it seem to **want** you to feel? Sneaking between the Great Pyramids can bring a sense of awe when you let yourself inhabit the moment. Hanging off the *Statue of Zeus in Assassin's Creed: Odyssey* (Ubisoft Quebec 2018) can feel transgressive. Interrogate the moment, because in doing so you interrogate yourself. Consider the environment, and what it tells you – in the rush from goal to goal, we often forget to simply stop and think about how a game's mise-en-scene is communicating ideas to us.

Consider how landscape and terrain mirror emotional state in *Hellblade: Senua's Sacrifice* (Ninja Theory 2017) and how the auditory landscape of Senua's head is communicative of the mental health struggle at the heart of her characterization. Consider how graffiti in *Left 4 Dead* (Valve 2008) encodes important narrative clues in diegetic game elements, and how environmental storytelling (lights still on, car alarms still active) communicates important clues about chronology in the absence of exposition. Consider the many in-jokes in *Fallout 4* (Bethesda Game Studios 2016) that are contained in arrangements of in-game assets – a skeleton, an adventurer's hat and a revolver in a fridge brings to mind Indiana Jones escaping a nuclear test in *Indiana Jones and the Crystal Skull* (Fetterman 2022). The archaeology in *Tomb Raider* (Crystal Dynamics 2013). The alien artefacts in *The Outer Wilds* (Mobius Digital 2019). It's all there for a reason.

Simply stopping and reflecting on what is being implied by our environments, and how we **feel** about those implications – that's psychogeography. How do we feel when we hear a witch in *Left 4 Dead* (Valve 2008) and is it the same as how we feel when we hear a clicker in the *Last of Us* (Naughty Dog LLC 2023)? How do we feel when I Don't Want to Miss a Thing starts playing at a climactic scene in *Saints Row 4* (Deep Silver Volition 2013) versus the sparse, almost incidental musical doodles in Breath of the Wild (Nintendo EDP 2017)?

Often in games, sights and sounds are explicitly communicative. Someone is shooting, someone has been hurt, danger is near. However, it can also implicitly communicate simply by existing – where there is no game design goal being met, and the only intent is what we ascribe to it. When the goal of its inclusion is simply "ambiance".

Increasingly, games have started to focus on what two previous thesis students of mine described as **positive downtime** (Persson and Pettersson 2024), which are those staged "moments of zen" where games essentially enforce a pause for reflection. *Ghosts of Tsushima* (Sucker Punch Productions 2024) does this with its hot springs – the character enters a warm bath and reflects upon his feelings towards story beats or characters. *Persona 5* (ATLUS 2022) does it with moments of safety in the chaos of its dungeons. *The Life Is Strange* games have looping moments that act like a kind of meditative screensaver – Chloe and Max chilling on a bed after a stressful day (DONTNOD Entertainment 2015); Alex sitting on her roof admiring the scenery (Deck Nine 2021). This is usually accompanied by dreamy, wistful music. The only choice a player makes in these moments is when to exit and take up the mantle of responsibility once more. It brings to mind the pleasing torpor of a lazy Sunday in which there is no pressing reason for you to get out of your warm, comfortable bed. When you can abrogate the need to be a person in a complicated world, if only for a few restful moments.

Those moments are opportunities for contemplation. They are your chance to reflect upon the journey so far and the distance left to travel. But they are also psychogeographical interrupts – a specific opportunity for you to consider how you feel once the time for feeling has arrived. What is the soundscape? The landscape? The implied texture-scape, or the implied smell-scape? What exists in the mediation and what exists in the imagination (Nitsche 2008)? What is the game actually delivering to your senses, and what of the experience are **you** contributing?

The outputs of psychogeography tend to be eclectic. Some people use psychogeographical reflection to build up a profile of a time and place. Some might use it to delve into aesthetics, as per the MDA (Hunicke, LeBlanc, and Zubek 2004). Others might be inspired to fan-art, or poetry. Some might simply accept it as evidence of a "vibe". Sketches, or word clouds, or heat-maps – all of these are "research outputs" of the process of psychogeography. Guy Debord, one of the originators of the pseudo-scientific form the concept took in the fifties, described it himself as being "charmingly vague" (Debord 1955).

The magic circle is often talked about as if it's a pentagram – an occult sigil that protects us from the demons within its radius. Psychogeography is more like an exorcism – a way to grasp hold of the feelings a game instils in us and confront them directly. If a magic circle contains, then psychogeography reflects. The magic circle is a magnet, psychogeography is a mirror.

Permission to Feel Your Feelings

The experiential perspective is, first and foremost, about how games make us feel. It's much less about the mechanisms of a game, or the interpretation of narrative. It's about the way we **react** to games. And in this, there's an important rule – there is no right or wrong way to feel. What matters, as far as game scholarship goes, is your ability to articulate the **why** of how you felt that way.

We will return to the magic circle as we go through the rest of this book, particularly in relation to social contracts and the socioeconomic context of gaming. However, for now the important thing is to consider what the magic circle gives us as an analytical tool – a way to engage with a game in two different frames. One is what the game does and says, and the other is how that affects us as people. Constraining things to the confines of the magic circle gives us a powerful distancing tool. It permits dispassion, which is often important in analysis. Detachment is important to ensure that our claims are proportionate.

We're not robots though and games wouldn't be worth a damn if they didn't reach inside us and manipulate our emotional machinery. Can a video game make you cry? Of course it can. It can also make us angry, or sad, or fill us with existential angst. It can make us reflect on our behaviour, and on what the systems of play could do to us if transported into a real-world context. They can encourage the interrogating of our emotions, and how those emotions came to be. This tends to be a holistic approach, and often our feelings are not amenable to decontextualization. The game made us feel a way because the game made us feel that way. As game scholars though, we need to dig deeper. The **what** of your feelings is a guide to where we can direct interpretation, as Barrett pointed out in our chapter on critical reading of games. The **how** is interesting from a game design perspective. The **why** is what elevates the process into actual scholarship.

Notes

1 Adulterers might be more familiar with the sleazy slogan, "What happens in Vegas stays in Vegas".
2 And as the Good Place so convincingly argues, everyone hates moral philosophy professors.
3 I'm just making an observation. I'm not saying they were wrong to add this prohibition. Just to clarify, I want to be on the record as saying "you probably shouldn't kill children, whether you can or can't". Why are you staring like that? It's the "probably", isn't it? It's probably the "probably".
4 Lawful evil and Chaotic Evil, right? Or is it Chaotic Evil and Chaotic Neutral? Or Lawful Neutral and...
5 Neutral good, yeah? Or chaotic good?
6 Lawful good, surely? Or maybe lawful neutral?

References

Alexander, Larry, and Michael Moore. 2007. 'Deontological Ethics'.

Azoulay, Pierre, Christian Fons-Rosen, and Joshua S. Graff Zivin. 2019. 'Does Science Advance One Funeral at a Time?' *American Economic Review* 109(8):2889–2920. doi: 10.1257/aer.20161574.

Barrett, Terry. 2011. *Criticizing Art: Understanding the Contemporary*. 3rd edition. New York: McGraw Hill.

Benko, Steven A., and Andrew Pavelich. 2019. *The Good Place and Philosophy*. New York: Open Court Publishing.

Bridger, Alexander John. 2013. 'Psychogeography and Feminist Methodology'. *Feminism & Psychology* 23(3):285–98. doi: 10.1177/0959353513481783.

Brons, Lajos L. 2015. 'Othering, an Analysis'.

Consalvo, Mia. 2009. 'There Is No Magic Circle'. *Games and Culture* 4(4):408–17. doi: 10.1177/1555412009343575.

Contato, Andrea. 2019. *Through the Moongate. The Story of Richard Garriott, Origin Systems Inc. and Ultima: Part 1- From Akalabeth to Ultima VI*. 1st edition.

Corey, James S. A. 2019. *Tiamat's Wrath*. New York: Hachette.

Dancy, Jonathan. 2017. 'Moral Particularism'. in *The Stanford Encyclopedia of Philosophy,* edited by E. N. Zalta. California: Metaphysics Research Lab, Stanford University. https://plato.stanford.edu/cgi-bin/encyclopedia/archinfo.cgi?entry=moral-particularism

Debord, Guy. 1955. 'Introduction to a Critique of Urban Geography'. *Les Lèvres Nues* 6(2):23–27.

Driver, Julia. 2011. *Consequentialism*. London: Routledge.

Ellard, Colin. 2015. *Places of the Heart: The Psychogeography of Everyday Life*. New York: Bellevue literary press.

Fetterman, Justin. 2022. 'The Absurd Hero: Indiana Jones, God, and Sisyphus'. Pp. 53–64 in *Indiana Jones and Philosophy*, edited by D. A. Kowalski. New Jersey: Wiley.

FOOT, PHILIPPA. 1985. 'Utilitarianism and the Virtues*'. *Mind* XCIV(374):196–209. doi: 10.1093/mind/XCIV.374.196.

Gamboa, Mafalda, Michael James Heron, Miriam Sturdee, and Pauline Belford. 2023. 'Screenshots as Photography in Gamescapes: An Annotated Psychogeography of Imaginary Places'. Pp. 506–18 in *Proceedings of the 15th Conference on Creativity and Cognition, C&C '23*. New York: Association for Computing Machinery.

Granic, Isabela, Adam Lobel, and Rutger C. M. E. Engels. 2014. 'The Benefits of Playing Video Games'. *American Psychologist* 69(1):66–78. doi: 10.1037/a0034857.

Harman, Gilbert. 1978. 'What Is Moral Relativism?' Pp. 143–61 in *Values and Morals*, edited by A. I. Goldman and J. Kim. Dordrecht: Springer Netherlands.

Heron, Michael James, and Pauline Helen Belford. 2014. 'Do You Feel like a Hero Yet?' *Journal of Games Criticism* 1(2).

Heron, Michael James, and Pauline Helen Belford. 2015. 'All of Your Co-Workers Are Gone: Story, Substance, and the Empathic Puzzler'. *Journal of Games Criticism* 2(1).

Heron, Michael James, and Pauline Helen Belford. 2024. *A Case Study for Computer Ethics in Context: The Scandal in Academia*. Florida: CRC Press.

Holloway, Philippa. 2022. 'Walking in Imaginary Shoes: Psychogeographic Approaches for Fiction Writing'. *Writers in Practice* 7(2021):74–89.

Hunicke, Robin, Marc LeBlanc, and Robert Zubek. 2004. 'MDA: A Formal Approach to Game Design and Game Research'. P. 1722 in *Proceedings of the AAAI Workshop on Challenges in Game AI*. Vol. 4. San Jose, CA: Association for the Advancement of Artificial Intelligence.

Keogh, Brendan. 2023. *The Videogame Industry Does Not Exist: Why We Should Think Beyond Commercial Game Production*. MIT Press.

Lathrop, Gail, and David O. Sutton. 2014. 'Elements of Mise-En-Scene'. *Retrieved on January* 3.

March-Russell, Paul. 2013. '"And Did Those Feet"? Mapmaking London and the Postcolonial Limits of Psychogeography'. Pp. 79–95 in *The Postcolonial Short Story*, edited by M. Awadalla and P. March-Russell. London: Palgrave Macmillan.

Mazlish, Bruce. 2014. 'The Flâneur: From Spectator to Representation'. Pp. 43–60 in *The Flaneur (RLE Social Theory)*, edited by Keith Tester. Abingdon: Routledge.

Nitsche, Michael. 2008. *Video Game Spaces: Image, Play, and Structure in 3D Worlds*. Cambridge: MIT Press.

O'Rourke, Karen. 2021. *Psychogeography: A Purposeful Drift through the City*. Vermont: The MIT Press Reader.

Persson, Sara, and Enna Pettersson. 2024. 'Positive Downtime: An Exploration of an Underplayed Gameplay Style and the Importance of Immersion in Games'. Masters Thesis, Chalmers University of Technology/University of Gothenburg.

Richardson, Tina. 2015. 'The New Psychogeography'. *Walking Inside Out: Contemporary British Psychogeography* 241–54. Rowan & Littlefield Publishers: London.

Rittel, Horst W. J., and Melvin M. Webber. 1973. 'Dilemmas in a General Theory of Planning'. *Policy Sciences* 4(2):155–69. doi: 10.1007/BF01405730.

Russell, Nathan J. 2006. 'An Introduction to the Overton Window of Political Possibilities'. *Mackinac Center for Public Policy* 4.

Self, Will. 2007. *Psychogeography: Disentangling the Modern Conundrum of Psyche and Place*. New York: Bloomsbury Publishing USA.

Sinclair, Iain. 2003. *London Orbital*. London: Penguin.

Smith, Phil. 2010. 'The Contemporary Dérive: A Partial Review of Issues Concerning the Contemporary Practice of Psychogeography'. *Cultural Geographies* 17(1):103–22. doi: 10.1177/1474474009350002.

Software, From. 2014. *Dark Souls: Design Works*. Illustrated edition. Udon Entertainment: Udon Entertainment.

Stenros, Jaakko. 2014. 'In Defence of a Magic Circle: The Social, Mental and Cultural Boundaries of Play'. *Transactions of the Digital Games Research Association* 1(2). doi: 10.26503/todigra.v1i2.10.

Sweller, John. 2011. 'Cognitive Load Theory'. Pp. 37–76 in *Psychology of learning and motivation*, edited by Jose Mestre and Brian Ross. Vol. 55. Amsterdam: Elsevier.

White, Dennis L. 1971. 'The Poetics of Horror: More than Meets the Eye'. *Cinema Journal* 10(2):1–18. doi: 10.2307/1225234.

Wu, Tim. 2016. *The Attention Merchants: The Epic Scramble to Get Inside Our Heads*. Erscheinungsort nicht ermittelbar: Knopf.

Ludography

2K Boston. 2K Australia. 2007. Bioshock [video game] [Microsoft Windows]. 2K.

ATLUS. 2022. Persona 5 Royal [video game] [Microsoft Windows]. Sega.

Bethesda Game Studios. 2008. Fallout 3 [video game] [Microsoft Windows]. Bethesda Softworks.

Bethesda Game Studios. 2015. Fallout 4 [video game] [Microsoft Windows]. Bethesda Softworks.

Bethesda Game Studios. 2016. The Elder Scrolls V: Skyrim Special Edition [video game] [Microsoft Windows]. Bethesda Softworks.

Bioware. 2003. Star Wars Knights of the Old Republic [video game] [Microsoft Windows]. LucasArts.

Bioware. 2008. Mass Effect [video game] [Microsoft Windows]. Electronic Arts.

Bioware. 2010. Mass Effect 2 [video game] [Microsoft Windows]. Electronic Arts.

Bioware. 2012. Mass Effect 3 [video game] [Microsoft Windows]. Electronic Arts.

Crystal Dynamics. 2013. Tomb Raider [video game] [Microsoft Windows]. Crystal Dynamics.

Deck Nine. 2017. Life is Strange: Before the Storm [video game] [Microsoft Windows]. Square Enix.

Deck Nine. 2021. Life is Strange: True Colors [video game] [Microsoft Windows]. Square Enix.

Deep Silver Volition. 2013. Saints Row IV: Re-Elected [video game] [Microsoft Windows]. Deep Silver.

DONTNOD Entertainment. 2015. Life is Strange [video game] [Microsoft Windows]. Square Enix.

DONTNOD Entertainment. 2018. Life is Strange 2 [video game] [Microsoft Windows]. Square Enix.

Favaro, Peter. 1986. Alter Ego [video game] [Commodore 64]. Activision.

Freebird Games. 2011. To The Moon [video game] [Nintendo Switch]. Freebird Games.

Houser, Scott. 2020. Trial by Trolley [board game]. Skybound Tabletop.

FromSoftware. 2011. Dark Souls [video game] [Microsoft Windows]. Bandai Namco Entertainment.

Larian Studios. 2023. Baldur's Gate 3 [video game] [Microsoft Windows]. Larian studios.

LucasArts. 1997. Star Wars Jedi Knight: Dark Forces II [video game] [Microsoft Windows]. LucasArts.

Lucas Pope. 2013. Papers, Please [video game] [Microsoft Windows]. Lucas Pope.

Mobius Digital. 2019. The Outer Wilds [video game] [Microsoft Windows]. Annapurna Interactive.

Naughty Dog LLC. 2023. The Last of Us: Part I [video game] [Microsoft Windows]. Playstation Publishing LLC.

Ninja Theory. 2017. Hellblade: Senua's Sacrifice [video game] [Microsoft Windows]. Ninja Theory.

Nintendo EDP. 2017. Breath of the Wild. [video game] [Nintendo Switch]. Nintendo.

Obsidian Entertainment. 2010. Fallout: New Vegas [video game] [Microsoft Windows]. Bethesda Softworks.

Origin Systems. 1985. Ultiva IV: Quest of the Avatar [video game] [Microsoft Windows]. Origin Systems.

Origin Systems. 1988. Ultiva V: Warriors of Destiny [video game] [Microsoft Windows]. Origin Systems.

Origin Systems. 1990. Ultiva VI: The False Prophet [video game] [Microsoft Windows]. Origin Systems.

Rockstar Games. 2019. Red Dead Redemption 2 [video game] [Microsoft Windows]. Rockstar Games.

Rockstar North. 2013. Grand Theft Auto 5 [video game] [Microsoft Windows]. Rockstar Games.

Simogo. 2019. Sayonara Wild Hearts [video game] [Microsoft Windows]. Annapurna Interactive.

Sucker Punch Productions. 2024. Ghost of Tsushima Director's Cut [video game] [Microsoft Windows]. Playstation Publishing LLC.

Team Ico. 2005. Shadow of the Colossus [video game] [Microsoft Windows]. Sony Compter Entertainment.

Telltale Games. 2012. The Walking Dead [video game] [Microsoft Windows]. Skybound Games.

tobyfox. 2015. Undertale [video game] [Microsoft Windows]. Tobyfox.

Ubisoft Montreal. 2013. Assassin's Creed IV: Black Flag [video game] [Microsoft Windows]. Ubisoft.

Ubisoft Quebec. 2018. Assassin's Creed: Odyssey [video game] [Microsoft Windows]. Ubisoft.

Valve. 2008. Left 4 Dead [video game] [Microsoft Windows]. Valve.

YAGER. 2012. Spec Ops: The Line [video game] [Microsoft Windows]. 2K.

ZA/ UM. 2019. Disco Elysium [video game] [Microsoft Windows]. ZA/UM.

7

The Melancholy of Hollow Knight: *A Study of the Dichotomy between Charm and Tragedy in the Artistic Elements of* Hollow Knight

Klara Aune

Introduction

Hollow Knight (Team Cherry 2017), one of the most beloved indie games, is a classic Metroidvania platformer. The success of the game might be due to its snappy and responsive fun, but I would argue that the attachment many feel to *Hollow Knight* points to something more than just good gameplay. The storytelling in *Hollow Knight* is often vague, but there is a sense of compulsion to explore – a drive to persist even in the face of its challenging difficulty. In this contributed chapter, I try to put a finger onto that nagging feeling which I describe in the context of melancholy, and I attempt to pinpoint the key narrative and artistic elements which contribute to this aesthetic. This paper might be useful to those who, just like me, are fascinated by the eerie and the pensive, aiming to apply a similar atmosphere in their work.

Melancholy, initially considered a medical disease, was brought to the attention of scholars at a time when "thinking" and "feeling" were in conflict. Identified symptoms included, amongst other things: troublesome dreams; heaviness of heart; and continuous fear. The condition was seen as a side effect of critical thinking – that the melancholic individual was in fact a "utopian dreamer who had higher hopes for humanity" (Boym 2008).

In this regard, melancholy very much overlaps with another complex territory of feelings, which is that of nostalgia. Nostalgia, like melancholy, was also considered a medical disease, and shared many of the symptoms. It was first reported in the 17th century and often befell various displaced people and soldiers fighting abroad, especially those who were longing for a return to their homes. In fact, the very word "nostalgia" reflects this, *nostos* – return home, and *algia* – longing.

Here again we see the "utopian dreamer" of the melancholic. However, whereas the melancholic individual considered the larger context, the utopia of the nostalgic was on an individual plane – guilty of an intellectual hazard, succumbing to what was

DOI: 10.1201/9781003530282-7

described at the time as "erroneous representations" of the past. Nowadays, we might call this "romanticizing" the past.

Our definition of nostalgia has expanded somewhat since the 1700s. The contemporary use of "feeling nostalgic" does not necessarily have to involve one's own past. It is not uncommon that one can feel a sense of nostalgia for something they have not even experienced, such as for certain cultures or periods in time. Aside from this, our ideas of nostalgia and melancholy have largely maintained their philosophical meaning, even if they are no longer medicalized. Melancholy mourns that which could have been, and nostalgia longs for that which is no more. Though melancholy is not exactly a positive emotion, it is more complex than being purely "blue". It has been noted that the pensive sadness associated with melancholia is commonly accompanied with a level of compensatory positive feelings about such appreciation. A dichotomy of feelings is present, which makes melancholy nuanced in its manifestation. It is intrinsically linked with nostalgia in that it romanticizes that which could have been, and furthermore appreciates the presence of that sadness itself. In the book *The Anatomy of Melancholy*, Robert Burton writes about melancholia (and what we now perhaps would call clinical depression). The abstract of this book includes the following lines by the author (Burton 1850):

> When I build castles in the air, Void of sorrow and void of fear, Pleasing myself with phantasms sweet, Methinks the time runs very fleet. All my joys to this are folly, Naught so sweet as melancholy.

Hollow Knight evokes the feeling of melancholia via both its storytelling and artistic elements, particularly its music and art style. The story of *Hollow Knight* follows an insectoid warrior fighting its way through a former glorious kingdom that has fallen into disease. The player controls a character, the eponymous *Hollow Knight*, see Figure 7.1. Not much is known of the fallen kingdom, but the thread to the past is gradually unravelled via interactions with its inhabitants, many of which have grown insane and hostile. One character the player encounters early, which closely relates to the poem of Robert Burton, is the small insectoid *Zote the Mighty* with his sword *life ender*. The small Zote,

FIGURE 7.1   The main character of *Hollow Knight*, "The Hollow Knight".

despite his boast of being a mighty warrior, is initially found trapped by the weakest of enemies. As the player helps him out, Zote berates our main protagonist as being beneath him, serenading his own greatness while doing so. It is a stark sense of delusion that has befallen the (supposedly) great warrior. In refusal of facing the present, he surrounds himself with the "erroneous representations" of what is his past. Zote is a reoccurring character, as the player often needs to save him from various situations.

Although Zote is clearly something of a comic-relief character, it is characters like Zote which help the player gain an understanding of Hallownest (the kingdom of *Hollow Knight*) and its past. Though the storytelling of *Hollow Knight* is further discussed in its own subchapter, Zote is a good example of the dichotomy between charm and tragedy present throughout the game. Coping with weakness, he surrounds himself with Burtonesque "phantasms sweet" of greatness and "air castles". He is in that sense manifesting nostalgia, and it is up to the player to believe if there is truth to his "mighty" tales or if he is simply surrounding himself with ideas of what he could have been.

There are many examples in both the narrative and artistic elements of *Hollow Knight* which convey a sense of what the old kingdom used to be. We will return to some of these later in this chapter. By meeting the nostalgic creatures of Hallownest, one finds oneself at risk of becoming the melancholic who mourns the lost future of Hallownest's past.

Although the character of Zote is a specific example, the aim of this work is not to list out all the characters and describe their potential melancholic qualities. Rather, this chapter aims to discuss and highlight the general artistic elements and design decisions that made it possible for characters like Zote to contribute to the general melancholic aesthetic of the game. This chapter can be seen as study of melancholic design, with the aim to provide understanding of how this profoundly human experience can be expressed within a game.

Storytelling in *Hollow Knight*

There are four aspects to storytelling that I consider here: story, narrative, setting and theme (we saw these discussed in this book, in the chapter on other perspectives). Story and narrative may seem similar, but there is a distinction to be made. The story is what is taking place, and the narrative is how the story is framed. In other words, the narrative is essentially what allows the player to piece together knowledge of the story.

The debut of Zote the Mighty also happen to be a good example of the storytelling employed in *Hollow Knight*. Rarely does the game outright tell the player the particulars but instead hints at them via narrative clues; "Why is 'Zote the Mighty' called 'the Mighty' when he clearly is not? Did he used to be? Is he lying?". *Hollow Knight* is a game within the genre of Metroidvanias, which put heavy emphasis on exploration. Hidden powerups, backtracking, and map-based navigation are the core of the Metroidvania genre. These make it especially suitable for **environmental storytelling**. Environmental storytelling is when a game relies heavily on environmental narrative rather than simple exposition of story. Here is the first piece of the story given to players by a character Elderbug at the entrance of Hallownest:

> The other residents, they've all disappeared. Headed down that well, one by one, into the caverns below. Used to be there was a great kingdom beneath our town. It's long fell to ruin, yet it still draws folks into its depths.

> Well watch out. It's a sickly air that fills the place. Creatures turn mad and
> travellers are robbed of their memories. Perhaps dreams aren't such great
> things after all…

Given this information, the player knows that there is a disease running rampant,
infecting those who enter Hallownest and causing them to go mad and turn hostile.
Not much else is known however, and much is left up to player inference. The player
rarely receives clear answers as to who "the Hollow Knight" is or what happened to
bring them to Hallownest. Environmental storytelling elements, discovered by exploration, allow the player to absorb information at their own pace. These also allow for
the player's perception to be shaped through their own investment and experience.
This has the additional effect of ensuring the interpretation the player makes gains
personal meaning (Ofner 2021). The player gets to familiarize themselves with the
kingdom of Hallownest by pulling together their own understanding of narrative. This
makes the world self-reinforced and immersive. In other words, the full story is not
known to the player until a late stage in the game, although the fundamental story
beats – such as that the kingdom is overcome by an infection and you possibly have
something to do with it – become clear early on. The rest is for the player to try and
piece together themselves via narrative clues such as "lore tablets"; artefacts in the
in-game environment; and dialogue with non-player characters (NPCs).

That players get to shape the narrative and colour it with their own investment and
experiences is likely part of why *Hollow Knight* elicits certain emotional response.
However, the storytelling by itself conveys little of meaning in *Hollow Knight* without
the aspects of *setting* and *theme*. Setting here is referring to the context in which a
story is taking place, and theme being an underlying unity between elements – again,
as we saw in this book on the chapter regarding other perspectives. Both setting
and theme carry expectations from the players. In *Hollow Knight,* the setting is
Hallownest, a disease ridden fallen kingdom and all its different biomes. Given this
setting, it is likely that players expect a grim story with potentially horror-adjacent
elements. The theme of *Hollow Knight* however is open enough to permit personal
interpretation. Some may interpret the overlying theme being about perseverance over
death and overcoming adversity, others may interpret the theme to be that of sacrifice
or free will. There are also plenty of subthemes, as Hallownest has many biomes and
characters with varying narratives of their own. For the purposes of this chapter, I will
outline the overlying theme of *Hollow Knight* as being interpreted as "overcoming
adversity" and "sacrifice", although other equally valid interpretations are possible.

Combining the aspects of storytelling thus far, some theories as to why *Hollow
Knight* "feels" the way it does can be put forward. For one, the environmental storytelling relying heavily on narrative and player exploration gives way for immersion
and personal interpretation. Secondly, the grim setting of *Hollow Knight* combined
with its themes of overcoming adversity provides the player with a context in which
the in-game characters exist and this colours the way that the player may perceive
them. Overcoming adversity combined with what is a grim setting is a powerful combination, fitting with the bittersweet melancholic mourning for something that has
been lost: The grandeur and health of the kingdom and its inhabitants.

The narrative gradually reveals the tragedies that the infection of Hallownest has
wrought, and the setting and story are apocalyptic in tone. If given only the story of
Hollow Knight, it is easy to imagine it as a zombie-like horror. We can see this in other

examples of games, such as Dark Souls (FromSoftware 2011), a series which has very similar themes and settings, married to an entirely different atmosphere – one that is intentionally depressing and full of dread. Though some aspects of dread do exist in the corners of Hallownest, overall this is a much more sympathetic tragedy. It is tentative sadness and eerie wonder that dominate the aesthetic of *Hollow Knight*. This is where we find an important juxtaposition to the grim theme of the game, specifically its artistic elements and the visual depiction of the setting and narrative.

Art Style and Visual Elements

The visual art of *Hollow Knight* is part of its atmosphere and complements the environmental storytelling of the narrative in several important ways. The light shifts as the player traverses deeper into Hallownest. The illumination is often dim with muted colours. This helps to create an isolated and lonely ambiance for the player.[1] And yet the game's visual art can generally be described as quite cartoony and cute. The characters usually have distinct big head, eyes and round shapes (see Figure 7.1) and are drawn with thicker black lines. The environment has distinct foregrounds, middle grounds and backgrounds (see Figure 7.2). The players may find themselves being slightly uncomfortable killing the cute characters in the game, especially given the narrative that they have succumbed to infection and are not actively choosing to be hostile. This dichotomy between aesthetic style and the more sombre, grimmer theme, and setting helps convey a few aspects of *Hollow Knight*. For one, given the horror-adjacent zombie setting of the infected kingdom, the visual aesthetic helps convey that the story being told is not one meant to invoke fear. Rather, the tragedy of the Hallownest inhabitants is highlighted by juxtaposing the theme with the whimsical and sympathetic art design. It comes together to make one feel empathetic for what has befallen the kingdom. This can also be said for the general environment of the many areas in Hallownest. The muted colours and musical themes convey that the story being told is a tragedy. There is little triumphalism in your conquests.

Much of the environmental storytelling is conveyed with artistic choices such as bug shells, skeletons, and statues. Areas are covered in moss and cracks in the background to convey the history of Hallownest. The narrative to be found in the visual elements is more prevalent in some areas than others, such as in the example of Soul Sanctum (Figure 7.3) where understanding of the area is available to be gleaned via visual clues. In most of the Soul Sanctum, there is evidence pointing to this being a place for scholars and experiments – implied by the university and library reminiscent

FIGURE 7.2 The biome "Queen's Garden" with distinct foreground, middle ground, and background.

FIGURE 7.3 Left, the soul sanctum, a sub-area of the city of tears. Right, the soul sanctum background littered with bugs.

FIGURE 7.4 The enemies "Mistakes" of the soul sanctum.

rooms. There are also additional narrative clues scattered in the form of lore tablets and journal entries. These further paint a picture as to what could have taken place here. Again, much of this is down to player interpretation.

> "The mind still limits us so. How to break past its constraints? To attain a pure focus, is it even possible?" - Soul Sanctum lore tablet
>   "Hoarded soul hoping to stave off Hallownest's affliction." - Soul Master Hunter's Journal entry

Some of the enemies, deformed ghastly figures, bear names such as "mistakes" and "follies" (Figure 7.4). Other past denizens of Hallownest seem to have been more successful in their experimentation, transforming instead into "soul warriors" (as shown in Figure 7.3, left). In the final room, where the player faces the boss "Soul Hunter", the background is littered with the empty husks of cast-away bugs (Figure 7.3, right). One can draw many conclusions here.

The player may understand via these visual clues that this area has a sinister past, which is further highlighted by its ominous music. Could the "mistakes" and "follies" be the failed experiments of the scholars trying to fight the infection? Why the many empty husks of bugs in the background of the "Soul Hunter"? The Soul Sanctum is a good example of the stark contrast of visual aesthetic and theme in *Hollow Knight*, as it is particularly grim in its implications. If the same story were to be told via film or realistic first person with 3D models, such as in Dark Souls, the atmosphere would likely invoke horror and disgust. However, the deformities of the enemies, such as the "mistakes", do not in particular invoke these feelings due to their cartoony style.

If not fear or disgust, then what emotional response takes their place? What do we *feel* unravelling the horrific narrative of these creatures? As many things, it is somewhat open for personal interpretation, though I believe much of the power of this aesthetic lies in how it softens the blow. Instead of fear, it evokes a sense of eeriness or the uncanny. Instead of disgust, we find ourselves often sympathetic of the blob-looking "mistakes".

Juxtaposition of aesthetic and theme here fills two seemingly contradictory, yet complementary, aspects. The first aspect is that it highlights the tragedy of the creatures in Hallownest by making them funny, cute, and/or charming in style. The intent seems to be to invoke sympathy and curiosity as to their fate. The second aspect is that the aesthetic style creates distance from the tragedy and horror that has taken place, softening the edges of fear to give way for eeriness to flood into the corresponding parts of our limbic system.

Music and Composition

Coupled with the visual aesthetics of *Hollow Knight* is its equally solemn, dark, yet elegant, and charming music. In his book *Music, Sound and Multimedia: From the Live to the Virtual*, Jamie Sexton observes that sound has some qualities which vision does not, such as being able to surround and immerse the player and blend together in ways visual information cannot emulate (Sexton 2007). Saxton identified three key areas of video game music in his analysis. These being:

1. **Environmental:** how music supports the perception of a game world
2. **Immersion:** how music supports the player's involvement in the game
3. **Diegetic:** How music supports a game narrative

Applying the reasoning of Saxton in his analysis and comparing it to *Hollow Knight*, we can observe some ways the composer, Christoffer Larkin, has used audio and music to immerse the player and convey the melancholic story of Hallownest.

Environmental Storytelling through Music

It is said that music was the first artistic medium able to communicate a dynamic sense of being in a different place (Sexton 2007). Melodies in video games convey a characterization of the areas (or levels) in games and are therefore important for our perception of the gameworld and the environment. *Hollow Knight*'s music, as such, dictates how the different areas of the Hallownest are *felt* by the player (Koelsch 2010). Most prominent is the leitmotif of *Hollow Knight*. This sets a vital tone for the player experience and is prevalent throughout the game. As noted by eight-bit Music Theory on YouTube: "the instrumentation of the piano and viola duet, coupled with the slow tempo and natural minor harmony set the stage for an intimate, yet solemn; dark yet elegant, adventure".[2]

One of the first biome themes in *Hollow Knight* is that of Dirtmouth, the area above Hallownest. There are no enemies in Dirtmouth, which lies beyond the infection as of now. It provides a place of rest, which is made clear for the player with the tones of a peaceful, yet serious, soundtrack. The contrast between this and the ambient, uneasy music of the dangerous, and dark Deepnest is stark. The low vibrating base with shaky violin gives you a sense of unease and paranoia. In terms of the specifically melancholic atmosphere of the game, the capital of Hallownest, City of Tears, and its theme are arguably a perfect example. The city having lost its original name to history is a husk of its former self. Yet it still conveys its decaying grandeur via its music. This is the only theme with a wailing choir. The choir evokes a sense of something that is divine or revered. Powerful. It also contributes an eerie, ethereal quality of loss and mourning. The capital's sub-area Soul Sanctum is accompanied by a similar theme which shares a consistent leitmotif. The choir is gone, however, replaced by an organ and a more sinister arrangement. The revered and sacred has become corrupted and sullied. This is fitting – this is the area in which bug scholars conducted experiments to draw out the souls of the citizens. As the player perceives the world of *Hollow Knight* and what the different biomes and areas might mean for our character, and by extension ourselves, the music plays a vital role – corroborating our visual perspective and offering depth to the emotional resonance.

Musical Immersion

When talking about immersion, we can mean several things. We might mean being immersed as in having a heightened sense of a particular aspect of a person's immediate surroundings – such as the act of threading a needle, or the sensation of being transported into a mediated alternate reality (Sexton 2007). One might argue that the latter type of immersion cannot exist without the first.

One factor particular to audio perception is the ability to focus on one sound in a larger group of sounds, a phenomenon also known as the cocktail party effect (Kuyper 1972). One reason why music is so important for the immersion in video games is this ability to allow the brain to only focus on the sound from the game – preventing the brain from searching for stimuli elsewhere. Such distractions risk creating a "wall of sound" effect between the player and their alternate reality (Collins 2014).

Some have argued that this wall of sound effect means it doesn't matter how music is presented to the player. It is, in of itself, the source of the immersion. Though this may be true in some instances, counterpoints can be marshalled against this idea. Considering the two different types of immersion, one can see how the wall of sound effect can contribute to the former kind – being that of shutting out other stimuli. However, this would not necessarily help with the latter type of immersion of transporting the player into an alternate reality. It can be argued that wrong type of music is detrimental to the **type** of reality the developers want to achieve. In Deepnest, an area of Hallownest meant to cause unease, it would contradict the reality of the space if the sombre and peaceful music of Dirtmouth was to play. There are times when juxtaposition of music can be effectively used to achieve an uncanny effect (Cook 2006). We might think of horror films and games using lullabies or children's songs to create uncanniness and unease – the presence of innocence within sinister contexts (Link 2009). In the case of Deepnest and *Hollow Knights*' use of music in general however, one could argue that this would not quite work. The reason for this is that the musical experience of Hallownest is usually an extension of the narrative. In other words, *Hollow Knight* is musically "reliable" in the sense that it generally does not make use of these juxtapositions for jarring and uneasy effects that contradict the story. Instead, they are used to highlight the visual and narrative clues of the various areas. In this way, the music of *Hollow Knight* is also a vital part of immersion for players.

Diegetic Music

The way narrative immersion is achieved in *Hollow Knight* via audio perception has some particular highlights. There are interesting ways *Hollow Knight* uses and rearranges some of its prominent tunes to connect certain characters. For example, the White Lady and its theme with the same name, and the character The Pale King with its theme "White Palace". However, as it is out of the scope of this chapter to discuss the story of *Hollow Knight* in detail, there will not be any deeper look at how specifically the diegetic aspect of the music fits into the narrative. However, one can point out the aforementioned City of Tears and how its theme is twisted in the sub-area Soul Sanctum as an example of a narrative shift expressed through the music. The Soul Sanctum, being part of the City of Tears, has a very similar melody and tone, although of a more slow-paced and dark nature to fit the story of its sinister past.

Other Contributions to Aesthetic

While this chapter does not focus on mechanics of the game, there are other elements of its design that contribute to its broader aesthetic. *Hollow Knight* can generally be described as a difficult and fast-paced game which requires high concentration and skill from the player. This is especially true in challenging areas such as the Deepnest or during complex boss battles. Yet it is also true when casually exploring the different areas of the Hallownest. As YouTuber Razbuten points out in his video essay "Vibe checks in video games", it is easy to get caught up in progress towards the goals of a game, especially in intense games such as this one.[3]

In *Hollow Knight* the prominent player motivation can be to discover new areas and develop new abilities; to progress the story; or to simply fill up a completion percentage. Because of the high motivation and intensity associated with these explicitly gamified tasks, there is a risk that a player may be caught up in consuming a game, rather than **experiencing** it. This is one of the reasons why certain games implement moments to check where the player is at, emotionally. This can be argued as being especially important for games using environmental storytelling, as the narrative often requires active interrogation from the player. These moments of rest most commonly take the form of "save points", which not only mechanically save the game but also can allow the player to mentally benchmark and reflect on their progress. The most famous example of this is the bonfires in the game Dark Souls. These are a resting place mechanically as well as a moment where one can relieve the tension that comes from the constant threat of losing accumulated progress. They are also moments of rest in a literal sense – your character sits and warm themselves by a bonfire. This gives the player time to reflect and gather energy before moving on to yet another in an endless cycle of almost certain deaths.

Hollow Knight treats save points in a very similar fashion to Dark Souls, although in the form of benches instead of bonfires. Few things bring such relief as coming across one of these benches in game. This moment of rest is accompanied by a slow paced and delicate music theme fittingly enough called "Reflection". The art also underscores this. There is often a dedicated rest room for the bench, and the bench itself is moreover illuminated by soft atmospheric light, seemingly beckoning the player to take a moment's respite. These rest points are vital for the game's pacing as the intensity otherwise might be too much for the player to properly inhabit the more solemn and contemplative experiences of the game. Even the pacing in *Hollow Knight* can be argued to give room for melancholy to set into a player's bones.

Conclusion

Melancholy is a complex feeling that often involves a bittersweet sense of mourning or loss of something that could have been. Melancholy often occurs when mourning that a place can no longer be experienced, be that in time or space. It bears close resemblance to the feeling of nostalgia. The narrative of *Hollow Knight* itself can be interpreted as melancholic to the core. It tells the story of a once grand kingdom which has fallen into ruin. It provides plenty of visual elements regarding its grand history and its many inhabitants. The artistic visual elements further invoke charm and sympathy for its cursed denizens, contrasting the otherwise grim theme and setting. The dichotomy of this charm and tragedy gives ground for a complex duality of positive and negative feelings. This is part of the bittersweet melancholy that surrounds the player experience. I theorize that the visual elements not only allow for the player to sympathize more freely with the creatures of Hallownest, but that they also establish a distance from the fear and horror taking place. They are insulation from the otherwise grim apocalyptic setting.

As melancholy can be described as a pensive sadness, it could potentially be argued that this "emotional distance" that the visual and thematic dichotomy creates lends itself well to melancholic design. Furthermore, the environmental storytelling moments of rest used in *Hollow Knight* give the player space for interpretation and self-reflection. This creates a high sense of immersion, as the player sets the pace of the game. They offer moments to recontextualize experiences and story beats – periods of time where one is encouraged to create their own theories based on the narrative clues given.

The melancholy of the game is further established with the music and sound design being employed, and the use of leitmotifs does well to connect the underlying unity of narratives in the different areas. The cathartic blend of deeply saddening, solemn, yet uplifting and grandiose themes of the music highlights the dichotomy of the visual charm and tragedy of *Hollow Knight*.

Hollow Knight serves as an excellent template for those looking to inspire the sensations and aesthetics of melancholy in their audiences.

Notes

1 https://medium.com/3d-environmental-art/the-art-of-hollow-knight-f4c05dda3882
2 https://www.youtube.com/watch?v=5IZ6ObjdkPA
3 https://youtu.be/Mt5SKnUGHOY?si=aMTDvyuH0GfNjUxf

References

Boym, Svetlana. 2008. *The Future of Nostalgia*. New York: Basic books.
Burton, Robert. 1850. The Anatomy of Melancholy: What It Is, with All the Kinds, Causes, Symptoms, Prognostics, and Several Cures of It. in *Three Partitions, with Their Several Sections, Members, and Subsections, Philosophically, Medically, Historically Opened and Cut Up*. New Jersey: Wiley.
Collins, Karen. 2014. 'Breaking the Fourth Wall? User-Generated Sonic Content in Virtual Worlds'. Pp. 351–63 in *The Oxford Handbook of Virtuality*, edited by Mark Grimshaw-Aagared. Oxford: Oxford University Press.
Cook, Nicholas. 2006. 'Uncanny Moments: Juxtaposition and the Collage Principle in Music'. Pp. 107–34 in *Approaches to Meaning in Music*, edited by Byron Almen and Edward Pearsall. Indiana University Press: Indiana, USA.
Koelsch, Stefan. 2010. 'Towards a Neural Basis of Music-Evoked Emotions'. *Trends in Cognitive Sciences* 14(3):131–37.
Kuyper, Paul. 1972. 'The Cocktail Party Effect'. *International Journal of Audiology* 11(5–6):277–82. doi: 10.3109/00206097209072593.
Link, Stan. 2009. 'The Monster and the Music Box: Children and the Soundtrack of Horror'. Pp. 50–66 in *Music in the Horror Film*. Abingdon: Routledge.
Ofner, Claudia S. 2021. 'Play Me a Story: Storytelling in the Metroidvania Game Hollow Knight [University of Graz]'. Masters thesis, awarded by the University of Graz in Austria. https://unipub.uni-graz.at/obvugrhs/content/titleinfo/6712652/full.pdf.
Sexton, Jamie. 2007. *Music, Sound and Multimedia: From the Live to the Virtual*. Edinburgh: Edinburgh University Press.

Ludography

FromSoftware. 2011. Dark Souls [Video game] [Microsoft Windows]. Namco Bandai Games.
Team Cherry. 2017. Hollow Knight [Video game] [Microsoft Windows]. Team Cherry.

8

Other Perspectives in Game Studies

Michael Heron

Other Perspectives

In our previous chapters, we've covered three major perspectives that can help illuminate important things about games. This illumination, I hope, will help you dissect and analyse games in more fulfilling ways. The critical perspective lets you dig into what a game is saying. The systemic perspective helps outline how games work. The experiential perspective lets you talk about how a game makes you feel. As useful as these approaches are, they're not exhaustive. Really, you can analyse games using almost any intellectual framework that can be applied to media in general. In this chapter, we're going to do some sampling of other techniques, considerations, and concepts that show off the breadth of what game studies can be.

Often insight comes from examining games from an angle that others haven't considered. You'll see examples of that in the extended case studies that accompany this book. If you are coming to this topic from another discipline, one profitable tactic is to consider what tools you have already encountered and employ them in this new context. Almost all research is either taxonomic (relating to classifying or categorizing, like building up a knowledge base of every RPG ever); or applying a well-developed theory to a novel problem domain; or applying a novel theory to a well-understood problem domain. Juxtaposition is the heart of innovation. If you're an economist by trade, why not evaluate resources within a game through a Keynesian lens (Hill 2021) or delve into the pricing models of games and their microtransactions (Tomić 2018)? If you've studied psychiatry, then perhaps you can psycho-analyse the characters in a game (Banfi 2024). Or a game's environment. Or, indeed, the developers who made them. If you're into neurochemistry, you can explore the biological impulses of the brain during play (Bateman and Nacke 2010). An anthropologist might employ ethnography to learn more about the behaviours of gamers (Snodgrass 2016).

Indeed, my own original research field, as expressed through my PhD, was in accessibility for older adults in an ageing workforce (Heron, Hanson, and Ricketts 2013b, 2013a). Bringing the focus of the accessibility field into games (Heron 2012) – in my case, primarily board games (Heron 2023, 2024; Heron et al. 2018b, 2018a) – permitted me to do useful, novel work in which I played my own modest part in contributing original knowledge to the general sum of human understanding.

DOI: 10.1201/9781003530282-8

The sky is the limit, and I certainly don't want to imply that this book outlines the only valid approaches. Or even the best approaches. Or even a portion of the best approaches.

With that in mind, this chapter will take a whirlwind tour through some of the other perspectives you might want to take into account when developing your opinion on gaming properties, specific trends of games, and the people who play them.

Business and Social Context

Nothing is ever created in a vacuum. Barrett's principles of interpretation (Barrett 2011), as we know, explicitly frame products of art as being embedded in the context of their time and their creators. The simple fact of a thing existing is a statement of sorts about society – about what we prioritize as people, and what prevailing economic models reward. The move away from physical copies of games is a good example of that. You can come to all kinds of different conclusions:

- Digital, rather than physical products, are a net-plus for the environment since digital goods tend to be less polluting (Sorrell 2020). So, the shift is good.
- Digital games lose the link between purchasing and ownership since typically you don't buy the game, but rather a licence to play the game (Perzanowski and Schultz 2016). So, the shift is bad.
- Digital games are bound up in complex intellectual property frameworks, and our lethargic legal systems have not caught up with the reality of the field (Lowood 2009). Game preservation of digital goods is almost impossible legally (Newman 2013) and technically complex due to updates and patches. Thus, the shift is bad.
- Physical media is fragile and can be destroyed or damaged through simply existing in an environment. Anyone who ever had to blow on a Super Nintendo cartridge to get it to play knows what that's like. Digital goods are theoretically infinitely reobtainable. The shift is therefore good.

The extent to which individual arguments convince you as a reader depends on your own internal calibration of the issue. The real objective truth ends up being, "it's a complex mix of plusses and minuses, with no consensus being possible". This is true in anything beyond a trivial level of complexity. Modern social media discourse often reduces discussion to mere sloganeering, where ideologically entrenched activists on either side of an issue resort to yelling catchphrases rather than engaging in constructive debate. If you're reading a book like this, you're expecting better of yourself.

What we see in a game is always a compromise. The translation from what goes in the head of a designer to the implementation of a game is never clean and complete. A design document is never pure enough to survive the consequences of actualization. No game vision survives contact with the playtesters, and no artistic vision survives contact with the accountants.

When you take into account business models and the realities of capitalism, it brings to mind Jason Shrier's (2017) discussion with a game developer friend. Upon hearing the woes and troubles of a game in production, Shrier remarked that it was a miracle the game got made. "Oh Jason", replied his friend, "it's a miracle that **any** game gets made". Making artistic statements, such as in *Spec Ops: The Line* (YAGER 2012), must be viewed through a lens of pragmatism. It takes a brave publisher to agree to sell a game that keeps telling its players not to play it. Taking a stand is always risky too – regardless of where you land on the dividing line, we live in a world of polarization. The business of game design must take into account reaction versus reward. Diversity, equality and inclusion (DEI) initiatives are particularly sensitive in this context – in the wave of movements like Gamergate (Heron, Belford, and Goker 2014), some gamers take especial issue with titles they consider to be "Woke" (Postill 2024). It is an unwise game developer that doesn't take this into account when considering how to design, develop, market, and support a game in such a way as to return a multiple on their investment.

Even leaving this aside, there are other concerns that impact on how games manifest. Assets take time to develop and polish – one of the reasons Ubisoft gave for why it took so long for a playable female protagonist to appear in the *Assassin's Creed* games (Bailey 2017). Since game development is a wicked problem, the correct form of manifestation may not be obvious. And since games must begin development many years before they are released, the market may move on in the interim. Technology too will change – chasing the mirage of the "cutting edge" was one of the fundamental problems that plagued *Duke Nukem Forever* (Thompson 2009).

One of the games I created was a Multiuser Dungeon (Heron 2013) called Epitaph (Heron 2016). I knew going in that there was no market value in a text-driven game in the graphical MMO era. However, I wanted to do it for my own edification and because I had a vision – a post-apocalyptic zombie game. A fresh, innovative new take on a tired medium which was full to the gunnels of fantasy and sci-fi settings. I started developing the game in 2008. By the time it was ready to be opened to players five years later, zombies had not just become commonplace, they had more than overstayed their welcome.

If we are to hold games subject to the same standards of critique as we do for other works of creativity, all of this has to be considered to be in scope for analysis. We have to take into account the wider context and the business models that underpin that context.

You might then consider folding critique of business models into your analysis:

- Crunch, and working conditions for developers, is an endemic problem in the industry (Cote and Harris 2021, 2023). Talking about the ways in which games are made can be as relevant as focusing on the games themselves.

- Microtransactions, collectibles, expansions, lootboxes, DLC, and more all have a profound impact on the experience of play. Game designs are often altered in service of financial viability, and some games are essentially designed in the same way a gambling firm might build a slot machine (Xiao et al. 2024). You can explore that.

- The legal status of things such as *Actual Plays* and *Let's Play* series is complicated (Taylor Jr 2015; Tie 2020), and likely not as clear-cut as many popular Twitch streamers and YouTubers would like. Some companies, such as Nintendo, yield control of their intellectual property like a weapon (Ribaudo 2017). Others add dedicated streamer modes to their games, allowing them to be played for an audience without the streamer having to worry about, for example, receiving a copyright strike for broadcasting licenced music. Abandonware – games that no longer have clearly defined owners – is a similarly interesting area in terms of the application of the law. I was once part of the authorship of a paper where the legal status of the many screenshots was an issue for the programme committee (Gamboa et al. 2023). What are the rights of gamers, what are the responsibilities, and under what limitations do we function?

- Games are one of a handful of domains where the word "addictive" has a positive connotation rather than a negative one. The psychology of play overlaps uncomfortably with that of gambling, and the neurochemistry of fun is abusable for those who know the correct incantations (Kühn et al. 2011; Palaus et al. 2017; Yin and Xiao 2022). What are the ethical implications of designing for addiction?

We've spoken already about the idea of weighing evidence and making sure that your views are fully rounded, which sometimes makes people think that advocacy has no place in scholarly work. The need for dispassionate evaluation is really only something that applies in the "data gathering" phase of your work. Once the evidence is in, it's perfectly appropriate for you to advocate for a particular position. Your research has to be well grounded in its foundation, but if you're sure where you stand is solid, then you can push for whatever you like. You can bring your own value judgements into your work. Indeed, I'd even argue that some of the best scholars are so embedded in their advocacy that it is inextricable.

We might consider wider social contexts in a similar way to how we talk about business contexts. One frame to consider, as with accessibility, is "who is included, and who is not?". Who suffers from a decision? Who benefits? This is something threaded through a game's design and its business practices. We've already talked about how everything we do either upholds, subverts or inverts societal expectations. How does a game contribute to our understanding of what it portrays? When a game includes a "sanity meter" (Crawford 2019; Vozaru 2022), something you'll often see in horror games, what is it communicating about mental illness? What myths does a game debunk, and which does it reinforce? What messages is a game sending? Are they the messages you think it wants to send?

Concepts such as the magic circle are all well and good for scholars who are detached from the real world "heat" of play. It's easy to talk about this as an insulating layer that keeps virtual harm from becoming actual harm. We've already spoken about how the circle is porous, and nowhere is that truer than when we talk about the overlap between games and social impact. Can we really say that only virtual harm is done when we grief a player in an online game? An occasional bit of light-hearted mischief can easily be brushed off, but what if you make it a core tenant to hunt and kill Michael Heron every time you see him log onto GTA Online (Rockstar North 2013)[1]? In that circumstance – someone intentionally polluting my game experience – I'm probably not going to feel as if the magic circle is protecting me much.

The player communities of EVE Online (CCP Games 2003) are full of grand stories of the real-world and the game-world overlapping in uncomfortable ways. From literal spies to crushing financial penalties. This game of corporate space exploration and exploitation sure seems to leave a lot of actual people feeling as if they have been genuinely damaged as a result of play.

What happens when you betray a friend in a game? The board game Diplomacy (Calhamer 1959) is played through making political agreements that are as fragile as the paper upon which they are written. The Game of Thrones (Petersen 2011) board game is one of complex military alignments and shifting political allegiances. You might talk a friend into teaming up to defeat a third player, only to find that they took advantage of your agreement to move troops into your territory while you were otherwise engaged. Can you shake that off as being safely contained within the magic circle?

How do you feel about people cheating? In a multiplayer game? In an online game? In a solo game? In a board game? What about people who just aren't into a gaming session and stare at their phone? Does their indifference change the experience of the game for everyone else? Juul (2003), as we discussed in our section on "what is a game", might consider this to be a violation of "player attachment to outcome", but it's also perhaps a violation of the implied social contract of play. Reiner Knizia is quoted as saying "The goal of a game is to win, but it is the goal that is important, not the winning" (Rogerson, Gibbs, and Smith 2016). The implication being that everyone needs to **strive** to win, because that's an important aspect of keeping everyone engaged. A player on their phone is like plunging a sedative into the heart of the experience. Exploring the expectations of the social contract – implied and explicit – can reveal a lot about what people expect from games in their real lives.

We can explore this idea through the consideration of what are sometimes known as **pervasive games** (Montola 2005) – games where there is an elastic relationship between the states of "playing" and "not playing". We might consider persistent role-playing game campaigns, where players may run the same character for years or decades. A character dying in a one-off game is easy to shrug off. The permanent death of a character you have been developing for ten years has an altogether different emotional heft. Legacy board games, such as Risk Legacy (Daviau and Dupuis 2011); Pandemic Legacy (Daviau and Leacock 2015); and Gloomhaven (Childres 2017), represent a subgenre of board games that draw on this idea to create evolving experiences with consequences that carry over from one game to another. Decisions taken might have long-term ramifications and the decision to begin a legacy game is often one that comes with a social obligation of commitment.

These might be loose conception of pervasive games, but there are other clearer examples. *Pokemon Go* (Arjoranta, Kari, and Salo 2020) encourages players to sample their real-world environment for rare Pokemon and opposing trainers. The genre of Alternate Reality Games (ARGs) works by placing a fictive layer atop the world in which we live (Kim et al. 2009; Szulborski 2005). Consider *I Love Bees* (McGonigal 2008), an ARG that served as an advertising platform for Halo 2 (Bungie 2004). In this, a purportedly hacked website gave clues to diligent observers that led to messages available only at specific GPS co-ordinates or hidden through steganography in the bits of another file. Whole communities came together to gather data, analyse clues, and posit theories. The Jejune Institute (Daschke 2013) was another full-on ARG-cum-interactive art installation which consumed many of those who encountered it.

Assassin, which has been for a long time a popular game on university campuses, is an excellent example because spatial, social and temporal aspects are all intertwined into the experience. The game is relatively simple – assassinate your target while avoiding your own assassination. The specifics vary from game to game, but you might carry out an assassination by hitting your target with a water gun, or a paint gun, or a nerf dart. Sometimes it's enough to get the target wet, other times you must "dispatch" them with a specific piece of equipment. Some games run on the honour system, while some require documentary evidence.

The thing that makes this a pervasive game as opposed to a weaksauce version of the *Hunger Games* is that the "board" of the game is your whole life. Many of these games place restrictions on what counts as a valid assassination – for example, maybe you can't legally assassinate someone at work, or in a class, or on public transport. Everything that isn't restricted is fair. As a result, the boundaries of everything around you take on a liminal quality in that you can never be sure if you are playing the game or simply living your life.

Let's say there's a knock at the door. Is it a package delivery? An unexpected visit from a friend?

It could be! It could also be an assassin, looking to score a kill when you open the door. Your own home turned into a battleground. And so, perhaps you think about turning the tables. You pick up your water pistol. Carefully turn the handle. Throw the door open and start firing, only to find yourself face-to-face with an exceptionally disgruntled UberEats driver carrying a soggy paper bag that was once your anticipated dinner treat. Someone looking at you funny on the bus might be an assassin, or an informant. Or just someone aggrieved that you're watching TikTok without wearing headphones.[2] This is the kind of game that can turn anyone into a neurovore – which is to say they end up living on their own nerves.[3]

It is this pervasiveness that makes Assassin such a compelling game for many – an experience difficult to replicate in any other form. However, from the perspective of the magic circle, it's certainly a complicated game style to emotionally parse.

Accessibility

As you may have already gathered from references in this book, much of my work has been on the topic of accessibility in games. And primarily, accessibility within board games. And as a research lens **within** games, it's genuinely fascinating. Many games are unfortunately **inaccessible**, in that they are not playable by people who don't conform to the median expectation of physical and cognitive capability. When we consider people with disabilities, or those with less significant impairments, many games simply ask more than what someone might be able to provide.

An inaccessibility is a barrier – real or perceptual – that stands between someone and a goal they want to achieve. Many inaccessibilities come about as a consequence of things like visual impairment, motor control and so on. Others come from broadly "sociological" frames of accessibility – predatory business models; representation; and emotional design. The problem for game designers and scholars is that inaccessibility is where fun comes from. Activities are made into games by adding artificial obstacles between a player and a goal. As such, inaccessibilities are necessary for fun to emerge. However, it does not follow that **all** inaccessibilities are necessary. Sometimes we need to assess games in the frame of who they even permit to play – again, who is included, who is excluded, and to what extent is that a conscious design choice?

TABLE 8.1

The Grid of Enlightened Self-Interest

	Colour Blindness	Visual	Cognitive	Physical	Socioeconomic	Emotional	Communication
Permanent Always relevant, will probably never go away although severity may modulate	Protanopia Deuteranopia Tritanopia Monochromacy Ageing Brain Damage	Blindness Short sightedness	Dementia Alzheimer's	Loss of a limb	Social classification Under representation	An emotional control disorder	Deaf/HoH Mutism
Temporary Short term, will eventually go away	Concussion	Eye infection Wearing an eyepatch Getting used to new glasses	Being drunk Bad night's sleep	Broken arm Sprained ankle	Unemployment Forgotten your Wallet Being in "the wrong neighbourhood"	Received some bad news	Broken jaw A noisy bar
Situational Intermittent, will phase in and out of relevance	Bad lighting Wearing sunglasses	Bright sunshine in your eyes	Being distracted Being in an open plan office	Carrying something heavy On a juddery train	Contactless payments not working	Irritation at a loud conversation in the background	With a group of mixed-language friends

I want to stress here though that while disabled gamers are the most significant beneficiary of accessibility support, the largest beneficiary **is all of us**. We all benefit from more accessible design in the games we play. The curb cut effect (Lawson 2015) is the term used when accommodations made for people with disabilities turn out to be generally useful to everyone. Curb cuts – those depressions you find offering a gentle slope from the curb to a road and vice versa – were originally conceived as an accessibility support for people in wheelchairs. They turned out to be valued by parents with strollers, elderly people, mail carriers, cyclists… anyone who found it an inconvenience to experience a jolt as they stepped from the pavement into a road. As I get older and my knees get ever less reliable, I find myself grateful for them every day.

More than this though, all of us benefit from accessibility because we are all, at various times in our life, impaired across one or more of our key faculties. In the book *Tabletop Game Accessibility: Meeple Centred Design* (Heron 2024), I provide what I call the grid of enlightened self-interest. I reproduce it here as Table 8.1.

What this shows is that across eight distinctive categories of interaction (the ones that have emerged from my ongoing work in accessibility) we see manifestations that are permanent (what we'd normally think of when we think of disabilities), temporary (those that will over time fade away), and situational (as in, we move in and out of the condition of being impaired). The general rule is that ordinary people in extraordinary circumstances benefit from the same accessibility compensations as extraordinary people in ordinary circumstances (Newell 2011). Accessibility isn't a niche concern – it's something we all fundamentally need. Well-designed games are as accessible as they can be while retaining the core inaccessibilities that create the fun. It's quite a needle to thread.

Note here that I include poor representation as an inaccessibility. For a long time, you were more likely to see a sheep on the cover of a board game than you were to see a woman. That is something I would frame as an inaccessibility because of the cultural impact it has. We create subconscious associations based on the imagery with which we are confronted – that's pretty much the basis of the field of semiotics. Imagine yourself as a young Black girl walking into a board game shop and seeing only a sea of dead-eyed middle-aged white faces staring back at you from the shelves. I think you'd fairly conclude "this clearly isn't a hobby for me". If you don't see yourself represented in a hobby, I believe it's easy to assume you're not intended to be part of it.

Now, this is in itself a controversial claim (harken back to Chapter 1, where we talk about claims being proportionate to evidence – I'm honouring that here by framing this as an intellectual exercise). Someone who genuinely wants to be part of a hobby won't let a lack of representation stop them. People can identify with characters that don't conform to the idea of "people like them". Male players can resonate with female characters and vice versa. Nothing is ever so simple that we can make definitive, sweeping statements such as "representation is a moral necessity". Consider it through a pragmatic lens though – if you want a wider range of people to engage with gaming, including those that **do** see a lack of representation as a barrier, then you need to meet them half-way at least.

Related to what we've already talked about with regards to business factors, inaccessibility is also something that extends to economic factors. How much of a game are you genuinely buying with the retail cost? How much is locked behind DLCs or expansions?

The earliest incarnations of *Magic: The Gathering* (Garfield and Lezzi 1993) had a business model driven through booster packs that contained random cards. A pack might have a couple of cards you actually wanted. Or perhaps you'd want every card. Or perhaps you wouldn't want any of them. Swapping cards with friends became part of the social context of the game, but what if you were like me – growing up on a housing estate in a small Scottish town – and didn't have access to other people who played Magic? Or, indeed, didn't have any friends? You could find yourself compelled to spend beyond a reasonable amount to construct the decks that you wanted, and yet still may have no opportunities to play them.

Consider *Warhammer 40,000* (Games Workshop 2020) – a fun game by all accounts, but you need a lot of money to field a credible army – those miniatures don't come cheap. And if you want to play at a tournament level, you also need to invest in paints and all the other accruements that are part of The Hobby. Consider *Fortnite* (Epic Games 2017), a game which is free to play, but if you're the only one who doesn't have premium skins there's a reasonable chance you're going to get bullied for being a dirty, poor "default" (Reich and Steinnes 2023). The cost of buying into the intended experience of play can be an inaccessibility, and it's not always just the sticker price on a box.

Then there are the emotional aspects. We've spoken a bit about the experiential frame of games, but there are factors that perhaps fit more into an accessibility lens. Particularly when there are features of a game that work to make us feel bad. Consider chess – a game of perfect information where everything that happens is completely deterministic. A pure game of systems, and the mastery of those systems. Chess is a game for clever people. That particular connection is so embedded in culture that it's a narrative shorthand. Your genius supervillain will be great at chess. People who are great at chess are de-facto geniuses.

Why do you lose a game of chess? You lose because someone outplayed you. There's nowhere, psychologically, to hide. How does it feel in a game of *Scrabble* (Butts 1948) when you play out the word CAT for three points, and your opponent uses that to play out *ABDICATION* for 11 million points? It feels like you shouldn't be allowed to use words in the presence of other people.

On the other hand, when you lose a game of poker or Liar's dice, the randomness (inbound, white) gives you some shelter to retain your dignity. You had a bad hand of cards, you rolled a bad set of numbers. Chess requires you to be pretty secure in your separation of "game skills" and "real-life smarts" to maintain even a shaky hold on your ego. Other games don't need you to be quite so established in your own sense of confidence.

These are valid frames of analysis – reasonable concepts to bring into an evaluation of games. Trust me – I've been doing it for years and nobody has made me stop.

Autoethnography

Much of what people end up doing in the study of games is centring a personal perspective that is informed by individual experience. Some believe that this flies in the face of traditional models of science, where quantification, objective truth and cool dispassion are the rule of the day. However, games are inherently subjective experiences – one story, but many heroes. Anthropology has long relied upon a type of study known as an **ethnography**, which is the study of cultures from the perspective of the cultures being studied (Atkinson 2007). Ethnography focuses on interrogating the behaviour of participants within a culture with the intention of coming to some conclusion as to the meaning of their behaviour. Such studies rely heavily on observation, but also a kind of **situated** observation known as **participant observation,** in which the scholar performing the ethnography embeds themselves within the culture so as to observe it more intimately. This is contrasted with **naturalistic observation**, where a culture is observed from the outside so as to avoid injecting alien elements into their behaviour. Sometimes this kind of work is done in the open, and sometimes it is **disguised** so that the subjects of the observation are unaware of their status.

Ethnography is a tool for researching complex social relationships, with a plurality of subjects. While specific individuals may be a focus of analysis, the approach is intended to look at the systems in which they function and at the construction of meaning within those systems.

What happens though when the number of subjects is one – the participant-observer themselves? Then we have **autoethnography** (Ellis, Adams, and Bochner 2011) in which we engage in a meaningful analysis of our own behaviours and motivations. And it turns out, autoethnography is a powerful tool for interrogating our relationship to the games we play.

The act of exploring the personal has become increasingly popular in the wider academic literature over the past 20 or so years (Duncan 2004; Silverman and Rowe 2020). There is an old piece of received wisdom in scientific publishing – "the plural of anecdote is not data". In that respect, autoethnography as an inherently anecdotal form of research seems at odds with the mores of the traditional academic model as it is understood in many fields. Sara Pikelet on Twitter has perhaps the perfect counter perspective – "they're not anecdotes. They're small-batch artisanal data".

Pikelet's response recognizes the importance of the small scale, personally constructed narrative. Anecdotes cannot offer broad general insight on larger systemic issues. They are too mired in personal biases, in personal contexts, and in personal mindsets. The second-person techniques that drive much qualitative research have corrective procedures built into them to permit a researcher to draw actionable insight from multiple personal perspectives. Surveys, focus-groups, interviews, and so on must be constructed and conducted in ways that eliminate as much bias as possible if they are to offer rigour in their conclusions. Autoethnography lacks systemic "checksums" on its conclusions.

What the personal autoethnography offers though is an impeccable form of engaging with personal meaning (Jones, Adams, and Ellis 2016) and lived experience (Ngunjiri, Hernandez, and Chang 2010). Where the autoethnographic technique shines most brightly is in terms of capturing truly **authentic** and fine-grained data (Wiesner 2020). Its focus on self-interrogation (Desjardins and Ball 2018; Holmes and O'Neill 2010; Roy and Uekusa 2020) gives a tool through which otherwise unobtainable perspectives can be codified in the academic literature. The format has its inherent limitations (Jackson and Mazzei 2008; Wall 2008) – in order to have the most genuinely authentic research data, one must accept inherent constraints on generalizability. It is though in the very tight coupling of the personal to the subject that creates the value of the approach. The observations associated with that union **are** the research output, and no part of that output can survive deconstruction. That is both its methodological weakness and its methodological value – it is "one of the dominant and characteristic forms of literary self-expression" (Pascal 2015). When we spoke about the ideas of the New Games Journalism and psychogeography in an earlier chapter, we were talking about an informal version of a scholarly auto-ethnography.

Key to pulling off a successful autoethnography is that authenticity we have already indicated as one of the primary deliverables. Autoethnography is almost a form of self-therapy in which you connect deeply and meaningfully with the emotional consequences of your personal experience. The intention is to surface perspectives that are deeply individual and yet also offer illumination with regards to worldviews with which we may not have familiarity. An autoethnography should not merely narrate an experience (autobiographical research steps in there) – it should embed that experience in meaning and contextualize it within the wider scholarly literature. A focus on the person doesn't mean that we escape the need for rigorous documentation and evidenced claims – in fact, if anything, the general scepticism in the wider scientific community mandates that we hold ourselves to even greater standards.

However, autoethnography does offer one quality that relaxes the kind of proof we need to provide of our claims – our lived experience is a form of expert evidence in and of itself. As a general rule, people are very good at identifying what a thing makes them feel. The movie *Moana* made me, by turns, happy, sad, pensive, and then triumphant. The song Mister Blue Sky by the Electric Light Orchestra makes me cheerful. All Too Well by Taylor Swift makes me melancholy. I can say all of this without providing evidence – proof of our internal emotional machinery is impossible to provide, so we operate on a trust basis. If you tell me *Stardew Valley* (Barone 2016) stresses you out, I have to accept that even if I can't empathize with it.

However, what people in general are not good at identifying, or articulating, is the **why** of the **what.** This is something designers have to consider closely in playtesting. Players may provide the feedback that "the game is too difficult". That's how they feel about it, and they are 100% correct in how they feel. Nobody is ever wrong for feeling a particular way about a particular thing. It's a mistake though for a designer to see this feedback and say, "Okay, we'll make the game easier". Playtesters have identified a symptom – the game is too hard. What they haven't identified is the reason. Perhaps it's not actually to do with difficulty, but more to do with a lack of tools for managing that difficulty. Perhaps it's because they're approaching challenges the wrong way,[4] and the real solution is to communicate the philosophy of the game better. Teasing out the meaning of feedback is a task of considerable analytical sophistication, but it's vital.

We have to acknowledge that we are unreliable narrators of our own life. We don't need to prove we felt a way, but we do need to be careful in how we identify the **why** of it. That's where connecting to existing theories and a process of reflective practice can build rigour.

Let's say you want to do an autoethnography that is essentially a reflection on how the game *Unpacking* (Witch Beam 2021) made you feel nostalgic for your childhood. For those that haven't had the pleasure, Unpacking is exactly what it sounds like – a game of moving possessions from cardboard boxes into the locations they are supposed to occupy in your life. You begin in your childhood bedroom at some unspecified point in the 1990s (going by context clues), and then into increasingly grown-up bedrooms and houses as you age. In an autoethnography, you'd begin by describing what happened in the game when it triggered an emotional response. You might note particular details. You might annotate with screenshots. You might journal your experience, or narrate it. You'd talk about the context, and what it meant to you.

Inhabiting the moment is important here – something autoethnography has in common with psychogeography – you don't need to analyse or reflect on an experience as it's happening. Just record the what – what was the experience, what was the emotional or intellectual response, what was the context, what were the thoughts you had?

Once you've gotten to a sensible stopping point (end of a chapter, end of the day, whatever), you can take these observations and begin to analyse them. You'll already have captured how you were thinking and feeling at the time, and then you can contrast that against what you are thinking and feeling during analysis. If your reflections relate to an action you took within the game, you might consider evaluating the actions themselves. Are you happy with what you did? Disappointed? Maybe even confused[5]? Dig into that – **why** do you feel **what** you feel? Which parts of your experience leave you feeling vulnerable or emotionally raw? Those parts are likely where you should spend a greater proportion of your time exploring. That can be uncomfortable, but your discomfort is grist for the mill. This is the autobiographical portion of the process.

Next up comes integrating your reflections into the wider context – this is the ethnography part of the work. What do other games in a similar style evoke within you in similar situations? How have other people related to similar feelings in other contexts? What do friends and relatives have to say about the results of your contemplation, and might they have other insights of their own to lend to yours? What about theoretical models of storytelling, of aesthetic design, of experience, of narrative – how do these all inform the understanding you've built up of yourself?

Enough of these analytical vignettes will sum up to a series of insights. Perhaps interesting design observations. Perhaps truths you've realized about yourself. Perhaps lessons learned for the future. It's these insights that reflect the core of what you've gained from autoethnography. It's not critical that an autoethnography provides insight that is **useful** to other people, although I'd argue all scholarly work has an implied duty to add value to society. That value though doesn't have to be purely transactional – it doesn't have to be "I did X and here are ten guidelines for those that want to accomplish Y". Sometimes the value you give is in making it easier for us to experience empathy with people who approach life – and games – in a different way to us.

Stories and Narratives

One might consider the games that stories tell to be something best addressed within a critical frame, and I would agree entirely with that as a philosophy. However, stories and narratives are so integral to games that I think it would be a good idea for us to focus on this as its own, distinctive element. A lot of the techniques that work for critical analysis of stories in general will work for games, but there are some specifically "gamey" elements that deserve being plucked out and looked at more closely.

Before we do that, let's row back a little – perhaps all the way to the boathouse – to talk about what we **mean** when we talk about stories. And within this, we need to consider the impact of medium. What is the difference between a book and a movie? Between a movie and a video game? A board game and a video game? A tabletop RPG and a theatre performance?

Humanity, as a species, is made up of natural storytellers. There's plenty of research to suggest that storytelling evolved as a mechanism for survival (Bietti, Tilston, and Bangerter 2019; Gansel 2012) – to survive the world, we must understand the world. Stories are a tremendously "sticky" way of communicating dense information in an accessible way. Stories encode causality, consequence, and moral messaging. A scattered collection of facts and meaning don't embed themselves into our brains in the same way. For generations, stories have been a fundamental part of societal memory – even before the alphabet, we had ideogrammatic paintings on cave walls that encoded important life lessons.

Early societies built around institutional memory took storytelling seriously – what is an epic poem other than a way for society to reflect on its own history and mythography? Religious texts are often narrative. Folk talks, superstitions, and myths are all forms that stories have taken, and many of them still persist into the modern day. We may disagree on what the story actually **is** (there are for example conflicting theories on what the nursery rhyme ring-a-ring-o-rosies is actually about), but the stories persist.

So, let's begin with some simple definitions.

A story is a description of people and the events that happen to them. We can be quite widely inclusive about how we define "people" here. There are stories about things and concepts. There are stories primarily focused on places – in fact, that's what psychogeography is, as a discipline. But we tend to see stories being about people – even if those people are anthropomorphized cars.

"Michael wrote a book and everyone loved it"

That's a story. Just off the top of my head.

Stories represent the fundamental building blocks of how we make sense of a game. Stories are how we put the events that occur in a chronological, and often causative, context. Every game has a story, even if we sometimes have to make it up ourselves by making ourselves into the protagonist.

"The blocks kept falling. I managed to keep them ordered until finally the speed overwhelmed my cognitive processing, at which point catastrophe loomed".

Consider some examples:

- A somewhat stereotyped Italian plumber stalks an ape through the scaffolding of a building in order to rescue his girlfriend.
- A super-fast hedgehog has a golden ring addiction, and he will do anything to satisfy it.
- Space debris is everywhere, and only a lone pilot in a lone spaceship can protect the world from it.
- A warrior falls from the skies, and they alone have to best all opponents in a vicious battle in which there can be only one.
- An ageing cowboy follows a charismatic windbag far beyond any sense or reason.

These are simple stories. They're not exhaustive. They miss out on important elements. But they're enough, by themselves, to clue you in on what's actually being described. Games make it difficult for us to do anything like extract a meaning or a message – we often take an active role in shaping the story. There may be no such thing as a canonical story that everyone will experience (Heron 2017).

Stories – in our simple technical definition – lack most of the varnishing that makes them worth our time. Stories here are codifications of facts, people and the order in which events happened. There's a common legend (it's not actually true) that Ernest Hemingway, in order to win a bet with a friend, wrote a complete story in six words. "Baby shoes. For sale. Never worn". The story definitely exists, but it's almost certainly not something that Hemingway wrote – it likely originates after his death.

The key thing here though is that stories don't need to be **long** in order to be complete. And they don't need to be explicit in their events or characters. However, the more room a story has to breathe, the more sophisticated it can be. With regards to the baby shoes story, critics have often pointed out the fact that this story actually lacks causation and ordering, or even really a meaning other than what we project into it. The canonical reading is that this was the sad outcome of a family tragedy. But it could also be that they were an unwanted gift. Or simply the wrong size. Or the baby was born with hooves and thus needed shod rather than shoed.

However, baby shoes – as a story – is notable because it's also a **narrative.** Stories and narratives are terms often used interchangeably, but they actually have different meanings. Stories are the bones of the thing, and narrative is the framing. Narrative layers on implication and the ordering in which things are encountered by the reader/player – not the order in which things happened, rather how causal elements are expressed. A story is what happened, a narrative is how you tell it. Or, if a story is sensemaking, a narrative is framing things so that **meaning** can be extracted from the sense. A narrative describes the presentation – what events are related, and in what order, and from what perspectives. Narrative also encodes the rhetorical or visual flourishes you use to emphasize story beats, and the extent to which you emphasize them. A single core story can spawn an infinite number of narratives, and each of these might feel entirely differently because of the way they land with the receiver.

Let's look at another story.

A powerful member of high society takes a disadvantaged street person and transforms them into something grander by exposing them to another kind of life.

That's the story. And from that, we can see abundant narratives:

- Pygmalion, by George Bernard Shaw
- The film and musical My Fair Lady
- The movies Pretty Woman, She's All That, Educating Rita and Trading Places

The story is broadly the same. The emphasis, setting, context, medium, and storytelling methods all shift. As too does the coverage of the story – a narrative element can be how much of the story you actually tell and how much you leave open to interpretation.

Theme and Setting

Story and narrative are two of the major building blocks of how we make meaning about the events in a game. The third and fourth are **theme** and **setting**. Again, two terms that are often used interchangeably, but they have their own distinct meanings and roles to play.

Setting is the situated context. It might be "the wild west", or "medieval Europe", or "Scotland". It implies the look and "feel" and sound of a place. Setting a game in the

TABLE 8.2

Story Elements and What They Handle

Story	Narrative	Theme	Setting
Events	Chronology	Motifs	Time
People	Causality	Underlying ideas	Place
Things	Emphasis	Mood	Audience Expectations
	Completeness of	Context	
	Coverage	Intended audience	
	Drama and Rhetoric	Audience expectations	

Highlands of Scotland instantly conjures up a (largely stereotypical) idea of what it will be like to be in a place within the game. Brooding hills; skirling bagpipes; dark, foreboding skies.

Theme sets the mood of a piece. Theme implies an underlying unity between elements, and the lack of it is often something critique can explore. In its simplest conception, a theme represents an idea that is executed repeatedly through all the other elements. Narrative should reinforce theme. Story should reinforce theme. And, ideally, so should the setting. A story of grim desperation and the endless absurdity of an uncaring universe might be reflected in how the game is set on an abandoned, decaying spaceship. Simply looking out a window into an endless, infinite void is a way of stressing the theme of our cosmic insignificance. Setting the same game on a cheerful island surrounded by azure-blue waves might be a harder sell, although there's no reason you couldn't intentionally explore it.

Theme and setting **should** overlap, but they're distinct. As with a narrative, a single setting might be used as the starting point for many different themes. The best kind of cultural products won't even stop at one theme – they'll have subthemes, and counterthemes, and complementary themes. Some themes will be represented by character moments, others by the logic and aesthetics of the settings, and others as an outcome of narrative. Maybe you explore the abandoned quarters of your fellow astronauts to find bottles of empty whisky hidden under the sleeping bunk of the one you didn't know well. Multiple pictures of a happy family are shown, dating to ten years ago but with nothing more recent. All the books are by Camus, Nietzsche, and Schopenhauer. Nowhere does the Story come out and say "This guy is lonely and lost since his divorce, and has stared directly into the abyss to find it staring back". The implications speak for themselves, permitting the player or reader to ponder what it all means. Or, potentially, to not do the exploration and end up forever mystified as to why this astronaut took their helmet off during a spacewalk and precipitated the whole ordeal.

Table 8.2 shows the relationship between these elements and where you'd normally expect to find them handled. In a well-constructed tale, it will be difficult to extract any of these elements out of their context without reference to other parts because everything should reinforce everything else. That's another way to talk about intratextuality. It should be cohesive, or it will come across as disjointed. Can you have a setting without a theme? Sure, but the setting will set expectations as to what kind of themes will be appropriate, and so you can't autopsy one without comparing against the other. Can narratives exist without a story? Can stories exist without a setting?

The answer, perhaps surprisingly, is **yes**. In order to do it well though, you need to engage in an extended process of deconstruction – as with accessibility, everything that is done within a game narrative should be intentional. Telling a story about the small kindnesses of human society will be difficult to do if your setting is a shipwreck on a lonely island. The absence of that society will need to be carefully worked around, and indeed the theme might end up being that absence of society. It would be easier and more obviously cohesive though to tell a story like that in a city, where human society is omnipresent. That's not to say, of course, that easy is the best incentive.

As a scholar analysing this kind of thing, always ask yourself what themes are coming up in your engagement with the text, and what themes you'd expect to be there given the setting. Or as a counterpoint what any absence of theme says about the intention behind the story. Interpreting narrative, like any of the techniques we discuss in this book, requires nothing more than for you to think about things in particular ways.

Storytelling Structures

Story, narrative, themes, and settings – these are basic, functional definitions, but they don't tell us a lot about how they come together. As we've implied, there are ways to construct stories but also ways to deconstruct them – to break them down into their constituent bits so we can see how they fit together. Our discussion thus far has not really talked a lot about medium, but that's a critical part of how a story should be told. You can tell different stories in a game versus a book, but what about a game versus live theatre? Ayn Rand's "Night of January 16th" (Rand 1971) is a play where the audience act as a jury, and the decisions they come to impact the final conclusion of the story. Medium makes a big difference in terms of what it permits and prohibits, and sometimes edge-cases raise questions about what medium we're even working with. Netflix's Bandersnatch (Roth and Koenitz 2019), for example, is a *Choose Your Own Adventure* gamebook in video form. Is it a game? Is it a movie? Is it something different entirely?

The structure that is employed to tell a story comes into focus here.

The Three-Act Structure

You've almost certainly heard of the three-act structure as a way of constructing stories. It's practically the default of modern cinema, mainstream games, and culturally accessible literature. Here, a story gets broken down into three main sections, or "acts". Each of these is structurally linked to each other and has particular beats that tend to lead to satisfying stories. As a hint, if you want to sound like you really understand storytelling just say of something that it "clearly had a third act problem" and watch how many people nod along.[6]

Act one is the setup, containing the introductory context, the **inciting incident** (the thing that sets the story in motion), and then the protagonist wrestling with the consequences of being outside their comfort zone. Act one then ends in a climax that irrevocably commits the protagonist to a course of action.

Act two is the confrontation, in which we continually introduce obstacles that, in overcoming them, bring the protagonist to the mid-point of the story when a twist or complexity is introduced. These obstacles might be physical, emotional, or even internal. The idea is to build a sense of tension. This is followed by escalating action until we reach a disaster – success must always be met with a tragedy – which then leads into a crisis. At this point, we should feel as if the protagonist is doomed to fail. The climax of act two is a transformation, in which the character – having failed – comes to an epiphany regarding who they need to be to succeed in their goals.

And then act three is largely payoff as the story is resolved. The crisis is solved, often with a thematic message coded within. That often takes the form of a pre-climax – a satisfying resolution that sets the character on a path from which there is no return. The big antagonist and obstacle – probably the one that triggered the act two crisis – is confronted and overcome. The story wraps-up and the character returns to their beginning context, changed forever as a result of their adventure. This is the **denouement**, in which everyone must adjust to a new conception of normal.

This is an incredibly popular structure for several reasons. It's formulaic, sure, but it's also flexible enough that the skeleton of the system can be hidden from casual inspection. Media savvy people though will instantly be able to trace the arc of the story, perhaps down to the minute or page as to when particular things will happen. It has a long, long pedigree – Aristotle's Poetics, from around 350 BCE, is one of the first playwriting manuals, and it sets the template for how stories should be told. And despite its predictability, it's actually loose enough to put a lot of important aspects of the story into the hands of the storyteller. It doesn't require, for example, that all acts be of equal length.

It's also "moddable" – many variations exist. The two-act structure; a two-act structure where each act has three sub-acts; the nine-act structure; and so on. As such, you can often begin deconstructing a story in any medium – games included – by thinking of what's happening in each act.

The Building Blocks of Story

In his excellent book *Into the Woods*, Yorke (2014) identifies several fundamental building blocks of a story:

- **A protagonist**. This is the leading character. The hero or the anti-hero.
- **An antagonist**. This is the main opposing force. This is often the villain of the story but doesn't have to be.
- **An inciting incident**. We say this in our three-act structure – the thing that moves the protagonist out of their complacency.
- **A desire**. This is the thing that the protagonist wants. This may also be something the antagonist wants.
- **A crisis**. This is the thing that stops the protagonist gaining their desire. Perhaps the antagonist.
- **A climax** – a conflict between the antagonist and the protagonist over a desire.
- **A resolution** – a final conclusion where the desire is resolved appropriately.

These building blocks are all to be found in the three-act structure. As Yorke says:

> The three-act structure is the cornerstone of drama primarily because it embodies the simplest units of Aristotelean (and indeed all) structure: It follows the irrefutable laws of physics. Everything must have a beginning, a middle, and an end.

Stories don't neatly fall into our discussions of critical, experiential and systemic frames because they are smeared over all three perspectives. Sure, we can critically analyse a narrative, but we can't ignore the fact that we love stories because stories make us **feel** things. We can't ignore the fact that stories are as systemic as game mechanisms. Profitable analysis can be done in any of these frames. For example, consider a story in which the protagonist and the antagonist want the same thing (the best for each other) but have radically different interpretations on how it might manifest. What you have there is not a summer action blockbuster but the recipe for an intense character study. It's essentially the core of the movie Brave. You could dig into story structure in games from any number of angles.

Notable in the Yorke conception is that some of these building blocks don't have to have rich identities of their own. Sometimes stories are built around a completely artificial but narratively satisfying desire – often known as **Macguffins**. These are things that are deemed inherently desirable enough to drive the story even if they play no further role in the evolution of the protagonist. A thing to be gained, or lost, and nobody should care about the specifics. The Maltese Falcon; Big Whoop; The Blackwater Heist money.

Many of the fundamental building blocks in storytelling emerge from characters and characterization. Some authors talk of their characters behaving in unexpected ways as they try to write them – they refuse to conform, on the page, to the require-ments of the plot. That's because well-rounded characters have motivations and values that emerge independently of author intent. A believable character tends to behave in a way that is internally consistent to their values, and when they don't, it's a tension that must be resolved in the story. Consider the relationship between Arthur (the pro-tagonist) and Dutch (one of several interlocking antagonists) in *Red Dead Redemption 2* (Rockstar Games 2019).

Arthur is indebted to Dutch, who serves as a surrogate father. He is trusting, down to his bones, in Dutch's abilities and intentions. Arthur is optimistic, willing to believe that the bend of life is upwards. And he has a great **desire**, to make Dutch proud of him. Dutch on the other hand is intensely arrogant and has been made so **because** of the faith others have put in him. However, he is constantly beset by the cognitive dissonance (Harmon-Jones and Mills 2019) that comes from reconciling his meagre abilities against the myth of his own genius. He can resolve that dissonance by decon-structing the myth, or turning against those who provide evidence of his limitations. Dutch's great desire is to protect his own standing in the eyes of others. Thus, he doesn't engage in self-reflection.

Much of the storytelling in *Red Dead Redemption 2* comes from tensions like this. Arthur's desire is for Dutch to admire him, but Arthur's tendency to act in the com-mon good constantly puts him in conflict with Dutch's plans. Dutch sees this as a form of undermining, which puts Arthur between him and his own desire. Arthur wants something that Dutch will never give. In order for Dutch to acknowledge Arthur's status as a better man he'd have to accept what he perceived as a diminished posi-tion within his own gang. The inciting incident is the "off camera" failed Blackwater Heist, and it is this that starts Dutch and Arthur down their diverging character arcs. The other storytelling elements all emerge from the entangling of these arcs – the plot itself is largely just a backdrop. And yet, in the relationship between two beautifully written characters we see all the key elements that Yorke mandates.

Sometimes characters are archetypes rather than fully developed individuals. Their role is to achieve certain storytelling goals related to a setting or a theme. Stories where we see systems and how they destroy people are sometimes best considered in a sociological frame rather than a narrative one. Consider for example *Game of Thrones*, in which characters can be slotted in and out of roles because the overarching theme is that the system itself is what's being fed by conflict.

Dan Harmon, of Rick and Morty fame, has spoken about the story cycle used as part of that series. There is not so much a progression as there is an ever-recurring pattern, where the end of one story feeds into the start of another:

1. The character is in their comfort zone
2. But they want something
3. They enter an unfamiliar situation
4. They adapt to it
5. They get what they want
6. They pay a heavy price
7. They return to their familiar situation
8. Having changed.

But even in this, you can see the beats of a three-act structure, even if they are conceptualized and paced in a different way. Once you know you know, and all that.

The Monomyth

One of the most influential concepts in story structure is that of the **Hero's Journey**, or the **Monomyth.** This is an idea proposed by Joesph Campbell in his book *The Hero with a Thousand Faces* (Campbell 2004). He posits that all almost all myths (and many stories in general) share a common structure. They don't necessarily have every feature he identifies, but enough that we can draw meaningful comparisons. In other words, the monomyth is identified by familial resemblance – hello Wittgenstein! Some myths may have every element, others may focus on a smaller subset of the monomyth's moving parts. This idea has explicitly or implicitly inspired storytellers since its inception, and it's sometimes a very conscious decision to emulate it. Star Wars: A New Hope is an almost perfect implementation of the Hero's Journey, as an example. A full discussion of this is well outside the scope of this book, but Figure 8.1 shows the full 17 stage arc.

In the 90s, Christopher Vogler – a Hollywood producer – put out a memo giving a practical overview to the monomyth (Vogler 2007). He condensed it down into 12 significant stages:

1. The hero is introduced within their ordinary world.
2. There is a **call to adventure,** in which a quest is offered.
3. The hero is reluctant, unwilling to give up the comforts of their life.
4. The hero is encouraged to take up the call by a wise mentor.
5. The hero accepts (still reluctantly, probably) and crosses the threshold into a secret world they never knew.

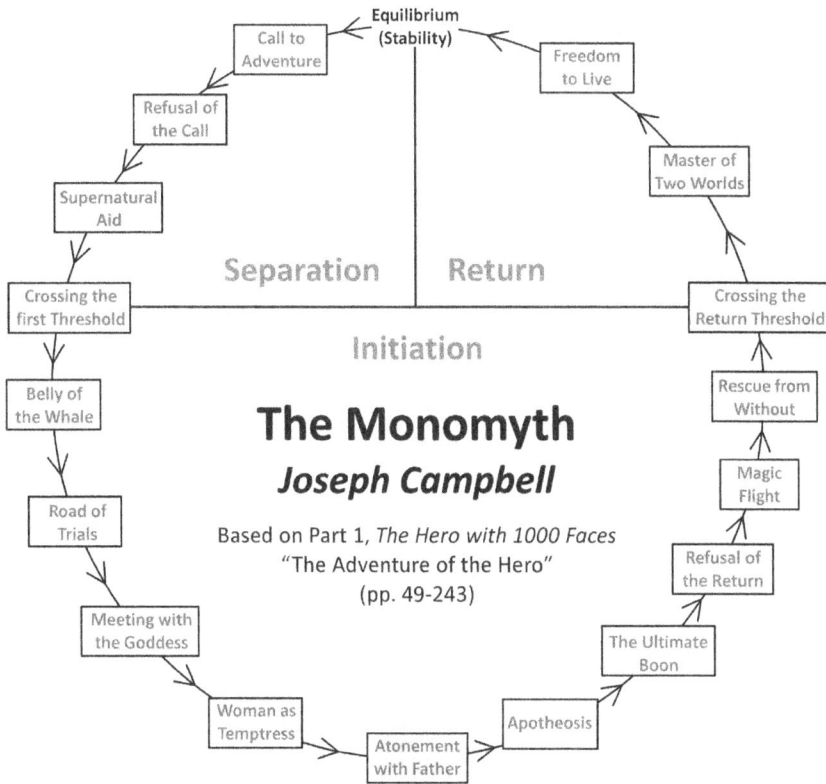

FIGURE 8.1 The Structure of the Monomyth. Available at https://commons.wikimedia.org/wiki/File:The_Monomyth_-_Joseph_Campbell.jpg, CC BY-SA 4.0.

6. The hero encounters tests and enemies and helpers.
7. The hero approaches the object of their quest.
8. The hero overcomes an ordeal.
9. The hero obtains the object of their quest.
10. The hero journeys back.
11. The hero faces a resurrected threat – the most dangerous one yet – and applies all he or she has learned to overcome it.
12. The hero returns having completed the quest.

We can see the monomyth, in many flavours, across all of classical antiquity. It's the story of Osiris. It's the story of Odysseus. It's the story of the Buddha. And the Vogler simplification can be seen across dozens of your favourite franchises. Luke Skywalker; Harry Potter; Katniss Everdeen; and Frodo Baggins – these are all relatively straightforward executions of the hero's journey. Paul Atreides too, in Dune, although that can perhaps be considered a subversion of the monomyth since in the end Paul is not a hero. If you want to understand the arc of stories in media – including games – then this is a great place to start thinking about it. Outline the major plot elements and map them on to the stages of the monomyth. Once again, things either uphold, reject or subvert expectations so the myth can be given its own flavour through **how** it is honoured – consider that too.

John Yorke (2014) again has something to offer here – he provides an evolution of the idea that works on a concept he calls **fractal storytelling.** This is a five-act structure which is focused on **thematic repetition**. The hero in this doesn't learn a single lesson; instead, they learn the core lesson several times in different ways in circumstances where the stakes keep getting higher. This is an ideal framework when examining complex characters in the context of the external challenges they face – consistent characterization becomes believable through the constant interaction and reaction between their reality and their motivations. Read Into the Woods if you're interested. And if you aren't, actually. It's fantastic. But Yorke's key message is that the small stuff shapes the big stuff – well-written stories allow you to consider thematic context in lots of different ways. We can mentally zoom out of small character moments to consider what they tell us about the larger narrative arcs.

Plots and Plotting

We've now spoken a lot on how to assess a story in terms of its plot, its structure, and the arcs that it is built upon. But what we haven't really spoken about is how a plot becomes a narrative – or rather, how we can say interesting things **about** narrative.

We're talking here as if a story has a plot and a character has an arc. In the best told tales, there are several plots and arcs that intersect and interact and interleave. Each arc is likely structured in a simple way, but the way they work together creates sometimes overwhelming complexity. Consider how difficult it is to just watch a modern Marvel movie without needing to watch three other movies as homework. Game of Thrones too, where each of its perspective characters has their own lens on the larger meta-narrative. Many soap operas function this way, as do movies such as Pulp Fiction in which parallel storytelling works together with non-sequential narrative to reward repeat viewing.

One of the simplest ways you see stories become narratives is through the execution of **linear plots** – things happen, one after another. They start at a certain point, and eventually they stop. Linear storytelling doesn't imply **sequential** storytelling though. The key thing is that we experience a story beat, and then another, and then another. Most books and movies work this way – our focus is always on the present.

One variant is the **nested story** structure, in which a story is told inside a story. The larger, overarching story connects these distinct and often self-contained tales together into something thematically coherent. Think of a Thousand and One Arabian Nights, in which the larger story is Scheherazade telling tales to a Sultan in order to survive, but each tale is self-consistent within that larger framing. House of Leaves (Danielewski 2000) is a book describing a documentary about a house, and both heavily reference supporting context from other sources. Assassin's Creed – the whole franchise – explores this in the context of the Animus (Vandewalle et al. 2023). Here, the framing is a modern-day secret society using a special machine to live through the genetic memories of those with particularly interesting ancestry. Every so often, the games lift you out of the fiction of, say, sailing the high seas in search of plunder – *Assassin's Creed: Black Flag* (Ubisoft Montreal 2013) – to force you through a sequence where you navigate office politics.

The card game *Once Upon a Time* (Lambert, Rilstone and Wallis 1993) is a good example of handing over the power to nest stories to the players. Players have a hand of cards that represent storytelling elements or plot points, and they weave a story playing down the cards when appropriate. Every player is trying to reach a particular conclusion, which requires them to carefully drive the story in a desired direction. The first to lay out all their cards wins. If you mention something in a story that relates to a card someone else has, they can interrupt and take control of the story. You can also be interrupted if you repeat yourself, hesitate, or say something that doesn't make sense. If you find it's difficult to push the story in the direction you want to go, you can simply "incept". "When the goblin reached the tavern, he met an old bard". The bard began to speak. "Once upon a time, in a faraway land, there was a princess…"

One very popular form of book in the early 1980s was the *Choose Your Own Adventure* line (Cook 2021). In this, I also include the abundant variants such as *Fighting Fantasy* (Traxel 2023) and *Lone Wolf* (Österberg 2008). The latter of these was my own personal favourite and still, I think, holds up pretty well even now. These books worked through branching and even sometimes looping narratives. The book would be broken up into numerous numbered passages. You'd start at passage one, and at the end you'd be given a choice such as "If you kick the dragon, turn to 88. If you run away, turn to 33". These books were wildly popular as they gave their intended audience (children) a chance to control a story in a way few would have otherwise experienced at the time. The book is a possibility space which collapses as the reader makes significant choices.

Many of these books included genuine game elements too – they weren't just jumbled-up narratives.

- Combat systems, as seen in Lone Wolf and Fighting Fantasy.
- Death and other failure states.
- Progression blocking via state management (as in, you can't go to section XX if you don't meet criteria YY).
- Character advancement (primarily in the Lone Wolf series).
- (Semi) persistent campaigns (again, primarily Lone Wolf).

The books form a genre of literature known as **ergodic cybertexts** (Aarseth 1995). **Ergodic**, because they are effortful to traverse. We must consider consequences and outcomes when we choose a branch. **Cybertextual** in that the outcomes that are produced are algorithmically defined by the inputs of players. That's a game framing but texts can be cybertextual without being ergodic, such as the *Tao Te Ching*. They can also be ergodic without being cybertextual, such as in *House of Leaves*.

This storytelling structure of branching and ergodic texts is reflected in many modern narrative games. You might have thought at this point that I'd forgotten this was a book about games – but here they were, lurking in plain sight all along!

One of the primary differences in game stories versus stories in other media is the implication of interactivity. Most classical entertainment forms (books, movies, plays, and so on) are heavily, and often exclusively, passive. You are the recipient of the story. Gamers, through the actions they take in a game, often have a profound impact on how a story is delivered. It's an almost quantum mechanism of storytelling (Heron 2017).

Games employ all of these different kinds of plot structures and conventions to tell stories. Some games enforce a linear plot where you start at the start, go on to the end, and then stop. Players here have control over the moment-to-moment story elements, but do not control the overarching story beats of the plot. You control your actions, maybe control your character, but you do not control the narrative.

Some games permit you to control multiple characters and swap between them at set points, or at your discretion – parallel storytelling in other words. Games as early as *Maniac Mansion* (Lucasfilm Games 1987) did this. Some games go down the story-within-story route, such as *What Remains of Edith Finch* (Giant Sparrow 2017).

Sometimes you only control the speed of the train, sometimes you also control the tracks. You might think to position a game on two axes. One is world versus game – how fully realized is the game versus the world? At one end, *Tetris* (Pajitnov 1985) – no world, only game. On the other hand, something like *Gone Home* (Fullbright 2013) – little game, almost all world. In a game like *Pacman* (Iwatani 1980), you need to invent your own reasons as to why you might want to eat a ghost.

Another axis is author versus player, in terms of who architects the story experience. At the author end, something like *Uncharted 4* (Naughty Dog 2016) where the story is the story and you can't meaningfully shape it. At the other, *The Sims* (Maxis 2000) where you are fully in charge of whatever story you want to tell. The major distinction here being between embodied stories (those put in by an external force) and emergent stories (those that arise out game mechanisms).

And Many, Many Others!

This isn't a book that is intended to be your one-stop shop for game scholarship. It's a map – an atlas, perhaps – to where you can find useful tools that can help direct your thinking towards productive ends. I'm trying to let myself off the hook here, because if given an unlimited page count I could literally go on and on and on. We haven't spoken about gamification, for example – how game thinking can create technologies that persuade people to interact with them. A lot of gamification theory is rank nonsense (Woodcock and Johnson 2018) – to much **ification** and not enough **game.** When well applied though, there's much to consider (Landers 2019).

We haven't spoken about games as educational tools or as vehicles for engaging with serious topics. Those are full academic disciplines of their own, and the interested reader will find an abundance of sources to dig into it.

We haven't spoken about play therapy or the idea that games can have therapeutic ends. There are plenty of case studies looking at how D&D helps troubled teens relate to the world (Chaplan-Hoang 2021; Li 2024), or how structured gameplay can help alleviate trauma in children (Quinones and Somers 2024; Wilson 2023), or even how playing games can keep our brains active and elastic long into old age (Bonnechère, Langley, and Sahakian 2020).

This book is not exhaustive, and while this chapter brings us to the end to our exploration of research perspectives, I would invite you to think of this as the start of your journey, and not the end of it.

Notes

1   It's fine, I don't play GTA Online. Whoever you're griefing won't be me. But... **I would** say that, wouldn't I?.

2 Stop doing that, you absolute monster.
3 As Terry Pratchett described the Bursar of Unseen University.
4 My first experiences with Fallout 3 were incredibly frustrating. I thought the game was **way** too difficult. The reason wasn't anything to do with the game, but how I was playing it. You're not supposed to play it like Doom.
5 This kind of self-reflection has a habit of revealing a number of moments where you ask, "Why on Earth did I do that?".
6 When you're caught out though, you'll have nowhere to hide.

References

Aarseth, Espen. 1995. *Cybertext: Perspectives on Ergodic Literature*. Bergen: University of Bergen.

Arjoranta, Jonne, Tuomas Kari, and Markus Salo. 2020. 'Exploring Features of the Pervasive Game Pokémon GO That Enable Behavior Change: Qualitative Study'. *JMIR Serious Games* 8(2):e15967.

Atkinson, Paul. 2007. *Ethnography: Principles in Practice*. sRoutledge.

Bailey, Veronique. 2017. 'Girls and Assassin's Creed'. *Journal of Games, Game Art, and Gamification* 2(2).

Banfi, Ryan. 2024. 'Disco Pinball: Declining Games and Depression in *Disco Elysium*'. *Games and Culture* 15554120241240018. doi: 10.1177/15554120241240018.

Barrett, Terry. 2011. *Criticizing Art: Understanding the Contemporary*. 3rd edition. New York: McGraw Hill.

Bateman, Chris, and Lennart E. Nacke. 2010. 'The Neurobiology of Play'. Pp. 1–8 in *Proceedings of the International Academic Conference on the Future of Game Design and Technology*. Vancouver British Columbia Canada: ACM.

Bietti, Lucas M., Ottilie Tilston, and Adrian Bangerter. 2019. 'Storytelling as Adaptive Collective Sensemaking'. *Topics in Cognitive Science* 11(4):710–32. doi: 10.1111/tops.12358.

Bonnechère, Bruno, Christelle Langley, and Barbara Jacquelyn Sahakian. 2020. 'The Use of Commercial Computerised Cognitive Games in Older Adults: A Meta-Analysis'. *Scientific Reports* 10(1):15276.

Campbell, Joseph. 2004. *The Hero with a Thousand Faces*. Commemorative ed. Princeton, NJ: Princeton University Press.

Chaplan-Hoang, Avery. 2021. 'Dungeons, Dragons, and Drama Therapy: A Digital Approach for Teenagers on the Autism Spectrum'. Masters thesis for Concordia University, Montreal.

Cook, Eli. 2021. 'Rearing Children of the Market in the "You" Decade: Choose Your Own Adventure Books and the Ascent of Free Choice in 1980s America'. *Journal of American Studies* 55(2):418–45.

Cote, Amanda C., and Brandon C. Harris. 2021. '"Weekends Became Something Other People Did": Understanding and Intervening in the Habitus of Video Game Crunch'. *Convergence: The International Journal of Research into New Media Technologies* 27(1):161–76. doi: 10.1177/1354856520913865.

Cote, Amanda C., and Brandon C. Harris. 2023. 'The Cruel Optimism of "Good Crunch": How Game Industry Discourses Perpetuate Unsustainable Labor Practices'. *New Media & Society* 25(3):609–27. doi: 10.1177/14614448211014213.

Crawford, Stella. 2019. 'The Ways Hellblade: Senua's Sacrifice Represents Mental Illness'. Bachelor thesis from Uppsala University, Uppsala. https://www.diva-portal.org/smash/get/diva2:1425591/FULLTEXT01.pdf.

Danielewski, Mark Z. 2000. *House of Leaves: The Remastered, Full-Color Edition*. New York: Pantheon.

Daschke, Dereck. 2013. 'The Institute'. *Journal of Religion and Film* 17(1).

Desjardins, Audrey, and Aubree Ball. 2018. 'Revealing Tensions in Autobiographical Design in HCI'. Pp. 753–64 in *Proceedings of the 2018 Designing Interactive Systems Conference*. Hong Kong China: ACM.

Duncan, Margot. 2004. 'Autoethnography: Critical Appreciation of an Emerging Art'. *International Journal of Qualitative Methods* 3(4):28–39. doi: 10.1177/160940690 400300403.

Ellis, Carolyn, Tony E. Adams, and Arthur P. Bochner. 2011. 'Autoethnography: An Overview'. *Historical Social Research/Historische Sozialforschung* 36(4):273–90.

Gamboa, Mafalda, Michael James Heron, Miriam Sturdee, and Pauline Belford. 2023. 'Screenshots as Photography in Gamescapes: An Annotated Psychogeography of Imaginary Places'. Pp. 506–18 in *Proceedings of the 15th Conference on Creativity and Cognition, C&C '23*. New York: Association for Computing Machinery.

Gansel, Carsten. 2012. 'Storytelling from the Perspective of Evolutionary Theory'. Pp. 77–109 in *Telling Stories/Geschichten erzählen*, edited by C. Gansel and D. Vanderbeke. Berlin: De Gruyter.

Harmon-Jones, Eddie, and Judson Mills. 2019. 'An Introduction to Cognitive Dissonance Theory and an Overview of Current Perspectives on the Theory.' Pp. 3–24 in (Ed.), *Cognitive dissonance: Reexamining a pivotal theory in psychology* (2nd ed.), edited by E. Harmon-Jones. American Psychological Association. https://doi.org/10.1037/0000135-001

Heron, Michael. 2012. 'Inaccessible through Oversight: The Need for Inclusive Game Design'. *The Computer Games Journal* 1:29–38.

Heron, Michael. 2013. '"Likely to Be Eaten by a Grue"—the Relevance of Text Games in the Modern Era'. *The Computer Games Journal* 2:55–67.

Heron, Michael, Vicki L. Hanson, and Ian W. Ricketts. 2013a. 'ACCESS: A Technical Framework for Adaptive Accessibility Support'. Pp. 33–42 in *Proceedings of the 5th ACM SIGCHI symposium on Engineering interactive computing systems*. London: ACM.

Heron, Michael, Vicki L. Hanson, and Ian W. Ricketts. 2013b. 'Accessibility Support for Older Adults with the ACCESS Framework'. *International Journal of Human-Computer Interaction* 29(11):702–16. doi: 10.1080/10447318.2013.768139.

Heron, Michael James. 2016. 'Ethical and Professional Complications in the Construction of Multi-Developer Hobbyist Games'. *The Computer Games Journal* 5(3–4):115–29. doi: 10.1007/s40869-016-0025-0.

Heron, Michael James. 2017. 'Pacman's Canon in C:A Quantum Interpretation of Video Game Canon'. *The Computer Games Journal* 6(3):135–51. doi: 10.1007/s40869-017-0036-5.

Heron, Michael James. 2023. 'Computer Supported Accessible Dexterity-Based Board Games'. *The International Journal of Games and Social Impact* 1(2):98–118.

Heron, Michael James. 2024. *Tabletop Game Accessibility: Meeple Centred Design*. Florida: CRC Press.

Heron, Michael James, Pauline Belford, and Ayse Goker. 2014. 'Sexism in the Circuitry: Female Participation in Male-Dominated Popular Computer Culture'. *ACM SIGCAS Computers and Society* 44(4):18–29. doi: 10.1145/2695577.2695582.

Heron, Michael James, Pauline Helen Belford, Hayley Reid, and Michael Crabb. 2018a. 'Eighteen Months of Meeple Like Us: An Exploration into the State of Board Game Accessibility'. *The Computer Games Journal* 7(2):75–95. doi: 10.1007/s40869-018-0056-9.

Heron, Michael James, Pauline Helen Belford, Hayley Reid, and Michael Crabb. 2018b. 'Meeple Centred Design: A Heuristic Toolkit for Evaluating the Accessibility of Tabletop Games'. *The Computer Games Journal* 7(2):97–114. doi: 10.1007/s40869-018-0057-8.

Hill, Geoffrey CE. 2021. 'Rethinking Economy-Building Video Games: How Might Designers Inspire New Economic Models through Video Game Mechanics?'. Masters thesis at the UOCAD University, Toronto. https://openresearch.ocadu.ca/id/eprint/3557/1/Hill_Geoffrey_2021_MDes_SFI_MRP.pdf.

Holmes, Prue, and Gillian O'Neill. 2010. 'Autoethnography and Self-Reflection: Tools for Self-Assessing Intercultural Competence'. Pp. 167–193 in *Becoming intercultural : inside and outside the classroom*, edited by J. Tsau and S. Houghton. Cambridge Scholars Publishing. http://www.c-s-p.org/flyers/Becoming-Intercultural--Inside-and-Outside-the-Classroom1-4438-2286-8.htm

Jackson, Alecia Y., and Lisa A. Mazzei. 2008. 'Experience and "I" in Autoethnography: A Deconstruction'. *International Review of Qualitative Research* 1(3):299–318. doi: 10.1525/irqr.2008.1.3.299.

Jones, Stacy Holman, Tony Adams, and Carolyn Ellis. 2016. 'Introduction: Coming to Know Autoethnography as More than a Method'. Pp. 17–48 in *Handbook of autoethnography*, edited by Tony Adams, Stacy Holman Jones, Carolyn Ellis. New York: Routledge.

Juul, Jesper. 2003. 'The Game, the Player, the World: Looking for a Heart of Gameness'. in *Proceedings of DiGRA 2003 Conference: Level Up*. Tampere: DIGRA.

Kim, Jeffrey, Elan Lee, Timothy Thomas, and Caroline Dombrowski. 2009. 'Storytelling in New Media: The Case of Alternate Reality Games, 2001–2009'. *First Monday*.

Kühn, Simone, A. Romanowski, C. Schilling, R. Lorenz, C. Mörsen, N. Seiferth, T. Banaschewski, A. Barbot, G. J. Barker, and C. Büchel. 2011. 'The Neural Basis of Video Gaming'. *Translational Psychiatry* 1(11):e53–e53.

Landers, Richard N. 2019. 'Gamification Misunderstood: How Badly Executed and Rhetorical Gamification Obscures Its Transformative Potential'. *Journal of Management Inquiry* 28(2):137–40. doi: 10.1177/1056492618790913.

Lawson, David Dyer. 2015. 'Building a Methodological Framework for Establishing a Socio-Economic Business Case for Inclusion: The Curb Cut Effect of Accessibility Accommodations as a Confounding Variable and a Criterion Variable'. Masters thesis from OCAD university, Toronto. https://openresearch.ocadu.ca/id/eprint/241/1/David%20Dyer%20Lawson%20Final%20MRP%20Report%202015.pdf

Li, Ben. 2024. 'Art Therapy Meets Dungeons and Dragons: Supporting the Development of Social Skills in High School Students'. Masters thesis from Lesley University, Cambridge. https://digitalcommons.lesley.edu/expressive_theses/892/.

Lowood, Henry. 2009. *Before It's Too Late: A Digital Game Preservation White Paper*. Lulu.com.

McGonigal, Jane. 2008. 'Why I Love Bees: A Case Study in Collective Intelligence Gaming'. *The Ecology of Games: Connecting Youth, Games, and Learning* 199–228.

Montola, Markus. 2005. 'Exploring the Edge of the Magic Circle: Defining Pervasive Games'. P. 103 in *Proceedings of DAC*. Vol. 1966. Citeseer. DAC 2005 conference, IT University of Copenhagen, Copenhagen.

Newell, Alan F. 2011. 'Ordinary and Extra-Ordinary Human Computer Interaction'. Pp. 107–14 in *Design and the Digital Divide, Synthesis Lectures on Assistive, Rehabilitative, and Health-Preserving Technologies*. Cham: Springer International Publishing.

Newman, James. 2013. 'Illegal Deposit: Game Preservation and/as Software Piracy'. *Convergence: The International Journal of Research into New Media Technologies* 19(1):45–61. doi: 10.1177/1354856512456790.

Ngunjiri, Faith Wambura, Kathy-Ann C. Hernandez, and Heewon Chang. 2010. 'Living Autoethnography: Connecting Life and Research'. *Journal of Research Practice* 6(1):E1–E1.

Österberg, Anders. 2008. 'The Rise and Fall of the Gamebook'. *Outspaced. Fightingfantasy. Net/.../Anders_-_The_Rise_and_Fall_of_the_G.*

Palaus, Marc, Elena M. Marron, Raquel Viejo-Sobera, and Diego Redolar-Ripoll. 2017. 'Neural Basis of Video Gaming: A Systematic Review'. *Frontiers in Human Neuroscience* 11:231323.

Pascal, Roy. 2015. *Design and Truth in Autobiography*. Abingdon: Routledge.

Perzanowski, Aaron, and Jason Schultz. 2016. *The End of Ownership: Personal Property in the Digital Economy*. Cambridge: MIT Press.

Postill, John. 2024. *The Anthropology of Digital Practices: Dispatches from the Online Culture Wars*. Florida: Taylor & Francis.

Quinones, Brian, and Shelby Somers. 2024. 'Utilizing Tabletop Roleplaying Games in Treating Trauma and Post-Traumatic Stress Disorder'. *Trauma Impacts: The Repercussions of Individual and Collective Trauma* 211:211–223.

Rand, Ayn. 1971. *Night of January 16th*. London: Penguin.

Reich, Clara Julia, and Kamilla Knutsen Steinnes. 2023. 'Barns Forbruk i Videospill Og Hvordan Det Påvirker Sosiale Relasjoner. Delrapport 2 Fra Prosjektet «Pay to Play»'. Oslo: Forbruksforskningsinstituttet SIFO, OsloMet.

Ribaudo, Nicholas. 2017. 'Youtube, Video Games, and Fair Use: Nintendo's Copyright Infringement Battle with Youtube's Let's Plays and Its Potential Chilling Effects'. *Berkeley Journal of Entertainment & Sports Law* 6:114.

Rogerson, Melissa J., Martin Gibbs, and Wally Smith. 2016. '"I Love All the Bits": The Materiality of Boardgames'. Pp. 3956–69 in *Proceedings of the 2016 CHI Conference on Human Factors in Computing Systems*. San Jose California: ACM.

Roth, Christian, and Hartmut Koenitz. 2019. 'Bandersnatch, Yea or Nay? Reception and User Experience of an Interactive Digital Narrative Video'. Pp. 247–54 in *Proceedings of the 2019 ACM International Conference on Interactive Experiences for TV and Online Video*. Salford (Manchester): ACM.

Roy, Rituparna, and Shinya Uekusa. 2020. 'Collaborative Autoethnography:"Self-Reflection" as a Timely Alternative Research Approach during the Global Pandemic'. *Qualitative Research Journal* 20(4):383–92.

Schreier, Jason. 2017. *Blood, Sweat, and Pixels: The Triumphant, Turbulent Stories behind How Video Games Are Made*. New York: Harper.

Silverman, Rachel E., and Desireé D. Rowe. 2020. 'Blurring the Body and the Page: The Theory, Style, and Practice of Autoethnography'. *Cultural Studies ↔ Critical Methodologies* 20(2):91–94. doi: 10.1177/1532708619878762.

Snodgrass, Jeffrey G. 2016. 'Online Virtual Worlds as Anthropological Field Sites: Ethnographic Methods Training via Collaborative Research of Internet Gaming Cultures'. *Annals of Anthropological Practice* 40(2):134–47. doi: 10.1111/napa.12097.

Sorrell, Steven. 2020. 'Digitalisation of Goods: A Systematic Review of the Determinants and Magnitude of the Impacts on Energy Consumption'. *Environmental Research Letters* 15(4):043001.

Szulborski, Dave. 2005. *This Is Not a Game: A Guide to Alternate Reality Gaming*. Seattle: Incunabula.

Taylor Jr, Ivan O. 2015. 'Video Games, Fair Use and the Internet: The Plight of the Let's Play'. *U. Ill. JL Tech. & Pol'y* 247.

Thompson, Clive. 2009. 'Learn to Let Go: How Success Killed Duke Nukem'. *Wired News*.

Tie, Anna-Lisa. 2020. 'Copyright Law Issues in the Context of Video Game Let's Plays and Livestreams'. *Interactive Entertainment Law Review* 3(2):121–30.

Tomić, Nenad Zoran. 2018. 'Economic Model of Microtransactions in Video Games'. *Journal of Economic Science Research* 1(1):17–23.

Traxel, Oliver M. 2023. 'The Reader as Traveller: Interactive Journeys within Fantasy Gamebooks'. *Travelling Texts–Texts Travelling: A Gedenkschrift in Memory of Hans Sauer* 14:417.

Vandewalle, Alexander, Rowan Daneels, Emma Simons, and Steven Malliet. 2023. 'Enjoying My Time in the Animus: A Quantitative Survey on Perceived Realism and Enjoyment of Historical Video Games'. *Games and Culture* 18(5):643–63. doi: 10.1177/15554120221115404.

Vogler, Christopher. 2007. *The Writers Journey: Mythic Structure for Writers*. 3rd edition. Moskva: Michael Wiese Productions.

Vozaru, Miruna. 2022. 'Reclaiming Agency: Engaging Non-Human Agency for a Nuanced Portrayal of Mental Distress and Recovery'. Pp. 63–76 in *Mental Health\Atmospheres\Video Games*, edited by J. Aguilar Rodríguez, F. Alvarez Igarzábal, M. S. Debus, C. L. Maughan, S.-J. Song, M. Vozaru, and F. Zimmermann. transcript Verlag. Copenhagen: IT University of Copenhagen.

Wall, Sarah. 2008. 'Easier Said than Done: Writing an Autoethnography'. *International Journal of Qualitative Methods* 7(1):38–53. doi: 10.1177/160940690800700103.

Wiesner, Adam. 2020. 'Contemplating Reflexivity as a Practice of Authenticity in Autoethnographic Research'. *The Qualitative Report* 25(3):662–70.

Wilson, Dava R. 2023. *The World of Dungeons and Dragons as a Therapeutic Approach to Complex Trauma*. Vermont: Liberty University.

Woodcock, Jamie, and Mark R. Johnson. 2018. 'Gamification: What It Is, and How to Fight It'. *The Sociological Review* 66(3):542–58. doi: 10.1177/0038026117728620.

Xiao, Leon Y., Laura L. Henderson, Rune K. L. Nielsen, Paweł Grabarczyk, and Philip W. S. Newall. 2024. 'Loot Boxes: Gambling-Like Mechanics in Video Games'. Pp. 1075–81 in *Encyclopedia of Computer Graphics and Games*, edited by N. Lee. Cham: Springer International Publishing.

Yin, Michael, and Robert Xiao. 2022. 'The Reward for Luck: Understanding the Effect of Random Reward Mechanisms in Video Games on Player Experience'. Pp. 1–14 in *CHI Conference on Human Factors in Computing Systems*. New Orleans LA: ACM.

Yorke, John. 2014. *Into the Woods: A Five-Act Journey into Story*. New York: Abrams.

Ludography

Barone, Eric. 2016. Stardew Valley [video game] [Microsoft Windows]. Chucklefish.

Bungie. 2004. Halo 2 [video game] [Microsoft Xbox]. Microsoft Game Studios.

Butts, Alfred. 1948. Scrabble [board game]. Hasbro.

Calhamer, Allan. 1959. Diplomacy [board games]. The Avalon Hill Game Company.

CCP Games. 2003. Eve Online [Video game] [Microsoft Windows]. CCP Games.

Childres, Isaac. 2017. Gloomhaven [board game]. Cephalofair Games.

Daviau, Rob, and Chris Dupuis. 2011. Risk Legacy [board game]. Hasbro.

Daviau, Rob, and Matt Leacock. 2015. Pandemic Legacy: Season 1 [board game]. Z-Man Games.

Epic Games. 2017. Fortnite [video game] [Microsoft Xbox]. Epic Games.

Fullbright. 2013. Gone Home [video game] [Microsoft Windows]. Fullbright.

Games Workshop. 2020. Warhammer 40,000 (Ninth Edition) [board game]. Games Workshop Ltd.

Garfield, Richard, and David Lezzi. 1993. Magic: The Gathering [board game]. Wizards of the Coast.

Giant Sparrow. 2017. What Remains of Edith Finch [video game] [Microsoft Windows]. Annapurna Interactive.

Iwatani, Toru. 1980. Pac-Man [video game] [Arcade]. Midway.

Lambert, Richard, Andrew Rilstone, and James Wallis. 1993. Once Upon a Time: The Storytelling Card Game [board games]. Atlus Games.

Lucasfilm Games. 1987. Maniac Mansion [video game] [Commodore 64]. Lucasfilm,Disney.

Maxis. 2000. The Sims [video game] [Microsoft Windows]. Electronic Arts.

Naughty Dog. 2016. Uncharted 4: A Thief's End [video game] [Sony Playstation]. Sony Computer Entertainment.

Pajitnov, Alexey. 1985. Tetris [video game] [Microsoft DOS]. It's Complicated.

Petersen, Christian. 2011. AS Game of Thrones: The Board Game (second edition) [board game]. Fantasy Flight Games.

Rockstar Games. 2019. Red Dead Redemption 2 [video game] [Microsoft Windows]. Rockstar Games.

Rockstar North. 2013. GTA Online [video game] [Microsoft Windows]. Rockstar Games.

Ubisoft Montreal. 2013. Assassin's Creed IV: Black Flag [video game] [Microsoft Windows]. Ubisoft.

Witch Beam. 2021. Unpacking [video game] [Nintendo Switch]. Humble Games.

YAGER. 2012. Spec Ops: The Line [video game] [Microsoft Windows]. 2K.

9

Animal Crossing: Turning a Space into a Place: A Reflection on the Psychogeography of Animal Crossing: New Horizons

Pauline Belford

Introduction

In this chapter, we will look at Animal Crossing: New Horizons (Nintendo 2020) through the lens of psychogeography, and of providing an ideal place to escape to from the harsh realities of the world. Psychogeography is an intensely subjective tool, and the nature of its application means it doesn't survive being extracted from the personal context. As such, this chapter is also structured as a personal autobiographical perspective about the nature of Animal Crossing. This chapter also draws on the concept of place attachment (Altman and Low 2012), which relates to the emotional relationship a person can develop towards a location. This could be due to one or more factors, or a complex blend of these, including nostalgia, familiarity, personal experiences, a sense of belonging, community, identity and security. If a space is defined as the where of a location, then a place is the why. A place is a space with meaning (Tuan 1979). I would argue that, through the work of shaping your island within Animal Crossing, we can explicitly build these emotional bonds, which deepen the more time you invest into making the space your place.

Psychogeography

Psychogeography has been described by Coverley (2018) as "the study of the influence of geographical environments – consciously organized or not – on the emotions and behaviors of individuals". Emotional resonance between people and their environment has existed for as long as humans have been fully conscious, and it has been a theme in literature stretching back at least to Victorian times. Psychogeography as a formal discipline only really began to emerge in the 1950s. The practice of psychogeography encompasses the derive (Debord 1955) – an aimless wander through a city, with the intention of being fully present and experiencing the sights, sounds, smells and activities which a

DOI: 10.1201/9781003530282-9

wanderer may observe around them. The intention is to arrive at objective conclusions regarding the psychological contours of the physical environment, although such objectivity is not actually possible within the intensely subjective focus of the approach. There is a gulf between the purported and observed scientific rigour.

Psychogeography is driven by the desire to extract meaning from how we, as people, exist within and without the external environments in which we find ourselves. As the psychogeographer Hou Je Bek said[1]:

> Psychogeography is the fact that you have an opinion about a space the moment you step into it.

The definition and practices of psychogeography are all usually based in the physical world. The prominent psychogeographers of our age are all consciously embedded in the materiality of real life and often specialize in the specifics of particular locales – London and Paris being two of the most common. And yet, there exist opportunities for leveraging the ideas of psychogeography in a wider sense, especially within the imaginary environments that make up the worlds of games and literature (Heron and Belford, in press).

Game environments can be deep, rich, multi-textured and vast spaces which have a strong impact on the emotions and psyche of the player. The psychogeography of game worlds has been largely unexplored, but for those who spend substantive amounts of time in these virtual locales, the emotional resonance (or dissonance) players feel is an important aspect impacting their desire to return to the game or not. It is this framing that is used in this chapter – the islands of Animal Crossing, by their very nature, represent psychogeographical playgrounds that uniquely link a player to their own constructed context.

Due to the unique nature of the relationship between place and person, psychogeography almost **has** to be autobiographical. The emotional resonance which a game environment is likely to create in a player will depend on a complex and unique blend of things dependent on both their in-game experiences and the life experiences they bring to the game. Due to this uniqueness, two players could experience the same game environment in completely different ways.

Games have a different emotional resonance depending on what previous games you have played. A player who has enjoyed Stardew Valley (ConcernedApe 2016) is likely to feel differently about Animal Crossing than one who hasn't, and the order in which they encountered the games will change how they interpret the differences. We are anchored (Welsh et al. 2014) by our life experiences. I loved the hills, trees, grass and mists of the Arathi Highlands when I played World of Warcraft (Blizzard Entertainment 2004) back in the 2000s. The resemblance to the Scottish Highlands brought to mind childhood memories of hiking with relatives and Sunday car rides through the landscapes of my youth. The zone was textured by those pleasant memories and the feelings of nostalgia I brought with me into the experience.

Animal Crossing: New Horizons

I began playing Animal Crossing: New Horizons in the spring of 2020, a little after COVID lockdowns had begun. As was true of most people, the places I could safely and legally visit in the real world were newly and unexpectedly constricted. Having only emigrated a few months prior, my closest friends and relatives were all out of reach. Part of the reason Animal Crossing: New Horizons became so explosively popular is probably the (fortuitous?) timing of its release (Lewis, Trojovsky, and Jameson 2021; Yee and Sng 2022). At a time when lockdowns were rampant, here was an opportunity to meet and hang out in a virtual space shared by millions. There was a real sense of community online, with many streamers and YouTubers showing what could be done with regards to island design, which in turn inspired players to create beautiful virtual islands of their own to which they could invite their friends. During 2020, far more friends came to visit Atlantis (the exceptionally unoriginal name I gave my Animal Crossing island) than came to visit me in my physical home. As the groove of visitors is worn into these virtual islands, an impersonal space can only ever grow into an emotionally resonant place. Those grooves contain memories, and those memories create connections.

Animal Crossing is a cosy game which affords the player an extensive level of control over what they do. Importantly for this topic, it offers opportunities to shape the environment – its physical geography and the non-player characters that inhabit it. Animal Crossing: New Horizons begins with your player character arriving on the island, alongside two other characters. All of you are looking to start a new life in this quiet, remote slice of paradise. You are elected as the residents representative, and begin living in a tent on the island. After a welcome bonfire, and some time spent tidying up the island, you begin working to pay off your relocation costs. The Nook employees (Tom, Timmy, Tommy and Isabelle) will give you some suggested tasks (quests) to do. Other villagers may also give you hints as to what you can do on the island. However, this is quite light-touch, and there is not much of a structured game after a few foundational tasks. After this, the game is largely what you make it.

Animal Crossing: Environment

The island in Animal Crossing is quite small. Excluding the beaches, they are just 80 by 64 tiles across. Players get to choose a layout for these tiles when their island is first created, but as time goes by, they'll be given the ability to shape the geography more profoundly. Whichever island layout you choose, the elements do not change. All islands have a town square with Resident Services, a river, ponds, beach, forests, and cliffs. The art style is cartoonish, with a warm colour palette and cosy feel. It's easy to feel charmed by the aesthetics.

On my arrival, the island (not **my** island, not yet) felt – okay. It was a largely blank space which spoke more of potential than anything else. The island is small – easily comprehensible – and as such even though it's a new environment, it's not overwhelming. It's impossible to get lost, even for someone as spatially challenged as myself. The art style is cartoonish but very polished, and the island looks pristine except for weeds and other easily dispensed with inconveniences. Jingly and comforting music accompanies your exploration. It all feels friendly and welcoming – a new pair of shoes just waiting to be broken in. There's no one unique factor that creates this impression – it's the combination of audio, visual, and geographical design that begins to wrap around you like a blanket.

The amount of exploration you can do on the island is kept very small to begin with. There are rivers which cut the island into sections – the layout you choose will affect how much of the island is available for you to explore. Initially, you are only able to access a single quadrant of the island; the rest is blocked off by rivers and cliffs. This too sets up an emotional resonance – that tomorrow may bring new opportunities that were not available today. The island is constantly promising to yield up ever greater secrets, the more we begin to make it our own.

This result is a very small area to explore, and this in turn keeps you close to resident services. It creates a kind of focal point around which all other development will naturally gravitate. It also means that you can't house the initial two villagers too far away from you to begin with. Whilst this can feel a little claustrophobic, it also increases feelings of community. You can't be a wild hermit in Animal Crossing, you must always be mindful of your neighbours.

The game progresses in real time based on the timezone where you are located. This means that if you log in at night, it is night in the game, and the main store (Nook's Cranny) will be closed if it is after 10:00 pm. The seasons also match the seasons in the real world, except that you get a more consistent and idealized version of these, rather than the erratic and turbulent weather you may experience in reality. If you visit your island in the middle of December (from a northern hemisphere country), you can expect the trees and ground to be covered in snow, and you can expect cherry blossoms on the trees in the first half of April. It's almost as if the island exists in your temporal reality – that it is tied to your own natural biorhythms and then of your physical location. Time in Animal Crossing is a property shared between the player and their avatar. This in turn builds on the sense of connection and nostalgia we experience towards the island – it is so neatly encapsulated into our own sense of space and time that it slots neatly into our expectations.

The downside of this is that our village operates according to its own schedule of opening times and availability of services. While it's not a problem for those lucky enough to maintain a life schedule that permits time for visiting their island during opening hours, it does create a sense of isolation for those who may be more inclined to nocturnal play. The relationship the player has with time is explicitly inconvenient. Animal Crossing may be a game of serendipitous neighbourly interactions in the bright sunlight or it can be a vaguely lonely and menacing game of darkened forests and spider attacks. However, if we dig into this, the game is perhaps telling us something about its own philosophy of spatiality and temporality – that it's important that we take time in our real lives to experience moments of relaxation in the virtual world. Everything in Animal Crossing happens in real time – absent glitches and playing with the console clock – which creates a friction in every activity. We are on island time now. Things take as long as they'll take. Patience is a skill you can train. My villagers sometimes tell me that I am always running around, and I should relax and enjoy the surroundings more. This gentle admonishment can be endearing if you have chosen your companions well.

This contrasts with Stardew Valley, where once you've done everything you wanted or needed to do that day, you can simply go to bed as early as you want, and watch time speed up until you automatically wake up at 6:00 am the next day. It's possible to speed-run a pastoral life in Stardew Valley. The Animal Crossing approach is closer to reality, and this does encourage you to spend time relaxing and enjoying the fruits of your labour.

As you engage with the activities of the island, new options will unlock. You'll get access to a vaulting pole on day two if you follow Tom Nook's orders. At this point, rivers become passable, and the rest of the "ground floor" of the island is opened up. After the claustrophobia of the first day, this creates a sense of almost transgressive freedom and awareness of greater potential. The island is now offering up more real estate for you to mould according to your desires. And, importantly, this also fulfils the implied promise that you will be rewarded for engaging with your island. If you get a pole today, what might you get tomorrow?

Once across a river you discover that there are upper, inaccessible, levels to the island. Moving the camera enables you to peek at the edges of the areas, and you can glimpse grass, trees, and, depending on the layout, a pond or two. Again, the psycho-geography of the island sends us a message – giving with one hand and taking away with the other. Still, the promise is there – if not today, then tomorrow. There is a sense of anticipation that new areas await to be explored, which nudges you to keep doing the tasks requested.

After building a bridge on the island (across a river) and creating house sites for some new villagers Tom Nook will give you the recipe for a ladder. Now you get access to the entire island, including the upper levels, of which there are two. The environmental aspects of these are the same as the ground level – grass, trees, a river, a pond or two, just in different configurations. It does give you access to more space, and to more resources with which to generate bells (the in-game currency) which you can use to pay for houses and infrastructure. These resources will also be used to create furniture and other items provided you have found or been given the recipes.

The Psychogeography of Animal Crossing: New Horizons

Small Space, with a Hideaway

While psychogeography is at least somewhat centred on the concept of a derive, the limited territory of an Animal Crossing island doesn't permit easy application of the idea. At least in an island's virgin state, it's hard to find an interesting path you never noticed when the layout is so easily navigated. There is however one hidden nook to find. There is a secret beach on the northernmost point of the island, which cannot be seen due to the location and the way the camera view works. Randomly exploring – much like a derive – will eventually lead the player to discover it. Alternatively, you may be not-so-subtly drawn to explore the unseen side of this cliff by the arrival of the scoundrel Redd's ship. This puffs out black steam that can be seen from some distance. Finding this hidden beach is enormously satisfying. It's satisfying too in a similar way to the payoff from a real-world derive when it leads you to happen unexpectedly upon a hidden gem in an otherwise mundane area.

As the other villagers do not climb ladders, it also gives you the option to have one small space which is completely your own. A location where you can enjoy solitude and where you are at almost no risk of being disturbed. Having such a space in the real world is very rare, so Animal Crossing offers a way to experience the tranquillity of isolation within the imaginary world you are gradually shaping over time. This spot gives you the opportunity to fully relax and just enjoy watching the ocean knowing that no villagers can come by to disturb your reveries. It has a certain meditative quality, like a hypnotic screensaver. You can largely relax in the knowledge that you will not be disturbed. This location can be a kind of emotional keystone in your island's development – a place where your own sense of elan can exist independently of the rest of the island's constraints. If Residential Services is the commercial heart of the island, this lonely outcropping can be the contemplative soul.

Incredible Customization Options for Your Environment

As time goes by, you as the player gain increasing opportunities to shape the island in the way you most like. You will accumulate greater numbers of recipes. You'll find new fossils. You'll get into the rhythm of discovery through quiet moments of interaction with neighbours. Flowers will cross-pollinate and spawn randomly, occasionally creating new and rare blooms. Shaking trees will reveal new recipes. Shells will wash up on the beach, along with messages in bottles. You never know, day to day, what will happen on the island and almost everything serves to incrementally expand the options you have for creating the unique resonance you want from the psychogeography of your surroundings. The geography and layout will remain reassuringly similar however until such time as you choose to make it otherwise. This brings the tension that can spark innovation and a desire for urban and rural renewal – a perfect environment which never changes can feel stultifying. The little changes and possibilities make the island feel a little more dynamic and help you remain mindful as you wander around – knowing there will always be a few surprises worth exploring for. It's largely all in service to the goal of allowing greater customization.

The gentle rewards for exploration create incremental incentive for **transformation.** At a certain point, your new options cohere in a way that creates an opportunity for a change in kind, rather than a change of scale. You'll find enough musical instruments that you want to set up a band-stand. Enough fish to create a public aquarium. Enough retro computing equipment to set up a special room in your home for it. Over time, your options begin to merge and intersect in a way that inspires grand, sweeping changes in your conception of your island. A limited set of options creates a limited set of horizons. The more options, the broader those horizons can be.

There are many games where you can customise a small part of the world: your character's house, farm, or stronghold. Animal Crossing is one of the few games primarily designed for solo play in which one might argue almost god-like control over the spatial environment is the core gameplay aesthetic. Getting to the point that terraforming is possible requires a deep engagement with your island, but at that point, you're also starting to feel a real ownership over the environment. Both the amount of work you invest in sculpting the island and the ability to design (and redesign) an island which closely matches the type of environment you need most at any point in time increase your feelings of place attachment.

However whilst there is an enormous amount of customization that can be done, it is all within the same art style or aesthetic. Although you can create mountains, the cliffs have to be built in tiers so that they can be climbed using a ladder or ramp. Each new level must be at least one square in from the edges of the base cliff. They will therefore always be accessible to you. You can round the edges of them, and change the appearance of the ground, but not of the cliff sides. This seriously limits your ability to create various landscapes and cityscapes, thereby limiting how you can impact on the psychogeography of your island, or the sense of place. You can't create brooding, inhospitable mountains or intimidating moors. You can't lock yourself into a horror aesthetic or a rustic Old West scheme. While the customization options are significant, they're not sufficient to allow all psychogeographical dreams to be realized. The plaza outside of Resident Services cannot be redesigned. You can't change the exterior of the museum or Nook's Cranny. If you want a wild, untamed wilderness this is not a game that permits you do this without some extremely clumsy workarounds such as dumping required buildings in inaccessible places and surrounding them with obscuring geological details.

Making Your Home Your Own

Partly due to the pandemic restrictions, my first terraforming was dedicated to the natural environment rather than townscapes. I enjoy spending time in nature surrounded by trees, rivers or lakes, birdsong, and as few people to share it with as possible. There is a spot called the Rocks of Solitude on the famous Blue Door Walk in Aberdeenshire where I have a very strong place attachment. I have been there countless times since childhood, sometimes with family, and occasionally with friends. I have often too been there alone.

I found the spot more spiritual and calming than a church, and it was one of the few places I could really switch off my brain. Mindfulness as a concept often stresses the restorative power of nature (Van Gordon, Shonin, and Richardson 2018) and much of our mental machinery is soothed by the soft, curving lines to be found in trees and lakes (Gómez-Puerto, Munar, and Nadal 2016). It was natural then that I sought to repurpose empty space on my island to reproduce an important place from my life. This involved building some cliffs, making a new and narrower river with a separate side stream running parallel, creating a multi-stepped waterfall, and adding some appropriate plants and vegetation. The fidelity of the island can only somewhat approximate the real-world geography, but it can still create a meaningful abstraction of the sense of the place – enough to trigger my brain to constantly bring to mind the positive associations with the inspirational landscape.

My Animal Crossing house has neither a kitchen nor a bathroom – the mechanisms of the game do not map onto our real-life biological necessities. This means that much of the space can be what I want it to be, rather than what I need it to be. As such, it contains both a library and a music room full of instruments – a way to capture some of the aspirational interior design that I associated with success in my childhood. I grew up in a small apartment where there was no space for such luxuries. I had one bookcase in my bedroom, and there were no other bookcases in the apartment. The walls were thin, and I could often hear the sounds of the television from two rooms away. As a quiet child who loved books, it was unsatisfying. I spent some time in the local library when I was studying for exams, and the sense of space, smell of books (biblichor), and relative quiet were something I have always wanted to be able to replicate in my own home.

While that hasn't always been possible, within Animal Crossing, my living environment can be whatever I want it to be, with whatever emotional resonances I feel are most necessary for a sense of happy ownership. I can imagine that the books in my library in Animal Crossing are the ones I have had to part with over the years. As a child, I also played the cello, which took up much room in my less-than-spacious bedroom. There was no room for a piano in my childhood apartment. The music room thus feels like a real indulgence, and the instruments remind me of some happier childhood times. I can hear classical music playing in my head whilst there. You unfortunately cannot play the instruments in the game, but the ability to sit surrounded by them is sufficient because they come with echoes and sounds that play directly in my head. They're important memories and longings, represented in pixels, and seared across my psyche.

In this though, there are limitations because Animal Crossing presents its mechanisms in an explicitly consumerist framing that requires the player conform to certain aesthetic expectations. Your island is judged by how well it meets certain criteria. If you want a true wilderness, complete with weeds and tents rather than shops, houses and a museum, certain aspects of the game will be closed off to you. If you don't collect or craft things to sell in order to pay off your debts, you won't be able to afford the upgrades you want for your island. If you want your villagers to become very close friends, this happens more quickly and easily if you give them regular gifts, and only if those gifts are above a certain value. Your Island Rating is based on a combination of things including how many upgrades you have made to the island, and how tidy it is. If you like weeds, wilderness, or even the convenience of leaving tools at useful spots on the island, you will get points deducted and have to listen to some negative feedback island inhabitants.

Similarly with your house, the Happy Home Academy scores and ranks your interior design skills based on categories such as having enough furnishings, placement of furniture, cohesiveness of theme, and use of seasonal items in decorating your home. If you like an eclectic home design or minimalist furnishings, you will not achieve the highest rank. You'll get nagging letters – each time they write to me, they give simple but irritating advice about colour schemes, furniture sets, and other things I have no interest in following. For a completionist, a lot of time could be spent to obtain highly graded interiors only to result in a home that doesn't feel like yours. Turning a place, in other words, into a space.

Where Everybody Knows Your Name

Another way in which you can tailor your island is through the selection of the other inhabitants who will live there. There are over 400 possible villagers, and you begin with two chosen at random. Three more will arrive early on in the game. Ten villagers is the maximum.

Forming relationships with your villagers is a prolonged process which feels a little more organic than in many other games. The process is similar to how you befriend townspeople in Stardew Valley – largely utilitarian and driven by given gifts. Occasional conversation. However, Stardew Valley's more flexible relationship with time means that you can speed-run everything from deep friendships to romantic entanglements. Animal Crossing's more sedate pace means that it takes time to develop friendships, which impacts on the extent to which we find them meaningful (Baumeister and Leary 2017). In return for building a friendship with a villager you'll find them visiting your house,[2] they'll give you gifts, ask you for favours, and provide you with new recipes and emotes. If you ignore them for a while, they'll react accordingly – becoming distant and passive-aggressive until you make it up to them. The unique mix of villagers may not impact much on the psychogeography of the island, but it is an important component in place attachment. There are vibrant online marketplaces where people spend real money to get access to the specific villagers they want. Everybody, apparently, loves Raymond.

Villagers also form relationships with each other to a greater or lesser extent, and you probably want to find ones who get along well together if you want the atmosphere on your island to be calm and harmonious. A friendly island is an island that is easy to love.

A Portable Paradise

Animal Crossing: New Horizons can only be played on a Nintendo Switch device. In addition to the psychogeography of this imaginary place, this also has implications for its real-world psychogeography. If this were a game designed to be played on a desktop PC, it would be tied to a room in your home, or wherever your computer was located. The fact that this imaginary world is found within a portable console means that you can take it with you anywhere. You can venture into this world wherever you might be in the physical world. For someone who gets restless when cooped up inside, doesn't have a lot of free time, and spends a lot of time commuting, this portability makes the island much more accessible.

One might harken back to the work of Nitsche (Nitsche 2008) and view this as a form of the **play** layer – where our environment is one of the places in which a game lives. There is a difference from sitting ramrod straight in an office chair versus lounged on a coach, idly hanging out with your virtual friends. The psychogeography here is more complex than in pure environments – the Switch itself is an almost psychogeographical device in that if you don't like the game you're playing, go somewhere else and see how it changes.

However, at odds with this idea are some of the dark patterns (Goodstein 2021; Zagal, Björk, and Lewis 2013) that are twisted through the game's otherwise wholesome design. You may only want to visit your island paradise occasionally, but the game has systems which coerce you into logging in more frequently – preferably twice per day. Some spawned items disappear if you don't log in, forcing a sense of Fear of Missing Out (Li et al. 2021), or FOMO. Resources are available daily and do not accumulate – use them or lose them. If you are seeking a particular island visitor – for unique inventory or services – you need to log in daily to check for them. Three random special items are available for sale in Nooks Cranny, and these change daily. Miss out on these and who knows when you will next get an opportunity to purchase them.

If you don't log in for a prolonged period of around one month, in addition to weeds and passive-aggressive villagers, the game will punish you by infesting your house with roaches. There is also pressure to log in during certain hours, not just for the things that happen twice per day, but due to shop opening times.

As such, despite the physical convenience of the Switch and its obvious opportunities for psychogeographically pleasing gameplay, the mechanisms in the game almost mandate an engagement that is less "pick up and play" and more "play or lose out". There is a considerable tension here between the technology, the medium, and the game design.

Conclusion

Animal Crossings: New Horizons is an interesting case study in the psychogeography of imaginary places. It provides you with a small, contained island world which you are free to explore and which, over time, you can craft and customize in an extraordinary number of ways in order to make it entirely your own. This is encouraged by altering itself subtly over time to provide regular opportunities to make new discoveries in the environment. It provides a largely blank space that you can transform into your ideal place, providing feelings of security and contentment whenever you visit it. Its release during a global pandemic meant it appeared at an ideal time when people were looking for an escape from the uncertainties and restrictions on exploration of the physical world.

It provided a welcoming, comforting space to retreat to, also offering a possibility of shared experiences with both your villagers, and an online community of players who were having similar experiences both within the game and in the physical world. Perhaps its most significant feature is that the game provides a place to retreat to away from the worries and restrictions of the physical world. A safe space in a world which otherwise has none.

Notes

1 https://thereader.mitpress.mit.edu/psychogeography-a-purposeful-drift-through-the-city/.
2 whether you want visitors or not – a nightmare for an introvert.

References

Altman, Irwin, and Setha M. Low. 2012. *Place Attachment*. Vol. 12. Berlin: Springer Science & Business Media.

Baumeister, Roy F., and Mark R. Leary. 2017. 'The Need to Belong: Desire for Interpersonal Attachments as a Fundamental Human Motivation'. pp. 57–89 in *Interpersonal Development*, edited by Rita Zukauskiene. https://www.taylorfrancis.com/books/edit/10.4324/9781351153683/interpersonal-development-rita-zukauskiene?refId=24f93d4d-87fd-44a3-bb58-0f5e536a9370&context=ubx

Coverley, Merlin. 2018. *Psychogeography*. Harpenden: Oldcastle Books Ltd.

Debord, Guy. 1955. 'Introduction to a Critique of Urban Geography'. *Critical Geographies A Collection of Readings*.

Gómez-Puerto, Gerardo, Enric Munar, and Marcos Nadal. 2016. 'Preference for Curvature: A Historical and Conceptual Framework'. *Frontiers in Human Neuroscience* 9:712.

Goodstein, Scott A. 2021. 'When the Cat's Away: Techlash, Loot Boxes, and Regulating" Dark Patterns" in the Video Game Industry's Monetization Strategies'. *University of Colorado Law Review* 92:285.

Lewis, Joanna E., Mia Trojovsky, and Molly M. Jameson. 2021. 'New Social Horizons: Anxiety, Isolation, and Animal Crossing during the COVID-19 Pandemic'. *Frontiers in Virtual Reality* 2:627350.

Li, Li, Zhimin Niu, Mark D. Griffiths, and Songli Mei. 2021. 'Relationship between Gaming Disorder, Self-Compensation Motivation, Game Flow, Time Spent Gaming, and Fear of Missing out among a Sample of Chinese University Students: A Network Analysis'. *Frontiers in Psychiatry* 12:761519.

Nitsche, Michael. 2008. *Video Game Spaces: Image, Play, and Structure in 3D Worlds*. Cambridge: MIT Press.

Tuan, Yi-Fu. 1979. 'Space and Place: Humanistic Perspective'. Pp. 387–427 in *Philosophy in Geography*, edited by S. Gale and G. Olsson. Dordrecht: Springer Netherlands.

Van Gordon, William, Edo Shonin, and Miles Richardson. 2018. 'Mindfulness and Nature'. *Mindfulness* 9(5):1655–58. doi: 10.1007/s12671-018-0883-6.

Welsh, Matthew B., Paul H. Delfabbro, Nicholas R. Burns, and Steve H. Begg. 2014. 'Individual Differences in Anchoring: Traits and Experience'. *Learning and Individual Differences* 29:131–40.

Yee, Andrew ZH, and Jeremy RH Sng. 2022. 'Animal Crossing and COVID-19: A Qualitative Study Examining How Video Games Satisfy Basic Psychological Needs during the Pandemic'. *Frontiers in Psychology* 13:800683.

Zagal, José P., Staffan Björk, and Chris Lewis. 2013. 'Dark Patterns in the Design of Games'. in *Foundations of Digital Games 2013*. Tampere: DIGRA.

Ludography

Blizzard Entertainment. 2004. World of Warcraft [Video game] [Microsoft Windows]. Blizzard Entertainment.

ConcernedApe. 2016. Stardew Valley [Video game] [Microsoft Windows]. ConcernedApe.

Nintendo. 2020. Animal Crossing: New Horizons [Video game] [Nintendo Switch]. Nintendo.

10

Domain Knowledge in Tabletop Roleplaying Games

Michael Heron

Tabletop Roleplaying Games

Before we get too deep into the woods here, we need to talk about what we mean when we say *Tabletop Roleplaying Game*, or TTRPG. Yes, I know – it's the definitions problem again but bear with me. Historically, I have found this to be one of the earliest points of bifurcation between what I'm talking about and what people **think** I'm talking about.

Let's take each part in turn.

These are games that are typically played physically – as in, around a table. Or at the very least, face to face. Zoom roleplaying sessions are increasingly common, and in fact, many of my favourite RPG sessions have been conducted that way. Synchronous play is the expectation. It is possible, albeit sub-optimal, to play through a forum, through Discord, or through some other remote, asynchronous medium.

I guess the tabletop part isn't actually that important.

Next, players take on the **role** of characters other than themselves. They inhabit these characters, deciding their motivations, their responses, and the actions they take within the fictive game world. You're not playing as yourself, you're playing someone completely different. Although many people do just transplant their own personality into the game, and live out their lives as a more exciting version of themselves. So maybe the role part shouldn't be emphasized either.

This definition process is going **terribly**.

TTRPGs are part of a tradition of **play**ful activities – we engage with the activity for entertainment, and not for a serious purpose. Except in all those circumstances where it's not true and we're playing to explore social dynamics, or crisis responses, or strategies for war, and so on. So, let's just write that bit down in pencil too.

Finally, they are **games**, which means that TTRPGs meet the characteristics of a game as we've already discussed in previous chapters. The actions you want to take as a player are governed by a set of rules that determine whether they are possible. And if they are permitted within the game world, the rules determine the extent of success and failure usually through relying on dice rolls or some other non-deterministic

DOI: 10.1201/9781003530282-10

mechanism. Except, even in the Juul model of games (Juul 2003), the flexibility of the rules – as in, when and where they apply – means that they're not clear-cut candidates for the clearest "game" definition. Oh no.

So, every single part of the descriptor is a lie, or misleading, or only partially true. Great stuff.

We'd be on firmer ground perhaps by talking about the expected features of a TTRPG – especially those most prominently embedded in popular consciousness. Oh look, it's familial resemblance again. There are many of these:

- **Pen and paper**, where players have sheets that contain the main character-istics of their character and update these through play.
  - There are though some RPGs that are entirely verbal, or played with only physical components.
- **Weird, complicated dice** representing the various Platonic solids.
  - Some RPGs however use cards, or rock-paper-scissors. Some use closed bidding and negotiation. Some have no randomness at all.
- **Fantasy settings** full of wizards and goblins and dragons.
  - These are very common, but all manner of settings is represented in the genre from the weird west to space paranoia to cyberpunk to the modern world. Some settings are striking in just how mundane they are.
- **An all-powerful referee**, usually known as a Dungeon Master (DM) or Games Master (GM)
  - There are a number of games though that have no referees at all, or where ownership of the GM role shifts as needed.
- **A persistent game world** with no fixed-end point.
  - Some games though are "one shot" – to be begun and completed in a single evening, or limited in scope to a few adventures.
- **Unclear winning conditions**, where success is driven by evolving character motivations.
  - Some RPGs have very clear set goals that must be accomplished, often in the form of the one-shot model mentioned above.
- **Development of character capabilities** over time.
  - Sometimes though characters don't become better over time, or their advancements are more nebulous, manifesting in conceptions such as "improved influence".

All of these features, and none of these features, are core to the TTRPG experience. As with most definitions, we find ourselves clenching sand that trickles through our fingers. There are many profitable debates to be had about what is the essential nature of an RPG, but we won't be having them here. Suffice to say, this is a broad medium and it often finds itself as the safe harbour for games that don't fit in elsewhere. Something that is often true of the people who play them. Historically, TTRPGs have been the province of social outcasts and misfits. I know, because I was one of them.

Where It Began

Let's go right back to the start… with chess. While chess isn't historically considered to be the first wargame, or even the **best** wargame – we'll talk about Chatarunga in the next chapter – it's certainly the earliest one that most of us would recognize **as** a wargame. And chess is what eventually evolved into the more formal, complex wargames – Kriegsspiel – that were used to train Prussian officers in the 18th and 19th centuries (Wintjes 2021). This is going to be relevant, I promise.

The thing about chess, if you want to consider it as a wargame, is that it suffers from its own design. Chess is fully deterministic, which is exactly what warfare isn't. Warfare is messy and unpredictable, and the world in which battles are fought doesn't necessarily conform to expectations (O'Keefe n.d.). D-Day was delayed by a weather forecast (Regnier and Feldmeier 2022). Command structures don't work properly in chaotic situations. Horses panic. Shots miss their mark. Knights fumble their swords. None of this is modelled in the systems of chess.

The wargames that evolved out of chess were stochastic – their outcomes were uncertain. Moltke the Elder once said "No plan survives contact with the enemy" and *Kriegsspiel* games were designed to accommodate that observation. The range of units was expanded to reflect military reality. The abstractions of chess – rooks, bishops and so on – gave way to light and heavy infantry, cavalry, riflemen, bombardiers and so on. Instead of elegantly gliding around an 8 × 8 board, they'd be mired in the physical terrain of a replica of the real world with all its hills, rivers and inconvenient forests.

Chess is a perfect information game, and war is all about imperfect information. You know where all your enemies are in chess, and you take a sporting approach where you attack and they attack. In a real battle, you don't know for sure how many opponents you're facing, where they are, and when they'll attack. You don't even necessarily know where your own troops are. This idea is codified into the concept of "fog of war", in which all participants in a battle have a different view on the lay of the land. To create a more useful training exercise, formal wargames would use a referee with a supporting staff of attendants. One "general" would issue their orders, based on a board that reflected their understanding of the battle. They'd leave the room, and the board would be restructured to represent the information possessed by the next player, who would issue their orders, and so on. Those orders would then be executed in secret, with each player being given a summary of what happened. "Your cavalry was routed but you did reveal the unit of riflemen in the trees on the ridge".

Dice were introduced to represent the uncertainties of battle. Troop morale, accuracy, the prevalence and consequence of weather – all of that stuff. If your low-morale, untrained conscripts fired a barrage of bullets at a charging cavalry unit, it was handled through a series of dice rolls which would be interpreted according to a range of considerations and modifiers. "You're firing at close range, so we'll use a twenty-sided dice. However, you're frightened so the roll will be at 2. Your lack of training is another -2. The enemy horses are tired and on the verge of panic, so +2. As long as you roll a ten or higher, with modifiers, your unit succeeds in hitting the enemy and then we'll work out how much damage you did".

The referee's job here was to interpret the rules, execute roles, and resolve ambiguity in a way that felt authentic to the experience. Poorly expressed orders might be ignored or interpreted in what **seemed** to be the most plausible ways. Any independent agents in the battleground, those too fell into the remit of the referee. They could introduce complexities as needed, and indeed standard scenarios with emerging narratives were often part of the experience (Wintjes 2017).

These were "serious games" in that they were put to the grim purpose of turning chaotic warfare into something approaching a science (Curry 2020). They weren't necessarily fun, and they certainly weren't designed for every-day people to set up and enjoy. The barrier to entry was high, and the command of military philosophy required to engage with it correctly was significant. These Prussian Kriegsspiel did though set a template for many formal military wargames (Lenoir and Lowood 2005), and the model has been replicated in modern and semi-modern scenarios. The Game of Birds and Wolves was used during the Second World War as a way of developing anti-submarine tactics against the high-stakes background of the Tonnage War (Parkin 2019), as an example.

It would take until 1913 before H.G. Wells (yes, of War of the Worlds fame) would publish the first "home" wargame. It was called Little Wars (Wells 1913), and it was designed around the use of the toy soldiers that were popular at the time. Many of us grew up with "little army guys" – plastic soldiers of varying specializations that could be used for imaginative play. Toy soldiers have been popular in Britain ever since the company William Britain devised a hollow-casting technique that allowed for producing soldiers that were considerably cheaper and lighter than those of their competitors (Toiati 2019).

Little Wars contained simple rules for various military units – cavalry, infantry, and artillery. It also included philosophical meanderings on the topic of war, along with suggestions for craft projects when it came to constructing convincing terrains for a battle. However, Little Wars was not intended to be a fun exploration of combat, but rather an advocacy game. Lizzie Magie attempted to convince players of the *Landlord's Game* (Magie 1904) that property ownership was a form of social decay (Pilon 2015). In a similar vein, Wells tried to convince the players of Little Wars that the cost of conflict was so high that the only rational response was pacifism (Peterson 2012). This was in the run up to the First World War, although it would have taken a remarkable pessimist to have referred to it that way at the time. "The Great War" was a more common contemporary phrasing. Tensions in Europe were at an all-time high, and the spectre of global conflict was looming. Wells wanted to de-escalate tensions with his own gentle exploration of the human cost of battle.

He did not succeed in that goal.

What he did manage to accomplish though was bringing a watered-down version of academic, professional war-gaming to a public audience that (eventually) found a lot of joy in the concept. It wasn't initially very successful, but over time, players fell in love with the tactility of play and its immediate conceptual accessibility.

By the time Little Wars had achieved its measure of popularity, it was also competing with a deep war-weariness in the civilian market. People were tired of conflict and had little interest in engaging in it recreationally. As the years passed though, the market for miniature wargames grew. More designers came along, theming wargame sets around specific scenarios (Kirschenbaum 2009). As the market grew, the community grew, and as the community grew the hobby started to gradually become more professionalized. Gamebooks, game variants and miniature models began to be developed in earnest. In 1955, Jack Scruby began to create the national and international networks that would eventually become the core of the hobby (Hyde 2013). No longer were potential wargamers separated by the tyranny of distance – technological innovations allowed for time to be sacrificed in exchange for a simulation of proximity. Telegraphs, letters, and phone calls all became the spine of the player experience.

This began to raise interesting logistical problems. *Play by Mail* games were very popular at a time before the Internet, but they often suffered from a trust deficit. If I mail you a letter saying "I rolled six d6, and every one came up with a six so I win", you are not exactly incentivized to believe me. Instead, conventions began to emerge such as "We will take the middle value of the stock price of this company, at this time, on this day, as the random number". While many of these workarounds cease to be relevant in the modern era, the culture of wargaming has never been stronger. The legacy of *HG Wells*, and *Kriegsspiel*, can be seen as clear as water in the design of everything from *Warhammer 40,000* (Games Workshop 2023) to the *X-Wing Miniatures* game (Fantasy Flight Games 2023) to Tanks (Gale Force Nine 2016) and *Fistful of Lead* (Wiley 2007).

A particular favourite pursuit of hobbyist miniature wargamers was to be found in replication – the design of scenarios, miniatures and rulesets to allow players to re-run famous battles. Many of these would be set in relatively contemporary theatres of war, where familiar conventions regarding the vocabulary of conflict could be relied upon. Many people would be familiar with how to model a cavalry charge in rules, but handling an elephant or an Egyptian war chariot would be a greater challenge. Over time, these small-scale reproductions would begin to be packaged up into stand-alone board games. Avalon Hill was a long dominant force in this area (Freeman 1980), and their interpretation of Gettysburg (Avalon Hill 1958) was the most widely played war-game for around a decade.

In 1956, Tony Bath began to develop a set of rules that allowed for games to be played in the medieval period (Peterson 2021). This was more than just doing a search and replace for "gun" to "bow". Not only do the physics of different kinds of weapons change, so too do the expected rules of engagement. Musket shots and machine gun fire are a far cry from swords and maces. Different models of armour (chainmail/plate-mail) required their own form of modelling in terms of encumbrance and protection. However, when codified, this opened up a whole new range of opportunities for wargaming, allowing for wargames around ancient warfare to be enjoyed as easily as for modern warfare. And, the canny reader may have already noticed... medieval settings tend to dominate TTRPGs.

The rules that Tony Bath put together would later go on to inspire Gary Gygax and Jeff Perren to create a system called Chainmail (Gygax and Peren 1971). This took the large-scale battles of other wargames and focused tightly down on the action of a few individuals. Instead of throwing a thousand horses at a thousand archers, you might have a handful of warriors who sneak into a keep to open the gates from inside. This is the core from which Dungeons and Dragons would eventually emerge (Peterson 2021).

Dungeons and Dragons

Gary Gygax is an incredibly important figure in the early days of D&D (Gygax and Arneson 1974), and his tempestuous relationship with collaborator and identified co-author Dave Arneson has been the subject of numerous deep dives (Peterson 2021; Riggs 2022; Witwer 2015). Chainmail eventually grew to accommodate a Fantasy Supplement – this added magic weapons, spells, and fantasy creatures. These were first expected to be incorporated into a larger war-game context. Eventually, it became obvious that the small-scale "heroic" focus on individual soldiers was perhaps the most interesting innovation in the system. This would morph into the first edition of *Dungeons and Dragons*. This was the first cohesive product we would think of as a TTRPG, and it set the framework for what would become a whole new medium of play. It is an absolute monster of the hobby – in the same way that every day people think "Monopoly" when you say "boardgame", they think Dungeons and Dragons when you say RPG. Although, as with anything, there is a geographical component too – different regions prioritize their own version of history.

Within *Dungeons and Dragons* though, we begin to see the formalization of a lot of core concepts. We see the idea of roleplaying introduced, along with the concept of a dungeon master. We see persistent characters that gained expertise as they accumulate experience points, with this expertise abstracted into the idea of a "level" in a "class". Classes included things like fighters, magic users but also dwarfs and elves. A first-level fighter was considerably less capable at the role than a fifth-level fighter, absent all other considerations. A lot of *Dungeons and Dragons* in its original incarnation looks awfully familiar to modern players, although not all of it. Over the years, TSR (the company that owned D&D) and then Wizards of the Coast (the company that bought TSR) have smoothed down its rough edges and tried to polish away some of the design legacy it brought from tabletop miniature wargames.

One of the ways that design legacy manifested was in an attempt to build a form of "simulationism" into the core of the game. Much of early D&D is almost fetishistically obsessed with the idea of arithmetic and lookup tables. Complex calculations were used in place of simple comparisons. Modifiers to rolls and specific situational adjustments were rife. The job of correctly working out how to apply the rules to a fictional scenario was complex. See Figure 10.1 for a few examples.

Perhaps nowhere is this more obvious than in the rules for working out whether an attack hits. Early versions of D&D used a system called THAC0, or "To Hit Armour Class Zero". Every player character (PC) and non-player character (NPC, controlled by the DM) began with an armour class (AC) of ten. The lower your armour class, the better. Characters would also have a THAC0 stat, which is the number they need to roll on a d20 to hit a target with an AC of 0. So, if your THAC0 is 10 and you are attacking an enemy with an AC of 0, you need to roll under ten. To hit an AC of −2, because of course they would go negative, you'd need to roll an 8 (10−2) or lower. To hit AC 5, you'd need to roll under a 15 (10 + 5). Seems… unintuitive? Yeah, no kidding.

Dungeons and Dragons did not start off strongly – sales were poor for a long time, and the survival of both the company and the game was regularly at risk (Peterson 2021; Riggs 2022; Witwer 2015). However, sales crept up as people began to discover it – often through direct engagement with Gygax himself. It wasn't long before the game became profitable enough to merit attention from other designers, and a swathe of other games came along to try and capture some of this budding new market. TSR, the company formed to manage *Dungeons and Dragons* and its ancillary products, was notoriously litigious in protecting its brand and its trademarks. That didn't stop competitors, although it did make them wary (Peterson 2021). Early alternatives to D&D included

I.B. ATTACK MATRIX FOR FIGHTERS, PALADINS, RANGERS, BARDS, AND 0 LEVEL HALFLINGS AND HUMANS*

Opponent Armor Class	20-sided Die Score to Hit by Level of Attacker									
	0	1-2	3-4	5-6	7-8	9-10	11-12	13-14	15-16	17+
-10	26	25	23	21	20	20	20	18	16	14
-9	25	24	22	20	20	20	19	17	15	13
-8	24	23	21	20	20	20	18	16	14	12
-7	23	22	20	20	20	19	17	15	13	11
-6	22	21	20	20	20	18	16	14	12	10
-5	21	20	20	20	19	17	15	13	11	9
-4	20	20	20	20	18	16	14	12	10	8
-3	20	20	20	19	17	15	13	11	9	7
-2	20	20	20	18	16	14	12	10	8	6
-1	20	20	19	17	15	13	11	9	7	5
0	20	20	18	16	14	12	10	8	6	4
1	20	19	17	15	13	11	9	7	5	3
2	19	18	16	14	12	10	8	6	4	2
3	18	17	15	13	11	9	7	5	3	1
4	17	16	14	12	10	8	6	4	2	0
5	16	15	13	11	9	7	5	3	1	-1
6	15	14	12	10	8	6	4	2	0	-2
7	14	13	11	9	7	5	3	1	-1	-3
8	13	12	10	8	6	4	2	0	-2	-4
9	12	11	9	7	5	3	1	-1	-3	-5
10	11	10	8	6	4	2	0	-2	-4	-6

FIGURE 10.1   A random sampling of lookup tables in early D&D (Image by author).

Tunnels and Trolls (St Andre 1975); *Traveller* (Miller 1977); *RuneQuest* (Stafford 1978); *Call of Cthulhu* (Petersen 1981); and many more. None would manage the same degree of market dominance. TSR grew to the point that mainstream wargaming companies such as Avalon Hill would find themselves squeezed out of what became the larger portion of what was still broadly considered the wargaming hobby.

There are certain conventions shared by a lot of TTRPGs at the time.

- There was an expectation that players would be proficiently numerate, capable of assessing probabilities and doing significant amounts of arithmetic. There were lots of calculation, lots of measuring, lots of estimating odds, and building strategies on the basis of likely outcome.

- There was a strong emphasis on realism of mechanism, if not necessarily a lot of realism of themes. Since slim rulebooks were easily pirated, an early form of ad-hoc copyright protection was simple weight of pages. However, the real reason was the momentum of design that came from wargaming, where realism was highly prized.

- Rules were mostly considered to be strict covenants, with the role of the Dungeon Master mostly being to deal with ambiguity and storytelling. Early conversations around D&D note that the DM role is about "rulings, not rules". There was little sense that the referee was engaged in a kind of collaborative game design. Rule Zero – the rule from which all other rules emerge – is sometimes used as a way to outline the scope of a referee.

Over the years, these conventions have been regularly challenged and revisited. *Dungeons and Dragons* is itself now in its fifth edition (Mearls and Crawford 2014), with a mid-edition refresh (known as D&D 5.5e) just completed as of the time of writing. It has undergone quite an evolution over the years – first with *Dungeons and Dragons* becoming Advanced Dungeons and Dragons or AD&D (Gygax 1977), then Second Edition AD&D (Cook 1989), the Dungeons and Dragons third edition (Cook,

Tweet, and Williams 2000), then the comically badly received fourth edition (Mearls and Wyatt 2008). Every single revision has resulted in rules changes, restructuring, and occasionally even reassessment of core philosophies. Certain elements remain largely true across all editions:

- D&D remains very mechanically focused – its focus is primarily on systems and integrations of systems as opposed to higher level narratives. Most of its three major rulebooks (*The Player's Handbook*; the *Dungeon Master's Guide*; and the *Monster Manual*) describe rules, spells, special abilities and character classes. Content that isn't mechanical tends to be de-emphasized.
- The DM/GM has full autonomy over the application of the rules. The DM is essentially the game engine upon which the rules run and how they are interpreted.
- The combat and magic systems are highly evolved, reflecting the mechanical focus of gameplay. The social and political systems – when they exist – are much more primitive and left to the DM's discretion or supplementary campaign settings.
- Each player is usually expected to have control over one main character as part of a group. Solo play is possible, but not generally encouraged. Players may also have mechanical control over hirelings and followers, but the "inner life" of both remains the purview of the DM.
- The game works on the assumption of a persistent campaign. As a result, character advancement in terms of gaining levels and equipment is one of the primary motivators for players.
- The game is expected to be broadly balanced, with everyone having a roughly equivalent amount of "cool stuff" they can do. In practice, this is sometimes a little ropey and over the years numerous philosophies of balance have fallen by the wayside. For a long time, the balancing principle was "Linear fighters, quadratic mages" – fighters would start strong and increase in power incrementally, while wizards would start weak and become exponentially more powerful as time went by. This meant that while the game was perhaps mathematically balanced over a whole campaign, it never felt that way in any individual moment.
- Magic is relatively free and accessible. Wizards and those who can channel the powers of the Gods or nature are not rare or extraordinary. This can create thematic weirdnesses in various settings – free access to spells that raise the dead or cure massive injuries has that effect.

D&D also tends to operate on a "setting agnostic" basis in that the rules are independent of the context in which they run. Not mechanically – we are still very much in the realm of sneaky thieves and noble paladins – but in terms of geography, politics and ecosystems. These tend to be offloaded into what are called **campaign settings**. Some of the notable ones include:

- **Greyhawk**, which was the campaign setting created by Gary Gygax for his own personal games.
- **Forgotten Realms**, which is perhaps the best developed and best loved of the settings. It's pretty much the archetypal D&D world. If you don't know

better, whenever you think of D&D you're probably imagining it in relation to the Forgotten Realms.

- **Dragonlance**, a high-concept setting where an overarching war between Good and Evil is raging between the gods and acted out by their agents on the world of Krynn.
- **Ravenloft**, a gothic horror setting full of vampires, ghouls and cursed souls trapped in their own personal hells known as the **domains of dread.**
- **Planescape**, a meta-setting that connects all the other settings together through the gateway city of Sigil, which is ruled over by the mysterious Lady of Pain and populated by zealous factions of remarkable ingenuity.
- **Dark Sun**, a largely discontinued post-apocalyptic setting in which metal is rare, magic is rarer, and life is a brutish battle for survival amongst the desert wastes.

Each of these campaign settings flavour the game, but they don't define it. They may introduce rules, new spells, new creatures and so on but they can't function independently. They do though allow players to choose the theme of their adventure through careful selection of the setting.

A Brief Tour of Alternate Systems

Since D&D is the 800lbs gorilla[1] in the room, it has a tendency to dominate conversation about TTRPGs. Its conventions and design choices are certainly massively influential. It is far from the only system out there, and there are plenty of others that have iterated upon its mechanisms and expectations, or even rejected them outright. We don't have space in this book to do more than briefly sample some of them, but the interested reader should certainly take time to explore systems that sound interesting.

Ars Magica

Ars Magica, first released in 1987 (Tweet, Rein-Hagen and Laws 1987) and 2023 in its most recent incarnation (Nephew 2023), has taken a completely different approach to how player dynamics should function in the game. No more were different player classes expected to be broadly equivalent in their ability to do "cool stuff". Here, wizards are vastly more powerful than anyone else, and magic is truly world-bending. The trade-off is that those who wield such powers must invest huge portions of their life in the preparation and execution of spells. They can't casually toss off fireballs into a bunch of charging orcs – magic is costly, and must be used thoughtfully. Wizards as a result are the most important characters, with everyone else bending the knee to them and the orders they serve. That seems like a recipe for imbalanced play. A party of characters is the heart of D&D in Ars Magica, it's the covenant's mystical stronghold that centres the experience. Everyone is in service of the long-term health of their home.

Since an effective party of wizards in Ars Magica is a functional impossibility given the way the role works, everyone plays a "troupe" of characters that are swapped in and out of stories based on narrative relevance. Perhaps you have a wizard, but also an experienced warrior and a thoughtful scholar who has devoted her life to the faerie world. When going hunting for supplies, your warrior steps into the frame, whereas your scholar is perhaps engaged in research activities for another player at the table. If none of your characters have a role to play, then you may take on the Story Guide (referee) role. Responsibility for running the game is shared around the table as needed. Character creation is complex and intricate, and easy to get wrong.

There's a lot more emphasis here on **players** rather than **characters**. Gratification is delayed in almost all of its main systems. The real resource you manage is not capability, but time.

Also stressed in Ars Magica is a complex socioeconomic structure. Mages exist only as part of an uneasy political convenience, acting as a counterbalance to the divine mandate of the church, and the otherworldly forces of the faeries and the infernal powers. This comes together in a setting often described as "Mythic Europe" where fairy tales and religious doctrines are held to be living, observable elements of the physics of the world. Managing these tensions is a major part of everyday activity, and it's usually the source of the "inciting incident" of the adventures that characters will embark upon. Narrative is chopped up in service of this, and time is often a discontinuous property.

It's a fascinating system, but perhaps not wholly approachable for newcomers.

Dread

You could argue that while the emphases in Ars Magica and D&D are different, they still draw from a number of common conventions and with effort, you could play a campaign designed for one in the ruleset of the others. Dread (Epidiah 2005) on the other hand is a horror RPG with game mechanisms that can't really be modelled in any system other than its own.

It's a (usually) **one-shot** system, where three to six players will take a few hours to play through a horror scenario from start to finish. Characters are not built mechanically, but rather narratively. Much as with *Ultima 4* (Origin Systems 1985), which we encountered in a previous chapter, we engage in a process of introspection through answering questions that outline personality. Questions are often specific to the scenario, but the rulebook gives a few examples of how they should be structured:

- Why will you betray the group if the going gets tough?
- What is the worst thing you've done to a loved one?
- Who else knows that you're a fraud[2]?

Notice the framing – not "will you betray?" but "**why** will you betray?". It forces players to create characters they may not like, which is exactly what you need for a game of this nature.

One of the emotions that tabletop games cannot easily deliver is **fear.** If people are the computers upon which the algorithms of an analogue game run, then you lose one of horror's main tools – the looming inevitability of the unknown. There are few genuinely frightening tabletop games, even if there are dozens of horror games. Dread understands that, and its mechanisms reach out from the heart of the magic circle to clasp you, the player, in their hands. Whenever you do something difficult in Dread, you don't roll the dice or flip a card. Instead, you pull a block from a Jenga tower.

The more difficult the thing, and the more contrary it is to your character's nature, the more blocks you have to pull. When the tower collapses, it is the end of the story – or perhaps, in longer games, the end of a scene. Nothing ends happily after the collapse of the tower. Played in a room with the right kind of ambiance, the mechanism can be thrilling.

Dread shows the power of game mechanisms to reinforce themes – powerlessness, escalation of tension, and the inevitability of defeat. Sometimes an effective game experience is built upon the back of a single clever system.

Blades in the Dark

Blades in the Dark (Harper 2017), henceforth BitD, is by far my favourite system for running a campaign. While it comes with its own extremely well-designed setting, I have used it most prominently for delivering a kind of grimdark version of *Terry Pratchett's Discworld* series – the city of Ankh-Morpork is in fact an almost perfect playground for the ruleset. My players were agents of the Patrician, sent into the city to do the kind of work to which he couldn't officially be linked. They were supposed to be covert. Unseen.

They were not.

At the end of every session, I'd write up a newspaper front page that included clues, lore, future adventure seeds, and nods to their exploits. Their activities were often... prominent.

I mentioned this not to get it on the record in the hope someone asks me to write an official Discworld in the Dark supplement for Blades in the Dark.[3] Rather, it is to show the kind of scenario for which this system excels. Several key concepts are core here:

- The system is rules light. A couple of pages of A4 can hold everything a player needs to learn.
- No forward planning is necessary on the part of players. Instead, players get a "load" of equipment, and you can choose the exact composition of inventory on a "just in time" basis. If you need a lockpick and you have an item of load left to allocate, then you have that lockpick. Similarly, you decide on the rough parameters of how your team will "approach" a heist, and the story begins *in media res*.
- Nobody, including the GM, knows what's going to happen. It's a form of **fiction-first** gaming in which you collaboratively develop the story beats.
- Problems are solved backwards. Every player has a supply of "stress" which is used to buy access to "flashbacks". Say you encounter a guard in front of the door you need to use. You can spend some of your stress to "flashback" to the time you followed him to the pub from work and slipped him some money to look the other way during your mission. Every game becomes like a heist movie.
- In systems such as D&D, it is the DM who decides how uncertainty is to be resolved. "Give me an athletics check, with advantage". In BitD, the referee and player decide collaboratively on what skill applies. The player has to give credible reasoning, but if it makes sense, it's applicable.

- The better you are at a skill, the more six-sided dice you roll. You take the best result from the pool. One to three are fails, six is a success, and four to five is the more interesting "success with a complication".
- Tension is generated through the use of clocks – segmented circles that are filled in at the referee's discretion.

What these rules together create is a framework for lightning-fast gameplay. No need to spend two hours planning an assault on the castle, you just say "We're going to sneak in as part of the serving staff, calling on our friend Jenny who is in charge of the kitchen". Roll the dice to see how it goes, and then smash-cut to the outcome.

'So, you're all standing on the execution block, nooses around your necks…'

The combination of systems lends itself well to feed-forward gameplay. In explaining how someone might want to use their "wreck" skill in order to convince a shopkeeper to give up some pertinent information, it sets its own context for complications and narrative. "I'll use wreck, smashing items at random until they talk". "It's a success with a complication. The noise from your wrecking has attracted the attention of a police officer in the street outside". This pushes the story in unexpected directions and almost always escalates the drama. It's a much more collegiate way to run a campaign rather than having a GM who is clearly the boss.

Ten Candles

Ten Candles (Smith 2015) is a one-shot, **zero-prep** game in which the player's job is to narrate the story of a character's death. Something terrible has happened. Nobody is sure to begin with what it is, but the nature of the incident will become known to you as you progress through the scenario. That's where the zero-prep element comes in – nobody has to plan anything out in advance, the game rules allow the narrative to emerge organically. Characters are defined with a virtue, a vice, a secret that someone else at the table knows about them, and a character defining **moment** that allows them to find a brief speck of hope in the endless bleakness of the world. Characters also have a **brink,** which represents them at the absolute ragged end of themselves.

Ten candles (literal candles, ideally) are lit in a circle. These represent ten little vignettes of story that will form the entire arc of the experience. To begin with, players have a shared pool of ten six-sided dice that they roll to indicate if actions their characters take succeed or fail. Success depends on the presence of a six in the roll. No six, and the outcome is failure. Traits can be burned (literally) to reroll any ones but in doing so a player must explain how their trait came to bear on the story. If they were cowardly, for example, they need to explain why cowardice played a role in the vignette.

Any remaining ones in the roll are placed to the side, unavailable until the next storytelling vignette. The GM at this point rolls the dice in their poll (none to begin with). Whoever has the largest number of sixes in their roll gains **narration rights**. The dice say whether things went well or poorly, but it is the person with narration rights who decides exactly **how** it went.

In the event of a failed roll, the GM always narrates the outcome, and one of the candles around the table is extinguished. As the game goes on, it becomes darker in tone, but also **literally** darker. The pool of dice that players have is refilled, but only up to the number of candles remaining lit. The rest go to the GM. Over time, successes become rarer and control over the narrative begins to be ceded to the referee. The traits, moments, and brink are stacked in a particular order, and only the top-most one is available. When a **moment** is lived, players get an additional **hope die** that doesn't get abandoned on the roll of a one, and persists after a candle is extinguished. When they reach the end of their stack, players can embrace their brink – repeatedly – to reroll every die in front of them.

It's a simple system, but incredibly effective. Players are told in advance their characters won't survive, and the only "successful" outcome is to achieve a meaningful death. The focus on a gradual siphoning of dice away from players and towards the GM creates a genuine sense of powerlessness as the game progresses. The candles – not just metaphorical, but literal – burn away everything their characters are as people in service of the goal of survival. And against it all, an unseen and unknowable threat continues to plague them – in the abstract to begin with, but increasingly as a directly malevolent entity that has a dark intelligence focused on their failure.

Brrr.

However, the element I have found most psychologically effective in *Ten Candles* isn't anything to do with its mechanisms, but is rather a storytelling flourish that book-ends the experience. Once characters are created, everyone records an audio message that represents their final hopes and expectations – their last official message to the world. They might talk about how they hope to survive, or ask that whoever finds the message seek out a family member. It might be a reflection on fate, or on death, or on hope. It's usually a little bit awkward, as it would be in the real world if you had to reflect upon your imminent demise without any opportunity for preparation and in the direst circumstances.

At the conclusion, when the final candle is extinguished and every character has met their end, everyone sits in silence for a moment and then those messages are played back. It is a stark moment where everyone reflects on the narrative arc of these people they were playing. Even the silly, nervous messages are underscored with a profound, helpless sadness. Perhaps **especially** the silly, nervous messages. You'd need a heart of stone not to have a tear in your eye at the end.

LARPs and Megagames

We also have to think about games that exist in entirely different liminal spaces, but share philosophical roots. These include *Live Action Roleplaying Games* (LARPs) in which dice-rolls are sacrificed for physical embodiment of actions. Where you have to rely on your own rizz[4] rather than your character's charisma modifier. These games are as much about the non-diegetic elements as they are anything else – they often rely upon a huge ecosystem of activity outside the game (Kamm and Becker 2016; Stark 2012b). Making costumes, developing character backstories, generating props (Simkins 2014; Stark 2012a). Similarly, much of the "resolution" that would traditionally be handled by a DM in response to dice rolls is handled outside of the session and the consequences reported on asynchronously. Some LARPs especially worth looking into include:

- **Conquest of Mythodea** (Live Adventure Event GmbH 2003) – a huge-scale campaign that has been running annually for over 20 years. Over 6,000 players and 2,000 NPCs. It takes place over five days, neatly blending a game world with a literal festival.

- **Monitor Celestra** (Bardo AB 2013) – set aboard a Swedish naval destroyer and inspired by Battlestar Galactica. It doesn't run any more, but the high production values were married to considerable amounts of digital automation to make people feel like they genuinely were aboard a spaceship.
- **Empire LRP** (Profound Decisions 2013) – a UK-based game that runs four times a year and is almost inextricable from its focus on political intrigue and courtly diplomacy. Imagine joining in on an episode of Game of Thrones right in the middle.

We should also in this frame consider megagames, which are situated in the vague orbit of LARPs (Johansson et al. 2024; Nicholson and Cable 2020). They generally have less emphasis on cosplay and also more tightly defined conceptions of winning and losing. They can be mechanically loose (more like a roleplaying game) but procedurally strict (such as a board game). They can also be incredibly intense.

Watch The Skies (Harrison 2014) is an excellent megagame with which I have personal experience. Within this, teams of four or five represent various countries, corporations, newspapers, aliens, or other discrete political entities. The aliens and the humans may, or may not, be in open conflict but they can't directly communicate. Individual organizations can only work with the information they can gather, which will be a tiny subset of the information actually available. The pace of play means that all intelligence gathered is partial, misleading, and perhaps complete disinformation that cannot be easily debunked. Members of a country will have internal roles, such as managing science or military disposition. Others may be responsible for conducting diplomacy, or acting as the public face to the press. Some others still might be responsible for leading the country and setting its strategic goals.[5] Essentially, *Watch the Skies* is a game of information silos, in which partial information and paranoia are the currency of the day. It's great fun.

Some other megagames worth exploring:

- **The Pirate Republic** (Megagame Makers 2016) – raid ships, manage commerce, raise settlements, and fight off other pirate crews.
- **Light the Skies** (Megagame Makers 2020) – Watch the Skies, but instead of aliens it's a brooding re-interpretation of the international distrust endemic during the Cold War.
- **The System has Already Won** (Engelstein 2022) – A corporate dystopia in a world of mega-corporations and industrial warfare. You have to work within an organizational framework to achieve personal and professional goals that may be at odds with those of your colleagues. Also see **Generic Office Roleplay** (Nothing Up My Sleeve 2018).
- **Rebel Country** (Megagame Makers 2021) – Star Wars, but with all the serial numbers filed off.

There are fuzzy boundaries between LARPs and megagames – they largely exist along a spectrum of their own. Megagames are often more structured, with turns and action sequences that must be executed within timing constraints. Often, one of the game masters will come by your desk and demand you roll a die or make a decision, and you might have no idea of the consequences or the context. The resolution happens soon afterwards and feeds into game state. LARPs can be more leisurely, with the social component often being more important than the "game".

LARP characters tend to be highly individualized, with complex characterization and backstories, and they may evolve over many instances of that LARP. In a Megagame, it's more likely that you inhabit a role with specific defined responsibilities. "Leader of the Alien Faction", or "President of the United States".

Megagames, necessarily, are highly abstracted from their context. Military forces for a whole country might be reflected by a small handful of tokens. In a LARP, you will likely have much finer-grained resolution – perhaps several players might be playing individual units of the Kingsguard within a military force within a country, which is a unit of organization that simply is too low-level to be captured in any sense in a megagame. Larger scale abstractions tend to be modelled and resolved outside of the game sessions themselves.

Many Others!

There are so many amazing systems out there, and nothing close to enough room in this chapter to cover them. All I can really do is throw some names and brief summaries out there in the hope you are interested enough to find out more.

How about the *Generic Universal Role-Playing System* (Jackson 1986, 2023) – GURPS – which is not just campaign agnostic but systems agnostic? The same rules work for space exploration and dungeon crawling; for fantasy cities and for espionage. Most systems are tightly bound to certain expectations of setting (see our discussion regarding Chainmail for an example as to why). GURPS rejects that convention entirely.

What about *Monsterhearts 2* (Avery 2017), a game billed as being about the messy sex lives of teenage monsters? Imagine Buffy the Vampire Slayer meets Degrassi High. This is a game about relationships, power dynamics, identity, and sexual discovery.

Then there's Vampire the Masquerade (Rein-Hagen 1991, 2023), which is a fascinating system of political, courtly intrigue set in the hidden world of urban vampires. New York, London, Paris – these are your playgrounds. The important thing is that you maintain the Masquerade – you must always leave the mortals in a position where they can credibly deny your existence. If you really want to give into the hunger, think of *Thousand-Year-Old Vampire* (Hutchings 2020), a "solo journalling RPG" in which you use narrative prompts to build the story of an absolute monster you won't be able to believe you created. In a similar vein, English Eerie (Hutchinson 2016) is also a solo-journaling RPG but you document your own story of the haunted countryside. *Frame 352* (Kent 2020) is a photo journaling game of finding cryptids in the real-life photographs you take.

There's World Wide Wrestling (Leary 2014), in which kayfabe (Laine 2018) and antagonistic promos are the way in which you set the context for a match to come. Or Night Witches (Merz 2015), which is about Russia's 588th Night Bomber Regiment – a military aviation unit made up entirely of women. There's Dialect (Fox and Hazzan 2017), which looks at the rise and fall of language and how context informs vocabulary.

That's only off the top of my head. If you want to focus your scholarship on TTRPGs, you'll find a massively rich and intricate family tree which you can explore and from which you can draw endless inspiration.

Social Contracts at the Game Table

A little more history now. The modern acceptance of TTRPGs is not a natural feature of the hobby. From the start, it has often been vilified as something profoundly antisocial and occasionally even dangerous (Gagné 2024; Wilson 2019). We've seen moral panics before in this book – early arcades being a prominent example, and violent video games being another – but none of them really match the sheer fervour of the public response to *Dungeons and Dragons*. To be fair, early versions of the game didn't shy away from explicitly occult content – they regularly talked of making deals with demons, and petitioning dark, evil spirits to selfish and self-aggrandising ends. This led a number of people to believe that the game itself was *Satanic* (Laycock 2015; Martin and Fine 2017; Wilson 2019). That must have come as quite a surprise to Gygax, Arneson, and the others at TSR who were often committed Christians themselves (Peterson 2021). The Satanic panic, as it is often known, is a defining moment in D&D's history and evolution.

Much of the backlash can be traced to a single incident in 1979. A teenage college student by the name of James Egbert disappeared one night from his dorm room in a Michigan university (Peterson 2021). The private investigator hired by the family was convinced that Egbert's many D&D books were a major clue. And he seems to have also been convinced there was likely money in that fact – for him and for everyone else involved. Preying on the fact that people had no idea what the game was, he began to make outlandish and incoherent statements about the nature of its design. This was amplified and expanded upon by journalists who seemed baffled by this new campus craze. Some spoke about it as if the game involved being locked up in a dungeon and then forced to solve puzzles to earn your freedom – a kind of mash up of Fifty Shades of Grey and an escape room.

The truth of the matter was more mundane. Egbert suffered from serious mental health issues and had hidden himself in the steam tunnels of the university during a depressive incident. He later killed himself, with the press citing his fascinating with D&D as a causative factor (Peterson 2021; Riggs 2022).

In 1982, a high school student by the name of Lee Pulling shot himself. His mother – Patricia Pulling – blamed the suicide on her son's interest in D&D, reflecting upon the Egbert incident. She first attempted to sue the school, and then she launched a suit against TSR – the then publishers of D&D. Her claim was that her son believed that a curse laid upon his character was real, and that he believed suicide was the only way to lift that curse.

Both of these cases were unsurprisingly dismissed, and in response Pulling's mother founded the group Bothered About Dungeons and Dragons (BADD) in 1982. This public advocacy group spent many years working with conservative Christian activists to publicly denounce D&D, TSR, and Gary Gygax specifically (Waldron 2005). Their mission was to make the brand so toxic that nobody would want to be associated with it and they did have numerous successes in that regard. Pulling is quoted as describing D&D thusly (Waldron 2005):

> A fantasy role-playing game which uses demonology, witchcraft, voodoo, murder, rape, blasphemy, suicide, assassination, insanity, sex perversion, homosexuality, prostitution, satanic type rituals, gambling, barbarism, cannibalism, sadism, desecration, demon summoning, necromantics, divination and other teachings.

I don't know about you, but I've never been so interested in playing a game in my life.

Jon Quigley, of the Lakeview Full Gospel Fellowship, is quoted as saying (Bean and Connell 2023):

> The game is an occult tool that opens up young people to influence or possession by demons.

Many parents did heed these warnings. They put pressure on schools, and their children, to eschew TTRPGs. Their children, on the other hand, didn't seem quite so keen to boycott this system that all the adults seemed so anxious to ban. The Streisand Effect (Jansen and Martin 2015) came into full effect – in attempting to suppress interest in the game, anti-D&D activists instead created an almost intoxicating sense of the taboo.

As a result, Dungeons and Dragons **exploded** in popularity. It went from $2.2m (about $8.7m in today's money) in revenue in 1979 to $8.3m in 1980 – worth around $36m in 2024. These relatively small numbers must be understood in the context of what was, at the time, a tiny industry.

However, TSR was stung by the criticism and worried that there might be a longer-term negative impact on the brand. Gygax in particular found it wearying to be forced, as the public face of the game, to constantly defend his creation against baseless allegations (Peterson 2021). Quietly, in the background, TSR began to "de-problematize" much of the game. Demons – out. The assassin character class – gone. Evil characters – well, we'll keep them but make them mechanically difficult to play. This shying away from challenging content would continue until Wizards of the Coast (who purchased TSR in 1997) relaxed the restrictions. Increasingly, D&D now faces criticism from the nebulous group known somewhat derisively as "The Woke". Wizards of the Coast and their parent company Hasbro have begun to resurrect more censorious impulses as a response to prominent controversies regarding representation. D&D, it seems, will never have the luxury of an untainted public perception.

That brief history lesson is largely an introduction to **why** tabletop publishers are so concerned about the social context of their games. There is a long-lasting consequence – far beyond any particular crisis – that ensures publishers take the public perception of RPGs seriously. One of the ways this is done is through a bifurcation of play into that which is "official" (at tournaments and the like) and that which is at "home".

Part of this is seen through a growing emphasis on ensuring that inclusive practice is established both in the rulebooks and the culture around a game. Increasingly, rulebooks devote considerable space to the importance of mutual consent at the game table – that's something that relates to content; to mechanisms; to themes; and to interpersonal relationships. Some of this is genuinely to embed an appreciation of "best practice", but some of it is also to stave off future PR problems.

This though raises an interesting question – what **are** your rights at the gaming table? How do you feel when you know your DM is fudging rolls behind the protection of a screen? Do you trust they are doing so in service of the greater good, or are they trying to exert dominance? Some DMs lust after the idea of the "Total Party Kill", or TPK. They view the game as a competition in which it is Players vs DM. Others see themselves as cheerleaders for their players, and are looking to craft heroic stories around them. Does the philosophy of the DM impact on how kindly you look upon manipulation of randomness? We've talked about how Juul (2003) would expel RPGs to the periphery of "gaming" because the rules are flexible. So – to what extent is it okay to take advantage of this purported flexibility?

We're going to introduce a new name into our discussion – Erving Goffman and his concept of Frame Analysis (Goffman 1974). This was his way of providing a framework by which we might understand emerging social contexts in any situation. Every time we are in a social encounter, we are engaged in an ongoing process of assessment and re-assessment where we take in the evidence of what's happening and contextualize it. Our understandings of what is going on and how we feel about it will change and evolve over time.

Social circumstances are dynamic and often subtle – and often much disagreement is down to how different people interpret a common store of information. How do we know when a friendly conversation is gradually becoming a heated argument? How do we know a friend is joking, and when they are hiding criticism underneath a façade of comedy? How do we know if a touch on the arm is a gesture of attraction versus a gesture of affection? When should we act as if **our** understanding of a situation is **real**?

Goffman contextualizes this into the idea of a "frame", which is an evolving, changing analysis of the context of our experience. Our friend laughed when we made a joke about our heated discussion, so we're good. Except that laugh had an edge to it, so maybe we're not good. When we tried to change the topic, they kept coming back to a point of contention. Their voice is getting louder. Mutual friends are trying to de-escalate things. Someone pulled a blade. We're not having a friendly conversation.

Frames can be social, such as in a game or conversation. They can also be natural, such as when we are talking about physical properties of the world. We might project our understanding, or interpretation, where it is not valid. We may ascribe malice to a thunderstorm, or a deep friendship to a distant colleague. Conflict between competing frames can be a problem, but so too can assuming that our own frame has a reality independent of our own mind.

However, frames can also be useful ways to create common ground between people. We can adjust frames by scoping relevant qualities or factors. Within a game of chess, one player might have gold pieces and the other may have tin pieces. We may frame this, within the game, in a way that means that all pieces have equal value.

If this sounds a lot like the magic circle again, you're right – the magic circle is an excellent example of frames in action. And it is perhaps in this that we see why the porosity of the magic circle emerges – it's often based on competing conceptions of what is and is not safely contained within. You may not have heard of the Gamer's Dilemma (Luck 2009), but it's a philosophical question that seeks to reveal the structural weakness of the magic circle as expressed through frame theory. It's basically this – "Why do most people believe violence in video games is fine, but would have severe problems with gamified child abuse"? It's the same thing, right? If a virtual murder has no real victims, then that's also true of virtual abuse. But… is that how it **feels**?

Frame analysis offers a way to conceptualize this in a more subtle way. We have agreed collectively on an irrelevance of violence within video games – that the magic circle is a semi-formalization of a set of common assumptions. We do not have those same assumptions when it comes to other topics. For those who find this too flippant a response, there are many answers to this question you can explore (Ali 2015; Bartel 2012; Coghlan and Cox 2023; Luck 2009; Montefiore and Formosa 2022; Ramirez 2020).

Ideally, competing frames align over time – independently and collectively. We might bridge our frames together, building upon compatibilities to focus on a common understanding. We might amplify one frame so as to exert its primary relevance over a competing frame. We might extend frames to bring in new context, people and viewpoints. And then we can transform them (Brenne 2005; Handelman 2006; Scheff 2005), which in the Goffman model is done through a process called keying. Goffman's original work identified four types of key:

- Make-believe
- Contests
- Ceremonials
- Technical Re-Doings

Each time we re-key a frame, it acquires a new layer. This process is sometimes known as **lamination**. We might watch children play-acting out a wedding rehearsal. The wedding rehearsal is a technical re-doing of a primary frame which is ceremonial, laminated to a second layer where the children engage in make-believe.

So, let's bring this back to TTRPGs. Imagine a scenario in which a player at the table is making another uncomfortable by having his character aggressively flirt with hers. Player A likely considers this fun, light-hearted roleplaying. Player B is perhaps interpreting this as a second-order form of sexual harassment – that harassing a character is also harassing its player. Here we have two competing frames, which must be brought into alignment for a mutually satisfying conclusion. Player A has laminated the primary frame of flirting into one of make-believe. Player B does not have the same lamination and is perhaps viewing this now as a kind of contest in which Player A must be shut-down. Others around the table will have their own interpretations. Perhaps Player C is viewing this as a commentary on social dynamics, and that Player A is actually "performing toxic masculinity" for the purposes of irony, which might be regarded as a keying into a ceremonial frame.

Managing all these competing frames can be disruptive to a game experience, and people often don't want to give up having fun in order to deconstruct toxic behaviour at the table. Increasingly this is being handled through the adoption of what have become known as **safety tools** (Quinones and Somers 2024; Valorozo-Jones 2021). These enforce a form of social contract around consent. The fifth edition incarnation of the D&D Ravenloft setting for example is a gothic horror campaign with an emphasis on the horror being kept to the fantastical and constrained within bounds. Even if someone being possessed by a ghost would be effective, the rulebooks stipulate it should only be executed upon if **permitted**.

This has profound conceptual implications for certain kinds of games. Call of Cthulhu (Petersen and Willis 2016) for example is built upon the idea of a loss of control in the face of cosmic entities of unfathomable unknowability. Their actions are alien and cannot be resisted, and probably not even understood. It's hard to imagine this kind of thing surviving the application of safety tools whole and intact. Cthulhu doesn't care about your consent.

Some popular safety tools include:

- **The X-Card**. This is placed in the centre of a game table. If a player touches that card during play, the current scene is skipped. No questions asked.
- **Lines** and **veils.** These are preparatory tools in which players pre-emptively identify topics, concepts or character types as a line (something they want

completely omitted from an adventure) or a veil (which can be encountered, but is handled "off-screen" and never directly)

- **Fade to Black.** At any point with this system, a player can ask that the scene "fades to black" and be resolved through implication so as to avoid having to engage directly with uncomfortable topics.

Some referees will use these tools regularly. Some will make their application a decision of the table. Some will reject them entirely. They have even been built into virtual tabletop platforms – as a mechanism for ensuring that nobody needs to feel uncomfortable when playing a game. However, we have already discussed numerous games where discomfort is an actual part of the intended experience – Dog Eat Dog (Burke 2012), for example. The extent to which such tools are necessary is something that everyone is likely to understand within their own frame. We cannot expect all players at a table to be able to compartmentalize what happens in play. Trauma tends not to be contained within the magic circle.

Systemic Models for Understanding RPGs

Finally in this chapter, let's talk about a few systems with which we can understand the structure and style of roleplaying games. Here, we're looking at ways to communicate mechanical and conceptual ideas about TTRPGs in a way that can generate greater clarity as to their design.

The Mixing Desk

The mixing desk was originally pitched as a design tool for creating LARPs (Koljonen et al. 2021), positing a series of sliders that could be used to give clarity on what kind of experience was intended, and how a game should be designed to meet that goal. Imagine a mixing console, of the kind you might see in a sound studio. Imagine it has numerous faders which can be positioned along a spectrum. Each of these represents a decision you need to make about the design of a system, although within a somewhat limited framing (Hook 2014).

- **Communication style**, from verbal to physical. Do people mostly **say**, or do they mostly **do**, and how do you communicate and enforce that in your design?
- **Openness,** from transparent to secret. How available is information about the game – are the broad strokes of the game available to everyone or do you need to tease it out from context clues?
- **Scenography,** from full to minimal. How all-encompassing is the environment for the game? Is everything you see part of it, or is it only a subset of things that are considered to be within scope?
- **Character creation responsibility,** from organizer to player. Do people get dealt characters with elaborate backstories, or are players rocking up to the game having created them themselves?

- **Game mastering**, from active to passive. Who is responsible for jollying the experience along? Does the game get started and then it's up to the players, or are there referees who will be influencing the flow of action throughout?
- **Storytelling**, collaborative versus competitive. Are people working together to tell a story, or are they working against each other to accomplish a goal?
- **Setting fidelity**, from playable to plausible. To what extent are players restricted based on fidelity to the setting? Would there authentically be such a thing as a female blacksmith, or a Black property owner, and if not does that make a difference to what players can do in the game?
- **Bleed**, from personal to impersonal. Should characters draw from real-life or be fully insulated from it? To what extent is the character the same as the player?
- **Representation of theme,** from abstract to simulation. Is the setting simply for ambiance or is it a rigorous replica? Is it loose enough to encompass the introduction of "alien" ideas, or should it be self-consistent?
- **Meta-Techniques**, from intrusive to discreet. How is information given to players, and to what extent do players need to enforce their own distinction between what they know and what their characters know?
- **Player pressure**, from hardcore to pretence. How do you model mechanisms such as hunger, exhaustion, or damage? Are players expected to eat, drink, and have sex in service of the story or do you simulate it through fake food, fake drink, and fake intimacy?

You can hopefully see how this would be useful as a design tool, but in my view, it is also excellent as an analysis tool. Much like with the MDA Framework (Hunicke, LeBlanc, and Zubek 2004), you can use this top to bottom as well as bottom to top. Start with a system of your choice, D&D for example, and position the sliders where you feel they belong as a consequence of your experiences. Cross-reference this with others and see where you have agreement and disagreement. There's a starting point for meaningful scholarship.

The GNS Model

You can profitably combine the mixing desk above with a concept known as the GNS Model (White 2020) to "chunk" a game into where it fits according to three broad categories:

- Consider how much of it is in service of a **game**, where players are expected to overcome challenges through skill or ingenuity. How much does winning matter, and how is winning reflected in terms of mechanical systems? How much of the system is in service to the mechanisms?
- Consider how much of it is in service of **narrative** – how well supported are players in developing interesting characters, exploring complex motivations, and evolving their characters through engagement with external forces? Or, how much of the system is in service to the story?
- Consider how much of it is in service to **simulation** – to what extent is a game system internally consistent, and how do the game systems ensure outcomes that are appropriate for the setting? How much of the system is in service to the world?

Every game becomes a data-point within a triangle here. Or perhaps, we might argue that every game **system** occupies a certain morphable region within the triad (see Figure 10.2 for a representative, not definitive example). Different players and different DMs will lead to different experiences. Some DMs for example are driven primarily by what's called the **rule of cool** – if players suggest doing something awesomely heroic then the DM will bend the mechanisms of the game to permit it to happen. This is in stark comparison to the principle of RAW, or **Rules as Written**. Under the rule of cool, you might permit a player to cartwheel off of a mezzanine onto a swinging chandelier, then leap off to ambush a villain underneath. Maybe you do that as a single athletics check with disadvantage (as in, players roll twice and take the worst result). Properly, there are a lot of individual mechanisms that come into play when doing it authentically. The official rules in a TTRPG, as we have discussed, are malleable, and it's one of the things that keeps them on the periphery of almost every formal definition of games.

The GNS model gives you a way of conceptualising a truth of TTRPGs – not every system works equally well for all kinds of settings. It's also the way we can bring in some of the insight of the "Engineer's Triangle" into game analysis – you know the old rule, "Fast, Cheap, Good – pick any two". Here, extreme service to one point of the triangle inevitably impacts on the others. Games that are all about internal moments and character triumphs will find it hard to be true to a simulation of the world. Games that are all about simulation will find it hard to support organic and believable moments of extraordinary heroism. Everything is a trade-off.

Rules Frameworks

We've already spoken a little bit about the idea of where a game lives. Informally in discourse we sometimes talk about tabletop games being **rules heavy** or **rules light**

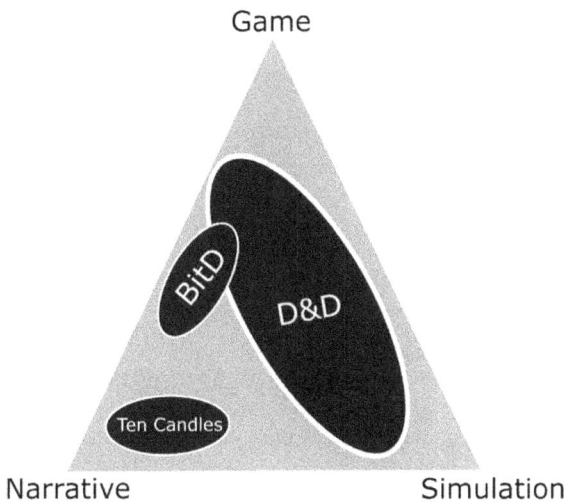

FIGURE 10.2 An example GNS analysis of Ten Candles versus D&D versus Blades in the Dark (Author's image).

(whether they are primarily mechanistic or narrative). The word "crunchy" is sometimes used in board game discourse to talk about the way in which the mechanisms of a game interlock (think of gears crunching against each other). The book *Rules of Play* (Tekinbas and Zimmerman 2003) offers an interesting lens on what rules are, and what goals they are supposed to accomplish. In this model, there are three categories:

- **Operational rules**. These are the formal written rules, or "rules of play", that outline how the mechanisms are supposed to function. The systemic part of games.
- **Constitutive Rules**. These are the formal structures that underpin the game. "Do this, and X is the consequence". This is where emergence usually lives.
- **Implicit Rules**. These are the social rules – be a good sport, narrate your turns, no takebacks.

This is a way of thinking about "the rules of the game" versus the more general "rules of gaming". We tend to think of rules in many games as inviolable – they must be followed in order to be playing a game at all. Partly this is down to the impact of deviation from game rules – even small, seemingly inconsequential changes can have a huge impact. "Take a card from the centre" and an end-of-round rule to "replenish centre cards" versus "Take and replenish a card from the centre" can massively change the flow and impact of a game. In one, if you get to take two cards from the centre, the second time you have a diminished set of options. In the other, your options always scale to the number of cards you are permitted to take. The distinction between "play a card face up" and "play a card face down" can completely recontextualize strategy. Bjork and Zagal (Björk and Zagal 2018) address some of the competing design challenges that come with formalizing rules:

- The familiar versus the novel
- Licenced content versus original content
- Rules versus setting
- Improvisation versus formalism

One of the things that RPGs and board games permit in a way that isn't so true of video games is that they are almost infinitely moddable. Video game modding certainly exists but it has a relatively high barrier to entry – you must learn the software development kits; master a programming language; develop code that interacts cleanly with the SDK; and integrate a mod with all the other possible mods someone may employ.

On the tabletop though, what you have is a perfect laboratory for investigating systemic aspects of a design. The mechanisms are there for you to modify and twist and bend. Few things are more illustrative of the intention behind a rule than removing it to see what happens. House ruling games are often a way to solve perceived problems, but few house-rulers are actually formally interrogating design consequences. As such, new copies of Monopoly now come with an insert that makes it clear that many common rules aren't actually real rules.

The final tool you have, as far as this chapter goes, is experimentation. If the best way to learn how a watch works is to take it apart, you can perhaps expand that logic to tabletop games. See what happens if a mechanism is altered or removed and assess the impact it has on the way the game plays. What happens in Poker if every other card in your hand is face up? What happens if you get to roll three dice in Monopoly and pick the two you like best?

Meddling without thought is an easy way to break a game. And a watch. Intentional and thoughtful modification of the structure of a game and how changes impact on the design – well, that's a different matter entirely.

Notes

1 363kg gorilla to those of us more comfortable with the metric system.
2 Everyone. I once gave a talk at a seminar on imposter syndrome in which I declared my status as a fraud out loud. I figured nobody could fire me for it once I'd gotten it on the official record.
3 But just in case – heronm@chalmers.se.
4 Kids, did I use that right?
5 This was me, and it gave me a massive amount of sympathy for real world leaders because I never once knew what was happening, or what we should do about it.

References

Ali, Rami. 2015. 'A New Solution to the Gamer's Dilemma'. *Ethics and Information Technology* 17(4):267–74.

Bartel, Christopher. 2012. 'Resolving the Gamer's Dilemma'. *Ethics and Information Technology* 14:11–16.

Bean, Anthony, and Megan Connell. 2023. 'The Rise of the Use of TTRPGs and RPGs in Therapeutic Endeavors'. *Journal of Psychology and Psychotherapy Research* 10:1–12.

Björk, Staffan, and José P. Zagal. 2018. 'Game Design and Role-Playing Games'. Pp. 323–36 in *Role-Playing Game Studies*, edited by Sebastian Deterding and Jose Zagal. Abingdon: Routledge.

Brenne, Geir Tore. 2005. 'Making and Maintaining Frames: A Study of Metacommunication in Laiv Play'. Master's Thesis.

Coghlan, Thomas, and Damian Cox. 2023. 'Between Death and Suffering: Resolving the Gamer's Dilemma'. *Ethics and Information Technology* 25(3):37. doi: 10.1007/s10676-023-09711-z.

Curry, John. 2020. 'Professional Wargaming: A Flawed but Useful Tool'. *Simulation & Gaming* 51(5):612–31. doi: 10.1177/1046878120901852.

Freeman, Jon. 1980. *The Complete Book of Wargames*. New York: Simon and Schuster.

Gagné, Alex. 2024. 'In Defense of Imagination: Canadian Youth Culture and the *Dungeons & Dragons* Panic in Canada, 1980–1995'. *Games and Culture* 15554120241276931. doi: 10.1177/15554120241276931.

Goffman, Erving. 1974. 'Frame Analysis: An Essay on the Organization of Experience'. *Northeastern UP*. Boston: Northeastern University Press.

Handelman, Don. 2006. 'Framing'. Pp. 571–82 in *Theorizing Rituals, Volume 1: Issues, Topics, Approaches, Concepts*, Jens Kreinath Jan Snoek, and Michael Stausberg. Boston: Brill.

Hook, Nathan. 2014. 'A Critical Review of the Mixing Desk'. *The Cutting Edge of Nordic Larp* 51. Knutpunk.

Hunicke, Robin, Marc LeBlanc, and Robert Zubek. 2004. 'MDA: A Formal Approach to Game Design and Game Research'. P. 1722 in *Proceedings of the AAAI Workshop on Challenges in Game AI*. Vol. 4. San Jose, CA: Association for the Advancement of Artificial Intelligence.

Hyde, Henry. 2013. *The Wargaming Compendium*. Philadelphia: Casemate Publishers.

Jansen, Sue Curry, and Brian Martin. 2015. 'The Streisand Effect and Censorship Backfire'. *International Journal of Communication* 9:16.

Johansson, Karin, Raquel Robinson, Jon Back, Sarah Lynne Bowman, James Fey, Elena Márquez Segura, Annika Waern, and Katherine Isbister. 2024. 'Why Larp? A Synthesis Article on Live Action Roleplay in Relation to HCI Research and Practice'. *ACM Transactions on Computer-Human Interaction* 31(5):1–35. doi: 10.1145/3689045.

Juul, Jesper. 2003. 'The Game, the Player, the World: Looking for a Heart of Gameness'. in *Proceedings of DiGRA 2003 Conference: Level Up*.

Kamm, Bjorne-Ole, and Julia Becker. 2016. 'Live-Action Role-Play or the Performance of Realities'. Pp. 35–51 in *Simulation and Gaming in the Network Society*. Vol. 9, *Translational Systems Sciences*, edited by T. Kaneda, H. Kanegae, Y. Toyoda, and P. Rizzi. Singapore: Springer Singapore.

Kirschenbaum, Matthew. 2009. 'War Stories: Board Wargames and (Vast) Procedural Narratives'. pp. 357–71 in *Third Person: Authoring and Exploring Vast Narratives*, edited by Pat Harrigan and Noah Wardrip-Fruin. MIT Press: Massachusetts, USA.

Koljonen, Johanna, Jaakko Stenros, Anne Serup Grove, Aina D. Skjønsfjell, and Elin Nilsen. 2021. *Larp Design: Creating Role-Play Experiences*. Copenhagen: Landsforeningen Bifrost.

Laine, Eero. 2018. 'Professional Wrestling Scholarship: Legitimacy and Kayfabe'. *The Popular Culture Studies Journal* 6(1):82–99.

Laycock, Joseph P. 2015. *Dangerous Games: What the Moral Panic over Role-Playing Games Says about Play, Religion, and Imagined Worlds*. California: University of California Press.

Lenoir, Timothy, and Henry Lowood. 2005. 'Theaters of War: The Military-Entertainment Complex'. Pp. 427–56 in *Collection - Laboratory - Theater*, edited by H. Schramm, L. Schwarte, and J. Lazardzig. Berlin: Walter de Gruyter.

Luck, Morgan. 2009. 'The Gamer's Dilemma: An Analysis of the Arguments for the Moral Distinction between Virtual Murder and Virtual Paedophilia'. *Ethics and Information Technology* 11(1):31–36.

Martin, Daniel, and Gary Alan Fine. 2017. 'Satanic Cults, Satanic Play: Is "Dungeons & Dragons" a Breeding Ground for the Devil?' Pp. 107–24 in *The Satanism Scare*, edited by James Richardson, Joel Best and David Bromley. Abingdon: Routledge.

Montefiore, Thomas, and Paul Formosa. 2022. 'Resisting the Gamer's Dilemma'. *Ethics and Information Technology* 24(3):31. doi: 10.1007/s10676-022-09655-w.

Nicholson, Scott, and Liz Cable. 2020. 'Unlocking the Potential of Puzzle-Based Learning: Designing Escape Rooms and Games for the Classroom'. Los Angeles: Sage Publications Ltd.

O'Keefe, MAJ Patrick. n.d. 'You Need to Play Wargames'. https://www.benning.army.mil/armor/eARMOR/content/issues/2023/Summer/3OKeefe23.pdf.

Parkin, Simon. 2019. *A Game of Birds and Wolves: The Secret Game That Revolutionised the War*. London: Hachette.

Peterson, Jon. 2012. *Playing at the World: A History of Simulating Wars, People and Fantastic Adventures, from Chess to Role-Playing Games*. San Diego, CA: Unreason Press.

Peterson, Jon. 2021. *Game Wizards: The Epic Battle for Dungeons & Dragons*. Cambridge: MIT Press.

Pilon, Mary. 2015. *The Monopolists: Obsession, Fury, and the Scandal Behind the World's Favorite Board Game*. New York: Bloomsbury Publishing USA.

Quinones, Brian, and Shelby Somers. 2024. 'Utilizing Tabletop Roleplaying Games in Treating Trauma and Post-Traumatic Stress Disorder'. *Trauma Impacts: The Repercussions of Individual and Collective Trauma* 211:211–223.

Ramirez, Erick Jose. 2020. 'How to (Dis) Solve the Gamer's Dilemma'. *Ethical Theory and Moral Practice* 23(1):141–61.

Regnier, Eva D., and Joel W. Feldmeier. 2022. 'D Minus Months: Strategic Planning for Weather-Sensitive Decisions'. *Decision Analysis* 19(1):1–20. doi: 10.1287/deca. 2021.0434.

Riggs, Ben. 2022. *Slaying the Dragon: A Secret History of Dungeons & Dragons*. New York: St. Martin's Press.

Scheff, Thomas J. 2005. 'The Structure of Context: Deciphering *Frame Analysis*'. *Sociological Theory* 23(4):368–85. doi: 10.1111/j.0735–2751.2005.00259.x.

Simkins, David. 2014. *The Arts of Larp: Design, Literacy, Learning and Community in Live-Action Role Play*. Jefferson: McFarland.

Stark, Lizzie. 2012a. *Leaving Mundania: Inside the Transformative World of Live Action Role-Playing Games*. Chicago: Chicago Review Press.

Stark, Lizzie. 2012b. 'Mad about the Techniques: Stealing Nordic Methods for Larp Design'. Pp. 71–76 in *Wyrd Con Companion 2012*, edited by Sarah Lynne Bowman and Aaron Vanek. California.

Tekinbas, Katie Salen, and Eric Zimmerman. 2003. *Rules of Play: Game Design Fundamentals*. Cambridge: MIT press.

Toiati, Luigi. 2019. *The History of Toy Soldiers*. Philadelphia: Casemate Publishers.

Valorozo-Jones, Caleb. 2021. 'Neurodiversity, Dungeons, and Dragons: A Guide to Transforming and Enriching TTRPGs for Neurodivergent Adults OR The Neurodivergent Player's Handbook'. Masters Thesis from OCAD University, Toronto, Canada. https://openresearch.ocadu.ca/id/eprint/3498/1/Valorozo-Jones_Caleb_2021_ MDES_INCD_MRP.pdf.

Waldron, David. 2005. 'Role-Playing Games and the Christian Right: Community Formation in Response to a Moral Panic'. *The Journal of Religion and Popular Culture* 9(1):3–3. doi: 10.3138/jrpc.9.1.003.

White, William J. 2020. 'Forge Theory: From GNS to the Big Model'. Pp. 123–75 in *Tabletop RPG Design in Theory and Practice at the Forge, 2001–2012*. Cham: Springer International Publishing.

Wilson, Austin. 2019. 'Demons & Devils: The Moral Panic Surrounding Dungeons & Dragons, 1979–1991'. PhD Thesis, Department of History, University of Kansas.

Wintjes, Jorit. 2017. 'When a Spiel Is Not a Game: The Prussian Kriegsspiel from 1824 to 1871'. *Vulcan* 5(1):5–28.

Wintjes, Jorit. 2021. 'A School for War – A Brief History of the Prussian *Kriegsspiel*'. Pp. 23–64 in *Simulation and Wargaming*, edited by C. Turnitsa, C. Blais, and A. Tolk. Wiley. New Jersey.

Witwer, Michael. 2015. *Empire of Imagination: Gary Gygax and the Birth of Dungeons & Dragons*. New York: Bloomsbury Publishing USA.

Ludography

Alder, Avery. 2017. Monsterhearts 2 [roleplaying game]. Buried Without Ceremony.

Avalon Hill. 1958. Gettysburg [wargame]. Avalon Hill.

Bardo AB. 2013. Monitor Celestra [LARP]. Bardo AB.

Burke, Liam. 2012. Dog Eat Dog [roleplaying game]. Liam Burke Games.

Cook, David "Zeb". 1989. Advanced Dungeons & Dragons (2nd Edition) [roleplaying game]. TSR.

Cook, Monte, Jonathan Tweet, and Skip Williams. 2000. Dungeons & Dragons (3rd Edition) [roleplaying game]. Wizards of the Coast.

Engelstein, Geoff. 2022. The System Has Already Won [megagame]. Megagame Coalition.

Fantasy Flight Games. 2023. X-Wing Miniatures Game [wargame]. Fantasy Flight Games.

Fox, Kathryn Hymes, and Tim Hazzan. 2017. Dialect [roleplaying game]. Thorny Games.

Gale Force Nine. 2016. TANKS [wargame]. Gale Force Nine.

Games Workshop. 2023. Warhammer 40,000 [wargame]. Games Workshop.

Gygax, Gary, and Dave Arneson. 1974. Dungeons & Dragons (Original Edition) [roleplaying game]. TSR.

Gygax, Gary, and Jeff Perren. 1971. Chainmail [wargame]. Guidon Games.

Gygax, Gary. 1971. Fantasy Supplement for Chainmail [wargame]. Guidon Games.

Gygax, Gary. 1977. Advanced Dungeons & Dragons (1st Edition) [roleplaying game]. TSR.

Harper, John. 2017. Blades in the Dark [roleplaying game]. Evil Hat Productions.

Harrison, Jim Wallman. 2014. Watch the Skies [megagame]. Megagame Makers.

Heinsoo, Rob. 2003. Dungeons & Dragons (3.5 Edition) [roleplaying game]. Wizards of the Coast.

Hutchings, Tim. 2020. Thousand Year Old Vampire [roleplaying game]. Self-published.

Hutchinson, Scott Malthouse. 2016. English Eerie [roleplaying game]. Trollish Delver Games.

Jackson, Steve. 1986. GURPS (1st Edition) [roleplaying game]. Steve Jackson Games.

Jackson, Steve. 2023. GURPS (4th Edition, most recent) [roleplaying game]. Steve Jackson Games.

John Nephew et al. 2023. Ars Magica (5th Edition) [roleplaying game]. Atlas Games.

Kent, Tayler. 2020. Frame 352 [roleplaying game]. Self-published.

Leary, Nathan D. 2014. World Wide Wrestling [roleplaying game]. Nathan Paoletta Publishing.

Live Adventure Event Gmb H. 2003. Conquest of Mythodea [LARP]. Live Adventure Event GmbH.

Magie, Elizabeth. Monopoly. 1933 [board game]. Self-published.

Magie, Elizabeth. 1904. The Landlord's Game [board game]. Self-published.

Mearls, Mike, and Jeremy Crawford Wyatt. 2008. Dungeons & Dragons (4th Edition) [roleplaying game]. Wizards of the Coast.

Mearls, Mike, and Jeremy Crawford Wyatt. 2014. Dungeons & Dragons (5th Edition) [roleplaying game]. Wizards of the Coast.

Megagame Makers. 2016. The Pirate Republic [megagame]. Megagame Makers.

Megagame Makers. 2020. Light the Skies [megagame]. Megagame Makers.

Megagame Makers. 2021. Rebel Country [megagame]. Megagame Makers.

Merz, Jason. 2015. Night Witches [roleplaying game]. Bully Pulpit Games.

Miller, Marc W. 1977. Traveller (1st Edition) [roleplaying game]. Game Designers' Workshop.

Nothing Up My Sleeve. 2018. Generic Office Roleplay [megagame]. Nothing Up My Sleeve.

Origin Systems. 1985. Ultima IV: Quest of the Avatar [video game] [Microsoft Windows]. Origin Systems.

Perkins, Chris. 2024. Dungeons & Dragons (5.5 or One D&D Edition) [roleplaying game]. Wizards of the Coast.

Petersen, Sandy, and Lynn Willis. 2016. Call of Cthulhu (7th Edition) [roleplaying game]. Chaosium.

Petersen, Sandy. 1981. Call of Cthulhu (1st Edition) [roleplaying game]. Chaosium.

Profound Decisions. 2013. Empire LRP [LARP]. Profound Decisions.

Reed, Epidiah. 2005. Dread (1st Edition) [roleplaying game]. The Impossible Dream.

Rein-Hagen, Mark. 1991. Vampire: The Masquerade (1st Edition) [roleplaying game]. White Wolf Publishing.

Rein-Hagen, Mark. 2023. Vampire: The Masquerade (5th Edition) [roleplaying game]. Renegade Game Studios, in collaboration with Onyx Path Publishing.

Smith, Stephen Dewey. 2015. Ten Candles [roleplaying game]. Cavalry Games.

St. Andre, Ken. 1975. Tunnels and Trolls (1st Edition) [roleplaying game]. Flying Buffalo.

Stafford, Greg. 1978. RuneQuest (1st Edition) [roleplaying game]. Chaosium.

Tweet, Jonathan, Mark Rein-Hagen, and Robin D. Laws. 1987. Ars Magica (1st Edition) [roleplaying game]. Lion Rampant.

Wells, Herbert George. 1913. Little Wars [wargame]. Self-published.

Wiley, Jaye. 2007. Fistful of Lead [wargame]. Wiley Games.

11

The Tension of Blades in the Dark

Anna Brannen and Edvin Skog

Introduction

Blade in the Dark is about **heists**.

> Blades in the Dark is a game about a group of daring scoundrels building a
> criminal enterprise on the haunted streets of an industrial-fantasy city. There
> are heists, chases, escapes, dangerous bargains, bloody skirmishes, decep-
> tions, betrayals, victories, and deaths.

(Harper 2017a)

Thus begins the text of *Blades in the Dark* (*BitD*), setting the standard for what to
expect from the game. *BitD* is a tabletop roleplaying game (TTRPG) wherein players
roleplay underdog characters, fighting against forces both mundane and supernatural
to vie for resources in the city of Doskvol. As a bunch of scoundrels and scallywags,
the players do this usually through deceit and thievery. Players and the gamemaster
(GM) collaborate on making a story that emerges from the gameplay elements and
improvisational roleplay.

The game is structured such that there are distinct phases of play, with a heist as the
focal point of any given session. Characters have certain customizable traits and roles
(known as *playbooks*), and rolling dice based on these (and other) characteristics is
a primary way to interact with the game. The outcome of these dice rolls determines
a given action's degrees of success or failure and their efficacy. However, fitting for a
game about underdogs, the dice are weighted against the characters, and the weight of
failure and its repercussions is fated to accumulate.

Heist Tropes

Typically, heist narratives have three acts: planning, execution, and the aftermath
(Leach and Sloniowski 2017). This maps to the intended flow of *BitD*, where the game
progresses through several phases. These are *free play*, the *engagement roll* (which
starts off the heist), the *score* itself, and *downtime* where progress is awarded and consequences assessed. The *free play* act, despite being positioned for it, is not perfectly

DOI: 10.1201/9781003530282-11

analogous to the idea of planning and scheming; it is a mix of choosing a target and choosing a category of plan for that target. The actual planning for the heist occurs in real-time, as players declare the retroactive solutions to problems through the use of flashbacks. This style of handling preparation is emblematic of the cinematic flourish of heist movies, where characters "reveal" their historical preparations for whatever exact scenario is currently at hand. Other mechanics support this playstyle, and it is an intentional part of the typical *BitD* experience.

Furthermore, the archetypes of playable characters (the *playbooks*) in *BitD* correspond to the tropes of characters prolific in heist movies. For example, if we translate the stereotype of a group's "muscle" to *BitD*, it would be the playbook of the *Cutter*, just as the group's mastermind is the *Spider* playbook. Combine these archetypes and you get a formula for creating the perfect circumstances for a pop-culture definition of a group of rogues up to no good. Although there are still choices a player can make for crafting or specializing their characters, it is expected that they will not deviate significantly in terms of their moral framing. Playing as bad people in a worse world is the draw of the *BitD* setting.

Another example of this is seen when specifying the crew types for the characters – a kind of overarching framing that binds these rogues together. This is a step of the character-building process where all the players should be on the same page. A crew type essentially specifies which "flavour" of antagonism their characters will have in their gang; whether they operate more overtly or subtly; and what kinds of gigs they are most qualified take on. The shared experience of creating the crew works twofold – both adding an element of customization and plotting for the players, but also serving as a mechanical tool for onboarding the players into knowing the "what" and "how" of the kind of encounters and characters they are preparing to engage with in the game. Needless to say, the crews that are described in the rules also embody those of your typical heist, caper, or gangster organizations.

When playing *BitD*, there's a kind of specific meta of engagement that emerges. Thus at the table, there should be a consensus in having a shared vision of this heist formula, *and* embracing it.

Rules and Ludonarrative

As we have just discussed, *BitD*, at a glance, has certain elements which align the game with the principles of a heist. But there is more to discuss in terms of how *BitD* supports this through its *ludonarrative*. A ludonarrative can be summed up as:

> [...] synchronization between mechanics and narrative that create a consistent and realized experience or story

> *(Despain and Ash 2016)*

Some may see the term mechanics as analogous to "rules", but that terminology is not all-encompassing. Rules can be broader than acting explicitly as the mechanisms that change state within a game. One framework for categorizing rules is to separate them into three categories (Tekinbas and Zimmerman 2003). The first of these is **operational rules**, which are the so-called "rules of play" for a game – mechanics would be covered by this category. The second are the **constitutive** rules which are formal structures of logic, which may not always be explicitly outlined. Lastly, there are the **implicit** rules which govern behaviour, etiquette, sportsmanship, etc.

In essence, rules are that which compose a game's formal identity (Tekinbas and Zimmerman 2003), and this also influences the way a player of a game will engage with them. This trifecta of rule categories can be taken into consideration when trying to define what *BitD* is at the systemic and mechanical level.

We would make the argument that, as a system, the rules and ways player behaviour is encouraged with *BiTD* matches the ludonarrative it purports to have. By having the players make characters that match the tropes, we can see one example of how the game encourages living up to its heist-theme. Yet there is more depth to consider: for example, the way the dice rolls mathematically don't favour the players' pure success, or the design of the inventory system. There are other mechanics one can take into account, but one specific cornerstone unique to *BitD* that merits consideration is the setting itself.

What defines *BitD* as a coherent world is the setting-specific material for Doskvol included in its ruleset (Harper 2017a). Blades in the Dark is in itself an implementation of a general set of rules known as the *Forged in the Dark* system – the latter is encountered as a system reference document (SRD) (Harper 2017b) pruned to be setting-agnostic barring examples noted as being for reference purposes only. The incorporation of Duskvol within *BiTD* as a wider system suggests that the setting itself may be integral for delivering the intended experience. This implies setting as a form of rules. Consider the following excerpt:

> The arcane spirit bells at Bellweather Crematorium ring whenever someone dies in the city. They may only be heard by those near the site of the death, and by the Spirit Wardens, whose arcane masks are attuned to the bells. A deathseeker crow leaves the belfry and flies to the district where the dead may be found [...] circling ever closer to the corpse.

The above text informs the reader of an important consideration within the setting of Duskvol – whenever someone dies, it *will* be known. Note that killing is *not* expressly forbidden to the player characters – their player agency remains intact – but the consequences of killing are immediate and unavoidable. However, we can add an extra dimension to this scenario if we consider the city of Doskvol itself which has lore reasons for being largely closed off from the greater world. This results in an additional limitation both in the sense of the world-building and for the player characters (PCs) who cannot simply flee the city.

> [...] it's impractical to "leave town and wait for the heat to die down" after you pull off a score.

Again, it's not a mechanical constraint that says that a PC can't ever, under any circumstances, leave Duskvol, but it *is* a tenet of the setting. In many games, this kind of context setting can be discounted merely as "fluff" text; i.e., flavour text to describe the setting (Garrad 2019), and thus shouldn't be considered a rule under the lens we are applying. However, the direct impact that the setting-specific information has on a PC suggests that it has more substance than simply acting as an aesthetic framing.

But aren't those *rules*? Perhaps a rule of the world itself, but not one contained in the SRD – a rule specific to BitD but not in the scaffolding implied by the Forged in the Dark architecture. Yet, this type of setting rule would almost certainly inform player actions. If a PC knows that they can't kill without it being broadcast to the world, or without a homing beacon closing in on their location, within a city they won't be able to leave... knowing how to manage conflicts in-universe rises in priority. As the text is explicit in what it describes, one could also make an argument that it *is* an operational rule despite not having any mechanical enforcement.

These rules by which the world is constructed inherently support common heist genre conventions. No killing means that if there are witnesses to players' crimes, holding them hostage or trying to threaten or buy their silence is one of the first resolutions that they can turn to (or invoke a *flashback* over). Similarly, being stuck in the city invites chase sequences fraught with tension, turf wars with rival thug groups, lying low in a safe house, even double identities between their day and night lives. The framing essentially supports even more baseline heist tropes. Though *BitD* does also have mechanical rules that further supplement these aspects of the setting (such as how to expand *turf* or cultivate *status*), they feel like natural extensions. Those rules are not simply grafted on top of the game world as an afterthought, nor are they trivial; they affirm what the system is trying to achieve – they make *sense* for a game about heists.

In part, because *BitD* takes such pains to establish a baseline setting, it becomes easier for players to be aligned on what they can reasonably improvise in a scene or otherwise freely express through their agency. Specific set pieces can be in flux (a trapdoor here, a getaway cart there) as long as they reasonably feel, with the consensus of other players and the GM, that they are setting-appropriate.

Moreover, the malleability of these set pieces allows for a *theatre of the mind* (Banks, Bowman, and Wasserman 2018) approach to participation in the game. In this context, theatre of the mind refers to how the game takes place primarily in the imaginations of its participants, without necessitating real-world artefacts to support the edifice of the game's reality (Sturdee, Gamboa, and Heron 2023). Hence, there is no need to arrange objects in a physical space or devote time to refining the visual components that could accompany the game. The theatre of the mind approach also allows for improvisation, as a player can simply say "As I enter the room, I look for a window", which would otherwise not be as encouraged if they were given an exact printed depiction of the room that shows clearly that there are no windows.

> Rules non-intensive games have an implicit trust between the GM and the players, a sense of cooperation that was, and often still is, missing from earlier games. Players have the ability to dramatically edit the situations by adding elements and even taking narrative control over the scene.
>
> *(Snow 2008)*

BitD's rules match at least one scholar's way of characterizing a rules "light" (akin to rules non-intensive) game (Snow 2008). The power given to players, however, is *not* an oversight from a lack of rules, but rather *stems* from how the rules specifically grant them certain freedoms and privileges. *BitD*'s rules empower players to act, while simultaneously keeping them in a heist-themed sandbox.

From the perspective of a GM, this means that the way the rules are learned is also affected. The cognitive weight of learning *BitD* falls mostly on learning what could be appropriate for the setting and the players' capabilities. Similarly, because players have unique agency in this game, there's no possible way a GM can prepare for every eventuality. Even planning for the "big picture" can go awry due to the freedoms of the players, but this is *planned* by the system and supported by its mechanics (as will be described later). The majority of work in learning the system is focused on understanding how to facilitate the gameplay flow.

Ultimately, the combination of the factors outlined means that there's *less* time spent cross-referencing specific rules or certain referential loci (e.g. needing exact measurements for gauging distance) and fiddling with tangible components in the real world. There is correspondingly *more* emphasis on engaging with the improvisational play.

In short, the ways *BitD* engineers uncertainties for its players, and *even for the* GM, support its ludonarrative goals: what results from this is a mould for making fast-paced heists with new plot twists around every corner as the underdogs scheme their way to dubious success, every step fraught with unbearable **tension**.

Player-Driven and Play to Find Out

Player agency in TTRPGs can vary. A variant akin to how most video game RPGs work is that the player is in control of an avatar, which then interacts with the world. The avatar is a vehicle through which choices may be performed. That is also how another popular game, Dungeons & Dragons 5th Edition (*D&D 5e*) works (Svan and Wuolo 2021). The gamemaster tends to be the only proprietor of the world around the player characters – the ultimate authority on what is and is not permitted to happen.

BitD has several mechanics that break this dynamic, letting players at the table have agency over more than just their avatar's current circumstances. Although the gamemaster still arbitrates, the players have equal power to orchestrate story beats, items, locations, and NPCs. Improvisation is not only encouraged to play – it is essential. *Play to find out what happens* is a phrase that is repeated nearly a dozen times in the core book, and this principle applies to **everyone** at the table.

Flashbacks

One of the most defining mechanics *BitD* uses is *flashbacks*. These allow the player to take actions in the past, from the perspective of problems encountered in the present. A flashback can consume resources and is thus limited in that sense. The cost of a flashback is linked to its complexity and how mundane the action would have been to accomplish. More unconventional or convoluted prospects may come with a higher cost. Thus, there is a reason for a player to try to justify their flashback through a believable narrative.

Flashbacks allow a player to directly create solutions outside of their present avatar and context. For instance, a player may react to a guard chasing them by declaring through a flashback that they set up an escape vehicle around the corner. No foreknowledge of the surroundings nor the guard's existence was needed for that player to achieve that method of escape. Using that same example, the player could also have improvised that another person could have been in that scene, perhaps another lowlife was bribed to distract the guard; or they were running towards an alley they had pre-prepared with traps.

Essentially, the affairs that typically are in the GM's domain within other game systems are organically transferred into the **player's** toolbox in *BitD*.

Retroactive Inventory

A player's inventory in *BitD* is unknown to everyone at the table, including the game-master. Only the number of items carried is known. This amount depends on a player's chosen *load*, such as a normal load granting five potential items. Players can go light or heavy, with the GM correspondingly taking this into account when deciding the extent of successes and failures.

An item in this case is abstract – they are all represented within a points system. The specifics of the item are decided on the fly by the player, with larger and more specialized equipment choices costing more than one point of load. In practice then a player who wants to descend a cliff can declare that one of their items is a rope, retroactively deciding that their PC has been carrying it the whole time. This allows the player to forgo time trying to plan out their character's inventory in real-world time, as well as hand-waving away typical bookkeeping elements such as item weight or spatial occupancy. Items are available on demand as necessary. This helps maintain a fast pace for playing the game, and also allows the player to feel clever when they pull out "the right tool for the job". Nobody arrives at a heist in Blades with a hammer when they needed a wrench.

Negotiations at the Table

The player is also empowered by being the ones to choose which *action* (analogous to skills) they will be able to use during the game. Players have a rating in each of these actions that determines how many dice they may roll to gauge success. This is an inversion of the typical structure for actions, common to games like *D&D*, where the GM decides what action is appropriate. In those games, a player may *try* to argue that a certain skill or attribute is what they should be using, but the power dynamic is such that the GM has final say.

In *BitD*, the player is granted the authority to choose their action on a diegetic basis although the GM may have suggestions about how the player's selection may influence the scene. The GM does also have final say over whether the selection of action is appropriate for its circumstances. For example, using the *Wreck* action to create or build a new device may seem antithetical, but perhaps with the right justification from a player, possible: the context matters. One can imagine a scenario in which one might wreck a car to create a buggy, for example, or wreck a window to create a firing position.

The GM may then discuss the mechanical implications of what the player is attempting to achieve with their action roll (known as setting the *position & effect*). The action's position is, in a nutshell, the deciding factor for the tiers of success and failure and their complementary hazards (*consequences, complications, harm,* etc.). The effect encompasses the levels of impact the action will have. However, settling on where an action lies on these two scales is also usually posed as a negotiation wherein the player has tools to influence this encounter, potentially trading a level of *position* (thereby increasing the severity of consequences) for improving the potency of its *effect*.

BitD also includes the *"devil's bargain"* mechanic. When a player is about to roll their dice, anyone at the table can offer a bargain, allowing the player rolling to add an additional die at a mechanical or narrative penalty.

> You make the deal, pay the price, and get the bonus die. The Devil's Bargain is always a free choice. If you don't like one, just reject it (or suggest how to alter it so you might consider taking it).

The GM can arbitrate the bargain. Yet the mechanic itself allows for between-player negotiations to take place as well. The player can often have some level of influence over not only what and how they act, but also how much impact their choices will have.

There are subtler ways *BitD* encourages a player-driven style of gameplay. Most dice are rolled by the players, rather than the gamemaster, even in cases where NPCs are the ones taking action. Contrast this with *D&D*, where the gamemaster's monsters act mostly under the same structure and principles as player characters do. Similarly, *BitD* entices players to be attentive and reactive through its initiative system, specifically its *lack* of one. When a player has the opportunity to interject at any given time during a scene, instead of waiting passively to take their turn in some arbitrary order, they can be more engaged with the action as a result of the intentionally minimized downtime.

BitD's absence of battle-maps[1] also encourages the aforementioned theatre of the mind approach which lets players come up with details in the environment, not constrained by clearly defined (both literal and metaphorical) walls. In essence, this is much in keeping with the nature of flashbacks and inventory – details are supplied on a "just in time" basis.

Tension

Before sitting down at a table, without even knowing the overall story concept or having a character created, the *investment* required to play *BitD* is functionally non-existent.[2] Only as you start playing the game will the investment grow. The world, the characters, the story, and the surrounding problems will (hopefully) start to matter. External factors, such as the social contract between the people at the table to engage with the game, as well as the real time spent, are also forms of investment.

Only once the player feels invested will the player care for any of the problems the game offers – it is personal now. The player is emotionally engaged, meaning the game can offer memorable experiences. *Tension* is one of the key emotions *BitD*'s design induces, just as one would expect from a heist.

As *BitD* is focused on heists and similar high-stakes scenarios, its game mechanics' ability to generate tension comes in several forms. Tension, as it is an abstract concept in the form of an emotion (Lehne and Koelsch 2015), can be difficult to pinpoint in terms of exact meaning and might have different definitions depending on its context. For the purpose of analysing TTRPGs, we would define tension as a mixture of two vital factors evoked when players have an in-game problem – **caring** for a preferred resolution, and that resolution being **unpredictable**.

- The **caring factor** can be instantiated from several perspectives, be it the player's social or real-time playing, the player's immersion into the story stakes at hand, or the player's intellectual stimuli from overcoming a challenge. It is *centred* around being invested. Note that the caring factor is never binary, but affects tension as a scale.

- The **unpredictability factor** is that the player cannot *know* which outcome will happen when aware of a problem. They may have some suspicions about how the situation will unfold, but until the interactions at the table *actually* take place – be it through dice rolls, GM or other player responses, or generally any in-game action – the problem's outcome is not settled.

These factors combined create tension. The less that a factor is stressed, the less tension is present. For instance, the potential death of a character a player does not have an investment in caring for has reduced tension. A *guaranteed* death for a character a player *does* care for has reduced tension due to its predictability. One might consider here as another data point how such things work in Ten Candles (Dewey 2015), where every player is told at the start that their character is definitely going to die. In such cases, there is no tension, but instead a narrative momentum focused around making the inevitable death **matter**. In such a case, the player might feel other, more, tragic emotions instead.

An additional perspective to consider is how immersion can break or make tension. Thematic background music and lighting can elevate immersion, and the sudden stop of such can immediately take a player away from the game, and thus remove a lot of the tension they were feeling as their focus shifts away. Or, if such moments of quiet are timed to the action, they can instead massively ramp up tension.

To clarify, tension is **not** possible within the frame of random surprises. Players are required to be *somewhat* aware of what can happen, otherwise there is nothing to care for, and nothing to predict.

Imagine yourself playing the game, and at the opening of a seemingly innocent door, it explodes, and your character instantly dies. Was this unpredictable? Very much so, but it had zero *tension* attached to its outcome. A player needs to be aware of the potential bad outcomes in order for tension to work. Foreshadowing is key. In the previous example, hinting at the idea that the door was booby-trapped, or otherwise teasing the imagination of the player to account for that scenario, would have accomplished this.

In essence, the player is in a push-and-pull relationship with tension, where they are caught in a cycle of craving conflict (tension increases) and subsequent problem-solving (tension decreases; see Figure 11.1). We designed this model to depict some of the crucial elements to consider for navigating the relations around tension in the context of TTRPGs (and subsequently also *BitD*).

As an example, assume there is a player with high investment. The player's character has been in talks of joining a secretive criminal faction, as long as their character stays under the radar. This already means there is a *problem* with personal investment – their character cannot get caught – that the player has a reason to *care* for. If this is the only problem, it's actually quite predictable. The player can just hide in a basement and do nothing, thus reducing tension since there's no motivation to interact with the game. That problem has a predictable, safe solution. The player could choose to have their character be idle in hiding, but this is not fun. At this point, their natural curiosity would likely be leveraged to want to be involved with the ongoings, unless already pressured so by the gamemaster. There is a desire for emotion (i.e. tension). Let's imagine this would lead the player character to engage with a new problem: steal a gem from a high-security vault.

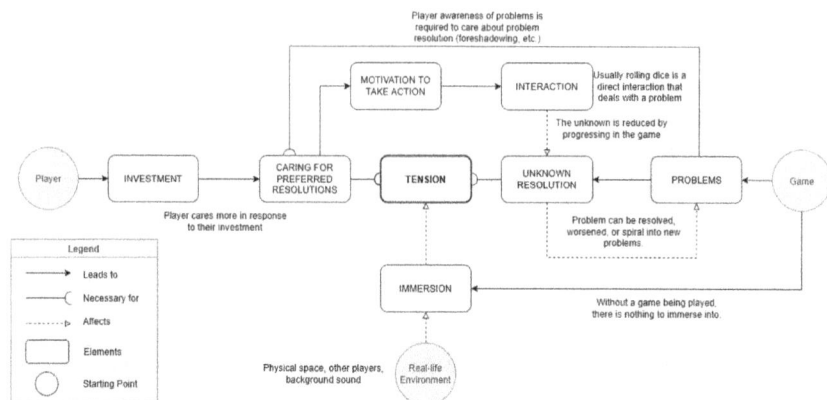

FIGURE 11.1   Our model of tension in a TTRPG context.

Now the problems work in tandem, as the hiding element is now *unpredictable* in its success due to the risks attached to the heist, thus allowing tension to rise. It is unpredictable whether or not these problems will resolve in the player's favour (didn't get caught, gem stolen) or the opposite (got caught, failed to steal the gem). The player will have a natural motivation to keep progressing in order to solve their problems and know their resolutions. Tension will remain until catharsis is reached, and the heist is over; or, if immersion is affected by the need to take a bathroom break.

Progress Clocks Are Foreshadowing

Foreshadowing can focus on different questions that may occur in a player's head regarding an outcome: what, how, when, why?

This is a strength *BitD* has with its *progress clocks*. These are set in motion at the discretion of the GM, who gives each a number of segments and fills these segments when narratively justified. These clocks provide players with meta-knowledge of what might occur. When a clock represents a problem, such as "the alarm will be triggered", the players have a constant reminder of consequences they need to avoid. The players can easily attach care to the problem, in this case stopping the alarm from being triggered. The problem is still unpredictable *when* and *how* it will happen, especially since the results of dice rolls and GM diktat tend to be what escalates the clock. The *what* is still known.

Progress clocks being tangible and visible give players access to engage with the game's pacing, as the Gamemaster's direction of the ludonarrative is not as vague as it would be without the clocks. This helps communicate clearly to the players what problems exist and puts all players on the same page with regards to which problems to focus on, thus granting room to generate tension.

Player-Driven elevates Investment

As we argued in an earlier section, *BitD* is player-driven, so in relation to building tension, there is a link to how agency affects the personal and subjective feeling of investment.

A vital factor of creativity is how the flashback and retroactive inventory mechanics allow the player to generate customized solutions on the fly. The player's own creativity being directly introduced into the game world ties the player and game together more, leading to a straightforward source of emotional investment.

These occurrences can create a cascade effect as well. When a player has a moment of control in which they make a decision, other players now have to deal with whatever they introduced. Even the GM may be blindsided and now have to incorporate the unexpected into the emergent narrative. When other players at the table also have the chance to do this, it gives a reason to pay attention because of that dynamic playing out: *their* world is *your* world. In essence, the player has a noticeable amount of power to influence the immediate scenes taking place, and also over the broader scope of the game's story. The devil's bargain mechanic explicitly allows anyone at the table to provide stake-enhancing dilemmas, furthering the creative input for the players.

For a brief moment, depending on the action, the player can feel like they are in the shoes of the gamemaster.

Flashbacks are an incredibly versatile tool for solving problems. *BitD* lacks a strict turn order, and flashbacks are something available to every character, and not limited in terms of physical distance or time. This opens up the floodgates for broader engagement with the scenario. It is also collegiate to interject with this mechanic, meaning there is plenty of opportunity to employ flashbacks, even if the problem to be solved belongs to another player. These opportunities to cooperate mean that there is a need to pay attention to all of the player's stakes in the game, as anyone can involve themselves with a literal action. Attention to the game retains the player's investment.

But if every problem can be solved with flashbacks, wouldn't that reduce tension as it makes the solution predictable? This would be the case if not for flashbacks being a resource, so players need to be careful not to waste them. There is tension around longevity of consequences, which we will describe later in this chapter. Furthermore, flashbacks are still fallible as they can involve dice rolls. Finally, players must actually have a creative solution that fits the problem, which inherently keeps a flashback unpredictable in its use cases.

From a gamemaster's perspective, there can be an issue with the players' ability to interject with their flashbacks, as perhaps the gamemaster is intending to build a specific kind of flow in regards to the game's tension. Having it be disrupted or quickly changing course can cause chaos in the game. However, the progress clocks maintaining a sense of clarity can ease this process to make sure that the players and the gamemaster don't end up in absolute conflict with the story's intention. In the end, this can vary a lot from table to table, as well as with the mindset and understanding of *BitD* when playing. A gamemaster should try and anticipate this phenomenon of player-driven abilities to maintain a cohesive and fun heisting experience.

Solving Problems Cause Problems

As long as a player is invested and immersed in the game, the outcomes will matter – certainly when it's a question of life or death regarding their favourite character. This means that the more problems, and the more potential outcomes there are, the more care the player can put into the game. This generates the most tension.

This is the beauty of *BitD*'s dice rolls, as the game is skewed towards consequences. On a six-sided die, the result of a one to three is a failure, a four to five is success with complications, and only on a six does the action fully succeed without strings attached. Luckily, players roll a pool of multiple dice and use the highest value as their result. Even then, it would require at least four six-sided dice to have a 52% chance of *not* having any negative consequence. And by employing judicious devils bargaining, even a clear success can have narrative impact.

The takeaway from this is that the longer the player group stays on a heist, mathematically, the more problems will keep arising as your primary solution will be to roll dice. Whatever the problem is it still needs to be explained in a more comprehensive manner than "You rolled a one, ergo that didn't happen". The choice of a particular action grants context to unfold into a narrative, thus, "It didn't happen **because** of [diegetic reason]". These organic narrative beats keep the player invested in the snowball effect of naturally cascading failures. It can feel fun to fail, especially since those fails can be the instantiation of a progress clock.

In *BitD*, problems cause more problems, and tension constantly escalates.

Additionally, some solutions require spending resources – such as *stress* and *inventory*. This in itself evokes the *longevity problem* of survival – a looming threat that if you are not careful enough, you might be completely screwed at the end of the heist. Replenishment of those resources *only* being available during downtime[3] in *BitD,* and even then in limited effectiveness, means that the consequences of solving a problem via those resources ultimately result in the longevity problem worsening. The consequences can be very dire too, as if enough stress is accumulated, the player's character will suffer permanent trauma – hence *caring* for this problem is elevated. Stress does not wipe away during heists; it is at best mitigated.

In a game like *D&D*, player characters can replenish resources through resting. This means the tension can be radically reduced since resting, while at GM discretion, is generally liberally available. In *D&D*, the longevity problem is *notably* less affected by spending resources from a mechanical point of view. However, in practice, the tension provided by the longevity problem is supplemented by the GM's ability to help foreshadow and provide clear consequences of spending resources, such as not letting players fully replenish deep inside a dungeon. The downtime restriction of replenishment in *BitD* gives an altogether more serious flavour to the cost of actions.

Conclusion

In a story, a (fun) heist should never go perfectly according to plan: complications and solutions are where the richness of its narrative lies. *Blades in the Dark* uses the template of a score for evoking problems, whilst ensuring its players have the focus as the ones always outwitting the game. The uncertainties guaranteed by the interplay present there grant room to generate tension, especially as the stakes get higher. Stakes have a tangible representation in the game (progress clocks, for example) and guide the player into the game's intended ludonarrative.

Players have a lot of control in solving these problems, providing reason to stay engaged in order to react at any moment: keeping the pacing high, retaining immersion and thus the feeling of tension within the heist taking place. Solving a problem in *BitD* is skewed towards escalating complications – there's a cascade effect of problems creating *more* problems. This means tension continues to build, creating a dramatic curve through its game mechanics. *Blades in the Dark*'s design and setting create a cinematic heisting experience for both players and the gamemaster, thus ful-filling its ludonarrative. Its effectiveness in this is largely without parallel and offers a template for introducing tense narrative beats and cinematic gameplay into TTRPGs of all different styles.

Notes

1 A map of which the layout and position of characters in an area are laid out, usually grid-based.
2 However, having taken the time to learn the rules can be a form of investment before these.
3 The time player characters explicitly spend between heists.

References list

Banks, Jaime, Nicholas David Bowman, and Joe A. Wasserman. 2018. 'A Bard in the Hand: The Role of Materiality in Player–Character Relationships'. *Imagination, Cognition and Personality* 38(2):61–81.

Lauryn Ash. 2016. Designing for ludonarrative harmony. https://www. academia. edu/34283487/Designing_For_Ludonarrativ e_Harmony.

Garrad, Jon. 2019, June 27–28. 'Fluff Ain't Rules: Absence, Presence and Haunting in RPG Design'. in *Absent presences*. Manchester, UK.

Leach, Jim, & Jeannette Sloniowski. (Eds.). 2017. *The Best Laid Plans: Interrogating the Heist Film*. Detroit: Wayne State University Press.

Lehne, Moritz, and Stefan Koelsch. 2015. 'Toward a General Psychological Model of Tension and Suspense'. *Frontiers in Psychology* 6:79.

Snow, Cason. 2008. 'Dragons in the Stacks: An Introduction to Role-Playing Games and Their Value to Libraries'. *Collection Building* 27(2):63–70.

Sturdee, Miriam, Mafalda Gamboa, and Michael Heron. 2023. 'TTRPG UX: Requirements & Beyond'. Pp. 1–9 in *Extended Abstracts of the 2023 CHI Conference on Human Factors in Computing Systems*. Hamburg Germany: ACM.

Svan, Oscar, and Anna Wuolo. 2021. 'Emergent Player-Driven Narrative in Blades in the Dark and Dungeons & Dragons: A Comparative Study'. Bachelor thesis from Uppsala University, Uppsala, Sweden. https://www-diva--portal-org.translate.goog/smash/record.jsf?pid=diva2:1576344&dswid=-3539&_x_tr_sch=http&_x_tr_sl=sv&_x_tr_tl=en&_x_tr_hl=en&_x_tr_pto=sc.

Tekinbas, Katie Salen, and Eric Zimmerman. 2003. *Rules of Play: Game Design Fundamentals*. Cambridge: MIT press.

Ludography

Crawford, Jeremy. 2012. Dungeons and Dragons 5th edition [roleplaying game]. Wizards of the Coast.

Dewey, Stephen. 2015. Ten Candles [roleplaying game]. Cavalry Games.

Harper, John. 2017a. Blades in the Dark [roleplaying game]. Evil Hat productions.

Harper, John. 2017b. Forged in the Dark [roleplaying game]. One Seven Design.

12

Domain Knowledge in Video Games

Michael Heron

Video Games

Now that we've discussed some of the many ways that we can analyse games, let's move on to building a little bit of domain knowledge. As with almost everything we're doing here, this isn't exhaustive. It's not even representative. It's barely scratching the surface. This chapter doesn't relieve you of your duty to master your subject matter – you'll still need to read, and play, and talk, and think. What we can do though is contextualize some of the things we've spoken about with regards to our Big Three types of game – video games, board games, and roleplaying games.

In the Beginning...

Scoping is important in research, so we're going to begin by doing a little of that. How far into the past do we have to go before we find something that is recognizably a video game?

There are many different candidates. Many authors will authoritatively state that it was Space War, in 1962 (Ivory 2015). Others say, "No, it was Tennis for Two" in 1958 (De La Cruz and Ryan 2015). Others will point to Bertie the Brain in 1950 (Rogaleva 2018), and others still will talk about the cathode-ray tube (CRT) amusement device in 1947 (Cohen 2012). Some point to the first pinball machines in 1931 as the earliest archaeological example (DeLeon 2012). As is often the case, the disagreement is down to definitions and what we're willing to accept "counts" as a video game.

The first pinball machine that most modern people would recognize was Automatic Industries' Whiffle back in 1931. Its scoring was handled electronically, it was coin operated, and it even had the plunger that is such an iconic part of pinball. However, most would baulk at the idea that pinball is a video game since the primary elements of play are mechanical – the flippers, the ball, the bumpers, and so on. It also lacks one of the keywords in the description – **video.**

Let's say that one of the characteristics that our first video game **needs** is video output – absent that, it's – by any definition – not a **video** game. Video itself is a word that means "the recording, reproducing, or broadcasting of moving visual images".

DOI: 10.1201/9781003530282-12

And we should probably insist that these are **cybertextual** (Aarseth 1995) – as in, their video output depends on non-trivial input from the player.

The cathode-ray amusement device is then our next credible candidate for being the first video game. Players would twiddle knobs on a CRT machine to adjust the trajectory of simulated artillery shells in order to strike targets that were overlaid onto the screen. The action was driven by an oscilloscope, and success or failure was largely determined through non-diegetic comparison. It was certainly a game, certainly electronic, and by a charitable definition, we might even say it's a video output, albeit one based on analogue signals rather than true moving images. The fact that most of the "game" part happens off-device though, since there was little true computation involved, leads many to disqualify it as a candidate. Bertie the Brain was a massive computer that played tic-tac-toe against a primitive artificial intelligence. However, it used a grid of lights rather than a video display – while clearly a game, and clearly running on a computer, it probably also doesn't count.

Tennis for Two returns us to the oscilloscope display we saw in the CRT amusement device. It doesn't offer any real technical innovation over what we've already seen, but some regard it as philosophically the first video game because it ran on a computer (again, an analogue one) and was explicitly designed as a game for the purposes of entertainment.

Spacewar! is probably the first time we see all the key elements line up in an uncontroversial way. It ran on a computer (originally the DEC PDP-1 minicomputer), was played through a Video Display Unit (VDU), and computation was all handled on-device. Two spaceships face off, attempting to destroy each other while avoiding the gravity well of a nearby star. Originally controlled through physical switches located on the CRT display, a forerunner of the gamepad was eventually developed to make it more fun.

One thing characterizes all of these early candidates to the crown – none of them were easily available to the wider public. They were aberrations, or test cases – used to show the power of a computer, or the interesting uses to which computing power might be put. Spacewar! was the first where **fun** was actually one of the expected deliverables of interaction– even *Tennis for Two* was primarily a research output. But the **reaction** to these games was telling. Spacewar! was massively popular, and it propagated far beyond its own limited user base onto computers all over the world. Tennis for Two was so enticing that hundreds of people turned up to play it when it was debuted. It was clear that there was an appetite out there for electronic gaming, and it wouldn't be long before someone came along to feed it. In 1971, Nolan Bushnell (heading up a company called Syzygy, which would later become known as Atari) tried to commercialize Spacewar! as an arcade cabinet. It was successful too, although not spectacularly so. Around 1,500 units were sold,[1] each costing between $1,000 and $1,500– between $7,750 and $11,650 in today's money. The sales built enough confidence for the newly incorporated Atari to release Pong in 1972. That sold at three times the price and would go on to sell around 8,000 units by the end of 1974 (Kent 2010). This is traditionally considered the end of the earliest era of video games as research oddities and the start of the commercial game era. Thousands of different game cabinets would be released in the next few decades.

Cafes, restaurants, pubs and clubs would install them in areas of high footfall. Sometimes they'd buy the machine outright, which involved keeping all the revenue but also paying for maintenance. Others would be leased by a "route operator" who would retain ownership but make available a percentage of the money generated (Lendino 2020; Meades 2022)

In 1972, Magnavox introduced the Magnavox Odyssey Series (Mazor and Salmon 2009). The idea for a home video game console dates back to 1966, when Ralph Baer and colleagues developed a series of workable prototypes (Bedi 2019). The Odyssey, released to the public, contained 12 hard-coded games. Swapping between them was done through changing "game cards" which acted as circuit boards that reconfig-ured internal electronic pathways to different ends. The display was primarily dots and lines, but that was sufficient – along with the provided dice, chips, cards, and overlays – to provide a range of recreational experiences. Magnavox went deep when it came to filing patents for the device, and this gave them considerable leeway over the next few years to wield the courts in protection of their commercial interests (Mailland 2024; Tannahill 2014).

These two innovations (Pong in the arcade and the Odyssey in the home) serve as the "creation myth" of two different conceptions of video games, driven by differ-ent commercial models. Physical cabinets, or **arcade machines**, relied heavily upon player turnover and games were designed in such a way as to ensure their commercial viability. Players would insert a coin to gain access to the play experience. This would be limited by a number of "lives" which were spent to recover from errors in play. As an operator, you wanted those coins to be inserted as often as possible, which would mean that games had a challenging needle to thread between difficulty and fun. Popular machines could make their operators a lot of money, and there was a lot of competition for those dimes and quarters. In the 70s, we saw Pong cede its domi-nance to *Space Invaders* (Taito 1978), *Galaxians* (Namco 1979), and *Asteroids* (Atari 1979) – games which were more exciting, and thus more profitable. Into the 80s, we see *Pac-Man* (Namco 1980), *Missile Command* (Atari 1980), *Frogger* (Konami 1981), *Defender* (Atari 1981), and *Donkey Kong* (Nintendo 1981), the latter being the first introduction of Mario to the world. Technological development was rapid, as was the physical design innovations around the cabinet. The first arcade games didn't even have colour screens – they used tinted overlays on top of monochrome VDUs to cre-ate colours. When games like *Spy Hunter* (Bally Midway 1983) and *Star Wars* (Atari 1983) were released, we had fully scrollable displays and wireframe 3D graphics. The costs, and potential profitability, began to ramp up.

In the 1980s, the average retail price of an arcade machine was $4,000 (~$16,000 in contemporary money), and especially profitable cabinets might cost as much as $20,000 (~$160,000). The commercial incentives to keep people playing became part of the vocabulary of game design, even in the home where the model of ownership and revenue was dramatically different. Lives and continues. Short, satisfying game loops. "Nintendo Hard" difficulty. When we spoke in an earlier chapter about hauntological elements in games, you can see these ghosts even in modern playing experiences.

The average arcade machine could cover its initial outlay within three or four months – if the game stayed hot. As new titles were introduced, a venue could only maintain the interest of its patrons if it boasted the best games. Venues would often have multiple games, and they in turn would be competing against each other. The ear-liest musical stings for arcade machines were less about creating a pleasing audiovi-sual experience and more about acting like a carnival barker, "Step right up folks and

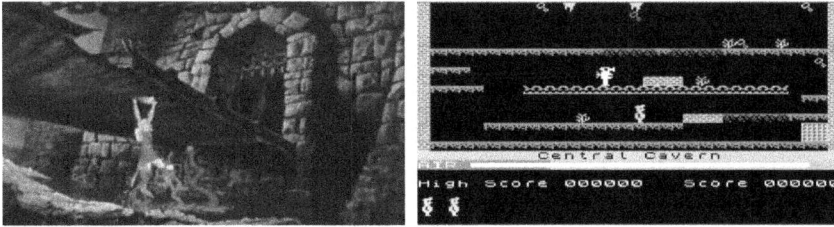

FIGURE 12.1 Left, Dragon's Lair in the arcade. Right, Manic Miner on the ZX Spectrum (Screenshots by author).

play!" (Heron 2015). Brash, bright colours, demonstration modes and more – all ways for games to yell "pick me" to a passing player.

At this time, we see arcade games attempting to wield their physicality in service of verisimilitude. You'd sit in the cockpit of an X-Wing when you played *Star Wars* (Atari 1983). *Afterburner* (SEGA 1987) – a game of aerial dogfighting – would lift and rotate on gimbals and pistons as you played. *Operation Wolf* (Taito 1987) used a replica Uzi as its controller. The bend of the arcade was towards **experience**, and you see that even now with modern arcade games. The physicality of play is something to be celebrated.

Arcade machines were typically single-game devices. They were engineered for playing a specific game in a specific way, and that allowed for them to take advantage of technological tricks, shortcuts, and developments in a way that home devices couldn't. By 1983, you might be playing *Dragon's Lair* (Advanced Microcomputer Systems 1983) in the arcade, and revelling in its full-screen cartoon graphics. Really, Dragon's Lair is little more than a series of QuickTime events that result in video files being played from a laser-disc, but it was hard to deny the effect was stunning for the time. At home in 1983, the Odyssey had long been supplanted by home computers and the earliest home consoles (Kirriemuir 2006). If you owned a ZX Spectrum, like my family did, you'd be treated not to a Disneyesque audiovisual experience but the primitive beeps and bloops of Manic Miner (Software Projects 1983). See Figure 12.1 for a comparison.

As home devices began to become cheaper and more powerful, and as developers learned how to leverage the hardware, this technological gap began to close. This became an existential threat to what had become a vibrant and booming arcade culture (Meades 2022), and this encouraged the developers of arcade games to go all-in on extravaganza.

By this point, arcade machines had become so popular that you no longer went to a bar or a café to play a game – you went to a dedicated amusement arcade which would contain dozens, if not hundreds of different cabinets. Despite their reputation as dens of spotty nerds and social outcasts, arcades were often intensely social places with their own social context, rules, and rituals. An argot emerged. You'd place coins and personal tchotchkes on a machine to act as an ad-hoc reservation. Conventions such as "winner stays on" would allow for easy navigation of social conflicts. Demonstrated skill, through high-score tables, would establish a pecking order of who gave way to who when multiple people wanted to play the same machine. If you were on a hot streak, you'd often find yourself playing to an audience as people huddled around.

All of this, in terms of how we've already spoken about games, is an experiential frame – or perhaps even meta-experiential. It's not so much about the games but about the experience of being a game **player**. Amusement arcades became so popular that wider society began to develop concerns (Hahn 2023; Meades 2019)

I spent as much of my formative years as I could in places like this, but it was always expensive. You'd feed your pocket money (or allowance, depending on your region) into a change-making machine and a few minutes later it was gone. At least, if you were as bad as I was at actually playing any of the games. It's only natural that serious gamers would want to replicate an arcade experience back at home, and so was born the idea of the "arcade conversion" in which popular games would be ported into home computer versions.

It… didn't always go well.

Home systems at the time – at least the ones affordable by most gamers – had severe technical limitations in terms of what they could replicate. Buying an arcade conversion was always a risky endeavour, because the chances were you'd end up with something only vaguely approximate to what you thought you were buying (Figure 12.2).

There were significant platform differences too. Computers like the Commodore Amiga (my love) and the Super Nintendo Entertainment System (SNES) were able to offer a greater fidelity, but the eight-bit systems that were cheaper and more popular would often struggle (see Figure 12.3 for the difference in presentation on four different systems for a single game).

The trend of gaming as a hobby has not been an uninterrupted upwards arc, though. There were moments where it seemed like its commercial viability was in question. People often talk about the Video Game Crash of 1983, which was the period between 1983 and 1985 when the early games industry collapsed and brought what seemed like a permanent end to an interesting and engaging fad (Ernkvist 2008). Revenues went from around $3.2bn (~$10bn in contemporary money) in 1983 to $100m (~$316m) in 1984. Many companies – software and hardware – perished as a consequence.

FIGURE 12.2 From left to right – *Street Fighter 2* (Capcom 1991), *Outrun* (Sega 1986), *Hard-Drivin'* (Atari Games 1989). Top shows the arcade, bottom shows the home conversion to C64 (*Street Fighter 2* and *Hard Drivin'*) and ZX Spectrum (Outrun). What the images don't show is just how poorly the games perform. (Image by author).

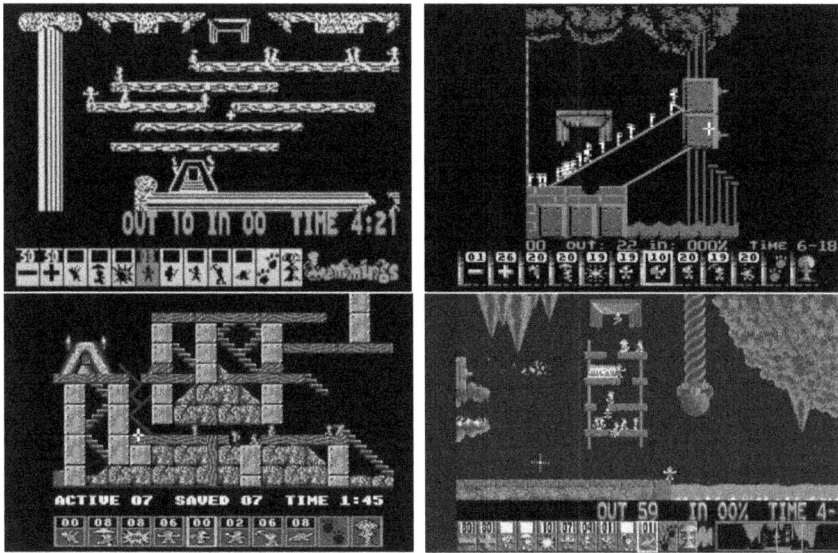

FIGURE 12.3 Lemmings (DMA Design 1990) on multiple different home systems ZX Spectrum top left, Commodore 64 top right. Nintendo Entertainment System bottom left, and the Amiga 500 bottom right.

In reality though, it's not quite as simple as a video game crash – really, there were multiple separate but tightly related crashes that fed and reinforced each other. Home consoles suffered from the price wars in the home entertainment market as many manufacturers struggled to convince parents to buy devices that could only be used to play games. Home computers, at least, have a nodding and winking relationship with home productivity and educational value (Lean 2014; Platt and Langford 1984). But home computers had their own problem, because poor consumer confidence and a lack of incentive to upgrade created a plateau for sales. Why buy a computer that is slightly faster than the one you already have when its actual promised benefits had likely failed to materialize? In 1983, suppliers in the UK had been caught out because the demand for computers dramatically outstripped supply. In 1984, they determined not to make the same mistake, but by that time everyone who wanted a home computer already had one. It would take decades for the industry to recover.

That though is a story for another day, and another book. This chapter isn't intended to be a history of video games – just a sampling of some special points of interest. Most of you likely didn't grow up with the sights, sounds and – yes – smells of the arcade. And if you want to explore hauntological principles in video games, knowing where the bodies are buried is a good start.

Genre

One of the things that was stressed in earlier chapters is the idea of **intertextuality**. One of the ways that gets expressed in video games is through the concept of **genre.** Whenever you are looking to put forward an argument about a video game, it helps to be able to situate it in context. It's a good idea to compare and contrast the game against others in similar genres.

Much as with our discussions on "what is a game", genre has more in common with cluster theory than it does a set rigorous definition. Wittgenstein again comes to our rescue – a game belongs to a genre when it ticks a certain number of familial features off of a checklist. That checklist likewise doesn't come from a Ministry of Genres or any formal body – genres emerge organically over time as a natural consequence of "the discourse" around gaming. Genres are not official, or even particularly consistent. They're often thrown around with a baffling range of variants and subvariants. They merge together. They split apart.

Consider the loose genre of **soulslike** games. There are certain features in a game that most of us would expect to be present. If a game has bonfires (or equivalent), then it gets a tick on its checklist. Rock-hard boss fights – tick. Minimal forgiveness in its learning curve, tick. Progress that must be reclaimed when you die, tick. Enough ticks, and you can be confident most people would agree that you have a soulslike on your hands.

So, Dark Souls (FromSoftware 2011) – tick, tick, tick, tick. Everything is present and correct. Jedi Knight: Fallen Order (Respawn Entertainment 2019) – well, it has its bonfire equivalent (meditation points). It has rock-hard boss fights (or does it? Sometimes you need to support your tick with evidence). It's perhaps too forgiving in its learning curve to merit that tick, but it does require progress to be reclaimed when you die (tick). Is it a soulslike? **Maybe.** If you're finding people aren't convinced, then it's because you haven't convinced them. Git gud.

Black Myth: Wukong (Game Science 2024) has all the features except for losing progression when you die. Is it a soulslike? Again, **maybe.** Elden Ring (FromSoftware 2023)? **Definitely.** Bloodborne (FromSoftware 2015)? **Definitely.**

Genres are a form of folksonomy (Li and Zhang 2020; Surinx 2023) – that is, they are defined bottom up through the gradual emergence of a vague consensus. The checklist I would expect for a soulslike may not be the one that you expect. You might want to focus on the key gameplay lesson of mastery through repetition. You might want to take into account the nature of boss battles – if they require study and consideration or if reactive button-mashing is enough. The entries on a checklist, as well as the point at which a sufficient number of ticks have been accumulated, are all a matter for debate. And some will strive for a definitional purity that simply does not exist. Some will split hairs on what counts as a **soulslike**, versus a **soulslite**, versus a **soulsborne**.

In reality, games rarely fit into a convenient category. Games are almost always a merging of genres where they only partially satisfy the commonalities. Games might even belong to seemingly incompatible genres. Golf Story (No More Robots 2017) is a sports-JRPG. Crypt of the Necrodancer (Brace Yourself Games 2015) is a rhythm roguelite, and *Bullets Per Minute* (Awe Interactive 2020) is a rhythm first-person shooter. *13 Sentinels: Aegis Rim* (Vanillaware 2020) is a mash-up of high-school life simulator and mecha real-time strategy. In many cases, the genre (or genres) is simply down to what you can convince people of through rhetoric. You as a scholar need to convince your reader. Game makers might instead have to convince a publisher, or the buying public.

Why does this even matter though?

Genres matter partly from a taxonomic perspective – we use them as ways of grouping together related things for the purposes of critique and analysis. As I've already hinted, genre relationships are a good place to begin exploring opportunities for meaningful intertextuality. They are also important from a marketing perspective – people tend to make buying decisions based, at least on part, on genre affection. Genres set expectations – if we sit down to play an RPG, we will have different expectations to what we'll have if we sit down with a 4X strategy game. Genres imply structure, which can be a useful perspective-building exercise when outlining the initial conception of a game design.

They're also useful in our normal frame of upholding, subverting, or rejecting conventions. Subverting genres can create opportunities for real innovation. Undertale (tobyfox 2015), for example, can be considered as a subversion of standard JRPG tropes. Identifying your genre and then rejecting its common framings can be a wonderful design exercise, as well as a delightful treat for those doing analysis of a game. Occasionally, they serve as a form of anti-innovation through cleaving to popular trends that have few unexplored avenues in their design space. Any time a game is described as "The Dark Souls of X", it genuinely makes me a little sleepy.

For our purposes though, it's the search for intertextuality that benefits the most. Genres are an easy way of identifying broad categories. Genres are multi-dimensional in that they can be framed in multiple ways to capture groups of games in different surrounding contexts. You might group games based on their systems, which is something you'd want to do if pursuing a systemic analysis of a game. What is inside, and outside, of your net determines how coherent your argument will be.

Imagine your research question is, "What are some of the most significant elements of similarity between the mechanisms of Dark Souls (FromSoftware 2011) and Disco Elysium (ZA/UM 2019)?". Does that question even make sense? Dark Souls is, well Dark Souls. Disco Elysium is an RPG game with a heavy focus on narrative implication and no meaningful combat system. How do you answer a question like this?

I'm not saying you can't (and if you do, drop me an email with your answer) but rather the lack of a genre connection means the answer will probably be inconsistent, incoherent, and impossible to draw a larger meaning from. What if you compare the systems of *Baldur's Gate 3* (Larian Studios 2023) to those of *Doom Eternal* (id Software 2020)? Again, a largely incoherent answer should be expected.

But what about *Bloodborne* (FromSoftware 2015) and *Elden Ring* (FromSoftware 2023)? Ah, now we're talking. The lens of genre, as expressed in commonalities of mechanisms, gives you a meaningful intertextual link to explore. You'd look at their similarities, their differences, and what the presence of both implies about the systems in the game and in the wider genre. A thoughtful scholar can spend many happy evenings wrestling with this analysis, and genre is the tool that made the connection.

You don't have to focus on mechanisms though. You can group things according to their themes and messaging – an evaluation of genre in terms of a critical lens. Here, you might find other kinds of meaningful links – I think it makes perfect sense to compare Dark Souls and Disco Elysium in the frame of what they are saying to the player. Consider a research question such as "What are some of the important things the desolation of Dark Souls has in common with the social collapse in Disco Elysium?". It's the scholarly equivalent of speaking in tongues to compare them mechanically, but critically we see much we can profitably say.

We can even think of genres in terms of experiential expectation – how they are intended to "feel" to their audience. You won't find a lot of systemic or critical links between *A Short Hike* (Whippoorwill 2019), *Stardew Valley* (ConcernedApe 2016), and *Spiritfarer* (Thunder Lotus Games 2020). They're all though conceptually grouped within the genre label of "cozy games". *Animal Crossing* (Nintendo 2020) was in many ways **the** game of the pandemic because of its experiential aspect. Plenty of us have turned in more recent times to games like *Unpacking* (SMG Studio 2021), *Dreamlight Valley* (Disney 2022), or *Arcade Paradise* (Nosebleed Interactive 2021) because of the warm, comfort of familiarity and nostalgia. Here we see again the hauntological, as we often do when nostalgia enters the picture.

Within the frame of scholarly work, genre can be considered too a useful starting point for identifying particularly rich areas of inquiry. Let's do a quick tour of some genres to see what games fall within their embrace and why they might be worth examining. As before, these genres aren't official or exhaustive – just common in the discourse.

Sports Games

We'll begin with the genre of Sports games. This is an appropriate starting place given the claim that *Tennis for Two* has to being the first interactive electronic game explicitly designed for entertainment. Games such as *Madden Football* (EA Sports 1988–2024), *FIFA* (EA Sports 1993–2023) and latterly, *EA Sports FC* (EA Sports 2023), *NBA Basketball* (2K Games 1999–2024), and *WWE/WWF Wrestling* (THQ 1999–2012; 2K Games 2013–2024) all fall into this category. So too do games like Rocket League (Psyonix 2015).

Some notable features of sports games as a genre include the business model, the licencing issues associated, and the expectations of the audience. Sports games are often **lifestyle games**, in that there are people who don't consider themselves to be gamers who will nonetheless buy every new edition of Madden and play it regularly and consistently. In the early days of computing, a gaming enthusiast would definitely have a football game, and a baseball game, and a wrestling game that they played in regular rotation with their other games. That's less true nowadays – you will find people who own a console and pretty much only play FIFA with their friends.

The business models too are interesting in that typically these games are driven by annual releases, which introduce a number of experiential aspects. The Fear of Missing Out is the term used to describe people who participate in something because the perceived cost (social, reputational, emotional) of non-participation is too high. Annual releases in which players constantly need to opt-in to the "real" version of the game can fall into this category. To feed that churn of versions, the game makers themselves need to draft in armies of volunteers to make sure that the new goalkeeper at your local club has stats that capture his capabilities. Up-to-date team rosters and such give players a sense of verisimilitude when they watch how teams function, and even the atmosphere of the games is important. FIFA's sound engine was so realistic that it was used to generate believable crowd noise in real football stadiums during COVID.

Sports are a big business, and the financial value of branding is important. The video game *Summer Games* (Epyx 1984) was clearly based on the Olympics but couldn't use that name because they weren't willing to pay the associated fee. That's exactly the same reason why FIFA is now EA Sports FC, because FIFA demanded around $250m–$300m a year to use their corporate dressing[2] and Electronic Arts were not convinced they needed it that much.

A genre exploration is also a good opportunity to talk about some edge-case questions that don't emerge in our broader discussions, and here we have an obvious one – what's the difference between a game and a sport? And the answer is – difficult to pin down. One obvious difference is that we tend to think of sports as stressing physical skills, but games as stressing mental skills. That doesn't explain then why the International Olympics Committee list chess and bridge as sports worthy of recognition.[3] Or why we call them the Olympic Games rather than the Olympic Sports. Some have argued the difference is whether professional play is regulated by a governing body, which then means everything from Scrabble to Magic the Gathering counts as a sport. I favour the informal definition that it's a sport if you're expected to change clothes when playing it. Even that becomes less convincing when we think of Yusif Dikec sauntering up to his Olympic shooting match in a t-shirt.

We might consider racing games to be a subset of sports games, if we consider F1 racing as being a sport and not a form of "extreme queueing". Like many sports games, they rely on speed, quick-reactions, and the ability to plan and execute upon skilful navigation of an environment. Often driven too by an intrinsic need to "git gud". These run the full gamut from cartoon cars to individually modelled stats on wheel nuts. *Dirt* (Codemasters 2007–2024); *Forza* (Microsoft Studios 2005–2021); *Gran Turismo* (Polyphony Digital 1997–2024); and even *Mario Kart 8* (Nintendo 2022) fall into this category. These are often the first games to be marketed when a new console generation comes along. Cars are both relatively easy to render and visually striking when that rendering is done correctly. They make excellent vehicles (lol) for demonstrating new lighting techniques and rendering improvements. Indeed, the rendering techniques for driving games often become the baseline for visual effects in movies – many of the cars you see spectacularly blown up in film aren't real cars at all.

Puzzle Games

If sports games are about a celebration of the physical, puzzle games are almost purely about the mind. They stress lateral thinking and the overcoming of obstacles via thought and creative analysis of the rules of the environment. Some significant titles here include *Myst* (Broderbund 1993); the *Professor Layton* series (Level-5, 2007–2021); *Portal* (Valve 2007); *The Talos Principle* (Croteam 2014); *The Witness* (Thekla Inc 2016); *Return of the Obra Dinn* (Pope 2018); *Baba is You* (Oy 2019); and *Chants of Sennaar* (Rundisc 2023).

While we're in the neighbourhood, it might be worth here talking about the difference between a puzzle and a game. It mostly comes down to solveability – puzzles have a solution, and when that solution is discovered, there ceases to be any "juice" left to extract. Who, for example, erases their lines in a word search so they can have the fun of doing it again? A puzzle, at least in this conception, is a building block of a game but also something that can be experienced independently of a game concept. The games listed above are all made up of interlocking puzzles, within a narrative context. Whether or not a jigsaw or a Sudoku puzzle counts as a game is something for you to decide for yourself.

Puzzle games are characterized often by long periods of doing nothing, or experimenting with the behaviours of the environment. Observation is critical, and environmental storytelling is a major feature. The player is constantly asking themselves questions like, "Why is that there?", "When did that happen?", "How did that get there?", and this begins to evolve into, "What happens if I do this?"

A player spends most of the playtime in their head, meditating upon what they know in an attempt to construct various hypotheses for how the puzzles may be solved. The specific mechanics of a puzzle may differ, but there are systemic links in terms of how we expect these hypotheses to be constructed and tested. However, in an experiential frame, it is the thoughtful cogitation that defines most of a player's experience.

Puzzle games come with an expectation too that there is an underlying consistency of the world, and that while puzzles are presented in an obfuscated manner, they still honour some basic rules of engagement. If you can't jump in 99% of the game, it would be considered unfair to have a puzzle that relies on you attempting to jump. I once got unreasonably angry when playing one of the Unlock (Carroll, Cauet, and Demaegd 2017) games because one puzzle explicitly breaks the fourth wall and requires you to look at the box, rather than the components in the box. Since nothing prior to this had required anything similar, I felt this was breaking the player contract. A similar puzzle in the Exit games (Brand and Brand 2016) was much less egregious because it had gradually included the box and other real-world elements into the language of its puzzles.

Strategy Games

Strategy video games can often trace their lineage back to the conventions of board or war games. They have a strong emphasis on analysis and evaluation, which culminates in the execution of a strategy, hence the name.

What's a strategy, though? You will find this word, along with its sibling, "tactic", referenced continually in discussions about games. Like narrative and story – or theme and setting – these are words often conflated and confused. Strategy refers to the broad, overarching goal that someone is attempting to achieve. It's the long-term principle that defines whether you succeed or fail – it's the encapsulation of your goal state, and what you need to do to move from where you are to where you want to be. Tactics are the individual, short-term steps that you take in order to follow a strategy. "We have to defeat the hated English and cast them from our homeland, which we will do by making them pay for every inch of the country they have conquered with the blood of their people"[4] is the strategy. "Sack and burn Nottingham, salting its fields so nothing new may grow" is a tactical move.[5]

Resource management, which we discussed in our chapter on systems, is one of the primary ways in which achieving a strategy is made difficult – time, money, energy, research capacity, war weariness – all of these are currencies that different games force players to manage in pursuit of their goal. Sometimes these are short-term, tactical resources, and sometimes they have effect across the entire theatre of play.

Significant examples here include XCOM (1994, and then rebooted in 2012). Here, long-term and short-term considerations serve as independent, interlocking game systems. You send soldiers on missions where they manage ammo, health and time limitations in pursuit of a tactical goal. The spoils of those missions get fed into the larger world view, where research and industrial development create the equipment and strategic context for future tactical engagements. Sid Meier's Civilization series (Firaxis Games 1991–2016) integrates tactical and strategic considerations into a single lens on the game. *Into the Breach* (Subset Games 2018); *FTL* (Subset Games 2012); *Crusader Kings* (Paradox Interactive 2004), and *Duskers* (Undead Labs 2015) are all strategy games. Some are turn based, some real-time, but they all focus on careful management of resources in pursuit of grander aims.

Real-time strategy games, sometimes given the acronym RTS, have emerged as a very distinct subgenre of strategy games. They share many of the same goals, but the pressure of time as a ticking clock textures the experience considerably. *Herzog Zwei* (Technosoft 1990); *Dune 2* (Westwood Studios 1992), *Command and Conquer* (Westwood Studios 1992), *Warcraft* (Blizzard Entertainment 1994) and *Starcraft* (Blizzard Entertainment 1998); and *Total War* (Creative Assembly 2000- present) all fit the bill here.

Simulation Games

Simulations attempt to create an abstract model of the world and turn it into a game. Sometimes they stress accuracy, other times they take a looser approach to representing their intended domains. Strictly defined goals tend to be an afterthought, and internal consistency of systems is highly prized. *Sim City* (Weight 1989); *The Sims* (Maxis 2000); *Euro Truck Simulator* (SCS Software 2012); *Dwarf Fortress* (Bay 12 Games, 2002); and *EVE Online* (CCP Games 2003) are all examples of this genre.

We've already discussed the principle that all models are wrong, but some are useful. Some models are wrong, **useless**, but also fun. We've spoken about verisimilitude before in its experiential frame, but within simulations, we're looking for systemic verisimilitude. It doesn't really matter if the systems are accurate; they just need to **feel authentic.**

Platforming Games

You might think of platformers as a kind of puzzle game where traversal of a level is the challenge. Getting from A to B is the point of almost every moment of the game – navigating complex layouts and avoiding aggressive enemies on the way. Spatial complexity is a key element of the design of platforming games – levels must be difficult enough to be challenging, but not so challenging as to be discouraging. Here, the specific physics of movement are incredibly important – a pixel imperfection in jumping and landing can be enough to destroy the experience.

Increasingly, puzzle games also tier their experience by tying traversal to exploration, and rewarding progress with new ways to more conveniently traverse that environment. This encourages players to backtrack to unlock areas and to pick up collectibles they couldn't access until a new tool was opened up. The Metroidvania subgenre – a portmanteau of Metroid (Nintendo 1986) and Castlevania (Konami 1986) – is where you'll find this design ethos most explicitly expressed.

Some examples of platformers – *Manic Miner* (Software Projects 1983); *Super Mario Bros* (Nintendo 1985–present); *Sonic the Hedgehog* (Sega 1991–present); *Ori and the Blind Forest* (Moon Studios 2015); *Celeste* (Maddy Makes Games 2018); and *Astro Bot* (Japan Studio 2024).

First Person Shooters

If platforming games are focused on traversal of an environment, first-person shooters (FPS) are focused on domination of that environment. They're about eliminating, rather than avoiding, obstacles. Doom (id Software 2016) I have said before is a game where I think of it as a puzzle game with 60 puzzles per second, but every solution is a variation of "use gun on demon". I'm only being a little flippant – that puzzle is definitely there, it's just more visceral than it is cerebral. FPS games are all about precision – precision of movement, of placement. Of aiming, of shooting. Of timing. They're about seeking opportunities and exploiting them while minimizing the extent to which you expose yourself to risk.

They even occasionally have stories in them! However, the nature of the gameplay means that narrative tends to be punctuated – an occasional pause in the frenetic action. Sometimes, again using Doom as an example, they aggressively lampoon the heavy narrative you'll find in other games. Doom Guy, the protagonist of Doom,[6] treats diegetic exposition the same way as many of us treat interminable skippable cutscenes. Often when seeing a video call playing on a screen, he'll just push it aside or smash a fist into it. Here we see an expression of a tension – story as an unwelcome interruption to the experience of flow. This is common in many action-heavy games.

Notable examples here include the Wolfenstein games (Id Software 1992); Doom (Id Software 2016); Quake (Id Software 1996); Bioshock (2K Boston and 2K Australia 2007); Half Life (Valve 1998); *Left 4 Dead* (Valve 2008). Also all your Call of Duties (Infinity Ward 2003–present) and Halos (Bungie 2001–present) and Gearses of Warses (Epic Games 2006). It's a very popular genre.

Computer Roleplaying Games

One of the earliest genres to emerge in video games was the Computer Roleplaying Game (CRPG), due to the overlap of nerd interests between computers and *Dungeons and Dragons* (Barton and Stacks 2019). In this, gamers have been channelling the same plaintive desire for decades – "wouldn't it be great if we didn't need a Dungeon Master and could play as often as we liked?". As such, some of the first truly successful home games were to be found in this school of design. The genre has been popular the entire span of gaming, pre-dating home gaming and arcade gaming by a considerable margin. The game DND (Greenblatt 1975) was popular on the PDP-1 system, as an example.

Early CRPGs often struggled to capture the essence of a tabletop experience. Technical limitations in particular meant that story, nuance, and atmosphere had to be offloaded somewhere. Those who grew up in an era of relative computational abundance have never had to think about how much space text takes up, for example. A single-sided floppy disk for the MS-DOS system would be able to hold around 160KB of data. That's about a total of 82,000 words. Sounds like a lot, right? But a single eight-bit image of 16 × 16 would take up a full percentage of your available capacity and you still had to fit all the code into the storage too. As such, lengthy text passages would sometimes be offloaded into a book you got inside the box – in the SSI Gold Box games, this was known as the *Adventurer's Journal* and every so often the game would direct you to read a section of text. To avoid spoilers, the journal would also be full of red herrings and false leads. In-game maps would be replaced with

TABLE 12.1

Some Examples of CRPGs

Early Examples	Later Examples
Wizardry (1981–2014)	*Neverwinter Nights (2002)*
Ultima (1981–2013)	Later Fallout games (2008–2015)
Bard's Tale (1985–2018)	Divinity: Original Sin (2015)
Dungeon Master (1987)	Pillars of Eternity (2015)
The Gold Box SSI Series (1988–1993)	Undertale (2015)
Eye of the Beholder (1991)	Disco Elysium (2019)
Neverwinter Nights (1991)	Wasteland 3 (2020)
Fallout (1997)	Baldur's Gate 3 (2023)
Baldur's Gate 1 & 2 (1998–2000)	

actual paper – or sometimes cloth – inserts. Early games of this era were known for the feelies (Holmes 2012; Kocurek 2013) they included as part of the standard box set. Not the collector's edition – just the version everyone got.

As a result, early CRPGs tended to be good at simulating mechanical systems (combat, advancement, and so on) but terrible at emulating the interpersonal relationships and spirit of improvisation that defines the tabletop experience. They tended thus to play to their strengths – heavy emphasis on combat, little emphasis on roleplaying. CRPGs, in other words, are not simply TTRPGs but running on a computer.

As technology advanced, it became easier for computer RPGs to replicate the depth and complexity of tabletop storytelling. And, as the Internet moved into common usage, it even became possible to emulate the social aspects of TTRPGs more cleanly.

However, genres evolve according to their own constraints and while it's certainly now possible to play roleplaying games on a computer (through Virtual Tabletops (VTT) as an example), CRPGs have become their own very distinctive thing. While many features were drawn from traditional tabletop campaigns, a whole ecosystem of design conventions now defines the CRPG experience. And that's fine – it turns out there's still a large market for single-player oriented adventures in a tabletop mould.

As a sidebar – Neverwinter Nights (Bioware 2002; Strategic Simulations Inc 1987) appears twice in Table 12.1 because it's had two significant incarnations. The first was an AOL online game based on SSI's Gold Box engine (1991). You'd pay by the minute (eek) to engage in an early Massively Multiplayer Online Role-Playing Game (MMORPG) experience. Although massive might be stressing it, so perhaps just MORPG. In the period of 2002–2009, there was a modern reboot that used the D&D 3.5e ruleset to create essentially a playground for dungeon masters who wanted to play something more akin to the tabletop game. The 1991 variant had social roleplaying – you could trade items and fight and group up. The 2002 variant had a strong focus on module building and gamemaster tools, and a diligent DM could run a persistent campaign through it.

If you wanted a proper tabletop experience back in the days before *Neverwinter Nights*, you mostly had to look to Multiuser Dungeons (Heron 2013) and their offshoots.

Adventure Games

Adventure games focus on progression through a narrative. They're often, in themselves, a form of puzzle game, but the emphasis is usually on the story rather than the puzzles. Each of the puzzles needs to be justified in relation to the plot. Puzzle games like *Portal* (Valve 2007) require you to master the physics of momentum, and the *Talos Principle* (Croteam 2014) needs you to master positionality and line of sight. An adventure game is mostly driven by diegetic environmental puzzles (a locked door, an aggressive dog) which are resolved through interacting with objects specific to the obstacle. Many of these games are inventory based, where the player finds objects in the world and uses these to solve the problem – find the key, use it on the lock. This is a genre plagued with what are sometimes called **moon logic puzzles,**[7] where successive levels of obfuscation mean that the solutions to problems are rarely deducible in a meaningful sense. These games often lack consistent logic, and eventually all problems are solved through the heuristic of "rub everything against everything else". Use the frog on the lock. Use the rope on the lock. Use the butter on the lock. Use the credit card on the lock. Oh, right – now you're jimmying it open.

The earliest games in this category were text-based, from companies such as Infocom and level 9. Zork (Infocom 1980); Hitchhikers' Guide to the Galaxy (Infocom 1984); Wishbringer (Infocom 1985) – all examples of text adventures. These games added to the frustration of the moon logic by adding parser-based troubles – you'd try to explain to the computer what you wanted to do, and it would do its best to execute it (Montfort 2005). But you'd often find a game would go like this:

```
Look at the door
I don't understand 'the'.
look at door.
It's just a door.
open door
It's locked, you need a key.
use key in lock
I don't understand 'use'
turn key in lock
I don't understand 'turn'
kick door
I don't understand 'kick'
inventory
You are carrying: a key, some money, and a ticket to see Taylor
  Swift.
unlock lock
The lock doesn't work that way.
unlock door
You need to unlock the door with something.
unlock door with key
The key you have doesn't fit the lock.
```

At that point, maybe you just quit.

Graphical adventure games came along to help with this. First, games such as King's Quest (Sierra On-Line 1984) combined text parsers with graphics. Then along came Maniac Mansion (LucasArts 1987) in which the parser was replaced with a point and click interface, greatly simplifying the job of trying to make things happen. Monkey Island 2 (LucasArts 1991) came along and added graphical flair while simplifying the interface farther. However, this was a genre that struggled to maintain financial stability and gradually faded out of relevance before being resurrected in the Telltale Games style narrative adventure games. The Walking Dead

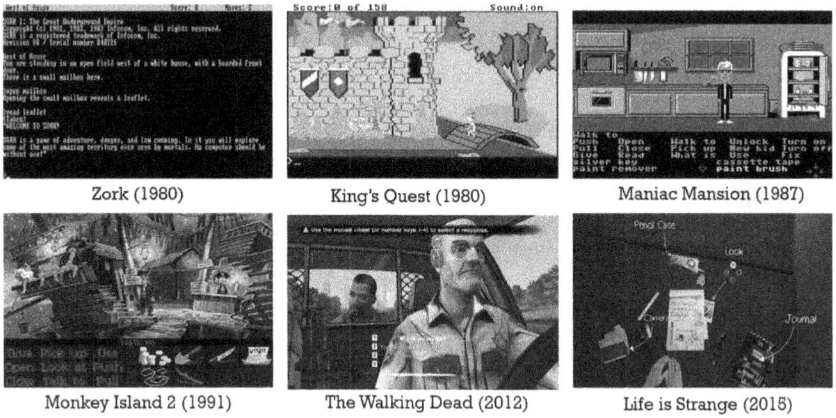

| Zork (1980) | King's Quest (1980) | Maniac Mansion (1987) |
| Monkey Island 2 (1991) | The Walking Dead (2012) | Life is Strange (2015) |

FIGURE 12.4   The Evolution of Adventure Games. Image by author.

(Telltale Games 2012) and Life Is Strange (Dontnod Entertainment 2015) further refined the narrative, simplified the interface, and gradually dialled down on the moon logic. To the point that you need to be of a generous spirit to consider many of the narrative obstacles to be puzzles at all.

The death and rebirth of adventure games shows an interesting feature of game genres too – they never truly go away they just reinvent themselves. Text adventures are still popular, although not as commercially viable as they once were. Games like *80 Days* (Inkle Studios 2014), *Fallen London* (Failbetter Games 2009), and others show that there is still an audience for literate games. At one point, you couldn't make a new isometric RPG for love nor money – then Kickstarter came along, Obsidian put *Pillars of Eternity* (Obsidian Entertainment 2015) up as a project (Schreier 2017) and now we have *Baldur's Gate 3* (Larian Studios 2023). Video game genres – like games in general – are difficult to kill.

Auteur Theory

The final topic for this whistlestop tour around video games is that of **auteur theory** (Wollen 2019; Wood 1977) – or, specifically, why situating video games as an auteur output is a problematic framing. We often talk of significant names in the games industry as if they are responsible for the games with which they are associated. In almost all cases, they are only partially responsible. Some people have a big role in setting the tone, concept and even design of a game, but we do a disservice to the legions of contributors when we omit reference to the role they play. The architect of a cathedral might be considered its author, because creative variation from the blueprints of a design is not really something we encourage of those working to a plan. We don't want a labourer to say "You know, marble is so over. I'm going to do this section in oak". The architect, or architects, lays down the plan which is to be strictly followed if the cathedral is to remain standing.

Video games aren't like that though. When we spoke about platform games earlier, I mentioned that pixel-perfect precision is important, and the feel of traversal is an important part of the experience. A senior designer might set down a guide that "movement must feel as if it has momentum", but the actual task of working out how movement should function is usually someone else's job. The directive sets a direction, but the implementation is the thing with which the player actually viscerally engages. That might be something mostly down to programming, or mostly down to perception triggered through animation. It might even be down to the sound design – players complaining of weak-feeling weapons might find themselves mollified not by an adjustment of damage but a change in the sound of the gun firing.

Liz England is a game designer who, among other things, is responsible for framing contribution in game design through what she called "the door problem".[8] In this, she gives a premise: you are making a game, and it has doors in it. And then she provides a series of questions about those doors to show just how complex even an everyday feature can be. Can the doors be opened? Can every door be opened? How does the player know the difference between closed doors that can be opened and those just for decoration? Do enemies spawn into the game from doors? Do doors lock behind players, and if so how do you handle that in multiplayer games? England has a lot of questions for developers, and they show the sophistication of thinking that underpins a lot of game design.

In addition to this, she lists the various roles at a big company and outlines exactly what they contribute to the solution. Three dozen individual roles, from the creative director ("yes, we definitely need doors in this game"), through to the sound designer ("I made the sounds the door creates when it opens and closes"), through to the lighting engineer ("There is a bright red light over the door when it's locked, and a green one when it's opened"), all the way down to the player ("I totally didn't even notice a door there"). Go read her article, it's a brilliant framing.

Leaving aside what this means for doors though, what this article shows is the way in which contribution within game design accumulates, and how nobody is necessarily more important than anyone else. Sometimes the "feels" you get from a game aren't linked to the most prominent names in the credits.

Auteur theory derives from a cinematic movement known as the **caméra-stylo** (Heinke 2017; Ray 2020), or "camera pen". This posits that film is an audiovisual language, and it is the director who writes the film with their camera. Other roles exist primarily in support of the director. You find this at play when a single creative is so unbound and omnipresent that they should be considered the "author" of a movie. Framing a movie in such a way allows for a critic to consider the themes, values, and stylistic flourish of the author in a way that a more full-bodied appreciation of contribution doesn't. While this has become a dominant viewpoint in film criticism, it's not without its own critics. Some believe the screenwriter is truly the principal author of a movie. Some argue that it is the main actor who is the primary author. Others argue that the concept lacks any kind of meaning in the age of the corporate cinema. Various producers, executive producers, and miscellaneous "suits" can interfere with the vision of a movie in service of commercial aims.

Nonetheless, this assumption that creative outputs have a principal author is one that has begun to seep into game criticism. Sometimes it's even true – board games in particular often have a handful of people involved in their creation, and the designer is habitually credited on the box. Increasingly so too are the artists that create the aesthetics of play, reflecting an increased awareness of collaborative credit. That's fair – I buy any game in which Maisherly Chan, the artist of Hanamikoji (Sen 2014), has been involved. I don't care what the game is, I just love her artwork.

In the early days of game development, games often were solo products. The "bedroom coder" of the United Kingdom was the lynchpin of the entire industry (Kirkpatrick 2017; Wade 2016) – a solo developer who took on responsibility for designing and developing the game before selling it as a unit to a publisher. Much like the author of a novel, game development for home computers in the 70s and early 80s was often a solo creative pursuit.

That hasn't been true for a long time though, and leaving aside a few notable outliers,[9] the idea that any game has a single visionary behind it has no real credibility. Yet, much of modern gaming discourse reflects this assumption. Video games are made up of many important creative roles, full of important creative people who are often underemphasized in discussion about games. And, importantly, this is not only a problem in terms of authentically capturing contribution, it also tends to erase the contribution of women due to the overwhelming concentration of "auteurs" in the XY chromosome camp. IGN's list of 100 top game creators lists one and a half women[10] in its roster of luminaries Danielle Bunten Berry, and then Roberta Williams shared a slot with her husband Ken Williams. PC Gamer in 2023 celebrated 30 years of video game history without naming a single woman.[11] When we think of those who have gained at least some attention as influential game professionals, or straight up auteurs, even professional periodicals struggle to recognize the many women who have been critical in creating the game experiences that so enervate us.

It's easy to notice Lucas Pope – both Papers, Please (Pope 2013) and Return of the Obra Dinn (Pope 2018) have been a part of our discussions so far. And to be fair, I do consider Pope to be one of, if not **the**, most innovative game designers working in the field. But what about Kim Swift who was a dominant force in the development of *Portal* (Valve 2007) and *Left 4 Dead* (Valve 2008)? Even in a world of Overwatch (Blizzard Entertainment 2016) and Valorant (Ropt Games 2020), I still consider *Left 4 Dead* to be the best squad-based shooter. She was a team leader for Portal, but also a level designer… and if you've ever played Portal you'll know just how significant the level design is to the experience of play.

It's certainly fair to elevate Sid Meier above almost all his contemporaries, although these days he is more of a brand than a hands-on designer. Even Sid himself would make it clear that his name on the marquee of a game is often more about marketing than anything else (Meier 2020). However, elevating Meier means that the actual lead designers of the mainline Civilization games are relatively obscure. Bryan Reynolds (Civilization II and Alpha Centauri); Soren Johnson (Civilization 4); Ed Beach (Civilization 6) – all had a larger role to play than the celebrated auteur.

Will Wright is the genius behind many games we have already discussed. He didn't invent simulation games, but he was certainly the one who made them obviously commercially viable. Sim City (Wright 1989) was a game that many publishers believed couldn't possibly succeed. No lives, no scoring, no enemies to kill. What, you need to take hours just to see a city start to function and yet you can't win the game? That won't play in Peoria. Still, he persevered and Broderbund gave him a shot (Kent 2010). The rest is history. You have probably heard of Wright, but maybe not Lucy Bradshaw who was a significant presence at Maxis during the early days of The Sims (1 and 2). Or what about Lyndsay Pearson, who is sometimes described as the "creative heart" of the series?

Shigeru Miyamoto is a clear candidate for auteur status, given that he is the likely architect of many readers' childhood. *Donkey Kong* (Nintendo 1981), *Super Mario*

Bros (Nintendo 1985), *The Legend of Zelda* (Nintendo 1986), *Star Fox* (Nintendo 1993) – he had a significant, even dominant, hand in all of them. Nintendo wouldn't be where it is today (a weird company that twirls to the right when everyone else waltzes to the left) without his influence. Indeed, we can see an impressive roster of Japanese names amongst those most often identified as stand-out figures in the gaming industry. Hideo Kojima is unabashedly self-promotional in his auteur status (Hartzheim 2023; Pettini 2015) – playing *Metal Gear Solid five* (Konami 2015) has every single mission you undertake book-ended by opening and closing credits that won't let you forget it. Death Stranding (Kojima Productions 2019) is widely considered to be his opus, and he self-inserts himself with comical regularity into the games he makes. Hidetaka Miyazaki is a core driving force behind FromSoftware. A creative visionary, to be sure, and someone worthy of his standing. Even if all he contributed to game design was his memorable note on the artistic direction of Dark Souls, he'd still have shifted the industry.[12]

We talk much less about Mari Shimazaki who created the striking look of Bayonetta (PlatinumGames 2019) – which I would argue is one of the main things that makes the game so camp and fun. Or Miki Higashino, who created much of the audio soundscape of the Suikoden series (Konami 1995). We hear a lot less about the women. Auteur theory, as a way of framing authorship, erases their contributions underneath the much more prominent senior figures in the industry, who just so happen to be overwhelmingly men.

This isn't though just an issue of sexism in critique. It's about the extent to which contribution is recognized proportionate to its impact.

Life Is Strange (Dontnod Entertainment 2015) is an immensely popular franchise, and I am equally immensely fond of it. Asking Google who the creatives were behind it gives me a list. Designed by Baptiste Moisan, Sebastien Judit and Sebastien Gaillard. Art by Michel Koch, Kenny Laurent, and Amaury Balandier. Written by Christian Divine and Jean-Luc Cano. Score composed by Jonathan Morali. All deserve the plaudits they get. But you know who it was who really made me fall in love with Life is Strange?

No, me either.

I **do** know it's whoever picked out the licenced music that accompanies the game. I have two major playlists in Spotify. They're called "Pre Life Is Strange" and "Post Life Is Strange". The former is made up of all the vaguely "dad rock" artists I grew up with. The other is a collection linked together in the genre of "sad emo girls being sad". *Life Is Strange* completely rewrote my musical tastes. There are certain songs I can't even listen to without feeling tears welling up. I don't even know who to thank for that – but if you're reading, you have my sincere gratitude.

Consider what Rhianne Pratchett did for the Tomb Raider reboot (Crystal Dynamics 2013) and for Rise of the Tomb Raider (Crystal Dynamics 2015), and what was lost when she didn't architect the story for the final entry in the trilogy. Consider how Amy Hennig directed Uncharted (Naughty Dog 2007) and how she was one of the major contributors who made you fall in love with Nathan Drake. Consider how 80 Days (Inkle Studios 2014) would have been a lot less compelling without Meg Jayanth's flair and philosophy underpinning much of the text.

Lena Raine is one of the regular features of my "Post Life Is Strange" playlist, and her wonderful compositions in Celeste are as much part of the storytelling as the writing and the animation.[13] Aleksander Rostov's bleak artistic style is part of the heart of Disco Elysium (ZA/UM 2019). Jackob Mikkelsen and Marta le Mendola are two of the most prominent level designers for Hitman (IO Interactive 2016-Present), and if you've ever played it you might believe – as I do – that they are employing some kind of witchcraft to accomplish the miracles of intricacy they pull off. Jade Raymond was one of the programmers and executive producers for games such as *Assassins Creed* (Ubisoft 2007), *Watch Dogs* (Ubisoft 2014), and *Far Cry 4* (Ubisoft 2014). Any time you drop from the sky and shank a Templar with your wrist-blades, you should pour a measure of whisky onto the ground for her.

Whether or not a single person puts a distinctive "stamp" on a game, I advise you to look at the credits of some of your favourite titles and try to work out how much each person contributed to your experience. You may find the proportion of your joy does not fall in line with the prominence of authorship. If games are the primary texts of our discipline, and I believe that is the case, then you have the same duty to recognize the contributions of the authors of a game the way you do authors in an academic paper. Games are too complex, made up of too many interlocking elements, for us to fall into the trap of thinking a single person is responsible for their success or failure.

Notes

1　Although the exact numbers and circumstances are uncertain. See the Videogame Historian for a fascinating deep-dive into this: https://videogamehistorian.wordpress.com/tag/syzygy-engineering.
2　See https://www.ign.com/articles/ea-sports-fc-fifa-split-reasons.
3　See https://olympics.com/ioc/recognised-international-federations.
4　In Sid Meier's Civilization series.
5　Again, in Sid Meier's Civilization series.
6　It has been convincingly – some might say conclusively – argued by Luke Westaway of YouTube channel Outside Xtra that Doom Guy is the same character as Link from Zelda.
7　https://tvtropes.org/pmwiki/pmwiki.php/Main/MoonLogicPuzzle.
8　https://www.gamedeveloper.com/design/-quot-the-door-problem-quot-of-game-design.
9　Both Undertale and Stardew Valley could be argued to have an obvious single principal author. Minecraft too, for a long time. However, even in this we should think of them as first authors, rather than solo authors.
10　https://www.ign.com/lists/top-100-game-creators/.
11　https://www.pcgamer.com/celebrating-30-years-of-pc-gamer/.
12　"Don't rely on the gross factor to portray an undead dragon. Can't you instead try to convey the deep sorrow of a magnificent beast doomed to a slow and possibly endless descent into ruin?" (Software 2014).
13　"It's a game where you're throwing yourself at these very difficult levels and you're failing over and over and over again – but the game and the music are not working against you. They're saying, you can do this, you can overcome this! The game literally tells you that. The way that it's designed is friendly towards retrying. The music doesn't try to punish you for doing badly, it encourages you" as she is quoted in Composer Magazine.

References

Aarseth, Espen. 1995. *Cybertext: Perspectives on Ergodic Literature*. Bergen: University of Bergen.

Barton, Matt, and Shane Stacks. 2019. *Dungeons and Desktops: The History of Computer Role-Playing Games 2e*. Florida: AK Peters/CRC Press.

Bedi, Joyce. 2019. 'Ralph Baer: An Interactive Life'. *Human Behavior and Emerging Technologies* 1(1):18–25. doi: 10.1002/hbe2.119.

Cohen, D. S. 2012. 'Cathode-Ray Tube Amusement Device–The First Electronic Game'. *About. Com*. https://patents.google.com/patent/US2455992.

De La Cruz, Angel, and John Ryan. 2015. 'Tennis for Two'. MIT bachelor thesis, Cambridge. https://web.mit.edu/6.101/www/s2016/projects/jackryan_Project_Final_Report.pdf

DeLeon, Christopher L. 2012. 'Arcade-Style Game Design: Postwar Pinball and the Golden Age of Coin-Op Videogames'. PhD Thesis, Georgia Institute of Technology.

Ernkvist, Mirko. 2008. 'Down Many Times, but Still Playing the Game: Creative Destruction and Industry Crashes in the Early Video Game Industry 1971–1986'.

Hahn, Eric. 2023. 'Coin-Op Conspiracies: Nostalgia and Moral Panic in the Video Arcade'. *The Journal of Popular Culture* 56(3–4):623–34. doi: 10.1111/jpcu.13250.

Hartzheim, Bryan Hikari. 2023. *Hideo Kojima: Progressive Game Design from Metal Gear to Death Stranding*. New York: Bloomsbury Publishing USA.

Heinke, Ralf Heiner. 2017. 'Between Caméra Stylo and the Making of Images: Hitchcock's Cinematographers'. Pp. 41–58 in *Reassessing the Hitchcock Touch*, edited by W. Schwanebeck. Cham: Springer International Publishing.

Heron, Michael. 2013. '"Likely to Be Eaten by a Grue"—the Relevance of Text Games in the Modern Era'. *The Computer Games Journal* 2:55–67.

Heron, Michael James. 2015. 'Everybody's Talking about Pop Music: The Evolution of the Cinematic Video Game'. *The Computer Games Journal* 4(1):3–17.

Holmes, Dylan. 2012. *A Mind Forever Voyaging: A History of Storytelling in Video Games*. Dylan Holmes.

Ivory, James D. 2015. 'A Brief History of Video Games'. Pp. 1–21 in *The Video Game Debate*, edited by Rachel Kowert and Quandt Thorsten. Abingdon: Routledge.

Kent, Steven L. 2010. *The Ultimate History of Video Games, Volume 1: From Pong to Pokemon and Beyond... the Story Behind the Craze That Touched Our Lives and Changed the World*. Vol. 1. New York: Crown.

Kirkpatrick, Graeme. 2017. 'Early Games Production, Gamer Subjectivation and the Containment of the Ludic Imagination 1'. Pp. 19–37 in *Fans and Videogames*, edited by Melanie Swalwell, Angela Ndallanis, Helen Stucket. Abingdon: Routledge.

Kirriemuir, John. 2006. 'A History of Digital Games'. Pp. 21–35 in Jason Rutter and Jo Bryce *Understanding Digital Games*. Los Angeles: Sage Publications.

Kocurek, Carly A. 2013. 'The Treachery of Pixels: Reconsidering Feelies in an Era of Digital Play'. *Journal of Gaming & Virtual Worlds* 5(3):295–306. doi: 10.1386/jgvw.5.3.295_1.

Lean, Thomas. 2014. '"Inside a Day You Will Be Talking to It Like an Old Friend": The Making and Remaking of Sinclair Personal Computing in 1980s Britain'. Pp. 49–71 in *Hacking Europe*, *History of Computing*, edited by G. Alberts and R. Oldenziel. London: Springer London.

Lendino, Jamie. 2020. *Attract Mode: The Rise and Fall of Coin-Op Arcade Games*. New Jersey: Steel Gear Press.

Li, Xiaozhou, and Boyang Zhang. 2020. 'A Preliminary Network Analysis on Steam Game Tags: Another Way of Understanding Game Genres'. Pp. 65–73 in *Proceedings of the 23rd International Conference on Academic Mindtrek*. Tampere Finland: ACM.

Mailland, Julien. 2024. *The Game That Never Ends: How Lawyers Shape the Videogame Industry*. Cambridge: MIT Press.

Mazor, Stanley, and Peter Salmon. 2009. 'Magnavox and Intel: An Odyssey'. *IEEE Annals of the History of Computing* 31(3):64–66.

Meades, Alan. 2019. 'The American Arcade Sanitization Crusade and the Amusement Arcade Action Group'. in *Transgression in Games and Play*, edited by Kristine Jørgensen and Faltin Karlsen. Cambridge: MIT Press.

Meades, Alan. 2022. *Arcade Britannia: A Social History of the British Amusement Arcade*. Cambridge: MIT Press.

Meier, Sid. 2020. *Sid Meier's Memoir!: A Life in Computer Games*. New York: WW Norton & Company.

Montfort, Nick. 2005. *Twisty Little Passages: An Approach to Interactive Fiction*. Cambridge: MIT Press.

Pettini, Silvia. 2015. 'Auteurism and Game Localization — Revisiting Translational Approaches: Film Quotations in Multimedia Interactive Entertainment'. *Translation Spaces* 4(2):268–88. doi: 10.1075/ts.4.2.05pet.

Platt, Charles, and David Langford. 1984. *MICROMANIA: The Whole Truth about Home Computers: With D.* London, Langford: Gollancz.

Ray, Robert B. 2020. 'The Automatic Auteur; Or, a Certain Tendency in Film Criticism'. Pp. 57–76 in *The Structure of Complex Images*. New York, Cham: Springer International Publishing.

Rogaleva, K. S. 2018. 'The History of the Development of Video Games'.

Schreier, Jason. 2017. *Blood, Sweat, and Pixels: The Triumphant, Turbulent Stories behind How Video Games Are Made*. New York: Harper.

Software, From. 2014. *Dark Souls: Design Works*. Illustrated edition. Udon Entertainment: Udon Entertainment.

Surinx, François-Xavier. 2023. 'For an Understanding of Video Games Genres through the Discourse of Players'. in *Abstract Proceedings of DiGRA 2023 Conference: Limits and Margins of Games*. Tampere: DIGRA.

Tannahill, Devon. 2014. 'Rise of the Machine: The Making of the Video Game Industry and Military Simulation'. PhD Thesis.

Wade, Alex. 2016. *Playback–A Genealogy of 1980s British Videogames*. New York: Bloomsbury Publishing USA.

Wollen, P. (2019). *Signs and meaning in the cinema*. New York: Bloomsbury Publishing.

Wood, Robin. 1977. 'Ideology, Genre, Auteur'. *Film Comment* 13(1):46.

Ludography

2K Games. 1999–2024. NBA Basketball Series [Video games] [Multiple platforms] 2K Games.

2K Games. 2007. BioShock [Video game] [Microsoft Windows]. 2K Games.

2K Games. 2013–2024. WWE Wrestling Series [Video games] [Multiple platforms] 2K Games.

Advanced Microcomputer Systems. 1983. Dragon's Lair [Arcade game] [Arcade]. Cinematronics.

Atari Games. 1989. 'Hard Drivin'[Arcade game] [Arcade]. Atari Games.

Atari. 1979. Asteroids [Arcade game] [Arcade]. Atari.

Atari. 1980. Missile Command [Arcade game] [Arcade]. Atari.

Atari. 1981. Defender [Arcade game] [Arcade]. Atari.

Atari. 1983. Star Wars [Arcade game] [Arcade]. Atari.

Awe Interactive. 2020. Bullets Per Minute [Video game] [Microsoft Windows]. Awe Interactive.

Bally Midway. 1983. Spy Hunter [Arcade game] [Arcade]. Bally Midway.

Bay 12 Games. 2002. Dwarf Fortress [Video game] [Microsoft Windows]. Bay 12 Games.

BioWare. 2002. Neverwinter Nights [Video game] [Microsoft Windows] Atari.

Blizzard Entertainment. 1994. Warcraft: Orcs & Humans [Video game] [Microsoft Windows]. Blizzard Entertainment.

Blizzard Entertainment. 1998. Starcraft [Video game] [Microsoft Windows]. Blizzard Entertainment.

Blizzard Entertainment. 2016. Overwatch [Video game] [Microsoft Windows] Blizzard Entertainment.

Brace Yourself Games. 2015. Crypt of the NecroDancer [Video game] [Microsoft Windows]. Brace Yourself Games.

Brand, Inka, Brand, Markus. 2016. EXIT: The Game Series [Board game] [Various platforms] Kosmos.

Brøderbund. 1993. Myst [Video game] [Microsoft Windows]. Brøderbund.

Bungie. 2001. Halo: Combat Evolved [Video game] [Microsoft Xbox] Microsoft Game Studios.

CCP Games. 2003. Eve Online [Video game] [Microsoft Windows]. CCP Games.

Capcom. 1991. Street Fighter II [Arcade game] [Arcade]. Capcom.

Carroll, Alice, Thomas Cauet, and Cyril Demaegd. 2017. Unlock! Series [Board game]. Space Cowboys.

Codemasters. 2007–2024. Dirt Series [Video games] [Multiple platforms]. Codemasters.

ConcernedApe. 2016. Stardew Valley [Video game] [Microsoft Windows]. ConcernedApe.

Core Design. 1996. Tomb Raider [Video game] [Sony Playstation]. Eidos Interactive.

Creative Assembly. 2000. Total War: Shogun [Video game] [Microsoft Windows]. Electronic Arts.

Croteam. 2014. The Talos Principle [Video game] [Microsoft Windows]. Devolver Digital.

Crystal Dynamics. 2015. Rise of the Tomb Raider [Video game] [Microsoft Windows]. Square Enix.

DMA Design. 1990. Lemmings [Video game] [Microsoft Windows]. Psygnosis.

Disney. 2022. Dreamlight Valley [Video game] [Microsoft Windows]. Disney Interactive.

Dontnod Entertainment. 2015. Life Is Strange [Video game] [Microsoft Windows]. Square Enix.

EA Sports. 1988–2024. Madden NFL Series [Video games] [Multiple platforms]. EA Sports.

EA Sports. 1993–2023. FIFA Series [Video games] [Multiple platforms] EA Sports.

EA Sports. 2023. EA Sports FC [Video game] [Microsoft Windows]. EA Sports.

Epic Games. 2006. Gears of War [Video game] [Microsoft Windows]. Epic Games.

Epyx. 1984. Summer Games [Video game] [Commodore 64]. Epyx.

Failbetter Games. 2009. Fallen London [Browser game] [Web Browser]. Failbetter Games.

Firaxis Games. 1991. Sid Meier's Civilization [Video game] [Microsoft DOS]. MicroProse.

Firaxis Games. 1994. XCOM: UFO Defense [Video game] [Microsoft Windows]. MicroProse.

Firaxis Games. 1996. Sid Meier's Civilization II [Video game] [Microsoft Windows]. MicroProse.

Firaxis Games. 2001. Sid Meier's Civilization III [Video game] [Microsoft Windows]. Infogrames.

Firaxis Games. 2005. Sid Meier's Civilization IV [Video game] [Microsoft Windows]. 2K Games.

Firaxis Games. 2010. Sid Meier's Civilization V [Video game] [Microsoft Windows]. 2K Games.

Firaxis Games. 2016. Sid Meier's Civilization VI [Video game] [Microsoft Windows]. 2K Games.

Firaxis Ganes. 2012. XCOM: Enemy Unknown [video game] [Microsoft Windows]. 2K.

FromSoftware. 2011. Dark Souls [Video game] [Microsoft Windows]. Namco Bandai Games.

FromSoftware. 2015. Bloodborne [Video game] [Sony Playstation]. Sony Computer Entertainment.

FromSoftware. 2019. Sekiro: Shadows Die Twice [Video game] [Microsoft Windows]. Activision.

FromSoftware. 2022. Elden Ring [Video game] [Microsoft Windows]. Bandai Namco Entertainment.

Game Science. 2024. Black Myth: Wukong [Video game] [Microsoft Windows]. Game Science.

Greenblatt, Richard. 1975. DND [Video game] [PDP–1] MIT.

IO Interactive. 2016-Present. Hitman Series [Video game] [Microsoft Windows]. IO Interactive.

Infinity Ward. 2003. Call of Duty [Video game] [Microsoft Windows]. Activision.

Infocom. 1980. Zork [Video game] [Microsoft DOS]. Infocom.

Infocom. 1984. The Hitchhiker's Guide to the Galaxy [Video game] [Microsoft DOS].Infocom.

Infocom. 1985. Wishbringer [Video game] [Microsoft DOS].Infocom.

Inkle Studios. 2014. 80 Days [Video game] [Microsoft Windows]. Inkle Studios.

Japan Studio. 2024. Astro Bot [Video game] [PlayStation 5]. Sony Interactive Entertainment.

Kojima Productions. 2019. Death Stranding [Video game] [Sony Playstation]. Sony Interactive Entertainment.

Konami. 1981. Frogger [Arcade game] [Arcade]. Konami.

Konami. 1986. Castlevania [Video game] [Nintendo Entertainment System]. Konami.

Konami. 1995. Suikoden [Video game] [Sony Playstation]. Konami.

Konami. 2015. Metal Gear Solid V: The Phantom Pain [Video game] [Microsoft Windows]. Konami.

Kosmos. 2016. Exit [Board game] [N/A]. Kosmos.

Larian Studios. 2023. Baldur's Gate 3. [Video game] [Microsoft Windows]. Larian Studios.

Level -5. 2007–2021. Professor Layton Series [Video game] [Nintendo DS, Nintendo 3DS, Nintendo Switch].

LucasArts. 1987. Maniac Mansion [Video game] [Personal Computer]. LucasArts.

LucasArts. 1991. The Secret of Monkey Island: LeChuck's Revenge [Video game] [Personal Computer]. LucasArts.

Lucasfilm Games. 1991. Star Wars: Dark Forces [Video game] [Microsoft Windows]. LucasArts.

Maddy Makes Games. 2018. Celeste [Video game] [Microsoft Windows]. Maddy Makes Games.

Maxis. 2000. The Sims [video game] [Microsoft Windows]. Electronic Arts.

Microsoft Studios. 2005–2021. Forza Motorsport Series [Video games] [Multiple platforms]. Microsoft Studios.

Moon Studios. 2015. Ori and the Blind Forest [Video game] [Microsoft Windows]. Microsoft Studios.

Namco. 1979. Galaxian [Arcade game] [Arcade]. Namco.

Namco. 1980. Pac-Man [Arcade game] [Arcade]. Namco.

Naughty Dog. 2007. Uncharted: Drake's Fortune [Video game] [Sony Playstation]. Sony Computer Entertainment.

Nintendo. 1981. Donkey Kong [Arcade game] [Arcade]. Nintendo.

Nintendo. 1985. Super Mario Bros [Video game] [Nintendo Entertainment System]. Nintendo.

Nintendo. 1986. Metroid [Video game] [Nintendo Entertainment System]. Nintendo.

Nintendo. 1986. The Legend of Zelda [Video game] [Nintendo Entertainment System]. Nintendo.

Nintendo. 1993. Star Fox [Video game] [Super Nintendo Entertainment System]. Nintendo.

Nintendo. 1996. Super Mario 64 [Video game] [Nintendo 64]. Nintendo.

Nintendo. 2020. Animal Crossing: New Horizons [Video game] [Nintendo Switch]. Nintendo.

Nintendo. 2022. Mario Kart 8 Deluxe [Video game] [Nintendo Switch]. Nintendo.

No More Robots. 2017. Golf Story [Video game] [Nintendo Switch]. No More Robots.

Nosebleed Interactive. 2021. Arcade Paradise [Video game] [Microsoft Windows]. Wired Productions.

Obsidian Entertainment. 2005. Neverwinter Nights 2 [Video game] [Microsoft DOS]. Atari.

Obsidian Entertainment. 2015. Pillars of Eternity [Video game] [Microsoft Windows] Paradox Interactive.

Oy, Hempuli. 2019. Baba Is You [Video game] [Microsoft Windows]. Hempuli Oy.

Paradox Interactive. 2004. Crusader Kings [Video game] [Microsoft Windows]. Paradox Interactive.

PlatinumGames. 2009. Bayonetta [Video game] [Sony Playstation]. Sega.

Polyphony Digital. 1997–2024. Gran Turismo Series [Video games] [PlayStation platforms] Sony Interactive Entertainment.

Pope, Lucas. 2018. Return of the Obra Dinn [Video game] [Nintendo Switch]. 3909.

Psyonix. 2015. Rocket League [Video game] [Microsoft Windows]. Psyonix.

Respawn Entertainment. 2019. Jedi: Fallen Order [Video game] [Microsoft Windows]. Electronic Arts.

Riot Games. 2020. Valorant [Video game] [Microsoft Windows]. Riot Games.

Rundisc. 2023. Chants of Sennaar [Video game] [Microsoft Windows]. Focus Entertainment.

SCS Software. 2012. Euro Truck Simulator 2 [Video game] [Microsoft Windows]. SCS Software.

SEGA. 1987. Afterburner [Arcade game] [Arcade]. Sega.

SMG Studio. 2021. Unpacking [Video game] [Microsoft Windows]. Humble Games.

Sega. 1986. OutRun [Arcade game] [Arcade]. Sega.

Sega. 1991. Sonic the Hedgehog [Video game] [Sega Genesis]. Sega.

Sen, Yugo. 2014. Hanamikoji [Board game]. EmperorS4.

Sid Meier. 1991. Sid Meier's Civilization [Video game] [Microsoft Windows]. MicroProse.

Sierra On-Line. 1984–2015. King's Quest series [Video games] [Personal Computer, Console]. Sierra On-Line, Telltale Games, The Odd Gentlemen.

Software Projects. 1983. Manic Miner [Video game] [ZX Spectrum]. Software Projects.

Strategic Simulations, Inc. 1987. Neverwinter Nights [Video game] [Apple II]. Strategic Simulations, Inc.

Subset Games. 2012. FTL: Faster Than Light [Video game] [Microsoft Windows]. Subset Games.

Subset Games. 2018. Into the Breach [Video game] [Microsoft Windows]. Subset Games.

THQ. 1999–2012. WWE/WWF Wrestling Series [Video games] [Multiple platforms]. THQ.

Taito. 1978. Space Invaders [Arcade game] [Arcade]. Taito.

Taito. 1987. Operation Wolf [Arcade game] [Arcade]. Taito.

Technosoft. 1990. Herzog Zwei [Video game] [Sega Mega Drive]. Sega.

Telltale Games. 2012. The Walking Dead [Video game] [Microsoft Windows]. Telltale Games.

Thekla, Inc. 2016. The Witness [Video game] [Microsoft Windows]. Thekla, Inc.

Thunder Lotus Games. 2020. Spiritfarer [Video game] [Microsoft Windows]. Thunder Lotus Games.

Ubisoft. 2007. Assassin's Creed [Video game] [Microsoft Windows]. Ubisoft.

Ubisoft. 2014. Far Cry 4 [Video game] [Microsoft Windows]. Ubisoft.

Ubisoft. 2014. Watch Dogs [Video game] [Microsoft Windows]. Ubisoft.

Undead Labs. 2015. Duskers [Video game] [Microsoft Windows]. Strangelite Studios.

Valve. 1998. Half-Life [Video game] [Microsoft Windows]. Sierra Studios.

Valve. 2007. Portal [Video game] [Microsoft Windows]. Valve.

Valve. 2008. Left 4 Dead [Video game] [Microsoft Windows]. Electronic Arts.

Vanillaware. 2020. 13 Sentinels: Aegis Rim [Video game] [Sony Playstation]. Atlus.

Visual Concepts. 1986. NBA 2K25 [Video Game] [Microsoft Windows]. 2K.

Westwood Studios. 1992. Dune II [Video game] [Microsoft Windows]. Virgin Interactive.

Westwood Studios. 1995. Command and Conquer [Video game] [Microsoft Windows]. Virgin Interactive.

Whippoorwill. 2019. A Short Hike [Video game] [Nintendo Switch]. Whippoorwill.

Wizards of the Coast. 1974. Dungeons & Dragons [Tabletop game] [N/A]. Wizards of the Coast.

Wright, Will. 1989. Sim City [video game] [Commodore Amiga]. Maxis.

ZA/UM. 2019. Disco Elysium [Video game] [Microsoft Windows]. ZA/UM.

id Software. 1992. Wolfenstein 3D [Video game] [Microsoft Windows]. id Software.

id Software. 1996. Quake [Video game] [Microsoft Windows]. id Software.

Id Software. 2016. Doom [video game] [Microsoft Windows]. Bethesda Softwarks.

id Software. 2020. Doom Eternal [Video game] [Microsoft Windows]. Bethesda Softworks.

inkle. 2014. 80 Days [Video game] [Microsoft Windows]. inkle.

tobyfox. 2015. Undertale [Video game] [Microsoft Windows]. tobyfox.

13

How Chants of Sennaar *Creates Intriguing Gameplay around Learning Culturally Infused Languages*

Luise Donat and Julius Lilie

Introduction

In the video game *Chants of Sennaar* (Rundisc 2023), the player finds themself in a strange world as a faceless person who neither speaks nor seems to have a backstory. The game starts with a relatively simple puzzle – pulling a lever to open a gate. However, there is one challenge: The description of said lever is written in strange glyphs, and presented without any translation given to guide as to their meaning.

This is how the game immediately throws the player into its mysterious environment. During the game, you will explore different places, meet people of various cultures and classes, and initially never understand the language in which they communicate. This is where the game's challenge arises: trying to understand the language and its context through the actions and speech bubbles of the inhabitants; through paintings with inscription; or notebooks lying around the world. The game simulates a person being placed into a strange culture and needing to understand the language in order to navigate an unfamiliar environment.

Chants of Sennaar has a very enticing way of engaging the players: Its core gameplay relies on translating strange glyphs with the help of a notebook. These translations are completely up to the player – any word can be entered as a definition for any glyph, with a few starter translations provided to help. This creates an engaging and fun playing experience as it can make the player feel like a linguist deciphering a lost language, or a puzzle solver needing to understand their environment to reach their goal. This combination of clever puzzle-solving mechanics and a visually pleasing aesthetic is reflected in its broadly positive perception in the eyes of critics.

What makes the language-solving mechanic of *Chants of Sennaar* stand out is how each of the five languages is uniquely constructed. Not only do they each incorporate core grammar rules (negation, pluralization, and the order of verbs and nouns), but each language also has its own individual vocabulary which reflects their people's culture. This creates interesting game mechanics by making the translations more

DOI: 10.1201/9781003530282-13

difficult while also forcing the player to reflect on how cultures shape languages. It's a powerful form of implicit storytelling – it is possible, by engaging with the languages in the context of their culture, to deduce the meanings of glyphs if one is reflective and observant.

Background

In order to analyse the game's mechanics and put them into perspective compared to other games in the genre, this section will provide an overview of existing literature and media focusing on language-related gameplay.

Apart from *Chants of Sennaar*, other games have previously explored the themes of deciphering languages and understanding foreign cultures. These games often introduce a fictional language, usually in combination with made-up symbols for scripture, and prompt the player to decipher its meaning to advance in the game.

Heaven's Vault (Inkle 2019), one of the core inspirations of *Chants of Sennaar,* features a similar game mechanic of translating unfamiliar symbols into words to learn more about ancient cultures and people. The player takes on the role of an archaeologist who investigates multiple moons to learn more about their forgotten past. In this game, a hieroglyphic language has to be uncovered by choosing between different translations for each symbol the player encounters while exploring the environment. Contrary to *Chants of Sennaar*, the player does not have complete freedom in their translations, but limited options as to what a symbol might mean. On one hand, this makes the translations a little bit easier – you do not have to figure out whether a symbol is a preposition or a noun, but only which one makes the most sense within the given context. If one sees a particular symbol often appear alongside running water, one may assume that it has some relation to water. However, Heaven's Vault never tells you whether your choices were correct – on the contrary, the protagonist's analysis of the culture is influenced by these translations whether they were accurate or not.[1] In *Chants of Sennaar*, there is a correct translation for each symbol which can be unlocked with the use of an in-game dictionary. Fully exploring the language and its structure is vital to solving the final puzzle of the game, which takes the form of a kind of "reverse tower of Babel" in which linguistic incompatibility must be addressed.

Captain Blood (ERE Informatique 1988); Observation (No Code 2019); and Sethian (Duang! Games LLC 2016) are other games focusing on learning fictional languages. All of these games implement language deciphering as puzzle mechanics, with the protagonist being a space explorer or an AI having to communicate with aliens to achieve certain goals. The game *Missing Translation* (AlPixel Games 2015) also uses fictional language learning in the form of a hand-drawn language. This though is only one of its challenges, not its core feature. Lingotopia (Lingo Ludo 2018) is a language learning game about being lost in a city where you don't speak the local language. It offers a variety of languages like Chinese, German, or Japanese to study. Language acquisition mainly happens by learning words one at a time through contextual clues. This is similar in many respects to the game Influent (Howland 2014).

In relation to games like Heaven's Vault, the terms *Archaeogaming* and *culturally significant presence* are sometimes used to describe games focusing on cultural heritage and archaeological aspects (Champion 2020; Hageneuer 2021). Archaeogaming is described as "an archaeological framework which, broadly speaking, includes the study of archaeology in and of video games, as well as the use of video games for archaeological purposes" (Reinhard 2018). Literature referencing this categorization of video games usually does not focus on the language part of the culture, but rather on the discovery of ancient places or cultural artefacts like art. Generally, most relevant research on language-learning games so far has been put into pedagogic games, not the gameplay mechanic of language-learning itself from a game research perspective. This represents a compelling knowledge gap that we attempt to address in this chapter.

Analysis

Looking at *Chants of Sennaar*, the game's mechanics and incorporation of culture and different fictional languages are what create an immersive game experience. *Chants of Sennaar* begins with the protagonist waking up in an ancient world without any information on how or why they got there. There is no tutorial provided regarding the game puzzles and language structures, only one for the basic controls relating to movement and interaction.

Language Acquisition

One of the main aspects of *Chants of Sennaar* is acquiring new languages. The player is introduced to new languages primarily by observation, trial, and error. At the start of the game, the first interaction with language is a gentle introduction. The player finds a closed door with a lever and an inscription. For the up and down position of the lever, the first symbols differ, and the second symbols are the same (see Figure 13.1). By flipping the lever, the door opens and closes. A likely meaning then of the differing symbols could be *open* and *close* or *up* and *down*. The common symbol for the two positions could represent the words *door* or *lever,* and one might even argue that ideogrammatically that's almost guaranteed. Without any further information, the player is not able to know whether the inscription means *Lever up/down* or *Open/ close door* or even something completely different. We must deduce, infer, build, and test hypotheses.

After passing through the door, the newly gained knowledge about the unknown language and its symbols is applied in the first puzzle. The path the player needs to take is blocked by water. Next to the path, there are six levers which open and close the water faucets below them and a note containing the symbols shown in Figure 13.2 can be found. By pushing the levers into the upper position, the faucets open and water starts flowing. The solution to the puzzle is to flip the levers into the position

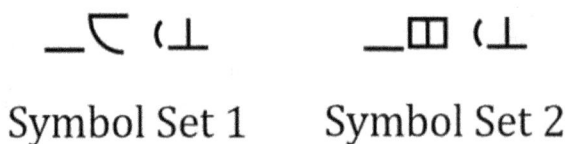

Symbol Set 1   Symbol Set 2

FIGURE 13.1   Symbol sets in Chants of Sennaar.

_⊏ _⊏ _⊡ _⊏ _⊡ _⊏

FIGURE 13.2 The solution to the puzzle.

Ⴑ

LI I _o⁹l⊓

LI I _⊏(⊥

FIGURE 13.3 Three short phrases.

corresponding to the symbols on the note as read from left to right. Because of this design choice, it does not matter in this case whether the symbols got interpreted as *Open* or *Up* and as *Close* or *Down* by the player. The acquired knowledge is enough to solve the puzzle without requiring explicit definition. After the puzzle is solved, the player can decipher the true meaning of the symbols through later context clues.

Another way language is acquired in *Chants of Sennaar* is by interpreting spoken words, gestures or nonverbal communication by other characters. Words are also encountered in inscriptions of paintings and statues. After the first puzzle is solved, the player enters a room where they are greeted by another character. The character says the three short phrases shown in Figure 13.3. An initial guess could be that the first is some sort of greeting. The symbols that begin phrases two and three are identical. The third phrase also contains the words "Open Door", which we know from solving the earlier puzzle. The second phrase only contains unknown symbols. It seems like the other character is stuck, providing a possible translation: *Hello. You help me. You open door.*

Language Dictionary

The dictionary in *Chants of Sennaar* has multiple use cases. It is used to take notes on unknown symbols, it unlocks the true meaning behind symbols, and it offers a layer to translate between the languages spoken by the different cultures. When a new symbol is discovered by the player, it appears in the dictionary. The player can write down a possible meaning of that symbol which, to begin with, is largely an aide memoire and tentative translation. The language spoken by the other characters is also displayed as symbols – a differentiation between written and spoken language is not present in *Chants of Sennaar*. The player can also assign the different symbols to drawings in the dictionary. If all of the assigned symbols match the correct drawing on one page in the dictionary, the true meanings of the symbols are unlocked and the need to guess the correct meaning is eliminated. This enables the player to continue learning the languages without involving an unreasonable amount of guesswork. Over time, player translations become concretized through successful application.

Language Translation

After acquiring the first language and completing the first level, a new page in the dictionary appears (see Figure 13.4). This is the translation section of the dictionary, in which known symbols from one language can be linked to symbols from a different language. If all of the symbols are correctly assigned, their true translation is revealed, similar to how language acquisition is concretized.

Puzzles

The puzzles in *Chants of Sennaar* are closely related to the languages discovered during gameplay, only becoming solvable after the required symbols have been translated. One example of such a puzzle is found at an early stage in the game, where the player has to point statues in a cemetery in a specific direction. In a church, the player can learn about the correct directions by solving a simple puzzle and reading the text that appears. This is only possible if the correct translations for the symbols have already been discovered. Many other game mechanics in *Chants of Sennaar* also use puzzle elements.

FIGURE 13.4 The translation part of the dictionary.

The language acquisition/translation itself can be seen as a puzzle that stretches across the whole game, requiring constant attention and unlocking more and more pieces as the game progresses. Sometimes players are progress blocked until they discover glyphs and symbols elsewhere in the game's often rambling levels. As such, finding ways to fill out the symbols in the dictionary is an overarching puzzle that requires understanding cultural context as well as possessing a thirst for exploration.

How *Chants of Sennaar* Connects Language and Culture

Another way *Chants of Sennaar* provides gripping gameplay lies in its clever tie-in of culture into the game world. In the game, the player has to manoeuvre through different levels – quite literally, since each world is higher up in the tower than the last. Each world has a unique culture of people inhabiting it: The Devotees, the Warriors, the Bards, the Alchemists, and the Anchorites. These different cultures are presented like castes – the further you proceed in the game, the more privilege and technical advancement you encounter. Lower caste cultures will look up to and even mythologize higher cultures, whilst higher cultures often disdain the lower ones, going so far as to dehumanize them in their language. This is an example of how *Chants of Sennaar*'s main game mechanic – understanding the fictional languages – ties into the cultural part of the game: Not only are the languages of all five different cultures diverse, but the vocabulary also reflects on their statuses, their beliefs, uniqueness and the way in which they perceive the other cultures.

Devotees

The first caste you encounter as a player are the Devotees. They live on the lowest part of the tower, right before its actual entrance, and believe in a god-like being inhabiting the top of the building. Their language, being the first you come across and thus also serving tutorial purposes, consists mainly of basic vocabulary. However, some translations reflect on their beliefs: The glyph for *up* is the same one used for *great*, mirroring their reverence to their god on the top of the tower. The devotee's language is also the only one with a word for *god*, and does not have words for any castes other than the warriors, who guard the entrance to the tower and prohibit them from entering.

The glyphs of the Devotee's language often consist of lines and curves fencing in other symbols or standing on a border of another. Their glyph for themselves (*Devotee*) is a combination of the symbol for *human* and a simplified version of the symbol for *god*. The symbols are drawn in imperfect angles, suggesting the aesthetics of a hand-drawn scripture rather than a typed one. This in turn symbolizes their technological limitations and comparatively undeveloped environment. They resemble the ancient writing system known as cuneiform due to their serifs and sharp lines[2] and are inspired by the Ge'ez script, used for several languages in Ethiopia and Eritrea (Hetzron 2006).

Warriors

The warriors are the second culture group the player encounters in the game, right after sneaking into the tower. They primarily live in the first part of the tower,

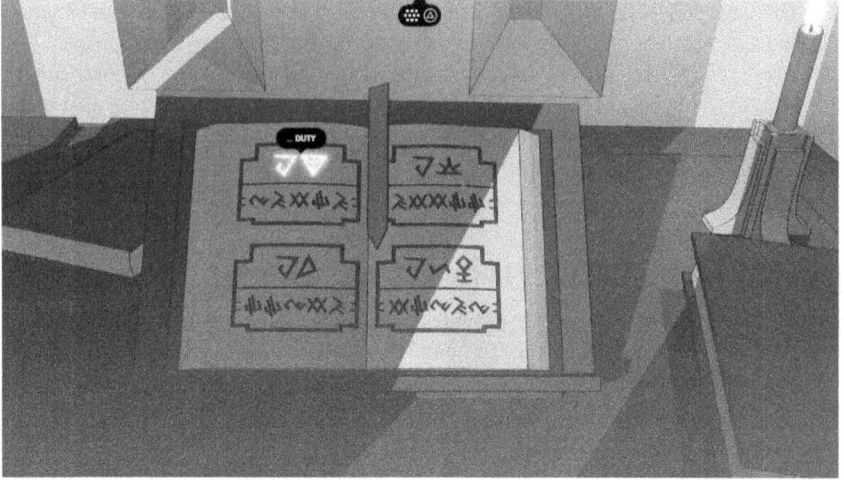

FIGURE 13.5   The warriors' language.

a fortress, which mainly features the colours white, black, grey and red. These colours immediately convey a feeling of coldness and visualize a change to the players, who were introduced to a yellowish colour palette in the Abbey where the Devotees reside. The Warriors' main purpose is to guard the tower and prohibit the Devotees from entering, as well as to protect the higher castes. The warriors harbour strong admiration for the Bards, whom they call the *Chosen* in their language, and they keep the Devotees, whom they refer to as the *Impure*, locked outside to protect the Bards from their unwanted influence.

Their identity is strongly connected to the word *Duty,* and their vocabulary mainly consists of basic words, with more focus on manual and military tasks compared to the other languages. The glyphs of the language are drawn in straight lines with no curves, representing their strictness and inability to bend to other people's wishes – such as listening to the Devotees. The symbols often have lines drawn through them to cross them out, which creates a brutal aesthetic, resembling the remnants of scars or weapons (see Figure 13.5). Regarding real scriptures, the Warrior's glyphs bear a strong resemblance to Runic scripture (Mees 1999) used amongst others by the Vikings, whom the warriors resemble due to their martial strengths.

Bards

As soon as the player crosses the Fortress, they are introduced to a contrasting environment: The lush garden of the Bards. This culture's main focus lies on art and music – the cherishing of *Beauty*, which is the word they use most. Their vocabulary consists mainly of words on that focus, as well as more light-hearted words like *idiot* or *play*, words that no other culture reference. The word *idiot* can be used by the Bards as both a literal meaning for a foolish person, but also for people of the subclass that exists within that culture – those who are treated as servants by the higher-ranking Bards. As they are a comparatively high-ranking culture, this vocabulary is a reflection of how privileged they are compared to the lower castes and how they have spare resources to support their focus on art and beauty for self-fulfilment. The Bards are

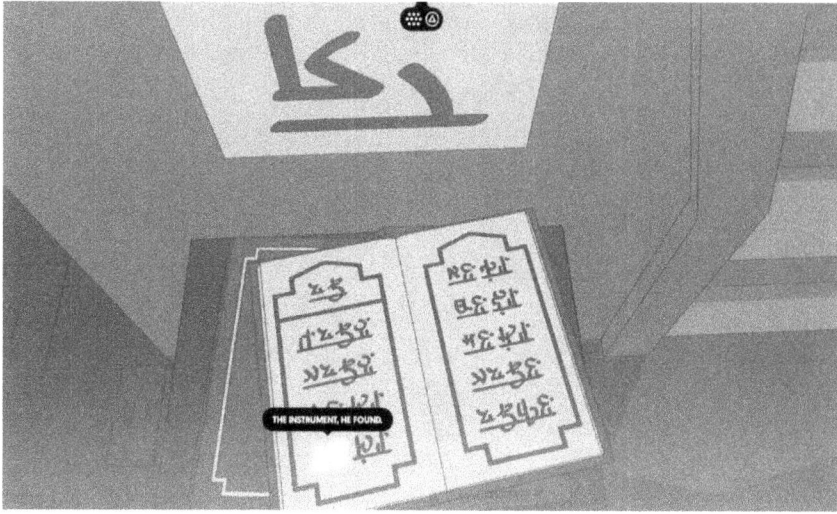

FIGURE 13.6 The bards' language.

characterized as rather narcissistic and selfish people, calling the Devotees *monsters* and keeping servants for manual and physically exhausting tasks. Their glyphs aesthetic bears a strong resemblance to the Devanagari (Salomon 1998) and Arabic scripture.[3] The symbols work with many curves, lines, and dots, thus tapping into an artful and graceful aesthetic which ties back to their culture (Figure 13.6).

Alchemists

The second-highest caste in *Chants of Sennaar* are the Alchemists. Their love of science characterizes their culture: They live in laboratories and the word most commonly used in their language is *Transformation*. Their vocabulary introduces the concept of numbers and chemical elements such as gold and silver. It also features words for reading and studying related tasks. It visually resembles alchemical formulas or sigils. In contrast to being a very scientifically advanced culture, their word for the highest caste, the Anchorites, is *fairies*. This underlines their reverence for these people by using a supernatural word to describe them, placing them outside the laws of the physical world that are otherwise the natural domain of the Alchemists.

Anchorites

Advancing to the final level of the game player encounters the culture of the Anchorites – tech-savvy people who once built the tower and now consider it doomed. Their symbols consist of thin, stacked lines, which give them a mechanical and digital appearance, consistent with their culture and abilities (see Figure 13.4).

The script is also inspired by Agglutinative languages, in which multiple morphemes are tied together for meaning, each representing a single syntactic feature (Durrant 2022). Their most commonly used word is *Exile* – the name of the computer AI /controlling them and keeping them artificially alive. Their vocabulary does not introduce new categories but features yet unseen words such as *revive*, which relates to their

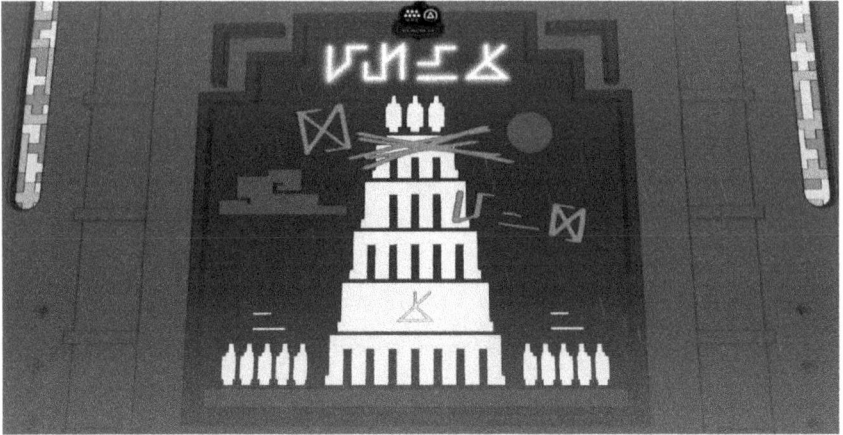

FIGURE 13.7   The anchorites' language.

TABLE 13.1

The Grammatical Rules of Each *Chants of Sennaar* Language

	Devotee	Warrior	Bard	Alchemist	Anchorite
Word Order	SVO	SVO	OSV/VS	SVO	SVO
Plurality	Reduplication	Prefix	Suffix	Suffix	Morpheme
Negation	Head-Initial	Head-Initial	Embracing	Head-Initial	Morpheme
Question	–	–	Embracing	–	–

immortality. There are no words for any other caste in the Anchorites' language as they do not interact with the rest of the world – instead, they are self-obsessed and insular, experiencing reality through VR headsets (Figure 13.7).

Despite all the differences between these in-game cultures, some lingual overlapping can be found. All five languages feature distinct grammatical rules for word order, plurality, negation and in one case questions (see Table 13.1).

Regarding word order, the Bard's language features a different structure from the rest of the languages: It changes the order from Subject-Verb-Object (SVO) like the Devotee's and Warrior's language to Object-Subject-Verb (OSV) or, respectively, Verb-Subject (VS) if there is no Object in the sentence. The forming of a plural differs in almost all of the languages: The Devotees use reduplication (repeating the same word); the Warrior's language uses a prefix symbol; the Bards and Alchemists use a suffix symbol and the Anchorites form morphemes – adding a symbol with the meaning of *plural* to an existing symbol to indicate plurality. Negation is also featured in different forms: The Devotees, Warriors, and Alchemists negate with head-initial rules – using a *not* symbol in front of the verb they want to negate. The Anchorites once more form morphemes, this time with a small symbol meaning *not* which is added to the respective verb. The Bards use embracing grammar for negation: Putting the negation glyph at the start and end of a sentence. They also use the same embracing rule for forming questions – a grammar rule not featured in any other language.

Discussion

The combination of varying glyphs and differing grammatical rules of each language in *Chants of Sennaar* creates a challenging gameplay experience for each translation level of the game. Especially advancing from the Warriors to the Bards language confronts the player with an almost entirely dissimilar grammar, creating an additional challenge to understanding the vocabulary's meaning. It also furthers the feeling of learning a real language connected to culture – as in real life, different languages from different environments have unique grammar and do not abide by the same rules. This supports the game mechanics by rendering the gameplay more challenging and strengthening the player's immersion into the game world by making the languages more believable. The additional real-life inspirations of each scripture further this believability. By recognizing parts of symbols as ancient human writings and easily connecting the aesthetics of the glyphs to each culture, the player is more invested in understanding the meanings of each language. They promise a logical consistency that is a hook to deductive reasoning.

The game features one more cultural tie-in for all different scriptures. There is one symbol in each language that looks similar. The word *God* for the Devotees, *Duty* for the Warriors, *Beauty* for the Bards, *Transformation* for the Alchemists and *Exile* for the Anchorites. At the end of the game, this is the symbol which ties all five cultures together and allows them to finally communicate with each other. This is explained by the game's implied Tower of Babel myth: The language of the Anchorites was once the only one spoken in the tower before other people from different cultures started populating the lower levels. People would not communicate due to fear, and the castes were formed as a consequence. One last remnant of this past remains – the recurring glyph for each language representing their most cherished value. This final revelation is another example of the well-thought-through in-game culture of *Chants of Sennaar* connecting all of the game's featured languages.

This research offers several practical applications across game design, linguistics and language education.

Our findings highlight the potential of integrating language mechanics as an engaging gameplay element. By combining language learning with puzzle solving, game designers can create an immersive and rewarding player experience. The gradual and ongoing discovery of vocabulary and grammar through context-driven interactions leads not only to entertaining but also to cognitively engaging gameplay.

For linguists, this paper could provide a starting point for examining fictional languages in games in relation to real-world linguistics. By comparing the fictional languages in *Chants of Sennaar* to real languages, linguists could analyse how game-based languages might be constructed and which properties they share with natural language. This comparison could reveal common linguistic strategies used in fictional language creation.

Our findings could also be applied to the field of language education. Educators could develop interactive language learning games that encourage students to learn through context, interaction and discovery rather than only through memorization. The puzzle-like approach of *Chants of Sennaar* provides an entertaining and rewarding method for language acquisition. This approach allows students to deduce vocabulary, grammar and syntax organically and at their own pace as they progress through the different levels.

Conclusion

Chants of Sennaar is a game about deciphering strange glyphs, solving puzzles and learning about different languages and cultures. Each language has its own vocabulary and grammar, which not only adds to the challenge of the mechanics but also strengthens the player's immersion, making the languages feel more believable within the game world. The immersion is further emphasized by the five different cultures the player encounters – each with their individual social hierarchies, beliefs and aesthetics. This unique combination of engaging language-learning mechanics and cultural storytelling demonstrates the potential for fictional languages to drive narrative immersion.

Notes

1 https://adventuregamers.com/games/view/34658.
2 https://smedium.com/@jonlangcommissions/show-nottell-an-analysis-of-chants-of-sennaar-4e283252558d.
3 https://medium.com/@jonlangcommissions/show-nottell-an-analysis-of-chants-of-sennaar-4e283252558d.

References

Champion, E. 2020. 'Culturally Significant Presence in Single-Player Computer Games'. *Journal on Computing and Cultural Heritage* 13(4):1–24. doi: 10.1145/3414831.

Durrant, Philip. 2022. *Corpus Linguistics for Writing Development: A Guide for Research.* Abingdon: Routledge.

Hageneuer, Sebastian. 2021. 'Archaeogaming: How Heaven's Vault Changes the "Game"'. *Pearls, Politics and Pistachios. Essays in Anthropology and Memories on the Occasion of Susan Pollock's 65th Birthday* 631–42. Berlin: Abingdon.

Hetzron, Robert, ed. 2006. *The Semitic Languages.* London: Taylor & Francis Ltd.

Mees, Bernard. 1999. 'The Celts and the Origin of the Runic Script'. *Studia Neophilologica* 71(2):143–55. doi: 10.1080/003932799750041696.

Reinhard, Andrew. 2018. *Archaeogaming: An Introduction to Archaeology in and of Video Games.* New York: Berghahn Books.

Salomon, Richard. (1998). *Indian epigraphy: A guide to the study of inscriptions in Sanskrit, Prakrit, and the other Indo-Aryan languages.* Oxford: Oxford University Press.

Ludography

AlPixel Games. 2015. Missing Translation [Video game] [Microsoft Windows]. AlPixel Games.

Duang! Games. 2016. Sethian [Video game] [Microsoft Windows]. Duang! Games.

ERE Informatique. 1988. Captain Blood [Video game] [Amiga]. Infogrames.

Howland, Rob. 2014. Influent [Video game] [Microsoft Windows]. Three Flip.

Inkle. 2019. Heaven's Vault [Video game] [Sony PlayStation 4]. Inkle.

Lingo Ludo. 2018. Lingotopia [Video game] [Microsoft Windows]. Lingo Ludo.

No Code. 2019. Observation [Video game] [Sony PlayStation 4]. Devolver Digital.

Rundisc. 2023. Chants of Sennaar [Video game] [Nintendo Switch]. Focus Entertainment.

14

Domain Knowledge in Board Games

Michael Heron and Pauline Belford

Board Games

There has been a major renaissance in the area of analogue gaming over the past few decades, starting roughly at the point Settlers of Catan (Teuber 1995) was released in the west and extending to the present day largely without interruption. We are in a golden age of board games – or at the very least, there has been a clear and extended period of recent time in which board games have been in the ascendence. It's always difficult to tell when things – such as a gaming renaissance – begin and end while you're enveloped within them.

This would be reason enough for us to spend some time talking about board games, but the growing quality and professionalism of tabletop game design is only one small part of it. Remember the dirty little secret we talked about earlier in the book – board games matter less than the people playing them. Play a bad game with good people and you'll have a good time. Play a good game with bad people, and you'll have a bad time. It's like the old adage – add a cup of wine to a barrel of oil and you end up with sludge. Add a cup of oil to a barrel of wine, well – you still end up with sludge.

It is though in that frame that I believe board games are most interesting – in their manifestation as a kind of cardboard computer. Board games are formal systems that run on the imperfect hardware of human beings. We are the CPU, the memory, the motherboard. Rules flow from the manual into our heads and get executed upon the organic matter of those around the board. The components are the user interface, the rules the software. It's a peculiarly symbiotic kind of game. Board games in the end are interesting because **people** are interesting.

As usual, let's put a little scoping around this chapter and talk about what we mean by a board game. It seems like the descriptor should be enough, right? A game which you play on a board? Surely, for once, we can just call it a day and move on?

Come on, you know better than that by now. What do we mean by a **board**, buddy? Does it have to be a Monopoly (Magie 1933) style folded piece of cardboard that acts as the game world? What if it's not, and it's made up of cards distributed around a table, but each of those cards acts in the same way as a space on a Cluedo (Pratt 1949) board? What if it's not cards, but instead **tiles** that are laid out randomly at the start of play? For that matter, what's the difference between a **tile** and a **card**[1]?

DOI: 10.1201/9781003530282-14

Let's do our usual hand-waving and just talk about some properties that are commonly shared, and let familial resemblance do the rest of the work for us. Board games **usually** have:

- Some kind of central state, represented by a game board or several game boards. That game board might be discontinuous, in that it's made up of individual discreet cards or tiles. Players too may have their own independent game boards.
- An expectation of one or (usually) more human players. This differentiates digital implementations of board games from board games themselves.
- Some resources that are gathered and spent by players, and rules for managing how those currencies function.
- Shared and/or individual game states that are modified through application of formal mechanisms.
- Clearly defined goals and clearly defined rules.
- A way of assessing winners and losers.

The Internet's best and largest collection of taxonomical information about board games is debatably BoardGameGeek, and it contains at the time of writing over 160,000 titles in its database. And within this collection, you'll find most games tick off almost all of these traits. However, the most stark and visible trait – the eponymous board – is actually the one that is most often honoured in the breach rather than the observance. Games that are played entirely using cards and tokens to represent resources, for example, are regularly welcomed under the banner of board games. Jaipur (Pauchon 2009); Arboretum (Cassar 2015); Hanamikoji (Nakayama 2013); Innovation (Chudyk 2010); One Deck Dungeon (Cieslik 2016); Targi (Steiger 2012) – all examples of "board games" that have no board and are accepted, largely uncritically, as being part of the modern renaissance of board game design. Surely though they are **card games**? You'd certainly get some funny looks from most people if you referred to Poker, in any of its variations, as a board game. Similarly for Solitaire or Patience or Canasta.

What we're basically talking about here is not just emergent genres, such as within our video game chapter, but rather emergent **traditions**. Card games are their own cultural property, often considered largely independent of any other form of gaming. They tend to work using one or more standard decks of playing cards and have a legacy that derives as much from historical social mores as from formal game design. Many card games are so embedded in the culture as a kind of social lubricant that people often won't intuitively think of them as games. Ask an elderly relative if they are a gamer, and you'll often be told "no" even if you know they're regularly playing *Gin Rummy* or *Bridge* with their friends. They're more widely considered to be "pastimes" than they are to be thought of as "games" – literally, pleasant ways to **pass the time.**

And yet, there's a complexity to card games that shows the importance that evolving designs have played over the years. There's a bewildering array of styles and expectations. Parlett (2008) outlines a number of major categories, each with specializations. You've got trick-taking games, matching games, shedding games, and comparing games. At one point, Bridge was such a common pastime for the upper classes that families would hire Bridge tutors to teach young ladies and gentlemen the specialist argot necessary to play competently (du Sautoy 2023).

All of this is to say that, once again, we don't have the luxury of grabbing hold of a definition and using it to correctly include and exclude all the right things. Jaipur and Texas Hold'Em use exactly the same kinds of components (a deck of cards, some chips), but one is considered a board game (Jaipur) and the other variously, depending on who you talk to, a card game, a pastime, a sport, or a competitive activity. Cards Against Humanity (Temkin et al. 2011) – a board game. *Whist* – a card game. *Bridge* – a pastime. And yet, each would also happily exist within any of these broad descriptors. As usual, we know it when we see it, and the real mark of correct categorization is how well you convince others that something is a natural fit.

Early Board Games

As is now traditional, we get into the meat here by looking at the early history of the medium to try and draw out a rough trajectory with regards to where it's going. Board games represent the earliest form of codified play, and the archaeological record is full of examples. However, the unpredictable nature of history means that sometimes we can only infer the existence of games through secondary evidence. One of the earliest games for which we have primary evidence is Senet. A painting of the game appears in the tomb of Hesy-Re (Crist 2019), circa 2613 BCE. Earlier artwork in the tomb of Merknera (Vyshedskiy 2014), somewhere between 3300 and 2700 BCE also shows something that looks remarkably similar. Fragments of the board itself have been found from dig sites dated to 3100 BCE, but it's only in the period of the Middle Kingdom (1782–2040 BCE) that we have found anything that could credibly be considered an intact board.

However, just because we found Senet game boards, it doesn't mean we have actually discovered Senet because the rules have – thus far – been lost to the winds of antiquity. Historians have reconstructed credible rulesets by stitching together disparate ancient sources, but these represent what are likely to be anachronistic patchworks. It's hard to believe the rules would have remained unchanged for millennia. In addition to the lost rules, we also have no consensus on the **purpose** of Senet – or even whether it had one. Some have argued that it was supposed to be a "playable guide to the afterlife", since Senet Net Hab (the full name) means "The Game of Passing Through". As with much of what we know of the early history of games, this is informed conjecture. It's entirely possible Senet was a simple pastime that was later afforded a spiritual purpose as it accumulated a palpable sense of veneration over the centuries it endured. Some things acquire a gravitas that is purely a function of time.

This is something to bear in mind when we talk about ancient board games. You can buy modern playable Senet sets. Despite being packaged up with admirable confidence, you are still going to be playing something inauthentic and artificial – a best guess reproduction that future historical finds will undoubtedly invalidate.

The Royal Game of Ur is an interesting counter-example of this. Archaeologists believe that the game originated in Mesopotamia around 2400 BCE to 2600 BCE – a board dated to that period is held at the British Museum. What makes it significant though is that in addition to the board, a partial clay tablet describing the rules was discovered at a separate site, which allowed Irving Finkel to do a translation of a simple version of rules as codified in the 2nd century BCE (Finkel 2007). While this is likely not the same ruleset that was used two thousand years prior, it's one of the rare examples we have of an ancient game manual. As to the purpose of the game – again, we can only infer. Some have argued it served a prognostication purpose, that the way players moved around the board was reflective of the fortune fate had in store for them. On the other hand, games are self-justifying – people don't need a reason to play.

Senet though is not the earliest game that we can situate in the historical record. Mancala is a game of picking up pieces and then redistributing them into a series of pits, with the intention of ending up with no stones on your side of the board. There is some evidence to suggest Mancala was played in Jordan around 6000 BCE – that evidence being indentations set into the flooring of neolithic dwellings (Rollefson 1992). As with anything in archaeology, this is a contentious claim and the debate rages on (De Voogt 2021; Depaulis 2020). However, part of the problem of situating Mancala in the archaeological record is the transient nature of its components. A mancala game can be played using nothing more than soft mud and a few gathered stones – such components of convenience do not leave lasting archaeological evidence. The earliest Mancala boards we have discovered date from around the 4th century BCE although as ever there is little academic consensus. There is though no more eloquent example of the importance of medium than having potentially thousands of years of evidence washed away by the vagaries of time. And that just because the boards were made in the sand and the game was played with shells.

Depending on where you look, and how far back you look, and how much you're willing to squint at the evidence, we can find a rich legacy of board games back for thousands of years. Backgammon may have originated in the 6th century BCE (Finkel 1995). Hnefatafl, a game with some similarities to Chess, is perhaps dated to the 4th century BCE (Hall and Forsyth 2011). Games of dice, carved from the knucklebones of animals, were used for gaming and gambling as early as 3000 BCE (du Sautoy 2023). Interestingly, the six-sided die that dominates Western conceptions of randomness is likely to be a much more recent innovation than the four-sided die which is now more associated with Dungeons and Dragons (Gygax and Arneson 1981). Animal bones were more easily carved into pyramids than they were into cubes. Modern six-sided dice are arranged so that the sum of each opposite face is a seven – a six and a one, a five and a two, and so on. That's a historical marker too – a way to embed a degree of "fairness" into the uneven rolling of imperfectly carved cubes.

These ancient games were classified by David Parlett into four main categories of play (Woods 2012):

- Racing games, such as Pacheesi/Ludo. The goal is to be the first player to get your token(s) to the end location.
- Space games, such as *Noughts* and *Crosses*. The goal is to control an area of the board while preventing an opponent from doing the same thing.
- Chase games, such as *Hnefatafl*. The goal is to force opponents into a specified region of the game board with the intention of blocking their escape.
- Displacement games, such as *Chess*. Here, players take or remove other players tokens in order to achieve the winning condition.

The common perception of the history of board games is often pock-marked by stereotypical assumptions. Mah Jong for example is sometimes spoken about as if it were some ancient game from the mists of China's immense past. It actually originated in the 19th century (Greene 2015), and achieved a cultural dominance at an astonishing rapidity. Chess, as we know it, is largely a product of the same time although its roots are much deeper. We have to go to India for those, and the game of Ashtápada – a game so controversial it was banned by name by Gautama Buddha[2].

Appearing in the 2nd century BCE, Ashtápada was a two or four-player game played on an 8 × 8 board. Each player was given an equal number of pieces to play, and the intention was to move pieces around clockwise so as to enter special spaces marked out as castles, and then back again to reach the centre. Except – as with many properties of antiquity – there is a lot of disagreement as to exactly how it worked for sure. The rules as we know them had little similarity to what would become chess, but the board became a foundation for many games to follow – importantly in our case, Chaturanga which in itself became the base for everything from Chess to Shogi (Averbakh 2012; Cazaux and Knowlton 2017; Davidson 2012).

Chaturanga was a 7th-century BCE four-player war game, in which the playing pieces were set up to represent the four divisions of the Gupta Empire's military. Players had Padàti (infantry), which moved like contemporary pawns. Aśva (cavalry), which moved like knights. Ratha (Chariots), which moved like rooks. Gaja (Elephants), which moved like bishops. The Raja (King) was to be protected. Ships were also represented in some versions.

Unlike in chess, players could only move the pieces that were dictated by the throwing of a rod with four sides, which limited your choices and forced improvisation. Eventually, this randomness resulted in the game being categorized as a form of gambling, and players were instead simply permitted to choose which piece to move. You can see the bend of the game's evolution towards chess as we know it. Along the way, Chaturanga became Shah Mat in Persia; Xiangqi in China; Ajedrez in Spain. Each variant had its own regional flavours and would co-exist quite happily for centuries in different incarnations. Nobody ever had a hold on the rules of Chaturanga – it was never the intellectual property of a commercializing power – so it changed with the times and with the prevailing winds of history as it was introduced across the world through trade and war.

Many classic games were not actually intended to be fun, but rather as spiritual tools designed to teach about accepting a world governed by forces beyond our control. The concept of "roll and move" is often one that raises the hackles of modern gamers, but its roots are deep. *Snakes* and *Ladders* – a game which dates back to at least the 2nd century – was a meditation on the Hindu principles of Karma (destiny) and Kama (desire). The goal was to reach spiritual enlightenment on the final square, but the board also looped – if you overshot, you went back to the start (du Sautoy 2023). Ladders represented spiritual virtues, snakes represented vices. There were always more snakes than ladders, reflecting that the path towards enlightenment is full of setbacks. However, falling is not necessarily a bad thing, as certain squares on the board are mathematically more advantageous than others. This encodes the idea that sometimes we must fail in order to achieve greater success. The role of the player was to meditate upon the journey, not to beat the game.

We see similar moral coding in *The New Game of Human Life* (Newberry 1790). The original intention was to teach morality to children – to inculcate good social values through play. Players would spin a totum (dice being considered mostly tools for gambling and not appropriate for children). Each square was marked with an illustration, a descriptor, and in the rules, a set of instructions for what should happen when one lands on the square. From the instructions:

- The Studious Boy at 7 shall receive a Stake and shall proceed to 42, the place of the Orator.
- The Negligent Boy at 11 shall pay a Stake and shall remain two rounds without spinning.
- The Married Man at 34 shall receive two Stakes for his Wife's Portion and go to be a Good Father at 56.
- The Drunkard at 63 shall pay 2 Stakes and go back to the Child at 2.

The negligent boy will be held back. The drunkard will regress to childishness. The messages are not subtle, and serve to reinforce dominant norms of the time.

Other games in the 19th century were used to teach a version of history that was acceptable to the powers that be. They taught about the greatness of Kings and Queens. They expounded on the righteousness of Empire and how Imperial policies were actually good and humane. They presented wars and conflicts in jingoistic terms. Whether they were fun or not – well, that was never really the point.

Julie-Anne Lambert, of the Bodleian Library, said[3]:

Games which aim to teach history are particularly interesting as it is impossible to take an unbiased view of the past or the present, so the images, text and format of the games reveal much about the attitudes and perspectives that were prevalent at the time.

In this, one important perspective you have as a game scholar is situating a game not just in its academic context, but also in its historic context. Much can be learned by interrogating the assumptions and intentions at the core of games.

Folk Games

How do you learn a board game?

One of the first, instinctive answers is "by reading the manual", but if that's true it puts you in a minority of players in my experience. I'm usually the "guy who teaches the rules" in my groups, because I do this kind of thing for a living and people assume – incorrectly – that I can be trusted with correctly interpreting rulesets. Most people though learn games from other people.

Think back to your first experience with Monopoly (Magie 1933) – did you, as an eager child excited to play a game with your family, sit down and work your way through the instructions? Probably not – you had a parent, or an older sibling, or a friend explain them. And they likely were taught by someone else, who was taught by someone else. Thus, the broad confusion when you tell someone they don't get money back when they land on free parking, or when you introduce the auction when they don't buy a property. People generally don't play board games as they are written – they play them as they are taught. The alignment between the manual and the way people play may not be perfect. See Figure 14.1.

Folk games are those that are learned through oral tradition, and there's a reasonable case to be made that Monopoly is a **de facto** folk game even if it does have well-defined and unambiguous rules, such as how you get double money when you land on Go rather than pass it.[4]

Folk games are often part authentic and part homebrew – as in, they're a mix of rules as written and house rules that have been adopted intentionally or accidentally.

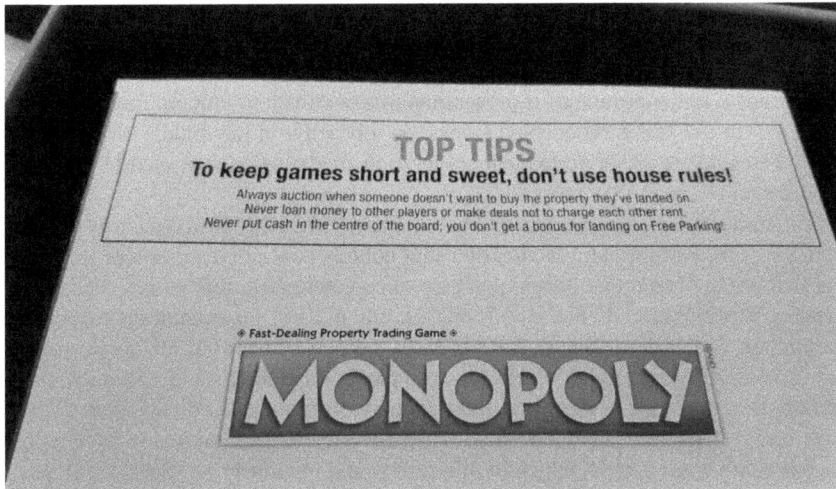

FIGURE 14.1 The first thing you see opening a new copy of Monopoly (Photograph by author).

Games, even if they are boxed products, don't exist pure and unsullied in the world. We see abundant evidence through the historical record that games undergo a form of convergent evolution, where the same game is invented in different regions and different times, but with cultural inflections unique to their epoch and geography (du Sautoy 2023).

For example, Americans who went to camp may well be a familiar with a folk game called Roll Call. While it doesn't conform to the concept of "game" as we've been using it, that's another important aspect of understanding definitions – people in the real world use words in a way that isn't beholden to academia.

Anyway, Roll Call is a "game" which is "played" at night. Everyone is lined up and told they're not allowed to speak unless called upon, and not allowed to look behind them. The exception is the person at the front who can, at any time, call for a "roll call". At that point, everyone in the line must shout out their name. The line marches around, in the dark, punctuating the silence with occasional call and response. One person playing is not in the line – that's the Taker, and their job is to steal away whoever is at the back of line – silently and ideally without anyone else noticing.

This is what you might think of as an intensely **experiential** framing of play. The whole point is to manipulate the emotions of everyone involved. The leader calls out "Roll Call" to find that the line is getting shorter and shorter every time, with no hint as to when it's happening. Someone in the line hears ten people behind them. Then nine. Then six. Every time anticipation builds for when a roll call results in no names being called. Nobody wins. Nobody save for the Taker makes any decisions. Everyone just… **anticipates.** It's like a real-life Among Us (Innersloth 2018) if it was played for horror rather than laughs.

Variations of the game exist throughout America, and versions are also found in plenty of other cultures. Nobody owns the rules. You can't buy a box of Roll Call. You just have a friend who at some point says, during a dark night in the woods, "Do you want to play a game?"

A similar kind of game is Down Mister President. This is a game you don't even know you're playing until you've lost. It works like this – in a group of likeminded friends, someone chooses to put a finger to their ear like they've just received a warning on an earpiece. The last person in a group to do this is designated as "The President". At that point, everyone else yells "Down, Mister President!" and bundles the President to the ground as if preventing an assassination. It doesn't matter where you are – in the street, on cobbled stones, on a beach – in the middle of teaching a class. The game is one of permanent observation and being on your guard – a bit like a version of Assassin that never ends.

Sometimes folk games are also called "car games". Eye Spy is an obviously popular one, but so is Mind Meld. I said earlier that nobody can sell you a box of Roll Call but that doesn't mean that people don't try to commercialize folk games. The boxed product Medium (Deley, Sherwood, and Thornton 2018) for example is essentially an attempt to sell the public domain back to the public. In Mind Meld, two people say a word. "Hound" and "Crime" for example. If they don't say the same word or phrase, they then say a word that links their two different words together. "Dog", says one. "Detective", says the other. Then they try to link these two new words together into a mind meld, which in this case would **obviously** be "Sherlock Bones". Learning of a folk game is often akin to being inducted into a form of secret regional history – a shibboleth of belonging.[5]

You can view much of the archaeological record of board games in this frame – lacking formalization. What is almost certainly true is that games evolved and changed and fell out of favour and were re-invented thousands of times in thousands of places. When we say we know how Senet was played, what we know – at best – is a snapshot of how a particular game was played in a particular location at a particular time. We have an endless array of folk games, with a reasonable argument to be made that even boxed products fall into this broader oral tradition.

Classic Family Board Games

Let's accelerate a little bit here into the era of classic family games by taking another swing at this book's favourite punchbag – 1933s Monopoly. Way back in our chapter on critical perspectives, I said baldly that Monopoly is an objectively bad game – part as provocation, part illustration of the expectations of evidence, and part foreshadowing. Monopoly is actually an excellent game – for what it was intended to be. Monopoly is not **fun** though, because that was never intended. Monopoly was originally a piece of anti-Capitalist propaganda which was originally released as *The Landlord Game* (Magie 1904). Elizabeth Magie designed and patented this in 1904 to make a case for the necessity of land reform. While all of the propaganda elements have been smoothed away, you can still see the core of its message in the mechanisms. You can still critically read, in other words, Magie's intent.

Consider what the systems of Monopoly are saying to us:

- It is the job of players to win by ruining their opponents.
- Wealth begets wealth – the richer get richer.
- Every cycle around the earth, honest labour provides a pittance of a wage. It is only property that provides real money.
- The legal system is arbitrary, and as the game progresses, crime is the best defence against ruin.

The Landlord Game is where these messages were first intentionally encoded into the rules. Monopoly is an appropriated counterfeit of the original, in which some of the most explicit messaging was softened in order to emphasize playability. The Landlord Game came with two rule-sets that were supposed to be played in sequence – the first showed the world as it was, and this is what became Monopoly. The other shows "the world as it could be" and was drawn from Georgist economic principles (Pilon 2015).

The elements in the original were more starkly presented than what would become Monopoly:

- "Go" was titled "Labour upon Mother Earth produces Wages".
- "Go to jail" was explicitly framed as trespassing, especially with regards to the foreign ownership of American soil.
- Poor and bankrupted players were sent to a public park (what is now free parking) to represent their expulsion to a Hooverville.
- The game had a fixed duration (how merciful!), and the winner was the player with the most money – in other words, a specifically capitalist framing of success.

The Landlord's Game, in Magie's words, "shows how the landlord gets his money and keeps it". She wanted players to "see clearly the gross injustice of our present land system" (Pilon 2015).

The original copies of the Landlord game were hand-made and spread through word-of-mouth and the painstaking copying of the board and its rules. An unemployed radiator repairman by the name of Charles Darrow happened upon one of these home-made copies at a dinner party. He borrowed the game, got a friend to improve the artwork, made a few tweaks and then sold it on to Parker Brothers in 1933, passing it on as his own invention. And the rest, as they say, is history – except that Magie's intellectual ownership of the game is something that, posthumously, is starting to become more widely known. The game is still wildly popular today, although the moral parable has been largely ignored. Still, the game's penetration in popular culture was such that even in the Second World War it was considered an acceptable item to be sent to German-held prisoners of war. That allowed military intelligence to smuggle supplies into POW camps by stitching them into the material of the board.[6] Play is a serious business.

In 1948, we see the release of one of my great loves – Scrabble (Butts 1948). Alfred Butts began developing the game during the Great Depression, analysing hundreds of newspaper articles to identify the frequency of occurrence of each letter of the alphabet. First, this was to determine how common letters should be, and then that later became linked to the score each letter would contribute. He was inspired by the emergence of crossword puzzles as a regular inclusion in newspapers and saw potential for the juxtaposition of these ideas. I would argue Scrabble is one of the most misunderstood games in the lexicon of "classic family games", because people insist on thinking of it as a word game. Some consider it a friendly game of making nice words and showing off their vocabulary.

Sorry, no. Scrabble has more in common with the Kriegsspiel of Prussian military academies than it does the pastime of constructing anagrams. Scrabble is a **war game**, where the primary ordinance you have are letters. The board is a battle-ground, special tiles are critical resources to be captured or burnt to the ground so no-one can use them against you. It's a game of playing economically and refusing to open the board up to an enemy.

I've never been able to work out why nobody will play Scrabble with me twice.

One interesting parallel between Monopoly and Scrabble is in how they both have abundant regional variants, but the actual impact of those variations is remarkably different. Monopoly primarily handles regional variation through "reskinning" – the UK version I am most familiar with plays identically to the American version, the only difference is in the names of each street. This means that there is little difficulty in making a Disney Monopoly (Parker Brothers 2001), or a Beatles Monopoly (Hasbro 2001), or a Warhammer 40,000 Monopoly (USAopoly 2019). The question really is whether or not you're playing the same game each time. You can learn a lot about how you think about the heart of games by asking yourself this question – if you changed all the pieces in Chess to be characters from Star Trek is that the same game as vanilla chess?

Scrabble, on the other hand, because regional variation introduces linguistic variation, changes substantively each time it is translated. In the English version of Scrabble, there are one each of the Q and the Z, and they're both worth ten points. In French, K, W, X, Y and Z are all represented by a single tile and they're all worth ten points. In German, a Y is worth ten points in comparison to the four it scores in English. In Irish Scrabble, there are no J, K, Q, V, W, X or Y tiles and both B and P are worth ten points.

And yet, understanding a language is not actually all that important when it comes to expert-level play – Nigel Richards, likely the greatest Scrabble player of all time, won the French-language championship without speaking French. He just learned all the Scrabble words that were valid in French Scrabble and worked from there. I mean, I say "just" but that's quite an accomplishment.

Cluedo (Pratt 1949) was inspired by the British murder mystery novels which had become incredibly popular in the UK between the two world wars. They were generally set in large country houses, harking back to better times, and the focus was on "the solve" rather than the grisly details of the murder. The British country house had come to represent something benign and comforting – an escape from the realities of an uncertain world. A place of continuity. Where better to stage a shocking murder?

The game is better known as *Clue in America* – *Cluedo* is a play on words (Clue and Ludo) that publishers did not feel would travel well across the Atlantic. A game of inquiry and deduction, this was one of the earliest board games to incorporate a sense of an unfolding story, albeit one that is actually very simple. It's also one of a handful of real board games to have been given a movie adaptation. Battleships and Ouija[7] share that particular distinction.

Twister (Foley, Guyer, and Rabens 1966) was a departure from tradition in that it was a highly physical game, and also sufficiently transgressive to receive its own mini moral panic.[8] It consists of a plastic mat with coloured circles arranged in a rectangle. A wheel is spun, and that determines which limb the current player must position on which colour of circle. Players are eliminated when their knee or elbow touches the mat. Usually, the game devolves into a series of bizarre, precarious human sculptures until a critical point is reached and everyone collapses. Like a human kind of Jenga (Leslie 1983) – the fun is in the catharsis of collapse (Heron 2023).

The moral panic was, predictably, due to the degree of physical contact – Twister is a board game that socially sanctions that most unacceptable of outcomes – teens rubbing up against other teens. 3M and Milton Bradley refused to publish it until persuaded of its potential marketability by more adventurous parties. Sears Roebuck refused to stock it. The media reported on naked Twister parties. Critics decried it as "sex in a box", once again showing a firm grasp on how to exactly not denounce a gaming product (Donovan 2018).

What these games tend to have in common, more than anything else, is a focus on younger audiences. Children, or families, are the primary target demographic. The games tend to be competitive, with a focus on player elimination or clear winners. Luck is a major element of play – even skilful games like Scrabble are, at best around 75% skill and 25% luck. Luck is a major balancing force when dealing with diverse skillsets, such as young kids playing against adults. As such, while these are certainly board games by all the metrics we use to describe them… they're not quite the same thing as the board games that are driving the modern renaissance.

When you say "board game" to the majority of people, you'll find the geeks and nerds will likely think of "Catan" and the wider populace will think "Monopoly". It's almost as if the last 90 years of evolution in board game design hadn't happened. Imagine if you suggested to a friend that you should go see a movie and they rolled their eyes and said "Urgh, the talkies? Aren't we a bit more sophisticated than that?"

This is a largely worldwide phenomenon, although perhaps it's less pronounced in countries such as Germany where hobbyist board games have a much greater prominence. "Board games are for kids", as a review of the hobby, bypasses how many games have adult themes and are not at all aimed at children. Consider Fog of Love (Jaskov 2017) as an example – a game of navigating adult relationships within the frame of a romantic coupling. Kids would certainly be able to handle the rules, but they wouldn't have the necessary understanding of the context. However, even within the classic family board game niche, we see a number of iterations and evolutions intended to bring gaming to a more mature audience.

The Ungame (Zakich 1973) was developed when its designer was left unable to talk due to polyps on her vocal cords. The idea was to get families to really talk to each other, using question cards as prompts – much in the style of Victorian parlour games that gave socially appropriate conversational prompts for young gentlemen to converse with young ladies. Some questions in the Ungame were trivial – "what is your favourite colour?". Others were more searching and occasionally transgressive. "How do you feel when people laugh at you?", or "Tell us about a time you hurt someone".

The Ungame was non-competitive, and had no clear end-point – it was an activity, rather than something where you won. It was credited by many as helping to save marriages, to navigate family tragedies, and getting children to communicate more with their parents. You can see its DNA in modern reinterpretations such as We're Not Really Strangers[9] (Koreen 2018) and Let's Get Closer[10] (Koreen 2022). Much like Roll Call, we might not think of these as games. They're ways to develop empathy and intimacy within an experiential context.

In the early 80s, Trivial Pursuit (Abbott and Haney 1979) took off and absolutely blew away almost every competitor in the market. This was the first mainstream game aimed squarely at adults rather than children. The juggernaut of *Dungeons and Dragons* (Gygax and Arneson 1981) stalled at this time directly as a consequence of the genuinely phenomenal success of Trivial Pursuit (Peterson 2021). It basically rewrote the market for quite some time. A game of trivia, where players were tasked with answering questions in a range of categories before beating each other to the centre to be crowned as winner – it was explicitly an "intellectualized" game for a mature audience. The questions were designed to appeal to the baby boomer generation, and served the important purpose of making people feel like their head full of largely irrelevant information had cohered into something genuinely useful. Twenty million copies of Trivial Pursuit were sold in its first year. In a good year, Monopoly sells around three million. It arrived at a time of increased adult leisure – supermarkets and labour-saving domestic appliances were starting to arrive in volume at homes. Trivial Pursuit managed to be seen as an adult pastime within a childish hobby – a way to responsibly spend the extra hours of recreation that technological advancement had brought.

In a similar vein, a Question of Scruples (Makow 1984) took direct aim at what its creator saw as the hypocrisy of the baby boomer generation – a generation he felt was high on condemnation but low on integrity. The game, much like the Ungame, asked players a series of questions, but these took the form of various moral conundrums:

- Would you admit you had smoked marijuana if asked by your child?
- Would you remind a waitress if she forgot to charge you for your drinks?
- Late one evening, your 19-year-old daughter asks permission for her boyfriend to stay over. Do you give it?

The game was a huge seller – by 1986 the game was selling faster than Trivial Pursuit, and by 1990 over seven million copies had been sold in the USA. Looking at it now, it feels like something of a time capsule reflecting what would now be considered rather conservative and racist assumptions. As of the time of writing, it hasn't received a modern update, but those looking to explore issues of social boundaries and expectations may find the game Billionaire Banshee (Bailey 2014) worth checking out.

It's roughly at this time when we start seeing an overlap between the games modern boardgamers consider part of the "hobby" and board games drawing from a more antique tradition. The very first board game recorded in BoardGameGeek – boardgame #1 in its database – is Die Macher and that dates from 1986. Design sensibilities had been evolving for a while, and the 1980s is when we see a lot of that start to truly bed in. And a lot of that comes down to a growing sense of professionalization stemming from, primarily, Germany.

The Rise of Hobbyist Board Games

Board games were taken seriously in Germany a long time before they achieved their current level of "cred" in the rest of the Western world (Woods 2012). Post-Second World War, in most nations, the board-game hobby was evolving only in small, incremental steps. Designers tended to cleave to the familiar templates set by Monopoly and Cluedo. A small minority would find themselves immersed in complex "chit and counter" wargames and strategic business games (Peterson 2021). Occasionally, an outlier such as HeroQuest (Baker 1989) would be released and become successful, but even they'd still often rely on bombastic presentation and crusty mechanisms such as roll-and-move.

In Germany, however, the attitude was different – perhaps as a natural byproduct of national self-reflection, the appetite of the time was for a form of wholesome togetherness (Donovan 2018). Board games represented an almost ideal way to spend meaningful time together in a socially acceptable way. Newspapers reviewed board games alongside films and books, and design sensibilities favoured player collegiality over competitive play in a way that made them very appealing for a conflict-averse sensibility. It's almost inevitable that this should form the nucleus of what would become one of the dominant design schools of board games – originally called "German style board games" but now mostly known under the label of "eurogames" (Woods 2012). Settlers of Catan (Teuber 1995) would become what many would identify as the tipping point between two conceptions of board games – between games as largely simple family affairs versus consciously designed and engineered formal systems worthy of cultural acceptance. Classic, or "mass market" board games – Monopoly, Scrabble, and so on don't really fall into the auspices of the hobby as it's understood by its devotees. You'd get strange looks if you called yourself a "hardcore boardgamer" if your experience was confined to Candyland (Milton Bradley 1949), Jenga (Scott 1983), Ludo (John Jaques and Son Ltd 1896), and Guess Who (Coster and Coster 1979). "Hobby" board games, or sometimes "designer" board games, are more niche, often greatly more complex, and tend to explore thematic and design territory that has been under exploited by mass market titles.

We might as an example compare Monopoly (a classic mass market game) against Chinatown (Hartwig 1999) which is a hobbyist, designer game. They have many of the same general mechanism and themes, but Chinatown has a much more intricate design that stresses long-term strategy and real-life negotiation skills. *The Game of Life* (Milton Bradley 1860) is a breezy, friendly and unchallenging journey through a fictional existence. *Fog of Love* (Jaskov 2017) on the other hand is to *Game of Life* what *Dungeons and Dragons* is to couples therapy.

There is no hard line at which we can draw a firm distinction – a common theme in this book – and there is considerable overlap between the simplest hobby games and the most complex mass-market games. Devotees of the former often look down on fans of the latter, but perhaps unfairly. There is no inherent value judgement that comes from separating board games into different streams. Both rough, broad categories are valid targets of inquiry. There's much of interest to be said of the mathematics behind Snakes and Ladders or the cultural biases embedded in Trivial Pursuit. You could certainly generate a meaningful research output on the social dynamics of Pictionary (Angel 1985), or how effective play in Scrabble can be viewed in the frame of military strategy.

It was though the rise of hobbyist games that was most critical to the emergence of Germany as a spiritual heart of the hobby. One of the reasons for that is that German hobbyist game designers were financially incentivized through an award called the Spiel des Jahres (SdJ). Founded in 1978, it had a primary remit to offer genuine recognition of excellence in board game design. As with all such endeavours it began with little market impact, but before long it would be considered prestigious enough to essentially act as a taste-maker for the industry. Winners would end up stocked in supermarkets, vastly boosting their visibility and commercial success. Nominees would be prominently listed in newspapers and supporting media, boosting their sales. Hard figures are difficult to come by, but conventional wisdom in the early 2010s was that a board game would be considered a success if it sold around 5,000 copies, and 10,000 would be considered a smash hit. An SdJ nominee at the time could be expected to sell 10,000, and a winner could easily hit the 500,000 mark. It was – and remains – a big deal.

From the point of its founding through to the release of Settlers of Catan, the Spiel des Jahres straddles the awkward separation of classic and hobbyist games. Many of its earliest awards go to games that do not fully belong in either of these groups. Rummikub (Hertzano 1979) – awarded in 1980 – and Scotland Yard (Burggraf et al. 1983) in 1983 are examples of "mass market" games that were recipients of the award, but then in 1985 we see an award for the German release of Sherlock Holmes Consulting Detective (Edwards, Goldberg, and Grady 1983), which is still a proper banger of a game even now and widely lauded in the hobbyist community. However, as we trend towards 1995, we see a real shift towards a focus on innovation, novelty and design elegance which then converts into an almost unbroken stream of sophistication. While the award is not always convincing in how it identifies truly stand-out design – these days it tends towards safe, family-friendly fare – it has had a remarkable impact on setting the standard for what excellence is. Notable winners include *Dominion* (Vaccarino 2008), *Dixit* (Roubira 2008), *Kingdom Builder* (Vaccarino 2011), *Hanabi* (Bauza 2010), *Camel Up* (Bogen 2014), *Colt Express* (Raimbault 2014), *Codenames* (Chvátil 2015), and *Azul* (Kiesling 2018). While the success of an SdJ winner is a self-fulfilling prophecy, it's almost unquestioningly the case that if you as an independent judge had a track record of backing winning plays remotely equivalent, you'd never want for work in your life. Your crystal ball would forever be in demand. That said, I'd personally rank *Concordia* (Gerdts 2013) or *Splendor* (Andre 2014) as much stronger candidates than *Camel Up*. Just to get that on the record.

In 1989, a special prize for children's games was introduced – the Sonderpreis Kinderspiel which eventually became the Kinderspiel des Jahres. In 2011, a category for experts and connoisseurs was introduced – the Kennerspiel des Jahres. Winners of the latter include *7 Wonders* (Bauza 2010); *Village* (Brand and Brand 2011); *Exit: The Game* (Brand and Brand 2016); and *Wingspan* (Hargrave 2019).

There are some interesting factors here though that complicate how to interpret the award. The first is that only games that have been published in the German language can be nominated, which creates a pressure for internationalization that may not be possible for hobbyist designers to meet. The award is decided upon by a jury, with the public having no ability to influence the results. The decision-making is private, so the basis of a decision is often only understandable through speculation. Games are occasionally chosen at odds with the public criteria. These are a focus on the game concept (originality and fun); the structure of the rules as determined by the rulebook; the layout and general quality of components; and the elegance of its design and implementation. When considered in that frame, certain winners are curious choices. Perhaps this can be explained away by one of the clear informal biases in selection – almost every winner of the SdJ and related awards is meaningfully enjoyable by **families**.

While it is not the only significant board-game award in the modern era, there is nothing that comes close to its level of significance or prestige, and it continues to be an important driver of design innovation. As a result of its influence, Germany was almost drowning in quality board games from the early 1980s onwards. If you were a serious board-gamer at the time, the chances were you imported your games from Germany and had them translated. Or, perhaps, you simply knuckled under and learned enough German to be functionally literate. There's a lot of parallels here to those who were JRPG or Anime aficionados in the early nineties.

It took a little longer for hobbyist designers in other countries to catch up, and many (myself included) attribute the recent explosion in the hobby's popularity to a set of games sometimes known as the "big four" – a perfect combo of titles ideal for introducing a newbie to the wonders of modern board game design. These are *Settlers of Catan* (Teuber 1995); *Carcassonne* (Wrede 2000); *Ticket to Ride* (Moon 2004); and *Pandemic* (Leacock 2008). The latter, of course, hits a little bit harder these days than it did when I first played it pre-COVID.

Settlers of Catan is the game most geeks will think of first when you say you're a board gamer. It was designed by Klaus Teuber, inspired by the tales he had read of Viking exploration and exploitation of resource-rich islands. He channelled this interest into a game that focused on what would happen if competing interests came to an unspoiled island, and how they might seek to develop it in their own favour. A series of hex tiles is used to build an island (either pre-set or randomized), with those tiles representing exploitable resources – wheat, clay, sheep, iron, and wood. Each tile is assigned a number between 2 and 12 – this is the number on which they will payout when two six-sided dice are rolled. Everyone who has a settlement touching a tile will receive a resource when its number is rolled, and those resources permit for roads, new settlements, armies and other innovations to be purchased. No-one will have exactly the blend of resources they need, and so trading is encouraged.

This was the first of what we might think of as eurogames that became popular outside of Europe, and as of the time of writing, the sales are around the 32 million units mark. As might be expected of something so popular, in the modern era it has come under intense criticism for its framing. A critical reading of its design is that it endorses the concept of "Terra Nullius" (Veracini 2013), or "Nobody's Land". Essentially, the idea that a resource-rich island ripe for exploitation would have nobody on it is really an expression of a colonialist mindset. It's a way of reframing the truth as "nobody of **consequence** was on it". Once again – games can be political without necessarily being ideological.

Carcassonne, recipient of the SdJ in 2011, is a tile and worker placement game. Everyone collaboratively works to build a pleasing countryside made up of villages, roads, open fields, and monasteries. In turn, players draw a tile and place it on the growing map. They then choose whether they want to play down one of their meeples (this is the game that first codified that term) in an attempt to claim it. When a feature is completed (a road linked between towns, or a monastery fully surrounded, and so on), the meeple(s) that have claimed it are reclaimed and the feature is scored. It's deceptively simple, extremely approachable, and amenable to clever strategies. You can play to advance your score, or to scupper the plans of an opponent. Or, more realistically, a little bit of both.

Ticket to Ride is probably the second most successful modern board game after Catan, with over 18 million copies having been sold as of 2024. Each player gets a set of hidden rail routes they need to build along a map of a particular region – the continental United States in the original, but there are many regional variants. Each completed route at the end of the game scores bonus points, and uncompleted routes attract a penalty. The rest of the game is about collecting cards of varying colours, and then spending those cards to complete sub-routes between major cities. Your job is to create the infrastructure you need while ensuring you stop your opponents from doing the same. Some versions of *Ticket to Ride* come with additional systems – stations that allow routes to be shared, or tech trees, or stock markets. The core game though is about developing the national infrastructure of the railway system.

What *Ticket to Ride*, *Carcassonne*, and *Catan* have in common is core to almost all eurogames – competition is indirect. You don't go in and smash up someone's train tracks or invade their city. Instead, you fight over efficiency – to be the first to do X, or to acquire Y before anyone else can. The theme in the games is often subservient to the mechanics – design elegance is a core feature of Eurogame design. But all three of these games are still competitions – there is a winner left standing at the end.

Pandemic is the first fully co-operative game many people will encounter as they get into hobby board-gaming – everyone wins, or everyone loses. While this wasn't the first game to focus on this, it's the one that is most responsible for popularizing the design. Instead of being Player versus Player (PvP), Pandemic is about Players versus the Environment (PvE). It's a perfect example of a design principle I call "four fires and three buckets", in which an ongoing triage of calamity requires the expenditure of resources in volumes greater than the supply can bear. Every turn of the game, disease cubes are added to random cities as indicated by a card draw. Threaded through the deck are **epidemic** cards which show an escalation in the severity of the pandemic. Each time an epidemic occurs, infected cities become more likely to be re-infected, and when a city reaches three disease cubes it spills out a cube to every adjacent city. If that results in another cascade, then the disease spreads and spreads. Your job as a team is to balance fighting the diseases while also trying to cure the underlying conditions which you do by using your special player roles in concert. The legacy version of the game adds to the tension by adding permanent consequences for mistakes.

These four games serve as an almost unbeatable primer to the delights in store for the hobbyist boardgamer, and over the years they have been directly responsible for introducing many into the domain of cardboard, dice and plastic meeple.[11] And between 2000 and 2024, it's certainly been true that many have been seduced by the lure of the tactile tabletop game. Part of this is clearly driven by an increase in general quality, but much as with the expansion of wargames much of it is also down to the enthusiasm of the community itself, and particularly as a result of the emergence of a number of media-savvy influencers. My own introduction to the hobby, in earnest, was thanks to Wil Wheaton and his YouTube show Tabletop. When I saw the first trailer for a game where various Internet celebrities play board games together, I thought it looked like some kind of grim practical joke – like YouTube's own version of the lethal movie from The Ring. However, it turned out that I was absolutely wrong and the show was both great and directly responsible for a trickle of board game purchases becoming a stream and eventually an unstoppable flood.

Eurogames are one of the major families of titles that made their way into the shelves I once held sacred for books, but the genre of **Ameritrash** is one that reflects a different sensibility. It's sometimes posited that there is a spectrum in board game design. Low conflict, mechanically elegant and thematically weak Eurogames at one end. Little randomness, and a big emphasis on analytical play. At the other end are the high-conflict, often mechanically shaky but thematically vivid games. Lots of pieces – miniatures, bright colours, fistfuls of dice. The essence of Ameritrash. Realistically almost every modern board game is a blend of these two sets of design considerations – we can see plenty of highly thematic games with elegant themes, or games with plenty of conflict yet no randomness. And, of course, any point between.

Harkening back to the GNS system we saw in the previous chapter (White 2020), we might argue that Ameritrash games are half-way between game and narrative, whereas Eurogames are half-way between game and simulation. In the no-man's land between these regions we find the bulk of modern games. For the final time in this book, we'll fall back to Wittgenstein and the concept of familial similarity

FIGURE 14.2 Exploration versus Exploitation (image by author).

(Wittgenstein 1958) – you're much more likely to find intertextual opportunities this way than by grouping games into two broad, largely stereotypical categories even if that's how the discourse will often frame it.

Some have identified other reasons for the staggering growth of the hobby in the past couple of decades – as a rejection of screens and a reclamation of co-located play, for example. In the 1980s, if you wanted to play a video game with a friend the chances were high you'd do it through some form of couch co-op. That is to say sitting together either playing at the same time or swapping the controller. That camaraderie ebbed away as the Internet began to turn co-location into remote-location. Yelling at teammates through a headset lacks much of the complex nuance of yelling at them face-to-face. Board games simply do some things better than video games – especially when it comes to social aspects of play.

We should also acknowledge too the explosion of range that has come as a consequence of Kickstarter and other crowd-funding platforms. The barrier to entry is tremendously low for a designer these days, and that is incredibly important when we discuss an industry where there are per-unit costs associated with every last thing. It's risky to drum up $50,000 to fund a print-run of an untested game, but you can spread out the risk by making a convincing pitch to an audience that agrees to support the project ahead of its delivery. For a long time, this resulted in an incredible diversity of games with truly innovative mechanics. However, nowadays there is a lot more money floating around the hobby, more professional careers dependent on a steady supply of novelty, and an increasing focus on monetization through brand crossovers and expansions.

We might argue that innovation has taken a backseat in recent years to the publisher's hope for sustainable, ever exploitable "evergreens". Given that board games are physical products, warehouse space and shelf presence are important factors when deciding on the size of a print run. Games regularly go out of print, and it is much better for a publisher to have a single title that sells well every year than a dozen titles that sell well one year and then fall out of public prominence. Speaking personally, it has been a while since I saw a board game that was genuinely pushing the envelope. In 2024, the only game I felt compelled to buy was *City of Six Moons* (Holland 2024) which presented itself as an opaque, almost aggressively inaccessible puzzle of translation which required hours of painstaking context-building before you could even get at the game within.

The situation is not yet dire, but it's certainly the case that the principles of hauntology seem to be, ironically, alive in the board-game space.

Games and Social Isolation

I'd like to end this chapter with a few observations about why board games matter in modern society. Many commentators and academics will say that we are currently – globally – in the middle of a loneliness epidemic (Cacioppo and Cacioppo 2018; Demarinis 2020; Hong et al. 2024). People have fewer friends than ever and the intimacy of those friendships has been plummeting. And in plenty of countries, it is incredibly stigmatic to admit to being lonely. Saying to someone, "I am lonely and would like to spend some time in your company" is a perfectly reasonable statement that will nonetheless get you a reputation for being weird and needy. Historically, this is something that is papered over through social ambiguity. "Hey, let's go for a pint" is an example in traditional "masculine" societies. It's primarily a way to de-emphasize the reason by shrouding meaning in a shield of interpretation. The social aspect can be relegated to a secondary benefit of lesser importance. This, is of course, not a great pattern in countries with a history of systemic alcoholism.

Social isolation is an endemic problem, and it's deeper than just loneliness. It's a form of **prolonged** loneliness without obvious redress. Sometimes that's a consequence of geography, or physical capability. Maybe it's down to estrangement. Perhaps it's down to mental health and low self-esteem. It's not as simple as an absence of friends or people around – it's possible to be isolated in the busiest and friendliest of cities. It's often linked to depressive episodes where the simple act of being around people is too much for someone to bear. Social isolation in those circumstances perhaps has its cruellest manifestation as it can be intermittently alleviated in the short term. In upbeat moments, someone might reconnect with friends and rekindle relationships only for them to become something to dread and avoid during intense depressive states. The ebb and flow of this creates its own frictions that can lead people to feeling even worse because of its irregularity. For others, the edge of ongoing isolation becomes dull through familiarity.

It's important to note here that social isolation isn't the same thing as solitude – it's possible to be alone without being lonely, and it's possible to be lonely while being surrounded by people. The proximity of humanity is only somewhat correlated with social isolation. It's about the connections we form, or not. It's not about the mere presence of others. Social isolation is a profound lack of intimacy – both physical and emotional.

It's caused by a large number of things. Disability is an obvious proximate cause because there are logistical and psychological barriers standing between people with disabilities and a full social life. It's sometimes caused by a change in life circumstances such as being unemployed, losing a partner, or financial distress. Sometimes it's inflicted from without, such in the case of domestic abuse – isolation is an incredibly powerful tool for abusers. Kids being bullied often avoid making friends with others because of the risk and stigma.[12] It can also happen because of a lack of appropriate transportation opportunities, or severe social anxiety. There are a lot of causes, but it all comes down to the same thing. It's being desperately alone when you don't want to be, but being with people isn't a possibility.

Where does board gaming come into this? Well, it comes in as a healthy way for a group of people to spend mindful time with each other. It's not the companionable silence of going to a movie, or the gradual quest for the oblivion of drugs or alcohol.

Remember our secret dark knowledge – in the end, the game doesn't matter. What matters is the people around the board – they're the ones who are going to determine whether you have fun or not. The jokes, conversation, and banter can have an alchemical effect on even boring, uninspiring games. They can make your time magical. That simple truth shunts a lot of criticism and review into the periphery of irrelevance. A lot of us don't like to admit that the quality of a game is, in the end, usually only a secondary factor in how much fun you'll have when playing.

To paraphrase Raph Koster, the game is "the grit around which the pearl forms". If the game is great, you get to enthuse about it. If the game sucks, you get to savagely roast it. You get to form a social connection that transcends the experience itself, and that can be a permanent bond that strengthens over time. It's easier to turn board-gamers into friends than it is to turn friends into board gamers as common hobby wisdom would put it.

Board games then can serve as an excellent "prop" that doesn't exacerbate the stigma of being lonely. Importantly, they also function better in this respect than a lot of the alternatives. You can drink alone. You can go "out on the pull" by yourself. You can't play (most) board games alone and so it can be framed as a thing of pure necessity. "I need three people to play this game, are you in?". That knocks down a lot of the psychological barriers. It gives you "cover". If you receive a rejection, you can also find comfort in the fact that maybe they just didn't want to play the game.

All of this is to say that in all of this talk about research lenses and experiential frames and so on, we run the risk of forgetting that **play** is at the heart of our discipline. We should make sure we don't forget that board games are interesting because people are interesting. You can't really understand board games in isolation. They're ways to spend meaningful time with the people that matter in our lives. Sometimes you just need to turn off analysis mode and simply experience the moment. And perhaps a reminder that if you see someone sitting by themselves and seemingly lost for human connection, perhaps invite them to play a game? Academic detachment and objectivity are well and good but social isolation kills (Friedler, Crapser and McCullough 2015; House 2001). Maybe you can save a life and make a friend at the same time.

Notes

1 Thickness, maybe?
2 Although that isn't much of a distinction – Buddha was famously not a fan of fun as outlined in The Intermediate Section on Virtue (*Majjhimasīla*).
3 https://www.ox.ac.uk/news/arts-blog/200-years-board-games-go-display.
4 Nope. That's another house rule.
5 A regional game that was played in Dundee, Scotland in my youth was called "feeks". Someone would run up to you, touch you, and yell "X has feeks!" and it was the job of X to pass on those feeks by touching someone else. Even now, there are Dundonians that have forgotten they still have feeks and walk around freely, a carrier unaware of their danger to the public.
6 https://www.snopes.com/fact-check/monopoly-games-escape-kits/.
7 Yes, for all its mystic and occult reputation – Ouija is a board game. The trademark is still owned by Hasbro.
8 For a topic historically considered so frivolous, we encounter moral panics surprisingly often in this book.

9 Sample question – "Do you feel hard to love"?
10 "What motivates you to get up each morning?"
11 Meeple is the plural term. The singular term is Merson. Yeah, I know. I hate it too.
12 It's a video game rather than a board game, but I've always found the not-game Loneliness (Jordan 2010) to be incredibly evocative here.

References

Averbakh, Yuri. 2012. *A History of Chess: From Chaturanga to the Present Day*. California: SCB Distributors.

Cacioppo, John T., and Stephanie Cacioppo. 2018. 'The Growing Problem of Loneliness'. The Lancet 391(10119):426.

Cazaux, Jean-Louis, and Rick Knowlton. 2017. *A World of Chess: Its Development and Variations through Centuries and Civilizations*. Jefferson: McFarland.

Crist, Walter. 2019. 'Passing from the Middle to the New Kingdom: A Senet Board in the Rosicrucian Egyptian Museum'. The Journal of Egyptian Archaeology 105(1):107–13. doi: 10.1177/0307513319896288.

Davidson, Henry A. 2012. *A Short History of Chess*. New York: Crown.

De Voogt, Alex. 2021. 'Misconceptions in the History of Mancala Games: Antiquity and Ubiquity'. Board Game Studies Journal 15(1):1–12. doi: 10.2478/bgs-2021-0001.

Demarinis, Susie. 2020. 'Loneliness at Epidemic Levels in America'. Explore (New York) 16(5):278.

Depaulis, Thierry. 2020. 'Board Games Before Ur?' Board Game Studies Journal 14(1):127–44. doi: 10.2478/bgs-2020–0007.

Donovan, Tristan. 2018. *It's All a Game: A Short History of Board Games*. London: Atlantic Books.

du Sautoy, Marcus. 2023. *Around the World in 80 Games: A Mathematician Unlocks the Secrets of the Greatest Games*. London: HarperCollins.

Finkel, Irving. 1995. 'Board Games and Fortune Telling: A Case from Antiquity'. AJ de Voogt, New Approaches to Board Games Research. IIAS Working Papers Series 3:64–72.

Finkel, Irving L. 2007. 'On the Rules for the Royal Game of Ur'. Pp. 16–32 in Ancient Board Games in Perspective, edited by Irving Finkel. London: British Museum Press.

Friedler, Brett, Joshua Crapser, and Louise McCullough. 2015. 'One Is the Deadliest Number: The Detrimental Effects of Social Isolation on Cerebrovascular Diseases and Cognition'. Acta Neuropathologica 129:493–509.

Greene, Maggie. 2015. 'The Game People Played: Mahjong in Modern Chinese Society and Culture'. Cross-Currents: East Asian History and Culture Review 1(17).

Hall, Mark A., and Katherine Forsyth. 2011. 'Roman Rules? The Introduction of Board Games to Britain and Ireland'. Antiquity 85(330):1325–38.

Heron, Michael James. 2023. 'Computer Supported Accessible Dexterity-Based Board Games'. The International Journal of Games and Social Impact 1(2):98–118.

Hong, Joanna H., Julia S. Nakamura, Sakshi S. Sahakari, William J. Chopik, Koichiro Shiba, Tyler J. VanderWeele, and Eric S. Kim. 2024. 'The Silent Epidemic of Loneliness: Identifying the Antecedents of Loneliness Using a Lagged Exposure-Wide Approach'. Psychological Medicine 54(8):1519–32.

House, James S. 2001. 'Social Isolation Kills, but How and Why?' Psychosomatic Medicine 63(2):273–74.

Parlett, David. 2008. *The Penguin Book of Card Games*. London: Penguin.

Peterson, Jon. 2021. *Game Wizards: The Epic Battle for Dungeons & Dragons*. Cambridge: MIT Press.

Pilon, Mary. 2015. *The Monopolists: Obsession, Fury, and the Scandal Behind the World's Favorite Board Game*. New York: Bloomsbury Publishing USA.

Rollefson, Gary O. 1992. 'A Neolithic Game Board from 'Ain Ghazal, Jordan'. Bulletin of the American Schools of Oriental Research 286:1–5. doi: 10.2307/1357113.

Veracini, Lorenzo. 2013. 'Settlers of Catan'. Settler Colonial Studies 3(1):131–33. doi: 10.1080/18380743.2013.761941.

Vyshedskiy, Andrey. 2014. *On the Origin of the Human Mind*. MobileReference.

White, William J. 2020. 'Forge Theory: From GNS to the Big Model'. Pp. 123–75 in Tabletop RPG Design in Theory and Practice at the Forge, 2001–2012. Cham: Springer International Publishing.

Wittgenstein, Ludwig. 1958. *Philosophical Investigations*. Oxford: Blackwell.

Woods, Stewart. 2012. *Eurogames: The Design, Culture and Play of Modern European Board Games*. McFarland & Co: North Carolina, USA.

Ludography

Abbott, Scott, and Haney, Chris. 1979. Trivial Pursuit [board game]. Selchow and Righter.

Andre, Marc. 2014. Splendor [board game]. Space Cowboys.

Angel, Rob. 1985. Pictionary [board game]. Hasbro.

Bailey, Steven. 2014. Billionaire Banshee [card game]. Breaking Games.

Baker, Stephen. 1989. HeroQuest [board game]. Milton Bradley and Games Workshop.

Bauza, Antoine. 2010. 7 Wonders [board game]. Repos Production.

Bauza, Antoine. 2010. Hanabi [cooperative card game]. Asmodee.

Bogen, Steffen. 2014. Camel Up [racing game]. Egmont.

Brand, Inka, Brand, Markus. 2011. Village [board game]. Eggertspiele.

Brand, Inka, Brand, Markus. 2016. Exit: The Game [board game]. KOSMOS.

Burggraf, Manfred, Dorothy Garrels, Wolf Hörmann, Fritz Ifland, and Werner Scheerer. 1983. Scotland Yard [board game]. Ravensburger.

Butts, Alfred. 1948. Scrabble [board game]. James Brunot.

Cassar, Dan. 2015. Arboretum [board game]. Z-Man Games.

Chudyk, Carl. 2010. Innovation [board game]. Asmadi Games.

Chvátil, Vlaada. 2015. Codenames [word game]. Czech Games Edition.

Cieslik, Chris. 2016. One Deck Dungeon [board game]. Asmadi Games.

Coster, Theo, and Ora Coster. 1979. Guess Who [board game]. Milton Bradley.

Deley, Danielle, Lindsey Sherwood, and Nathan Thornton. 2018. Medium [board game]. Greater Than Games.

Edwards, Raymond, Suzanne Goldberg, and Gary Grady. 1882. Sherlock Holmes: Consulting Detective [board game]. Sleuth productions.

Foley, Charles, Reyn Guyer, and Neil Rabens. 1966. Twister [board game]. Milton Bradley.

Gerdts, Mac. 2013. Concordia [abstract strategy game]. PD-Verlag.

Gygax, Gary, and Dave Arneson. 1981. Dungeons and Dragons [role-playing game]. TSR.

Hargrave, Elizabeth. 2019. Wingspan [board game]. Stonemaier Games.

Hartwig, Karsten. 1999. Chinatown [board game]. Z-Man Games.

Hasbro. 2011. Beatles Monopoly [board game]. Hasbro.

Hertzano, Ephraim. 1977. Rummikob [board game]. Alga.

Holland, Amabel. 2024. City of Six Moons [board game]. Hollandspiele.

Innersloth. 2018. Among Us [Video game] [Microsoft Windows] Innersloth.

Jaskov, Jacob. 2017. Fog of Love [board game]. Hush Hush Projects.

John Jaques & Son Ltd. 1896. Ludo [board game]. John Jaques & Son Ltd.

Kiesling, Michael. 2017. Azul [abstract strategy game]. Plan B Games.

Koreen. 2018. We're Not Really Strangers [card game]. Self-published.

Koreen. 2022. Let's Get Closer [card game]. Self-published.

Leacock, Matt. 2008. Pandemic [board game]. Z-Man Games.

Magie, Elizabeth. 1904. The Landlord Game [board game]. Self-published.

Magie, Elizabeth. 1933. Monopoly [board game]. Parker Brothers.

Makow, Henry. 1984. A Question of Scruples [board game]. Guilt Games Inc.

Milton Bradley. 1931. Battleships [board game]. Milton Bradley.

Moon, Alan. 2004. Ticket to Ride [board game]. Days of Wonder.

Nakayama, Kota. 2013. Hanamikoji [board game]. EmperorS4.

Newberry, Elizabeth. 1790. The New Game of Human Life [board game]. John Wallis.

Parker Brothers. 2001. Disney Monopoly [board game]. Parker Brothers.

Pauchon, Sébastien. 2009. Jaipur [board game]. GameWorks.

Pratt, Anthony. 1949. Cluedo [board game]. Waddingtons.

Raimbault, Christophe. 2014. Colt Express [train robbery game]. Ludonaute.

Roubira, Jean-Louis. 2008. Dixit [board game]. Libellud.

Scott, Leslie. 1983. Jenga [board game]. Irwin Toy.

Steiger, Andreas. 2012. Targi [board game]. Kosmos.

Temkin, Max, Josh Dillon, Daniel Dranove, David Munk, Eliot Weinstein, Ben Hantoot, and Eli Halpern. 2011. Cards Against Humanity [board game]. Cards Against Humanity LLC.

Teuber, Klaus. 1995. The Settlers of Catan [board game]. Kosmos.

Teuber, Klaus. 2015. Catan [board game]. Catan Studio.

USAopoly. 2019. Warhammer 40,000 Monopoly [board game]. USAopoly.

Unknown. 1860. The Game of Life [board game]. Milton Bradley.

Unknown. 1949. Candyland [board game]. Milton Bradley.

Vaccarino, Donald. 2008. Dominion [board game]. Rio Grande Games.

Vaccarino, Donald. 2011. Kingdom Builder [board game]. Queen Games.

Wrede, Klaus Jurgen. 2000. Carcassonne [board game]. Hans Im Gluck.

Zakich, Rhea. 1973. The Ungame [board game]. Talicor.

15

Conclusion

Michael Heron

So long!

The most fun I have ever had in my professional career is teaching Introduction to Game Research in my current role in Gothenburg. Some of it is just the topic – it's hard not to have fun in a course where I literally get to run D&D and Blades in the Dark adventure sessions **and** get paid for it. Most of it though is down to the sheer enthusiasm I see on the faces of my students at the end of the first lecture. Every year, without fail, I have a stream of students who come down to say some variation of "I had absolutely no idea that it was okay to talk about games like this". It's like they've been given permission to treat games seriously for the first time in their lives – to know that their passions can be explored without mockery. The work that comes out of this course is routinely excellent, and you've seen some of it in the contributed case studies. I emphasize again that this is an **introduction** to game research course, and yet I am endlessly enriched by the thoughts of everyone who takes it. It is a joy to be part of their journey. I owe this book to all those hundreds of students who have so inspired me to write it.

What I hope this book has been able to express is that having interesting and nuanced opinions about games is something well within the grasp of anyone willing to spend a little time thinking about things from different perspectives. And, importantly, that nobody needs to do a PhD in Advanced Gameology to feel confident in the rigour of their thinking. While this book does draw in academic theory and is abundantly referenced throughout, I'd hope you share my view that this has been a process of demystification – that the topic has been made accessible to a wider audience.

This is only the start of the journey though for an aspiring game scholar. You've considered things from multiple angles. You've lined up your evidence. You've been appreciative of context. You've been intertextual **AF** (as I believe you kids say). Your opinions aren't bullet-proof – there is no such thing as permanent knowledge – but they're believably defensible. However, until you test your analysis in the free market of ideas, you don't really know just **how** defensible. Research is partially about coming up with an interesting opinion, but it's also about revising and adjusting that opinion in the face of contradictory evidence or analysis. The process we have discussed in this book is where opinions are born. They **live** in analysis and review.

DOI: 10.1201/9781003530282-15

Nobody was ever diminished by changing their mind in the face of new perspectives. Most ideas don't die through criticism. They are **tempered** and made stronger. Brittle ideas may snap into a million pieces, but your ideas are stronger than that. Debate and discussion are how your ideas become **battle-hardened.** While we've looked at research in this book as a process, the truth is that research is an endless dialogue where we forever seek to ensure that our thinking today is better than it was yesterday.

Research is never completed. No idea is set in stone. It's on you to engage with the process. To be continually critical of your own thinking. Be endlessly curious about the thinking of others. Evaluate your thoughts from all angles. If you do that, regularly throughout your life, you'll never have an uninteresting thought again. I hope you have found this book a useful stepping stone in your journey to being an endlessly fascinating scholar of this rich and important form of popular culture.

Index

Note: **Bold** page numbers refer to tables; *italic* page numbers refer to figures.

For Product Safety Concerns and Information please contact our EU
representative GPSR@taylorandfrancis.com
Taylor & Francis Verlag GmbH, Kaufingerstraße 24, 80331 München, Germany

www.ingramcontent.com/pod-product-compliance
Lightning Source LLC
Chambersburg PA
CBHW060339220326
41598CB00023B/2753